Zoya Durdik

Architectural Design Decision Documentation through Reuse of Design Patterns

The Karlsruhe Series on Software Design and Quality
Volume 14

Chair Software Design and Quality
Faculty of Computer Science
Karlsruhe Institute of Technology

and

Software Engineering Division
Research Center for Information Technology (FZI), Karlsruhe

Editor: Prof. Dr. Ralf Reussner

Architectural Design Decision Documentation through Reuse of Design Patterns

by
Zoya Durdik

KIT Scientific Publishing

Dissertation, Karlsruher Institut für Technologie (KIT)
Fakultät für Informatik
Tag der mündlichen Prüfung: 27. Juni 2014
Referenten: Prof. Dr. Ralf Reussner
Prof. Dr. Barbara Paech (Universität Heidelberg)

Impressum

KIT Scientific Publishing

Karlsruher Institut für Technologie (KIT)
KIT Scientific Publishing
Straße am Forum 2
D-76131 Karlsruhe

KIT Scientific Publishing is a registered trademark of Karlsruhe Institute of Technology. Reprint using the book cover is not allowed.

www.ksp.kit.edu

Print on Demand 2016

ISSN 1867-0067
ISBN 978-3-7315-0292-0
DOI: 10.5445/KSP/1000043807

Abstract

Software design patterns are evaluated and recognised architectural solutions for recurring design problems. They are often described in pattern catalogues that contain known patterns for a certain application domain, for example, patterns for object-oriented software by Gamma et al. or patterns for distributed computing by Buschmann et al.. However, design patterns are still often misunderstood and inappropriately applied. While design decisions on the application of patterns involve complex trade-offs between desired functionality and various quality properties, such decisions are often spontaneous and do not follow a systematic process. Moreover, documentation of such decisions and trace links to related artefacts is usually insufficient or completely omitted. Finally, even if design decisions on pattern application are documented, there are often mistakes during the architectural modelling of design patterns or their implementation in code. Thus, some design decisions on the application of patterns may be misunderstood or overseen and overridden. Even worse, correction of design decision mistakes causes costs and overhead. All these factors negatively influence evolution of software systems.

The existing approaches usually focus only on one of the above mentioned aspects of the problem, such as documentation of design decisions or improvement of design pattern application in architecture or code. Hereby, the documentation of rationale and trace links has to be done and maintained manually.

The approach proposed in this thesis provides a support to overcome the above mentioned problems. It combines support for evaluation of design pattern application, semi-automated documentation of decision rationale, trace links between requirements, decisions and architectural elements, and support for goal-oriented architecture-driven requirements engineering. The contribution is the lightweight support of evaluation of decisions and the documentation of rationale for design pattern application. This approach is based on a new kind of design pattern catalogue, where usual design pattern descriptions are captured together with pattern-specific questions (question annotations to the patterns) and the information on architectural structure of patterns. The question annotations are sets of questions about the main properties of design patterns, which are fragments of a rationale for a potential pattern application. The contributions can be summarized as follows:

1. **A lightweight process for goal-oriented requirements engineering and simplified documentation of rationale for the design decisions on design pattern application:** Extension of the general development process with a process that supports the proposed approach. The process describes application of the developed catalogue for evaluation of decisions on pattern application and documentation of the rationale. Besides the documentation of rationale and elicitation of requirements, the developed process supports several other design and evolution scenarios. These sub-processes are incorporated into the main development process.

2. **A new type of design pattern catalogue with rationale question annotations:** A new kind of catalogue was developed, in which design patterns are stored together with question annotations. This allows for the documentation of rationale for design decisions, documentation of trace links between various project artefacts, such as design model elements and requirements, goal-oriented elicitation of requirements and evaluation of decisions on pattern application.

3. **An exemplary design pattern catalogue:** The exemplary catalogue contains 12 design patterns described according to the proposed ap-

proach (called AM3D, Architectural Modelling with Design Decision Documentation) and annotated with questions for rationale documentation and requirements elicitation. This catalogue was used during the approach's validation. The treatment group used it for design and evolution tasks to make and to re-evaluate design decisions on pattern application.

The benefits of this approach are: (1) Documented rationale of design decisions on the pattern application; (2) Semi-automated documentation of trace links between requirements, decisions, and architectural elements; (3) More appropriate use of design patterns and design pattern variants (reduced number of design mistakes connected to ungrounded design decisions on pattern application and pattern application design), especially by less experienced software engineers, through systematic pattern evaluation with the help of question annotations; and (4) Goal-oriented architecture-driven requirements engineering (a more goal-oriented and efficient elicitation and prioritisation of requirements that are highly-relevant for the design-phase).

The approach and contributions were published in the refereed conferences and workshops [1–15], as well as in technical reports [16, 17].

The validation of the proposed AM3D approach consists of three parts: (1) A survey with 25 engineers and students to validate the motivation of the approach and the feasibility of the annotated pattern catalogue as a potential solution for the problems with design pattern application and documentation. Motivation and feasibility of the catalogue were positively qualitatively evaluated. (2) Application on a CoCoME-based example (a Common Component Modelling example, which is a benchmark for modelling of the component-based systems) to demonstrate appropriateness of the AM3D approach, its artefacts and the process. Process and artefacts could be applied on the example without exclusions. (3) An empirical study based on a controlled experiment involving 20 students to validate the applicability and benefits of the approach. The empirical study validates that design patterns annotated according to the AM3D approach can be better understood and applied more correctly than the design pattern catalogue based on the standard approach. The validation results show statistically significant improvement over the control group. Furthermore, the study validates that a system architecture that is documented according to the AM3D approach can be better maintained,compared to a system documented according to the standard catalogue approach. The validation results show noticeable improvement over the control group; however, no statistically significant results were obtained.

Zusammenfassung

Software-Entwurfsmuster sind erprobte und verbreitete Lösungen für wiederkehrende Entwurfsprobleme. Entwurfsmuster sind in mehreren Muster-Katalogen, wie zum Beispiel in denen von Gamma et al. oder von Buschmann et al., beschrieben. Dennoch werden Architekturentwurfsmuster oft missverstanden und unpassend eingesetzt. Die Entscheidungen über den Einsatz von einem Muster beziehen zumeist komplizierte Abwägungen und Entscheidungen zwischen den unterschiedlichen Qualitätseigenschaften und der Funktionalität mit ein. Dabei sind die Musterentscheidungen oft intuitionsbasiert und unzureichend dokumentiert. Dazu können eine inkorrekte Entwurfsmodellierung in den Architekturmodellen und eine fehlerhafte Implementierung im Code kommen. Diese Faktoren erschweren eine spätere Systemwartung erheblich, wobei manche Entscheidungen zum Einsatz von Mustern einfach übersehen werden und von der ursprünglichen Entwurfsidee abgewichen wird oder die Fehlentscheidungen mühsam korrigiert werden müssen.

Die existierenden Ansätze konzentrieren sich hauptsächlich auf einzelne Aspekte dieses Problems. Entweder werden die Architekturentwurfsmuster umfangreich textuell beschrieben, um das Verständnis für die Muster zu ermöglichen – dabei braucht man aber viel Zeit für die Dokumentation – oder es wird die Entscheidungsdokumentation als Ziel gesetzt. Dabei werden die Entscheidungen nicht in Frage gestellt und die Begründung für die Entscheidungen wird oft entweder missachtet oder kann nur mühsam manuell angegeben werden.

Mein Ansatz geht alle diese Probleme an – die Evaluation der Architekturentwurfsmuster, die Dokumentation davon zusammen mit den semiautomatisiert generierten Begründungen und die Unterstützung bei der korrekten Modellierung der Muster. Der Beitrag meiner Dissertation ist eine Methode für die leichtgewichtigere Evaluation und Dokumentation der für die Architekturentwurfsmuster relevanten Entwurfsentscheidungen zusammen mit deren Begründungen. Die Methode basiert auf einer neuen Art eines Entwurfsmusterkatalogs, bei dem zusätzlich zu den textuellen Musterbeschreibungen auch die Entwurfsbegründungen in Form von Fragen zu den Mustern und die Informationen zu dem Architekturbau des Musters enthalten sind. Die Beiträge sind wie folgt zusammengefasst:

1. **Leichtgewichtiger Prozess für ein zielgerichtetes architekturgetriebenes Anforderungs-Engineering und eine erleichterte Dokumentation von Begründungen zu den Musterentwurfsentscheidungen:** Der Prozess beschreibt die Anwendung des entwickelten Architekturmusterkatalogs für die Evaluation von den Musterentwurfsentscheidungen und dessen Dokumentation zusammen mit den semiautomatisch aus den Fragen zu den Mustern erstellten Begründungen. Außerdem definiert der Prozess die notwendigen Schritte zur Erstellung eines Musterkataloges und für die Erstellung und Annotation von Fragen zu den Mustern.

2. **Neuartiger Entwurfsmusterkatalog mit den Fragen zu der Musterbegründung:** Es wurde eine neue Art des Entwurfsmusterkataloges entwickelt, der Fragen zu der Musterbegründung zusammen mit der Beschreibung der Entwurfsmuster enthält. Dieser Entwurfsmusterkatalog unterstützt die Dokumentation der Begründung von Entwurfsentscheidungen, die Dokumentation der Verfolgbarkeitsbeziehungen zwischen Anforderungen, Entscheidungen und Architekturelementen und ein zielgerichtetes architekturgetriebenes Anforderungs-Engineering.

3. **Exemplarischer Entwurfsmusterkatalog mit den Begründungsannotationen:** Basierend auf dem entwickelten Prozess und dem

Ansatz (genannt AM3D , “Architectural Modelling with Design Decision Documentation”) wurde ein initialer Musterkatalog erstellt, der die Entwurfsmuster und die Fragen zu dessen Begründung beinhaltet. Der Katalog wurde bei der Validierung eingesetzt.

Die Vorteile des Ansatzes sind eine verbesserte Systemevolution durch: (1) Leichtgewichtige Dokumentation von den Begründungen der Musterentwurfsentscheidungen; (2) die semi-automatisierte Dokumentation von den Verfolgbarkeitsbeziehungen zwischen Anforderungen, Entwurfsmusterentscheidungen und Architekturelementen; (3) Reduzierte Anzahl der Entwurfsfehler, vor allem durch weniger erfahrene Software-Entwickler, durch die systematische Evaluation von den Musterentwurfsentscheidungen mittels der im Katalog gespeicherten Fragen zu den Mustern und den Architekturvorlagen mit den OCL-Randbedingungen (OCL, Object Constraint Language); und (4) Das zielgerichtete architekturgetriebene Anforderungs-Engineering (die zielgerichtete Erhebung der Anforderungen, die für den Entwurf relevant sind).

Es wurden folgende begutachtete Konferenz- und Workshopspublikationen [1–15] und technische Berichte [16, 17] mit Beiträgen meines Dissertationsvorhabens veröffentlicht.

Die Validation der Arbeit besteht aus drei Teilen: (1) Eine Studie für die Evaluation der Idee des Ansatzes und exemplarischen Einträgen aus dem Katalog, basierend auf den strukturierten Befragungen (Structured Interviews, qualitative Untersuchungsmethode) mit 25 Software-Entwicklern und Studierenden. Die Motivation und die Idee konnten qualitativ positiv evaluiert werden. (2) Die Anwendbarkeitsuntersuchung anhand beispielhafter Instanziierungen des Kataloges mit den Mustern und Begründungen und der Anwendung der Methode an einem auf dem Common Component Modelling Example (CoCoME) basierten Beispielsystem. CoCoME ist ein Benchmark für die Modellierung von einem auf Komponenten basierenden Beispielsystem. Die Methode und der Katalog konnten ohne Ausnahmen angewandt werden. (3) Ein kontrolliertes Experiment mit 20

Studenten aus dem Software-Entwicklungspraktikum zur Validierung der Vorteile des annotierten Musterkatalogs im Vergleich zu einem klassischen Katalog, wie z.B. der von Gamma et al.. Der Vergleich erfolgte anhand zweier Szenarien: Entwurfsentscheidungen für den neuen Entwurf und die Re-Evaluierung von bereits getroffenen Entscheidungen während der Systemevolution. Bei den Aufgaben zu dem neuen Entwurf machte die Behandlungsgruppe statistisch signifikant weniger Fehler. Bei den Aufgaben zu der Re-Evaluierung machte die Behandlungsgruppe erkennbar weniger Fehler, die Ergebnisse der Validierung waren in dem Fall jedoch nicht statistisch signifikant.

Acknowledgements

I am truly and deeply grateful to the many people who have supported and encouraged me on this journey that culminates with the accomplishment of this dissertation project. I hope I am able to remember all of you.

First of all, I would like to express gratitude to my advisor Prof. Dr. Ralf Reussner for his support, motivation, understanding and encouragement as I studied for my PhD. His venerable advice and scientific supervision gave me many profound insights into both scientific work and the principles of good research.

I would also like to thank my secondary advisor Prof. Dr. Barbara Paech for her willingness to and expertise in co-supervising my thesis, as well as for the many helpful discussions and valuable feedback she provided. In addition to my advisers, I would also like to thank the members of the defence committee: Prof. Dr. rer. nat. Jörn Müller-Quade and Prof. Dr. Walter Tichy, who both kindly agreed to take on examiner positions.

Further thanks are due to the members of the SDQ group, the secretaries, and my colleagues at FZI for the fruitful discussions and wonderful company throughout my stay as a member. I would especially like to thank Franz Brosch, Thomas Goldschmidt, Anne Koziolek, Philipp Merkle and Tanja Rhode for their great company and advice; Erik Burger and Jörg Henß for the extremely helpful paper reviews and corrections of my endless article mistakes; and Klaus Krogmann for his good example and professional insights. I am also very grateful to my students for their contributions, specifically: Nelli Kaiser, Azim Khakulov, Markus Heller, Michael Tänzer, Anas Saber, Felix Schad and Sergej Werfel. I am certainly lucky to have met so many talented people. Outside of the SDQ and FZI, I would also like to thank Marco Konersmann for the great team-work experience.

I also want to express my special thanks to Raffaela Mirandola, Diego Perez, Alessandra Viale and members of the DEEPSE group for their kind reception, great work atmosphere, fresh view on the research, and, of course, all the great times I had in Milano. Cari Raffaella e Diego, molte grazie per il tempo fantastico passato insieme. Spero che questa collaborazione potrà continuare in futuro.

Additionally, I want to thank all of the dear friends who accompanied me throughout the years and put up with work-life balance, or lack thereof – especially these last few years. Many warm thoughts go to Mauro, who, by being there and providing care, encouragement, and guidance motivated me to see this dissertation through to completion. Thank you as well to Mauro's family for the wonderful time we spent together.

Finally, none of this would have been possible without the love, support, patience, and trust from my own family – especially from my mother Marina and grandmothers Zoya and Nadezda. I love you and appreciate everything you have done for me. I am deeply sorry that neither my father nor grandmothers, who were so proud of me and looking forward to my graduation, are not here to share this moment with me.

Karlsruhe, June 2014 *Zoya Alexeeva*

Contents

1. Introduction

Software design is of particular importance for the development of stable and easy-to-maintain software systems. Design decisions for the application of architectural solutions are an inevitable part of software design. Design patterns are established reusable solutions for common architectural problems, and design decisions for the application of design patterns are therefore one of the important classes of design decisions.

This thesis focuses on architecture-relevant design patterns[1] and design decisions for the application of design patterns. In particular, the focus lies on the evaluation of design patterns as suitable solutions for given design problems and on the documentation of decisions on pattern application or pattern withdrawal, together with the rationale for the decisions. The goal of the thesis is a step forward in establishing more correct and better documented designs in order to support the software evolution.

The remainder of this chapter explains the motivation for the work in Section 1.1, describes goals and contributions of the proposed approach in Section 1.2, and lists the application scenarios in Section 1.3. Section 1.4 provides an introduction to the validation of the approach, and, finally, Section 1.5 provides an outline for the rest of the thesis. The motivation described in Section 1.1 is based on our previous publications [1, 3, 4, 11].

[1] Unlike some related work, this thesis does not distinguish between the terms "Architectural design patterns" and "Design patterns". They are used as synonyms throughout the thesis.

1.1. Motivation

The proposed approach addresses the four following problems in system design and evolution:

1. **Poor documentation of the rationale for design decisions design pattern application:** The documentation of design decisions and their rationale supports the evolution of software systems, as it eases the comprehension of the design and enables easier implementation of changes [18, 19]. However, design decisions and the rationale for them are seldom explicitly documented. Instead, design decisions are usually implicitly captured in architectural design models in the form of applied architectural solutions, for example, in the form of applied patterns or components. The rationale is typically completely omitted [20–23]. Such implicit documentation is a problem, as design decisions are subjective and often based on the experience of the engineer designing the system. Therefore, capturing the rationale behind the decisions is of particular importance, as it is hard to grasp without proper documentation [24, 25]. If documentation for the decision's rationale is missing, the reasons for a decision are not clear, nor are the considered alternatives and constraints known [24, 25].

   However, documentation of design decisions together with the rationale requires significant effort when it is done manually [25]. Moreover, the documentation quickly becomes out of date, and its manual update is tedious as well [26]. The immediate benefit of the documentation is not clear and a high effort is hard to justify during the design time.

2. **Missing documentation of trace links between requirements, decisions and architectural elements:** Requirements to the system change during the course of the system's evolution. These changes requires new design decisions and render some of the already met de-

cisions obsolete. Such outdated decisions shall be replaced or modified. However, decisions are typically neither linked to the triggering requirements nor linked to the architectural elements implementing the decisions [21, 22, 24, 26, 27]. A manual documentation of trace links is tedious and error-prone [22, 26, 27].

Due to the lack of documentation of such links, design decisions and architectural elements may remain untouched in the architectural design or, even worse, may be easily overseen and accidentally modified [27]. Documentation of trace links between requirements, design decisions, their rationale, and architectural elements minimises such problems during the system evolution.

3. **Inappropriate use of design patterns and their variants:** Software design patterns are evaluated and recognised architectural solutions for recurring design problems [28, 29]. They are often described in pattern catalogues that contain known patterns for a certain application domain, for example, patterns for enterprise architectures by Fowler [30] or patterns for distributed computing by Buschmann et al. [31]. Pattern design solutions contribute to the system comprehension and to architectural knowledge reuse. They serve as a common language and a solution for common design problems. Therefore, from one side, design patterns enable better architectural designs, which are also easier to communicate and to maintain. Appropriately applied design patterns with an explicit documentation of their use help to stabilise software design during software evolution [32].

   From the other side, while design patterns may improve the comprehension and some non-functional properties of the system, they may also worsen other properties at the same time. For example, an additional flexibility achieved in design may result in performance bottlenecks or security issues. Moreover, the application of a design pattern not only solves design problems, but also infers costs in the form of a more complex design. If these are not properly documented, the system may be harder to understand and maintain. Inappropriately used design patterns only incur costs without having benefits or may even become anti-patterns in the system design.

There are several other potential problems connected to the pattern application. First, design patterns are often not well-understood by the engineers [1, 33]. While the main purpose of a design pattern may be clear, its properties and especially its potential negative influences may remain unnoticed [1]. This might be particularly true for the less-experienced software engineers, who expect design patterns to be well-evaluated solutions and, therefore, do not expect drawbacks from their application. Second, even if a pattern and its influences are properly understood, there might still be problems with its application in architectural models. The architectural structure of a pattern may be misinterpreted and wrongly applied in a model, leading to follow-up mistakes in the implementation [1]. In such cases, the intended properties of a pattern may be lost and unconsidered drawbacks may appear. Third, similar to the other types of design decisions, decisions on the design pattern application are often intuitive. Most engineers decide on the use of a pattern through a rather informal process. Their own experience and unevaluated estimates of the usefulness of design patterns are often the main guides of the process, instead of a rational approach. The above mentioned problems were also confirmed by the results of our survey, described in Section 6.4.

4. **Unfocused requirements engineering:** Software system development typically starts from a requirement specification. It is followed by stepwise refinement of available requirements through transferring them into the system architecture with the help of design decisions [11]. In such an approach, the granularity and the amount

of requirements to be elicited for a successful architectural design are not well understood [11, 34]. The later the important requirements are discovered, the more expensive their consideration may become [11, 35, 36]. Sometimes, an expensive re-design of subsystems may be required to be able to consider required properties of a system that were discovered later [36]. This is particularly true for the quality requirements, careful consideration of which is often neglected until the later design phases [34, 36–39]. Even if the quality requirements are elicited, their prioritisation may differ for the different subsystems. Quality requirements actually sometimes need to be re-prioritized for certain design decisions. However, this often remains unconsidered during the requirements engineering phase. Thus, some design decisions may become a result of an unauthorised and badly informed design process. Such a process results from insufficient requirements engineering, where effort was wasted on elicitation of irrelevant requirements.

Therefore, it is important to consider that not only does requirement engineering inform architectural design, but architectural design may also inform requirement engineering [40–42]. This is a relatively new direction of research, where system design contributes to the on-demand elicitation and prioritisation of requirements. Such requirements engineering is called goal-oriented architecture-driven requirements engineering [3, 43, 44].

The main directions in the related approaches on design decisions and design patterns are either ways of documentation of design decisions, including decisions on pattern application, rationale and trace links (e.g., [45–56], see also survey [57]); formalisation, capture and visualisation of design patterns (e.g., [28,29,58–68], see also the survey [69]); or selection and evaluation of design patterns (e.g., [23, 55, 70–75], see also surveys [76–78]). The goal-oriented architecture-driven requirements engineering is an emerging area of research, and there are comparably few related approaches (e.g., [40–43, 79, 80]).

To the author's best knowledge, none of the related approaches provides an integrated support to jointly overcome the aforementioned problems and to automate the documentation of rationale and trace links. In particular, there is no approach combining support for evaluation of design pattern application, semi-automated documentation of decision rationale and trace links between requirements, decisions and architectural elements, and support for goal-oriented architecture-driven requirements engineering.

1.2. Goals and Contributions

The main goal of the approach proposed in this thesis is to support and improve software evolution through: (1) Lightweight documentation of design decisions on design pattern applications together with the semi-automated generated rationale for the decisions, and trace links between requirements, decisions and architectural elements; (2) Reduced number of design mistakes, especially connected to ungrounded decisions on pattern application (through decision evaluation with the help of questions from the pattern catalogue) and design mistakes in the pattern application design (through OCL constraints check); (3) Goal-oriented elicitation of requirements, avoiding later consideration of relevant requirements, while wasting effort on elicitation and management of low-relevant requirements.

This goal is achieved with the help of the proposed approach, which focuses on the lightweight evaluation and documentation of design decisions on design pattern application, together with the semi-automated generated rationale for the decisions and trace links to requirements and architectural elements. The proposed approach is called AM3D (Architectural Modelling with Design Decision Documentation).

The approach is based on a new kind of design pattern catalogue, where usual design pattern descriptions are captured together with pattern-specific

questions and information on architectural structure of patterns. The pattern-specific questions are questions on general positive and potential negative properties of design patterns and their importance to the approach user. The target users of the approach are software architects and engineers. In particular, the approach shall be most beneficial to those having less design experience.
The questions concept has the following purposes: First, to provide a short reference on the characteristic properties of design patterns (both positive and potentially negative properties). Second, to support the evaluation of a pattern as a design solution for the given problem in a particular project context. The questions are actually design rationale fragments and reflect the properties of a pattern that were the most important for the user to make a decision on the pattern application or the pattern withdrawal. Finally, the questions support goal-oriented architecture-driven requirements engineering through triggering inquiries about missing requirements needed to take a design decision and thus supporting their on-demand elicitation. Details on the approach are described in Section 3 and Section 4.

To summarise, the contributions of this dissertation are the following:

1. Extension of the general development process with the *lightweight process for goal-oriented requirements engineering and simplified documentation of rationale for the design decisions on design pattern application.* Besides the documentation of rationale and elicitation of requirements, the developed process supports several other design and evolution scenarios, proving corresponding sub-processes to be incorporated into the main development process.

2. *A new type of design pattern catalogue with the rationale question annotations,* allowing for the documentation of rationale for the design decisions, documentation of trace links between various project artefacts, such as design model elements and requirements, goal-

oriented elicitation of requirements and evaluation of decisions on pattern application.

3. *An exemplary design pattern catalogue* is developed and provided to instantiate the proposed approach. The exemplary catalogue contains 12 design patterns described according to the AM3D approach, and annotated with questions for rationale documentation and requirements elicitation.

In the following, the contributions are discussed in more detail.

1. **Lightweight process for simplified documentation of rationale for the design decisions on design pattern application and goal-oriented elicitation of requirements.**

   - **Process for goal-oriented requirements engineering and rationale documentation through decision evaluation:** The general software development process is extended with the explicit support of goal-oriented requirements engineering, for decision evaluation and semi-automatic documentation of decision rationales. For this, the needs of the users are analysed with regard to the lightweight decision evaluation and documentation of the rationale. The sequences of required actions are defined as processes, and the corresponding processes are then incorporated into the software development process. In addition, the process defines actions for creation of such a design pattern catalogue with question annotations, and steps to annotate the design patterns in the catalogue with questions.

     The AM3D approach process is based on the reuse of design patterns and their rationale. Design patterns are reused to solve reoccurring design problems. The main properties of design patterns are formulated as questions to an architect wishing to apply a pattern, and are reused to document the rationale behind decisions on pattern application (the questions are fragments of design rationale).

The AM3D approach is easily incorporated into any software development process that has an explicit architectural design phase (for example into the V-model [81,82] or the RUP model [83]). It can also be incorporated into the agile processes, such as Scrum [84], because the approach supports the documentation of decisions on demand, which fits well with the philosophy of the agile methods.

- **Better supported processes for design and evolution scenarios:** The AM3D approach supports several other design and evolution scenarios, proving corresponding sub-processes to be incorporated into the development process. These scenarios include: Gaining information about a design pattern, choosing between similar patterns, pattern application, retrieving information about used patterns during system evolution (system maintenance), understanding architectural elements during system evolution (system maintenance), understanding pattern design decisions during system evolution (system maintenance), and checking architectural implementation violations of a pattern. The scenarios are explained in Sections 1.3 and 3.2.2.
- **Goal-oriented architecture-driven requirements engineering:** The AM3D approach process explicitly includes and triggers goal-oriented requirements engineering. During the evaluation of a design pattern as a potential solution to a given design problem, known requirements to the system might be insufficient or require a re-prioritisation in order to make a decision on whether to apply or to withdraw a pattern. In such a case, a user of the approach would be triggered to precisely acquire additional information about the system or to prioritise the already-available requirements. The trigger is released through the catalogue questions to design patterns, which describe the exact properties of a pattern. Such on-demand inquiries of requirements triggered by architectural decision-making processes contribute to a goal-oriented architecture-driven requirements engineering. There-

fore, the requirements are elicited and prioritised in a lightweight on-demand process, contrary to the extensive requirements elicitation phase at the beginning of the development. The latter simply tries to elicit as many of the requirements as possible, without consideration for if and when these requirements would actually be useful for the system design and development.

A detailed description of the application scenarios and corresponding process, together with the general process can be found in Section 3.2. More on the agile processes and architectural modelling can be found in our publication [10]. Goal-oriented requirements engineering with the AM3D approach is described in Section 3.4 and in our publications [11] and [3].

2. **A new type of design pattern catalogue with rationale question annotations.**

   - **Support in documentation of decision rationale:** The AM3D approach defines a new type of design pattern catalogue, which contains definitions of design patterns, together with the question annotations. These question annotations are the fragments of rationale for a design pattern application. They describe the goal, intents and consequences of a pattern, as well as the difference in properties between design pattern variants. While answering the questions, a user of the catalogue automatically generates a rationale for the decision to apply or to discard a pattern candidate. This rationale is then documented, together with the decisions. Thus, the user receives support in documentation of the rationale for the decisions.
   - **More appropriate use of design patterns:** The question annotations to design patterns in the AM3D pattern catalogue support the decision making process. While answering the questions, a user is triggered to explicitly think about the goal, intents and consequences of a pattern, and to compare these with the system requirements. Such sets of

questions can be seen as a check-list to be used before the pattern application. They reduce spontaneity and subjectivity of the decisions of a user, and the application of design patterns is no longer solely based on the user's own experience and opinion.

- **Semi-automated documentation of trace links between requirements and architectural elements:** Answers to the question annotations are justified with the existing requirements to the system. The user may select to provide IDs of the most important requirements, contributing to the answers to the questions. By doing so, the AM3D approach receives information about the connection between a decision to apply or to withdraw a design pattern and the requirements contributing to this decision. Moreover, if a decision is made to apply a design pattern candidate, the candidate is then instantiated in the architectural model. In this case, the design decision is related with the corresponding architectural elements.

  Thus, the AM3D approach supports establishing a connection between several project artefacts via documentation of trace links: First, the requirements in the requirement specification are related with the design documentation, and second, they are then related with the architectural model elements. The requirements are linked to the architectural elements via documented design decisions and their rationale.

3. **Exemplary design pattern catalogue.**

- **Support in instantiation of the AM3D approach in a project context to document design rationale and to establish trace links:** An exemplary design pattern catalogue with the rationale question annotations was developed based on the defined process and formalisation of the AM3D approach, and provides an initial starting point in the application of the AM3D process.

  The catalogue contains common design patterns from books by Gamma et al. [28] and Buschmann et al. [29] documented following the approach proposed in this thesis. Each of the patterns, besides the description based on the developed template (described in detail in Section 4.2), has question annotations attached to it. These questions are pattern-specific, but general enough to be project-independent. It means that they describe a design pattern in a way that the properties and consequences of a pattern can be understood independently of the project for which the design pattern is being considered. The questions are design rationale fragments describing expected pattern properties and assumptions, and they support the goals of the AM3D approach. In addition, each of the patterns in the catalogue has an architectural structure description based on the role-connector notation, described in Section 4.2.3. Such architectural descriptions allow for automated checks in component models in order to verify if the structure of the pattern is applied correctly and is not occasionally violated during the maintenance of the model. The catalogue is provided in Section 5.

- **Reference for creation of the catalogues based on the AM3D approach:** The developed exemplary catalogue provides a reference for the creation of the catalogues based on the AM3D approach, and can serve as a starting point for this purpose.

The developed exemplary catalogue was also used for the validation of the approach in the survey and in the conducted controlled experiment. The subjects used the catalogue during the experiment to solve tasks on design pattern application and maintenance.

1.3. Application Scenarios

Several application scenarios are considered for the proposed AM3D approach. The scenarios are independent from each other, however, they can be used in a sequence. While some of them require a complete application of the approach and related artefacts, others can be applied only with a part of them. The scenarios are the following:

- **Gaining information about a design pattern:** Reading the proposed pattern catalogue to get information about some pattern, similar to the classical approaches based on the book catalogues.
- **Evaluation of the design pattern suitability for a given problem:** Once there is a potential design pattern candidate to solve a given design problem, the candidate can be evaluated with the help of the AM3D approach. Such evaluation reduces the spontaneity of design decisions on pattern application.
- **Semi-automated documentation of decision rationale:** The information collected during pattern evaluation is used for semi-automated documentation of decisions to apply or to withdraw patterns together with the rationale for the decisions.
- **Selection between similar patterns for a given problem:** Evaluation of the design pattern suitability for a given problem can be done for several patterns, thus highlighting the differences in the expected properties of patterns and supporting the selection between them.
- **Goal-oriented requirements elicitation:** The questions in the catalogue explicitly ask details required for making a decision on a pattern application. If the information is insufficient or if the functional and quality requirements contradict each other, requirements elicitation and prioritisation are triggered. Such requirements engineering is goal-oriented and is driven through the system design and its architecture.
- **Retrieving information about patterns applied in the system:** Once the system has been documented according to the proposed

approach, it is possible to retrieve information on design decisions that have been made about the pattern application.

- **Understanding pattern design decisions during system maintenance:** Similar to the previous scenario, the rationale for the design decisions can be extracted from the decisions and supports an understanding of the pattern application.

- **Understanding the rationale of architectural elements through trace links to requirements:** If the rationale and decisions to pattern application were documented using the proposed AM3D approach, the semi-automatically created trace-links between requirements, design decisions and architectural elements could be used for understanding the architectural elements.

- **Tracing change of requirements during maintenance:** Similar to the previous point, captured trace links can be used to trace change of requirements through design decisions and their rationale for the architectural elements. In this case, deprecated design decisions and architectural elements can be updated on demand.

- **Architectural implementation violations checks:** The structural information is captured in the catalogue, together with design pattern descriptions and question annotations. It can be used to automatically check structural violation in pattern implementation at the architectural level.

Application scenarios are presented in detail in Section 3.2.2, together with the relevant process steps and artefacts.

1.4. Validation

This dissertation thesis defines four types of empirical validation for the architectural knowledge management research area, based on the three types of empirical evaluations for the model-based performance prediction methods proposed by Böhme et al. [85] and Koziolek [86]. The goal of the explicit validation type definition is to avoid ambiguities in the validation of the approach and its clustering the research area. These types shall provide a common language for the validation in the area and reflect the maturity of the proposed approaches in regard to their validation. The developed types are: Feasibility, Appropriateness, Applicability and Cost-benefit. They are described in Section 6.1 and were applied for the description of the carried validations of the AM3D approach in Chapter 6.

Overall, the proposed AM3D approach is validated in three parts (described in Chapter 6).

First, a survey was conducted to evaluate the motivation of the approach and to evaluate the feasibility of the proposed annotated pattern catalogue as of a potential solution for the problems with design pattern use and documentation. The survey research method was to use structured interviews, and the results were evaluated in a qualitative way. The survey and its results are described in detail in Section 6.4.

Second, the AM3D approach was applied on a common example to demonstrate the appropriateness of the AM3D approach, its artefacts and the process. It is described in detail in Chapter 4.

Third, an empirical study was conducted to validate the applicability and claimed benefits of the approach. The empirical study validates if design patterns annotated according to the AM3D approach can be better understood and applied more correctly as compared to the design pattern catalogue based on the standard approach. Further on, it is validated if a system architecture, which is documented according to the AM3D approach and, thus, is the result of development of the system using the AM3D approach, can be better maintained compared to the system documented according to the standard catalogue approach. The empirical study research method is a controlled experiment, which is a quantitative research method. The experiment is described in detail in Section 6.5.

1.5. Outline

The rest of this thesis is organized as follows:

- **Chapter 2** introduces concepts and terms required to gain an understanding of the approach. Section 2.1 gives an overview of the software development process. The requirements engineering and related artefacts are explained in Section 2.2. Section 2.3 provides an overview of the software architecture and software design. It explains software design decisions and their rationale. It introduces concepts of architectural styles and design patterns, and explains the difference between these. Section 2.4 deals with the foundations of model-driven development and explains the concept of a meta-model, model and model instance together with the hierarchy levels they undergo. Finally, Section 2.5 provides an overview of the additional foundations of the AM3D approach, such as Palladio Component Model (PCM), Common Component Modelling Example (CoCoME), and Controlled natural languages.

- **Chapter 3** gives an overview of the proposed AM3D approach and of all the related concepts. First, Section 3.1 provides an overview of the main concepts of the proposed approach. Section 3.2 introduces the developed process to use the proposed catalogue of design patterns. First, the base process is introduced, which is followed by a detailed description of application scenarios for the approach, and of the corresponding processes for these application scenarios. Section 3.3 describes the traceability support given by the AM3D approach. Section 3.4 explains the contribution of the AM3D approach to goal-oriented architecture-driven requirements elicitation. Section 3.5 highlights the differences between the proposed approach and expert systems in order to avoid ambiguities in the understanding of further sections. Finally, Section 3.6 introduces an example that is used to demonstrate the proposed approach.

- **Chapter 4** provides a detailed explanation of the proposed AM3D approach and details on the core of the approach – the AM3D pattern catalogue. Section 4.1 explains the purpose of the proposed pattern catalogue. Section 4.2 explains the structure of the catalogue, which consists of three blocks: General information on patterns, question annotations and architectural structure. Section 4.3 details the concept of question annotations, which are proposed as a solution for problems with pattern application and decision documentation. The purpose of the question annotation is explained in detail, followed by a discussion of the ways to formulate the questions, types of questions and supporting styles of formulating the questions. The section then provides a discussion of answers to the question annotations, and is concluded with a description of a process to add questions to the patterns in the proposed catalogue. Section 4.4 introduces a process to fill in the catalogue. The types of pattern in the catalogue are discussed in Section 4.5. A detailed presentation and discussion of the developed formalisation method for the approach based on the meta-models is provided in Section 4.6. Each of the subpackages of the developed meta-model is described in detail in the subsections. Section 4.7 concludes the chapter, highlighting the important details about the presented approach.

- **Chapter 5** presents an exemplary pattern catalogue, developed according to the proposed AM3D approach. The catalogue contains descriptions of 12 common design patterns, each of which is provided with question annotations. The catalogue was also used during validation of the approach. It concludes with a summary of experiences collected during the creation of the catalogue.

- **Chapter 6** introduces developed validation types for the architectural knowledge management area, gives details on the conducted validations and presents the results. The developed validation types are provided in Section 6.1. Section 6.2 discusses how and what was validated for the AM3D approach. Section 6.3 introduces the Goal Question Metric approach, which was used to formulate goals and the research questions for the conducted validations. Section 6.4 provides details on the conducted survey, its research questions and method, survey design, testing of the research method, and survey results. It discusses threats to validity and limitations of the survey and gives a summary of the results. Section 6.5 provides details on the conducted empirical study, based on the controlled experiment, its research questions, research method, experiment design, testing of the method, and experiment results. It discusses threats to validity and limitations of the experiment and provides a summary of the results. Finally, Section 6.6 concludes the chapter.

- **Chapter 7** provides an overview of the related work in the area and outlines the differences between the approach proposed here and other related approaches. First, Section 7.1 introduces the developed classification scheme for the related work approaches. It explains what areas of the related work research are in the focus of the AM3D approach. Further on, Section 7.2 provides a review of the related approaches in the formalisation and documentation of design patterns research area. The section is structured based on the underlying formalisation method used by the approaches. Section 7.3 provides a review of the related approaches in the formalisation and documentation about the design decisions research area. The section is also structured based on the underlying formalisation method used by the approaches. Section 7.4 provides a review of the related approaches that deal with the reasoning about and selection of design patterns.

The approaches are structured based on the mechanism used for the pattern selection, such as approaches based on the influence on non-functional properties and question-based approaches. Section 7.6 provides a summary of related approaches and points out the main differences between them and the AM3D approach.

- **Chapter 8** concludes the thesis with a summary of the most important contributions described in this thesis, of the approach benefits and of conducted validations (Section 8.1). Assumptions and limitations are discussed in Section 8.2. Open questions and future work are presented in Section 8.3, which is structured according to the three categories: Short-term user-relevant open questions and future work (Section 8.3.2); long-term user-relevant open questions and future work (Section 8.3.1); and empirical user-relevant open questions and future work (Section 8.3.3).

2. Foundations

This chapter provides foundations for the AM3D approach. The goal of the chapter is to enable uniform understanding of the concepts that are used by the AM3D approach and are required to understand the approach.

First, an overview of the software development process is given in Section 2.1. The requirements engineering and related artefacts are explained in Section 2.2. Section 2.3 provides an overview of the software architecture and software design main terms and concepts. It explains what is understood under software design decisions and their rational, what are the reusable architectural solutions, explains Styles and Design Patterns and difference between them, and provides a short introduction into main concepts of component-based software development. Section 2.4 deals with foundations on model-driven development and explains the concept of a meta-model, model and model instance together with the hierarchy they undergo. These concepts are used later on to formalise the proposed design pattern catalogue and the relevant project context. Finally, Section 2.5 provides an overview of the additional foundations of the AM3D approach, such as Palladio Component Model (PCM), Common Component Modelling Example (CoCoME), and Controlled natural languages.

2.1. Software Development Processes

This section introduces the concept of a software development process (in Section 2.1.1) and provides a brief description of agile process models (in Section 2.1.2).

2.1.1. Basic Concepts

Software development typically consists of several standard phases, such as: Requirements specification (elicitation, negotiation, prioritisation and capture of requirements to the system), Architectural design (transformation of requirements into architectural design, architectural design decision making and capture, architectural modelling, architectural evaluation), Implementation (transformation of architectural design into code), Testing (various level of tests to the system, such as unit, integration, system and acceptance testing), Deployment (installation of developed software on running productive systems) and Maintenance (implementation of change requests, new requirements and bug fixing).

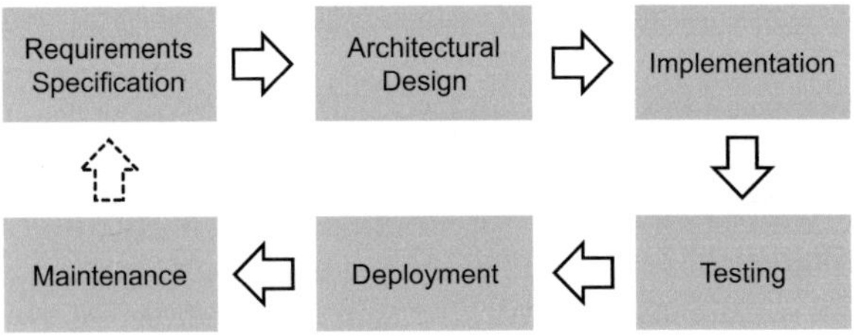

Figure 2.1.: Overview of General Software Development Phases (Adapted from [87])

The overview of these general software development phases is provided on Figure 2.1 (adapted from [87]). The arrows schematically depict possible order of connections between the development phases (please note that this is only one of the many process options). The dotted arrow schematically depicts the start of a new development iteration.

The development phases are interconnected in an order following one of the known development patterns. The order in which the phases are followed is defined by the selected development process model. Software development process model is "an abstract representation of a set of activities that leads to the production of a software product" [87]. According to

Sommerville [87], the generic process models are "not definitive descriptions of software processes. Rather, they are abstractions of the process that can be used to explain different approaches to software development".

Definition 2.1 Software Development Process Model [87]

Software development process model is an abstract representation of software process, which is a set of activities that leads to the production of a software product.

The order of activity phases defined by process models may be linear, non-linear, iterative, incremental or a combination of these. Lineal development might be well-suitable for short projects or projects in the known domain with clear defined and unlikely to change requirements, where final systems require a strict conformance with the specification and extensive testing, for example systems in a military domain. Iterative and incremental development is better suited for less known domain or domains with changing requirements that have to be reconsidered in design and implementation.

Some of the examples of the common process models are: Waterfall model [87], V-Model [81, 82], Rational Unified Process (RUP) [83] and so-called Agile Methods, such as Scrum [84, 88] or Extreme Programming [89]. Most of the process models can be considered frameworks, which define general rules and artefacts, and shall be tailored to fit a particular project.

The approach described in this thesis proposes a set of actions to extend any base process having explicit architectural design phase, and using artefacts form the requirements phase. More details on requirements engineering are provided in Section 2.2, and on architectural design in Section 2.3.

2.1.2. Agile Methods

A software process models family called "agile methods" was developed to anticipate the rapidly changing software developing environment.

Since there is no uniform definition for the agile methods, this thesis provides its own definition for the agile methods: Agile methods are software development process models that follow an iterative and incremental approach, are concentrated on a software development with a lowest possible management overhead and on execution of activities that are the most relevant for the project success at the current moment. Such development is called goal-oriented development.

Definition 2.2 Agile Methods

Agile methods are software development process models that follow an iterative and incremental approach, are concentrated on a software development with a lowest possible management overhead and on execution of activities that are the most relevant for the project success at the current moment.

The most famous agile methods are: Extreme Programming (XP) [89], Scrum [84, 88], Crystal Clear [90], Feature Driven Development [91] and Adaptive Software Development [92].

While classical software engineering methods, such as RUP [83] or V-Model [81, 82], require careful planning up-front, the agile methods concentrate on quick reaction and adoption to changes. Because of this, they became popular in the broader developer community, and there are a high number of success reports, especially for Scrum and XP [93–98]. The empirical studies on the quality and efficiency of these methods are less clear [99, 100]. It seems that agile methods improve well over ad-hoc processes. However, common practices, such as as pair-programming and test-driven development, are not demonstrated yet to improve over established classical software development quality assurance techniques, such as code and architectural reviews.

The agile methods are based on the agile manifesto and have the following common characteristics (from [10]):

- **Iterative and incremental process:** Developing software in steps and iterations over a complete process steps circle.
- **Lightweight process:** As few forward planning as possible with code being the main artefact, some classical practices, such as forward planning and architecture modelling are considered to be abundant.
- **Flexible:** Quick response to a changing environment, and new requirements are welcomed at any stage of development.
- **Goal-oriented:** Project value oriented, every development increment shall add value to the product.
- **Customer oriented:** Strong customer involvement.
- **Team-oriented:** The team has the main role in the development process and is self-organized.

These properties are not unique for agile methods, however the agile community is focused on them. The agile manifesto explicitly states the principles of agile development [101] as the following: Individuals and interactions over processes and tools; Working software over comprehensive documentation; Customer collaboration over contract negotiation; and responding to change over following a plan.

One of the key keywords in agile methods is a word "lightweight", which is typically used to characterise a low overhead of an action. Another one is a concept of "waste". As wastes are considered all the activities in the project that do not directly contribute to the project success. Therefore, architectural design and software documentation are often misinterpreted in waste, and are neglected.

An example of an Agile process is presented on Figure 2.2, which depicts a Scrum development process.

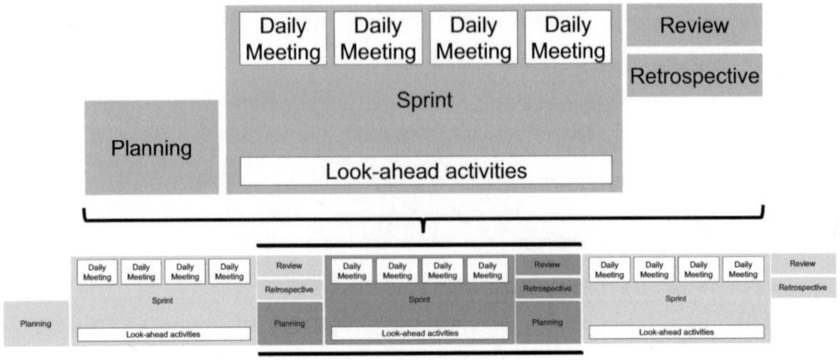

Figure 2.2.: Overview of Scrum Development Process

On the figure's upper part is depicted one Scrum process iteration. It consists of four steps, which are also associated with meetings in the Scrum process:

- **Planning:** Planning meeting to plan the development during the next Sprint, usually a 2-4 hours time slot.
- **Sprint:** A single development iteration unit, usually a 2-4 weeks time slot. During the Sprint there are Daily meetings every day. A Daily meeting is a meeting to briefly discussed planned activities for the day, to identify dependencies and to notify about impediments in the development, and look-ahead activities, such as contribution to planning of the next Sprint iterations and some organisational activities.
- **Review:** Review meeting to accept the development results of a past Sprint, usually a 2 hours time slot.
- **Retrospective:** Retrospective meeting to review good and bad practices during the past Sprint, usually a 2-4 hours time slot.

All of these four steps together are called one Sprint iteration. A sequence of such Sprint iterations comprises a Scrum process, depicted on the bottom of Figure 2.2.

The AM3D approach proposed in this thesis originates from the idea of more agile architectural design and documentation, as published in our publications [10, 13]. It includes definition of actions, which would simplify documentation of architectural design and reduce required planning up-front. In particular, one of the claimed benefits of the approach is the light-weight documentation of design decisions, their rationale and trace links. The other related benefit is a goal-oriented elicitation of requirements, whereby the AM3D approach stimulates elicitation and prioritisation of requirements relevant to the current design tasks. Thus, architectural design documentation and requirements engineering are more lightweight and require less overhead in terms of agile methods. Moreover, the AM3D approach helps to avoid waste in respect to improper design decision on pattern application, which make design more stable with less mistakes, which require correction.

2.2. Requirements Engineering

This section introduces the requirements engineering phase of a software development process. First, the basic concepts such as requirements engineering itself and requirements are described in Section 2.2.1. Then, Section 2.2.2 introduces classification of requirement types, which are used throughout this thesis. Section 2.2.3 introduces the concept of stakeholder in requirements engineering. Finally, requirement engineering process is explained in Section 2.2.4, together with the role of requirements engineer, ways to capture requirements, and the relation between requirements and architecture.

2.2.1. Basic Concepts

Requirements engineering is the first phase of a classical system development life cycle and is focused on the requirements to the system. However, neither an established definition of requirements and of requirements engineering exists, nor there is a consensus how to structure and to write requirements. The state of the art typically simply omits the definition of what is understood under requirements and requirements engineering in the proposed method.

This thesis uses the definition of requirements engineering by the IEEE 29148-2011 Standard [102], which defines the requirements engineering as "an interdisciplinary function that mediates between the domains of the acquirer and supplier to establish and maintain the requirements to be met by the system, software or service of interest". According to the IEEE standard, requirements engineering "is concerned with discovering, eliciting, developing, analyzing, determining verification methods, validating, communicating, documenting, and managing requirements" [102].

Definition 2.3 Requirements Engineering [102]

Requirements engineering is an interdisciplinary function that mediates between the domains of the acquirer and supplier to establish and maintain the requirements to be met by the system, software or service of interest. Requirements engineering is concerned with discovering, eliciting, developing, analyzing, determining verification methods, validating, communicating, documenting, and managing requirements.

The requirement is defined in the IEEE 29148-2011 Standard [102] as "a statement which translates or expresses a need and its associated constraints and conditions".

Definition 2.4 Requirement [102]

Requirement is a statement which translates or expresses a need and its associated constraints and conditions.

It is a formal and quite general definition. A more comprehensive definition is given by Sommerville et al. in [103], where a requirement is defined as "a specification of what should be implemented", and as "a description of how the system should behave, or of a system property or attribute". Thus, requirements are specifications of the system, which describe various aspects, such as functionality, quality properties, context, and constraints. This thesis uses the definition by Sommerville et al. in [103], as it includes attributes and properties as elements of requirements engineering.

Definition 2.5 Requirement [103]

Requirements are defined during the early stages of a system development as a specification of what should be implemented. They are descriptions of how the system should behave, or of a system property or attribute.

2.2.2. Classification of Requirements

The classification of requirements is an even more complicated and controversial topic. The most typical classification is to divide all requirements into functional (describing functions of a system) and non-functional (also called extra-functional, describing all other requirements). Sommerville et al. [103] provides the following explanation of funcitonal and non-functional requirements: "Functional requirements describe what the system should do and non-functional requirements place constraints on how these functional requirements are implemented." Following this classification, non-functional requirements describe quality features of a system, constrains on the system and its context, etc.. However, depending on how the requirements are formulated, a quality requirement might actually be rather a functional requirement and vice versa.

Another option to describe requirements is to associate them with system goals, as proposed for example in [44] van Lamsweerde. The requirements are then structured according to the goals and concerns at the different levels of abstraction, from "high-level strategic concerns to low-level technical details".

In this thesis, the first classification is used. In particular, the AM3D approach relies on the definitions and classification proposed by Glinz [104]. The classification proposed by Glinz [104] is based on the taxonomy of terms, that in their turn are based on concerns. According to Glinz, "the set of all requirements of a system is partitioned into functional requirements, performance requirements, specific quality requirements, and constraints" [104].

Definition 2.6 Classification of requirements types [104]

The set of all requirements of a system is partitioned into functional requirements, performance requirements, specific quality requirements, and constraints.

Here, Glinz [104] defines a functional requirements as "a requirement that pertains to a functional concern".

Definition 2.7 Functional requirement [104]

A functional requirement is a requirement that pertains to a functional concern.

A performance requirements is "a requirement that pertains to a performance concern" [104].

Definition 2.8 Performance requirement [104]

A performance requirement is a requirement that pertains to a performance concern.

A specific quality requirement is "a requirement that pertains to a quality concern other than the quality of meeting the functional requirements" [104].

Definition 2.9 Specific quality requirement [104]

A specific quality requirement is a requirement that pertains to a quality concern other than the quality of meeting the functional requirements.

And finally, a constraint is "a requirement that constrains the solution space beyond what is necessary for meeting" [104].

Definition 2.10 Constraint [104]

A constraint is a requirement that constrains the solution space beyond what is necessary for meeting.

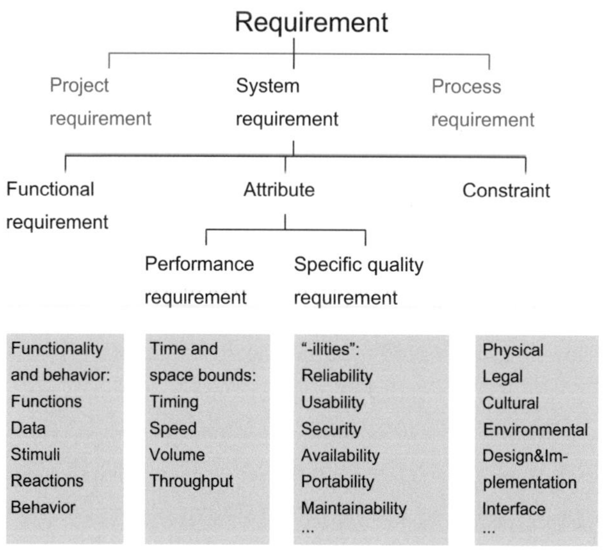

Figure 2.3.: A Concern-based Taxonomy of Requirements [104]

This classification (taxonomy) is presented on Figure 2.3. In the classification, the requirements are first structured according to their general role: Project requirements, system requirements and process requirements. Furthermore, system requirements are fined into: Functional requirements, attributes and constraints. The attributes consist of: Performance requirements, such as throughput, volume, etc., and specific quality requirements, such as legal requirements, cultural requirements, etc..

Compare this classification to the one provided by IEEE Standard [102] and depicted on Figure 2.4. The IEEE classification presents a much more flat hierarchy, with a larger consideration of human influence factor. Here, in addition to the types specified by Glinz [104], a performance requirement "defines the extent or how well, and under what conditions, a function or task is to be performed". A usability or quality-in-Use requirement "provides the basis for the design and evaluation of systems to meet the user needs". An interface requirement "defines of how the system is required to interact with external systems (external interface), or how system elements within the system, including human elements, interact with each other (internal interface)". And a human factors requirement "states required characteristics for the outcomes of interaction with human users (and other stakeholders affected by use) in terms of safety, performance, effectiveness, efficiency, reliability, maintainability, health, well-being and satisfaction". However, even though this classification might be more detailed, it is of less practical use for the AM3D approach.

The classification by Glinz [104] was selected because of its comprehensive overview and structure of requirements types. It contains all categories of requirements that are important in the context of design pattern selection, documentation and for the reasoning about patterns. It also contains a classification of quality requirements that are connected to the quality influence dimensions of the design patterns. This classification of requirements was used to structure the classes in the AM3D requirements meta-model, described in Section 4.6.

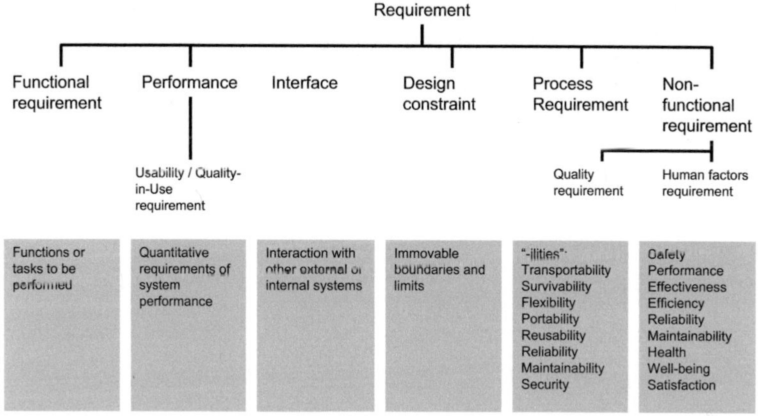

Figure 2.4.: An IEEE Standard Taxonomy of Requirement Types (Abstracted from Textural Description in [102])

2.2.3. Stakeholders

Another important attribute of requirements, besides the type classification, is the stakeholder. Sommerville et al. in [103] defines stakeholders as "people who will be affected by the system and who have a direct or indirect influence on the system requirements".

Definition 2.11 Stakeholder [103]

System stakeholders are people who will be affected by the system and who have a direct or indirect influence on the system requirements.

As clear from the definition, its focus lies on the system stakeholders. A more generic definition of stakeholders is provided by the IEEE 29148-2011 Standard [102] and includes system stakeholders as a subclass. According to the IEEE Standard, a stakeholder is "an individual or organization having a right, share, claim, or interest in a system or in its possession of characteristics that meet their needs and expectations" [102].

This thesis uses the definition by the IEEE 29148-2011 Standard [102], as it more precisely specifies influence by stakeholders on the system.

Definition 2.12 Stakeholder [102]

Stakeholder is an individual or organization having a right, share, claim, or interest in a system or in its possession of characteristics that meet their needs and expectations.

Stakeholders take active part in the process of requirement elicitation. Elicitation of requirements is "a process through which the acquirer and the suppliers of a system discover, review, articulate, understand, and document the requirements on the system and the life cycle processes" [102].

2.2.4. Requirements Engineering Process

An important part of requirement engineering process is requirement elicitation. It is a process through which the acquirer and the suppliers of a system discover, review, articulate, understand, and document the requirements on the system and the life cycle processes.

Definition 2.13 Requirement elicitation [102]

Requirement elicitation is a process through which the acquirer and the suppliers of a system discover, review, articulate, understand, and document the requirements on the system and the life cycle processes.

A requirements engineering process is "a structured set of activities which are followed to derive, validate and maintain a systems requirements document" [103].

Definition 2.14 Requirements Engineering Process [103]

A requirements engineering process is a structured set of activities which are followed to derive, validate and maintain a systems requirements document. A complete process description should include what activities are carried out, the structuring or schedule of these activities, who is responsible for each activity, the inputs and outputs to/from the activity and the tools used to support requirements engineering.

The requirement engineering process is a complex set of steps and requires a support of specially trained individuals – requirements engineers. A requirement engineer is "a person responsible for communication with stakeholders, and for the elicitation, capture, prioritisation, testing, update and communication of the requirements with or without them, depending on the organisational structure" [103].

Definition 2.15 Requirement Engineer [103]

A requirement engineer is a person responsible for communication with stakeholders, and for the elicitation, capture, prioritisation, testing, update and communication of the requirements with or without them, depending on the organisational structure.

There are multiple ways to capture the requirements. The most common way is to capture requirements in textual specification documents. In this case, requirements are captured as structured text (for example, as a Microsoft Word document or as a Microsoft Excel table), provided with identification number and textual description. A more advanced form of a textual description is a description template, for example the Volere Requirements Specification Template by Robertson et al. [105]. A process using this specification template is described in the book by Robertson et al. [106].

The Volere template proposes a fixed and use-proven structure to capture the requirements (also called Volere Atomic Requirement Template), which contains a set of fields describing the most common-used properties of requirements, such as ID, description, priority, etc.. In addition to this, it proposed a set of sections for the general process and context description, such as information about project stakeholders, context constraints, functional and non-functional requirements specified according to the Volere Atomic Requirement Template, project risks, etc.. For more information to the Volere Requirements Specification Template please refer to [105, 106].

Another way to capture requirements is to formulate them as User Stories. User Stories are very often used in Agile development to capture the requirements. A User Story is a kind of requirement description template, where requirements are described as short stories with an explicit actor, benefit for the actor, estimated required effort and priority. An example of a User Story is presented on Figure 2.5.

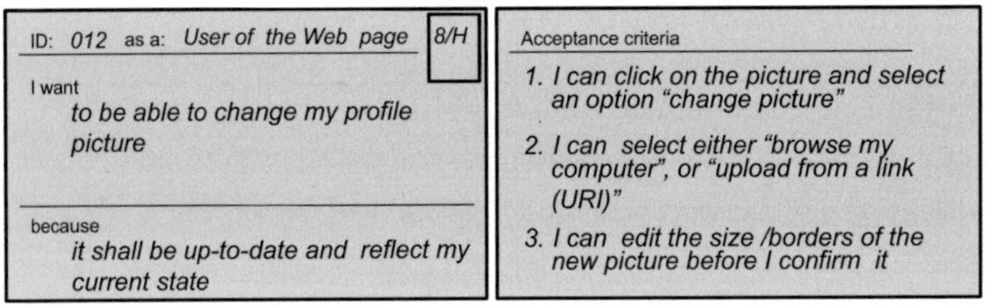

Figure 2.5.: An Example of a User Story

In the example, an actor of the story is a Web page user. The user wants to be able to change a profile picture on the Web page. A rationale for this requirement is that the user would like to keep his profile picture up-to-date, and the picture shall reflect the current state of the user's life and taste. The story has an estimate effort of 8 Story Points (a measure to estimate effort in User Stories, for more information on effort estimation refer to [107]), and a high priority. One of the most important fields in the User Story is the acceptance criteria block. These criteria are a kind of post condition, and describe conditions when a Story is considered to be implemented (finished). User Stories can have different granularity levels, from very large (Epic

User Stories) to very small (Working User Story). The latter are comparable to the detailed requirements in requirements specifications. For more information on User Stories refer to [107, 108].

The form of requirements description also depends on specialized tool support. The most famous commercial tools in the area are IBM Rational DOORS [109], IBM Rational RequisitePro [110], Polarion REQUIREMENTS [111]. Some of the open source tools in the area are: Open Source Requirements Management Tool [112] and Unicase [113] (a CASE-tool for modelling artefacts in a software engineering project).

Finally, even though requirements engineering is a first step of the system development life cycle, it is an ongoing activity throughout the whole life of a system. The new requirements and change requests trigger changes in the system design and implementation, and also system design and implementation actually trigger new requirements. In the latter case, the requirements are systematically elicited as a by-product, as very often information about certain expected properties, features or behaviour of the system is incomplete. Architects and developers often have to ask requirements engineers to elicit additional information on the missing features and properties.

As the focus of this thesis lies primarily in the area of architecture, and not in the implementation, a relation between requirements and architecture is of a primary interest. A two-way relationship between requirements and architectural design is schematically presented on Figure 2.6.

Requirements are important triggers for the feature demand in software architecture. Decisions on architectural design are taken based on the current requirement specification of a system, and requirements serve as a rationale for the taken design decisions. On the other hand, architectural design and architectural design decisions deliver a feedback back to requirements engineering, and constraint further requirement engineering or trigger updates in the existing requirement specifications.

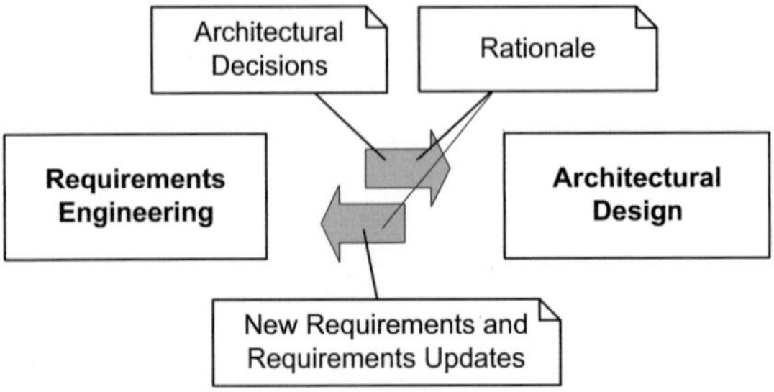

Figure 2.6.: Relation Between Requirements and Architectural Design

In the AM3D approach, the existing requirements to the system are linked to the taken or discarded pattern design decisions as triggers, constraints or rationale attributes. Change of the existing requirements is propagated through these trace links into the architectural model to warn the architect about changes and potential decision obsolescence, and also back to the requirements engineer to warn about the impact of change and about potential inconsistencies. For more information about relation of requirements and architectures please refer to [42, 114].

2.3. Software Architecture and Architectural Design

This section provides an introduction to the concept of software architecture, architectural design and modelling. It explains the concept of design decisions and design decisions rationale, reusable architectural design solutions, such as architectural styles and patterns, and gives an introduction to component-based software development.

The concept of software architecture is explained in Section 2.3.1. Design decisions and rationale are explained in Section 2.3.2. Section 2.3.3 introduces a concept of architectural styles, and Section 2.3.4 the concept of architectural design patterns. Finally, component-based software development is explained in Section 2.3.5.

2.3.1. Basic Concepts

This section is based on the books by Taylor et al. [115], Clements et al. [116], Rozanski et al. [117], Paulish [118], and on material collected in our previous publications [1, 9, 17].

2.3.1.1. Software Architecture Definition

The main term throughout this section is the term "software architecture". However, there is no acknowledged single definition available. In fact, there are multiple definitions of software architecture that are used throughout the research area.

Taylor et al. [115] provide the following definition of software architecture: A software architecture is "the set of principal design decisions made about the system".

Definition 2.16 Software Architecture [115]

A software system's architecture is the set of principal design decisions made about the system.

Clemets et al. [116] define architecture as "a high level abstraction of software".

Definition 2.17 Software Architecture [116]

A software architecture is a high level abstraction of software.

Paulish [118] replies on the definition of Soni et al [119], where software architecture is "concerned with capturing the structures of a system and relationships among elements ...".

Definition 2.18 Software Architecture [119] via [118]

Software architecture is concerned with capturing the structures of a system and relationships among elements.

Rozanski et al. [117] define software architecture as a "structure or structures of the system, which comprise software elements, the externally visible properties of those elements, and the relationships among them".

Definition 2.19 Software Architecture [117]

Software architecture is a structure or structures of the system, which comprise software elements, the externally visible properties of those elements, and the relationships among them.

The key concepts of these definitions are abstraction, design decisions, structure and relationships between elements. This thesis further on relies on the definition of Rozanski et al. [117], as it is simultaneously concerned with the system structure, properties and relations between elements.

2.3.1.2. Software Architect

The person responsible for the system architecture is called the system architect. In some cases, this role is merged with a more general role of software engineer. Taylor at al. [115] define software architect as "a person combining the skills of a domain expert, a software designer, a technologist, a standards compliance expert, and a software engineering economist". The authors point out that, unfortunately, a title of software architect is rather randomly assigned, which leads persons with insufficient experience to be responsible for important design decisions.

Definition 2.20 Software Architect [115]

Software architect is a person combining the skills of a domain expert, a software designer, a technologist, a standards compliance expert, and a software engineering economist.

The responsibilities of a software architect include [115]: Development of project strategies, system design, leading, and communication with stakeholders. Thus, the software architect can be seen as an experienced software engineer. In this thesis, the role of software architect is replaced with the role of software engineer. This is because the AM3D approach is not limited to the application by a professional software architect at the architectural level. It is also suitable to the application of software engineers, and in particular, less experience software engineers, who might profit the most from the approach application.

2.3.1.3. Architectural Design and Modelling

Software architecture is comprised of architectural design, which shall be documented in design documentation. This includes architectural models, textual descriptions, taken design decisions with the rationale for them. According to Taylor et al. [115], architectural model is "an artefact that captures some or all of the design decisions that comprise a system's architecture". Architectural modelling is "reification and documentation of those design decisions".

Definition 2.21 Architectural Model and Modelling [115]

Architectural model is an artefact that captures some or all of the design decisions that comprise a system's architecture. Architectural modelling is reification and documentation of those design decisions.

The architecture can be represented either visually in a model, for example with the help of the Unified Modelling Language (UML) [120], or formally with the help of Architectural Description Languages (ADL) [121]. Some of the ADLs also include a visual model representation. Depending on the definition of the ADLs, UML can be also considered an ADL.

An ADL is "any form of expression for use in architecture descriptions. An ADL provides one or more model kinds as a means to frame some concerns for its audience of stakeholders. An ADL can be narrowly focused, defining a single model kind, or widely focused to provide several model kinds, optionally organized into viewpoints. Often an ADL is supported by automated tools to aid the creation, use and analysis of its models" [122].

Definition 2.22 Architectural Description Language (ADL) [122]

An ADL is any form of expression for use in architecture descriptions. An ADL provides one or more model kinds as a means to frame some concerns for its audience of stakeholders. An ADL can be narrowly focused, defining a single model kind, or widely focused to provide several model kinds, optionally organized into viewpoints. Often an ADL is supported by automated tools to aid the creation, use and analysis of its models.

The ISO/IEC/IEEE 42010 standard [122] defines minimum requirements to an ADL: The identification of one or more concerns to be expressed by the ADL; The identification of one or more stakeholders having those concerns; The model kinds implemented by the ADL which frame those concerns; Any architecture viewpoints; and Correspondence rules relating these model kinds.

An opinion about documenting architecture presented by Kruchten [123], and also shared in this thesis, is that documentation of architecture is a matter of documenting the relevant views and then adding documentation that applies to more than one view. An architectural view is a representation of a set of system elements and the relations associated with them [116].

Definition 2.23 Architectural View [116]

An architectural view is a representation of a set of system elements and the relations associated with them.

The famous "4 + 1 View Model" by Kruchten "describes software architecture using five concurrent views, each of which addresses a specific set of concerns" [123]. The model is depicted on Figure 2.7. It consists of the logical view describing the functionality of the system, the development view describing static organization of software in the development environment, the process view describing design's concurrency and synchronization aspects, the physical view describing mapping of the software onto the hardware, and the scenarios describing system's use cases. The architectural model includes views on its static structure, such as components and connectors, the inter-component control flow and the deployment of components and connectors on virtual or physical resources (virtual machines or hardware knots).

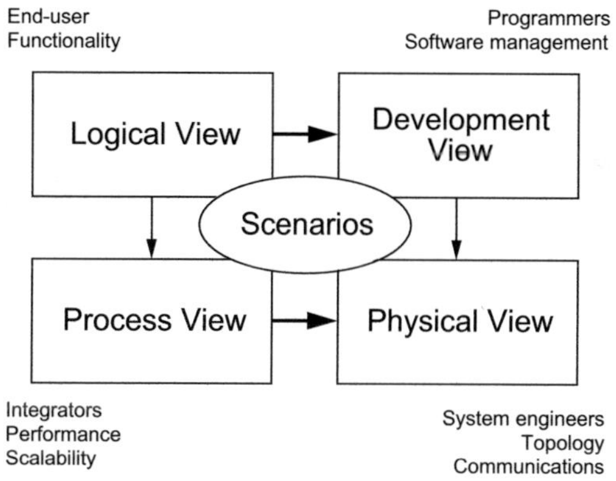

Figure 2.7.: 4 + 1 View Model [123]

Architecture and architecture modelling have the following benefits [10, 116, 124]:

- **Communication:** Software architecture may be used to focus discussion by system stakeholders, such as engineers, requirements engineers and customers.
- **Comprehension:** Architectural models ease comprehension of architectural design, and of complex dependencies in a system. The details are raised to the next abstraction level, which is easier to grasp than the very detailed descriptions or code. However, this requires (1) a common understanding of the used modelling formalism, such

as UML or of some other ADL, and (2) a correct definition of the abstraction level. The later is a subject of decisions of the software architect, and may be accordingly over- or under-detailed. There is no precise definition for the right level of abstraction and details in software architectures.

- **Analysis:** Software architecture allows for consistency checking, checks of conformance to constraints and to quality attributes, dependence analysis and others. Architectural models allow for a design-time analysis of quality properties of a system, such as performance or reliability. Such design-time feedback to the architect helps to avoid costly design mistakes, which are hard to correct at later development phases.

- **Reuse:** Architecture design stimulates reuse at multiple levels and across a range of systems. The reuse is achieved through reusable architectural solutions, such as styles, design patterns, components, frameworks or even code.

- **Management:** Architectural design demands practical and precise understanding of the requirements to the system. It typically leads to a much clearer understanding of requirements, design and implementation strategies and potential risks (cost-estimation, mile stone organization, dependency analysis, change analysis, staffing); evaluation of an architecture

- **Implementation support:** Architectural models and design provide a partial blueprint for development of system code by indicating the major components and dependencies between them.

- **Evolution:** Architectural design supports system evolution by definitions of the directions and dimensions along which a system is expected to evolve. Usually, a system design included pre-defined support for some evolution scenarios that were anticipated during the system design.

Often, there is no other documentation than the architectural models. Therefore, architectural design decisions are often documented in an implicit way, as elements of design models. Having significant benefits, architecture modelling has disadvantages as well. Architectural design and modelling require technical skills and domain knowledge. They cause significant overhead, and in particular, a significant overhead when maintaining the documentation and models. The value of the architecture modelling is not always understood (especially by the customers), as it does not directly contribute to the value of the product, while creating additional cost, time and effort overhead.

The architecture is strongly influenced by the context and by the persons designing the architecture. Thus, given the same set of system requirements and constraints, different architectural designs will be developed. These are called variants of software architecture. Usually, multiple valid variants of system design exist, and the task of a software architect is to optimise various properties of the system in design according to the quality requirements to the system (non functional properties).

2.3.1.4. Architectural Knowledge Reuse

Another key concept in architectural design is a reusable architectural design solution. A reusable architectural design solution is an architectural solution that can be reused in the context of multiple projects maintaining the solution structure, design details and expected positive and potential negative properties. Some examples of reusable architectural solutions are architectural styles, design patterns, reusable components, such as thirds-party components (COTS) or in-house components.

Definition 2.24 Reusable Architectural Design Solution

Reusable architectural design solution is an architectural solution that can be reused in the context of multiple projects maintaining the solution structure, design details and expected positive and potential negative properties.

The different levels of architectural reuse and reusable solutions are depicted on Figure 2.8.

Level	How
Domain	Reference Architectures, Standards, etc.
System	Product Lines, Architectural Styles, etc.
System Component	Design Patterns, Components, Interfaces, Services

Figure 2.8.: Levels of Architectural Knowledge Reuse and Corresponding Reusable Solutions

The reusable architectural solutions, such as design styles or patterns, services and components are low-level examples of knowledge reuse. In addition to them, there are reference or domain-specific architectures, software product lines, generative approaches, frameworks and design or domain standards. The latter provide a kind of framework, which an architect can then fill with more specific low-level design solutions.

The reuse of architectural knowledge is important due to several reasons. First, it saves effort through reuse of existing design elements and increases the design speed. Second, it contributes to improvement of quality through recognised and tested design solutions. Then, it improves comprehension through a common language based on the reusable design solutions. Finally, it allowed for more elegant design solutions also for less experienced architects Architectural design is a creative process, which highly depends on the experience of a software architect. Reusable architectural knowledge allows for achieving a certain quality level of design, allowing for a more predictable standard architectures and less deign mistakes. The advantage of architectural knowledge reuse is also grasped by this thesis, which emphasises on the advantages of reuse of design documentation based on the reusable architectural solutions.

2.3.1.5. Software Architecture and Evolution

Software architecture typically plays a key role as a bridge between requirements and implementation [124] and supports evolution of the system. The extent of the evolution support depends on the quality of the architecture and its documentation, and if the documentation properly maintained. Once defined, the architectural design usually does not remain stable. It has to be changed due to the change requests, bug fixes and implementation of new requirements. This is a natural process of software evolution, which includes architectural design evolution.

When code implementation of system is in process, it has to be monitored for its conformance with the defined architectural design. This comparison is called comparison between is- and should-architectures. If a system has been changed, the architectural design and its documentation has to be accordingly updated. Taylor at al. [115] introduce these types of architecture as prescriptive and descriptive architectures. A prescriptive architecture is a set of design decisions reflecting the intent of the software architect during design time. A descriptive architecture describes how the system has been realized, and design derisions relevant to this aspect.

Definition 2.25 Prescriptive and Descriptive Architectures [115]

A prescriptive architecture is a set of design decisions reflecting the intent of the software architect during design time. A descriptive architecture describes how the system has been realized, and design derisions relevant to this aspect.

If software architecture and its documentation are not maintained, they degrade over time due to the loss of architectural knowledge and due to the design decisions becoming obsolete and contradicting. Such degradation is called architectural erosion. Taylor at al. define architectural erosion as "the introduction of architectural design decisions into a system's descriptive architecture that violate its prescriptive architecture".

Definition 2.26 Architectural Erosion [115]

Architectural erosion is the introduction of architectural design decisions into a system's descriptive architecture that violate its prescriptive architecture.

For further reading on software architecture and design aspects please refer to the book of Taylor et al. [115].

2.3.2. Design Decisions and Rationale

Design decisions are a very important concept in software architecture. They comprise architectural design and influence functional and qualitative properties the system. As with many other architectural concepts, there is no accepted definition of design decisions. Most of the state-of-the-art works on design decisions simply do not provide any definition. Few others usually define design decisions though their main aspects. For example, design decisions "embrace all aspects of the development, such as system structure, functional behaviour, interaction, non functional properties and their prioritisation, and implementation" according to Taylor et al. [115]. Thus, the aspects included into the design decisions are the following [115]: System structure, functional behaviour, interaction, non-functional properties, and system implementation.

Definition 2.27 Design Decision (adopted from [115])

Design decisions are core elements of software development, which are concerned with its design and embrace all aspects of the development, such as system structure, functional behaviour, interaction, non functional properties and their prioritisation, and implementation.

Taylor et al. [115] distinguish between architectural design decisions and design decisions. According to the difference lies in a degree of importance and topicality, and their influence on the system architecture. Tyree et al. [125] define architectural decisions as "a primary representation of architecture". Jansen et al. [126] define architectural decisions though the set of elements, including rationale, design rules and design constraints, and additional requirements, where architectural design decisions are "the outcome of a design process during the initial construction or the evolution of a software system" [126]. For this thesis, a combined definition based on these two definitions is used.

Definition 2.28 Architectural Design Decision (adopted from [125], [126])

Architectural design decision is an outcome of a design process during the initial construction or the evolution of a software system and is a primary representation of architecture.

The person making architectural design decisions is a software architect, while design decisions are met by a software engineer or even a system developer. The focus of this thesis lies on the architectural design decisions, therefore, under design decisions in the rest of this thesis the architectural design decisions are understood.

An overview of main elements of design decisions by [127] (from [128]) is provided on Figure 2.9.

Element	Description
Issues	Design issues being addressed by this decision
Decision	The decision taken
Status	The status of the decision, e.g. pending, approved
Assumptions	The underlying assumptions about the environment in which the decision is taken
Alternatives	Alternatives considered for this decision
Rationale	An explanation of why the decision was chosen
Implications	Implications of this decision, such as the need for further decisions or requirements
Notes	Any additional information one might want to capture

Figure 2.9.: Elements of Design Decisions [127] (Taken from [128])

Despite their importance, the treatment of design decisions as of first-class entities is not self-evident. In fact, design decisions are often viewed as a by-product of software design and are implicitly documented in as model elements (e.g. components or services) in software architectural design models. One of the first proposals to treat design decisions as first-class entities due to their importance comes from Bosch [129] and Kruchten [130]. The idea is based on the previous idea from Perry et al. [131] (as stated in by Kruchten in Chapter 3 of [128]). According to it [50, 128], the architectural design together with design decisions form architecture and knowledge about it.

The decisions are met based on a rationale, which is an "explanation, justification or reasoning about architecture decisions that have been made" [122]. The rationale for a decision includes such aspects, as the reasoning behind a decisions, alternative architectural solutions, trade-off between these solutions, intent of a selected solutions and awareness of the possible negative consequences of a solution. Lee [132] defines design rationale, as "not only the reasons behind a design decision but also the justification for it, the other alternatives considered, the trade-offs evaluated, and the argumentation that led to the decision". This later definition is used throughout this thesis.

Definition 2.29 Design Decision Rationale [132]

Design decision rationale includes not only the reasons behind a design decision but also the justification for it, the other alternatives considered, the trade-offs evaluated, and the argumentation that led to the decision.

Other important aspects of design decisions are their types, relations between each other and their status in the development process. An overview of these is provided in Figure 2.10.

Type	Relationship	Status
Architectural	Constraint	Open
Design	Exclude	Taken
Component	Trigger	Reviewed
Deplyoment	Enable	Obsolete
Technology	Parent of	Replaced
Design Pattern	Child of	Conflicted
...		

Figure 2.10.: Possible Types, Relationships and Statuses of Design Decisions

These aspects are used for classification of design decisions, and are the following:

- **Types:** Design decision can be classified based on types. The most common types are above mentioned architectural and design decision types, component decisions, deployment decisions, decisions on style or pattern application, decision on a use of service, and others.
- **Relationships:** Design decision can be classified based on relations between each other. A decision may be a trigger for some other decisions, it may constraint or even completely exclude some other types of design decisions. A decision may include some sub-decisions (a parent-of relationship) or be a sub-part of some design decisions (a child-of relationship).

- **Status:** Design decision can be classified based on the status in development process. Design decisions go through several states of their status, since there is usually a review process accompanying architectural design. These are: Open, taken, reviewed, obsolete, replaced, and conflicted. A decision may become obsolete or conflicted due to requirements of other design decision changes (in particular, if it was dependant on some other design decision).

There are also other classifications of types, relations, and statuses available. For example, Babar et al. [128] provide a different classification of the status of a design decisions: Idea, tentative, decided, approved, challenged, rejected, and obsolesced. However, this thesis relies on the classification from Figure 2.10.

Independent of their type, the documentation of design decisions, their rationale and relations to each other is important, as it supports the evolution of software systems, eases the comprehension of the design and enables easier implementation of changes [18, 19]. However, documentation of design decisions causes effort and time prone. Therefore, documentation of all design decisions is not reasonable due to their high number and difference in their importance [128], and only significant design decisions shall be documented.

There are multiple ways proposed for documentation of design decisions. The methods include textual description templates, such as by Tyree et al. [45], ontologies, such as by Kruchten [130], meta-models, such as by Tang et al. [133], and others. A detailed overview of documentation and formalisation approaches is provided in Section 7.3.

2.3.3. Architectural Styles

This Section text is also used in the Section 4.3 “Architectural Styles” of the Chapter 4 “Architectural Reuse” of the book by Reussner et al. [134]. The author of the Section’s 4.3 text in the book is this thesis’s author. Architectural styles are one of the important classes of reusable architectural solutions, and are means of architectural knowledge reuse. Some famous examples of architectural styles are component-based 2.3.5, multi-tier [87], layered [87] or client-server styles [87].

The idea of architectural style originated from two observations. First that a certain problem context leads to a repeating set of architectural design decisions. And second that there are better and worse sets of solutions to satisfy the given problem. However, despite of the understanding of architectural styles origins, there is still no common understanding about where an architectural style starts and where it ends.

This variety results a wide range of architectural style definitions. However, in this book we rely on the definition by Taylor et al. [115]: "Architectural style is a named collection of architectural design decisions that (1) are applicable in a given development context, (2) constrain architectural design decisions that are specific to a particular system within that context, and (3) elicit beneficial qualities in each resulting system".

Definition 2.30 Architectural Style [115]

Architectural style is a named collection of architectural design decisions that (1) are applicable in a given development context, (2) constrain architectural design decisions that are specific to a particular system within that context, and (3) elicit beneficial qualities in each resulting system.

According to this definition an architectural style has therefore three important influence points on system architecture: Collective, restrictive and qualitative. In the following, these influence points are described in detail:

- **Collective:** Architectural style can be seen as a large coarse-grain design decision and it is followed by a collection of finer-grained design decisions. This coarse-grain design decision is based on the experience with similar problems in a similar context. It can be seen as a kind of "best-practice" to approach the solution in a general way.

- **Restrictive:** This coarse-grain decision immediately limits the design solution space. For example, decisions for a component-based architectural style forces structuring of the subsystem parts inside of smaller reusable entities - components. It limits all kinds of following design decisions, starting from management and organisational design decisions (e.g. which developers shall work on the project), to the technological decisions (e.g. decisions on deployment and frameworks).
- **Qualitative:** This is the most interesting property of the architectural styles from the point of view of this book. Architectural style is, to a certain extent, a warranty that the following to-be selected solutions are those, which are more suitable for the given problem in the given context. And although the final result still strongly depends on how the style was followed by the architect and development team, the architectural style creates borders for the potentially better architectural design. Therefore, the selection of style assures qualities and properties of the to-be built system.

The important property of the styles, on the contrary to the architectural design patterns discussed later in this thesis, is that architectural styles are not meant to be mixed. Once the architectural style is selected, it shall be followed throughout the system. Clearly, design of the large complex system includes several styles, but they are not mixed; precisely, they shall not be mixed at the same level of granularity. So for example, in a large system built according to the client-server style, the server side can be implemented following layered architectural style. This is not considered to be a mix of styles, as the styles are situated at the different granularity levels.

2.3.4. Architectural Design Patterns

This Section text is also used in the Section 4.4 "Architectural Patterns" of the Chapter 4 "Architectural Reuse" of the book by Reussner et al. [134].

The author of the Section's 4.4 text in the book is this thesis's author. While architectural styles are system-comprehensive, architectural patterns (also called design patterns) are a more fine-grained way of architectural knowledge reuse.

Similar to architectural styles, there is a high number of controversy for architectural pattern definitions and naming conventions – architectural patterns vs. design patterns. We do not distinguish between architectural and design patterns, but propose that these are just different names for the same architectural knowledge reuse concept. In this book we use the definition by Taylor et al. [115]: "An architectural pattern is a named collection of architectural design decisions that are applicable to a recurring design problem, parametrized to account for different software development contexts in which that problem appears".

Definition 2.31 Architectural Design Pattern [115]

An architectural pattern is a named collection of architectural design decisions that are applicable to a recurring design problem, parametrized to account for different software development contexts in which that problem appears.

In their principle, architectural patterns are similar to the architectural styles. However, while architectural styles shall not be mixed and provide a high-level restraint to the system design, multiple architectural patterns can be used in the same architecture and usually more than once, and can even overlap. While styles are more abstract and have more degrees of freedom in the realisation, architectural patterns are strictly defined and well-described. There is a plenty of pattern catalogues available, such as by Buschmann et al. [29], Schmidt et al. [135], Gamma et al. [28], Kircher et al. [136], Douglass [137], Fowler [58], Erl [138] and Schumacher et al. [61]. In catalogues patterns are grouped by the specific topic (security patterns, SOA patterns, etc.) and goals (organisational, behavioural, etc.).

These catalogues provide information on pattern's goals - which problem the pattern solves, details on pattern's structure - which set of design decisions is required, advantages and consequences of pattern application and implementation details. Some IDEs, such as Eclipse, have a built in support for common patterns. Some famous examples of architectural patterns are: Façade, Decorator, Model-View-Controller, Observer and Factory.

Similar to architectural styles, architectural patterns have three influence points on system architecture: Collective, restrictive and qualitative. Like architectural styles, architectural pattern is a collection of architectural design decisions. A decision to use architectural pattern at the same time constrains and enables design possibilities: While some solutions get excluded, some solutions get enables and can be used together only with the pattern.

Architectural pattern is similar to the architectural style a warranty to achieve certain qualitative properties in design. So, architectural patterns are tightly related with the non-functional properties, such as performance, security and maintainability. They usually influence several properties at a time, both in positive and negative ways. Therefore, their application is often a trade-off between non-functional goals of the solution. For example, a Façade pattern (a unified interface to a set of components in a sub-system) improves the maintainability of the system component, but at the same time might decrease its performance. The final quality influence of a pattern application, however, depends on how pattern is implemented in the system.

The application of architectural patterns brings several advantages to the system. The first advantage is improved system comprehension. Patterns can be seen as a common language between team members. Applied pattern tells information about problem that was to be solved, and details about its solution. Patterns can be seen a a way of system structure documentation. The second advantage is design quality. As patterns are approved solutions to the re-occurring problems, these solutions most probably bring a better quality and are less error-prone compared to the self-invented solutions. In face of architectural pattern one reuses available knowledge about architectural solutions. However, there are also drawbacks of the pattern application. The most common problems are pattern misuse and false implementation. Thus, instead of expected quality improvement and improved system comprehension, there are performance or maintenance problems and confusing implementation.

2.3.5. Component-Based Software Architecture

Components are one of the means of a reuse-driven software development. Szyprski [139] defines a software component as "a unit of composition with contractually specified interfaces and explicit context dependencies only. A software component can be deployed independently and is subject to composition by third parties".

Definition 2.32 Software Component [139]

A software component is a unit of composition with contractually specified interfaces and explicit context dependencies only. A software component can be deployed independently and is subject to composition by third parties.

Taylor et al. [115] defines a software component as "an architectural entity that (1) encapsulates a subset of the system's functionality and/or data, (2) restricts access to that subset via an explicitly defined interface, and (3) has explicitly defined dependencies on its required execution context". The software components are "embodiment of software engineering principles of encapsulation, abstraction, and modularity" [115].

Definition 2.33 Software Component [115]

A software component is an architectural entity that (1) encapsulates a subset of the system's functionality and/or data, (2) restricts access to that subset via an explicitly defined interface, and (3) has explicitly defined dependencies on its required execution context.

The above provided definitions of components all rely on a concept of an interface. There are two types of interfaces: Provided and required interfaces. A provided interface is the interface that "specifies the services that a component provides to its environment via a defined contract between a component and the users of the environment, and contains all information that users can rely on when interacting with the component" [139]. One component may have multiple interfaces, and such interfaces are access points to the components.

Definition 2.34 Provided Interface of a Component [139]

A provided interface of a component is the interface specifying the services that a component provides to its environment via a defined contract between a component and the users of the environment, and contains all information that users can rely on when interacting with the component.

A required interface of a component is "the interface to services provided by other components in a system on which this component depend for its ability to perform its operations" [115]. With the help of required interfaces a component explicitly specifies its needs to be able to function and provide functionality described in provided interfaces.

Definition 2.35 Required Interface of a Component [115]

A required interface of a component is the interface to services provided by other components in a system on which this component depends for its ability to perform its operations.

The components are related with each other via connectors. A software connector is "an architectural element tasked with effecting and regulating interactions among components though the interfaces" [115].

Definition 2.36 Component Connector [115]

A software connector is an architectural element tasked with effecting and regulating interactions among components though the interfaces.

Component-based software development is "development based on the existence of a significant number of reusable components . The system development process focuses on integrating these components into a system rather than developing them from scratch" [87].

Definition 2.37 Component-Based Software Development [87]

A component based software development is the development based on the existence of a significant number of reusable components. The system development process focuses on integrating these components into a system rather than developing them from scratch.

Finally, this thesis defines a component-based architecture as an architecture that is comprised of components and of decisions on use or reuse of those. The architecture of such system consists of a set of components and interfaces, and interaction between them.

Definition 2.38 Component-Based Architecture

A component-based architecture is an architecture that is comprised of components and of decisions on use or reuse of those, and interaction between them.

This thesis has a two-perspective connection to components and component-based software architectures. First, a component is one type of the reusable architectural solutions, and decision of component applications are, therefore, in the focus of the AM3D approach. Components can be handled by the AM3D approach to be annotated with questions in order to support design decisions documentation. Second, the architectural modelling of the AM3D approach relies on the Palladio Component Model, which is an approach for architecture-based performance and reliability prediction for the component-based software systems. Thus, the design decisions are instantiated in component diagrams in terms of the AM3D approach. These component diagrams are assembly models of the Palladio approach. Palladio Component Model is described in Section 2.5.1.

2.4. Model-Driven Software Development

This section introduces the model-driven software development together with its main concepts. In particular, the focus lies on the definition of the hierarchy of the models and meta-models, and on the explanation of the instances of the meta-models.

First, the basic concepts are explained in Section 2.4.1. Then, Section 2.2.2 introduces classification of requirement types, which are used throughout this thesis. Section 2.4.2 introduces the idea of meta-model and model in terms of model-driven development, and explains their hierarchy.

These concepts are used later on to formalise the proposed design pattern catalogue and the relevant project context. The information in the section is based on the book of Stahl et al. [140], dissertation thesis of Goldschmidt [141], and on the student thesis of Khakulov [142].

2.4.1. Basic Concepts

Model-driven software development (MDSD) is a software development methodology which goal is to improve development of systems though a shift from code-based development to the model-based development. The shift to the model-based development shall optimise and ease the development process. Thus, the system can be developed at a model level and the system code is afterwards generated from the models. The process of generation is often described as a transformation. Transformation can be executed from model to code, from code to model and between different models. The models, used during the development can be (partially) reused, as well as the transformations.

Another advantage of the model-driven development is its independence from the target platforms. The transformations from models to models and to code can be defined for various platforms based on various technologies. Thus, once a transformation is developed, it can be reused. The system, therefore, needs to be developed only once, and other implementation variants can be simply generated. The transformations also assure consistency of architectural and code level.

Moreover, the models used for the development of the system are easier to comprehend as code, and they serve as a documentation of a system and its architecture.

The problem is, however, the shift of complexity from code to the model level. The level of abstraction is much higher, and requires additional training in understanding. In particular, the complexity is shifted into the development of transformations. The transformations also require significant effort for their development and their regular maintenance, since the underlying technology changes.

2.4.2. Models, Meta-Models and Instances

The main artefact of the model-driven development is a model. The common definition of it according to Goldschmidt [141] is the definition by [143]: "A formal representation of entities and relationships in the real world (abstraction) with a certain correspondence (isomorphism) for a certain purpose (pragmatics)" (cited via [141]). This definition originates from the Stachowiak [144].

Definition 2.39 Model (in the MDD context) [143] via [141]

A model is a formal representation of entities and relationships in the real world (abstraction) with a certain correspondence (isomorphism) for a certain purpose (pragmatics).

Goldschmidt [141] further on names three main characteristics of a model by Stachowiak [144]:abstraction, isomorphism and pragmatism. Abstraction means that "a model has relevant selection of the original object's attributes" [142]. Pragmatism means that "a model needs to used for a certain purpose" [142]. Isomorphism means that "a model represents an original object" [142].

The next important artefact is a meta-model. Goldschmidt [141] provides the following definition by Ernst [145]: "A meta-model is a precise definition of the constructs and rules needed for creating semantic models". Thus, "a central task in MDD is the process of creating such meta-models for a modelling language, which is also called meta-modelling" [141].

Definition 2.40 Meta-Model [145] via [141]

A meta-model is a precise definition of the constructs and rules needed for creating semantic models.

The meta-meta-model is "the foundation of the meta-modelling hierarchy, which is used to define the meta-models" [146]. The Meta Object Facility (MOF) [146] is "a meta-meta-model, defined as a standard by the Object Management Group (OMG), which is used for the definition of meta-models" [141]. MOF is based on the UML and " uses class diagrams with its main constructs classes, attributes and associations as basis" [141].

Definition 2.41 Meta-Meta-Model [146] via [141]

The meta-meta-model is the foundation of the meta-modelling hierarchy, which is used to define the meta-models.

The third artefact, which is important for the AM3D approach, is the model instance. Instance is a real-life object which is described in terms of the model and is filled with the world-relevant information.

Definition 2.42 Model Instance
Model instance is a real-life object which is described in terms of the model and is filled with the world-relevant information.

An overview of these terms and their hierarchy is presented on Figure 2.11. The Figure also displays the corresponding models of the AM3D approach, which are depicted on the same level as the related MDD term.

Meta-Meta-Model	Meta-Model Framework	Ecore
Meta-Model	Domain Meta-Model	ADM3D Approach Meta-Model
Model	Domain Model	ADM3D Models (Requirements, Design Pattern Catalogue, Design Decisions, etc.)
Model Instance	Domain Model Instances	Catalogue Model Instances (Design pattern instances, Architectural Solutions instances, etc.)

Figure 2.11.: Hierarchy Structure of Models in Model-Driven Development and of Corresponding AM3D Approach Models

The first column on Figure 2.11 provides a hierarchy of the terms meta-meta-model, meta-model, model and model instance. It means, that while there is one meta-meta-model, it can be used to define many meta-models. On its own turn, one meta-model can be used to define multiple models. And finally, each model can have multiple instances. The middle column provides an explanation for the term of the first column. The third column provides corresponding models of the AM3D approach, related to each of the previously mentioned terms. So, the meta-meta-model used by the AM3D approach is the Ecore model [147]. The meta-model is the AM3D approach meta-model, which is used to formalise the approach, its supporting artefacts and related project context. Models in the context of the AM3D approach are instances of the meta-model, such as Requirements models, Design Decision models, Design Pattern Models, and others. Some of these models do have further instances, which is called a double-step instantiation in this thesis. In this case, some of the models, such as Design Patterns model and Architectural Solutions model, actually define types of design patterns and architectural solutions that can be reused. Thus, an instance of such a model is a concrete implementation of a design pattern or some other architectural solution in an architectural model. Thus, the moment a pattern is assigned to some component in the architectural model, it becomes a model instance of a particular patter type defined n the Pattern model.

Besides these artefacts, the AM3D approach makes use of the OMG Object Constraint Language (OCL) [148]. OCL is "a formal language used to describe expressions on UML models. These expressions typically specify invariant conditions that must hold for the system being modelled or queries over objects described in a model". An OCL constraint is a constraint on a model. It constraints the classes and relationships between the classes in the model and allows for automated check if the constraint was violated.

Definition 2.43 Object Constraint Language (OCL) [148]

Object Constraint Language is a formal language used to describe expressions on UML models. These expressions typically specify invariant conditions that must hold for the system being modelled or queries over objects described in a model.

The AM3D approach uses OCL constraints to support correctness of architectural implementation of design patterns. It allows verification, if all the roles and connectors of a pattern were defined in the architectural model, and if the connectors between the roles follow the direction and scheme defined in the catalogue. For example, if the View in the Model View Controller design pattern [28] is communicating directly with the Model, an architect can be warned about violation of the Model View Controller architectural structure.

2.4.3. Eclipse Modelling Tools

The AM3D approach relies on the Eclipse Modelling Tools to support the formalisation and development of the approach tooling.

The Eclipse Modelling Framework (EMF) [147] is used for the meta-modelling of the AM3D -relevant artefacts. EMF is an open source Eclipse-based framework, which support the model-driven development in the Eclipse environment. The EMF is "a modelling framework and code generation facility for building tools and other applications based on a structured data model. From a model specification described in XMI, EMF provides tools and runtime support to produce a set of Java classes for the model, along with a set of adapter classes that enable viewing and command-based editing of the model, and a basic editor" [147].

The EMF meta-model is called Ecore, which support "describing models and runtime support for the models including change notification, persistence support with default XMI serialization, and a reflective API for manipulating EMF objects generically" [147].

EMF includes support to generate tree editors for the models instantiated from the meta-models. The editor support can be further on extended with the help of the Graphical Editing Framework (GEF) [149] and the Graphical Modelling Framework (GMF) [150]. The Graphical Editing Framework "provides technology to create rich graphical editors and views for the Eclipse Workbench UI" [149]. The Graphical Modelling Framework "provides a set of generative components and runtime infrastructures for developing graphical editors based on EMF and GEF" [150].

2.5. Additional Foundations

This section introduces additional foundations required for understanding of the AM3D approach. The Palladio Component Model (PCM), which is used as an architectural modelling approach for the AM3D approach, is described in Section 2.5.1. A Common Component Modelling Example

(CoCoME) is introduced in Section 2.5.2. CoCoME is used as an example system to demonstrate the AM3D approach in this thesis. Finally, Section 2.5.3 explains the main idea of the Controlled Natural Languages and provides some examples. The AM3D approach uses a simplified version of one of the controlled English languages (SBVR Structured English [151]) to define the question annotations to design patterns (the definitions of the question annotations and the question styles concept based on the simplified SBVR Structured English is described in Section 4.3.3).

2.5.1. Palladio Component Model

The Palladio Component Model (PCM) is an approach for architecture-based performance and reliability prediction for the component-based software systems [152]. The goal of the PCM is to support architectural decision making through quantitative analysis of quality properties of architectural designs at design time. The currently supported quality properties are performance (throughput, response time, potential load of resources) [152] and reliability (mean time to failure, mean time to repair, reliability of the system) [153]. For each of these quality properties, the PCM has a defined set of analysis and sensors available. Sensors allow for a measurement and aggregation of the quality data at different points of system design. The overall view on PCM approach is presented in Figure 2.12.

The assumption for the analysis is that all of the architectural models are captured in PCM (or are transformed into PCM models). The models are UML-compatible views on the software system design from different perspectives, in the tradition of "4+1" model of architecture by Kruchten [123]. PCM supports five following views on the software architecture [152], which are depicted on Figure 2.13:

- **Component View (Repository Model):** The Component view is used for the definitions of components, interfaces (provided and required interfaces), and component-relevant information, such as op-

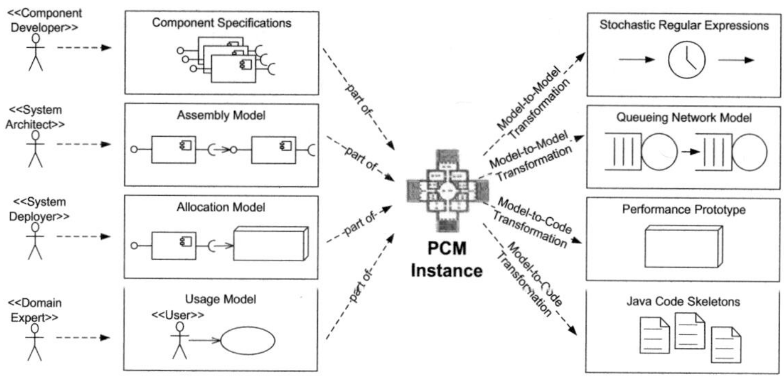

Figure 2.12.: The Overview of the PCM Approach [152]

erations (defined with SEFF models) and signatures. Interfaces are "first-class entities in the PCM and thus exist independently from components" [152]. The component and interface definitions are independent, and can be seen as reusable architectural solutions – reusable components. Once a component or an interface is defined, they can be reused in different projects from this repository.

- **System View (System Model):** In the System view, components and interfaces defined in the repository get instantiated and connected to form system architectures. Components and interfaces can be instantiated multiple times. The connections between the components are called AssemblyConnectors. They are attached to the Provided- and RequiredRoles of components. Finally, each system has provided and required interfaces, called SystemOperationProvidedRoles and SystemOperationRequiredRoles, which define interfaces to and from the system.

- **Behaviour View (SEFFs Models):** The SEFF Models define behaviour of operations of components, and therefore are a behavioural view on the system. Besides various possibilities for the behavioural specification, the recourse demands (e.g., required processor time or length of an operation) are defined in the SEFF to enable quality evaluation of the system design.

- **Allocation View (Deployment Model):** Once the system architecture is defined, it can be deployed in the allocation view on the defined computing resources. System can be deployed on one or through several hardware knots. The hardware knots contain definitions of the available processing resources, and can be connected through a network with a specified throughput.

- **Usage View (Usage Profiles Model):** In the Usage view it is possible to define typical usage scenarios for the system. The usage scenarios can be parametrised with type of the workload on the system, information on size of artefacts or their amount, etc..

For each of these views, the PCM defines an assigned role in the software engineering process. The definitions of the roles are independent from the definitions of the roles of software architect and requirements engineer provided earlier in this thesis, because the PCM roles are defined from the performance evaluation perspective. The PCM roles are [152]:

- **Component developer:** Component developers specify and implement components. They also specify the behaviour of the components and their required resource demands. Component developers are responsible for the Repository Model and SEFF Models of the system.

- **Software architect:** Software architect design systems using the component and interface definitions from the repository. They are responsible for the System Model.

- **System deployer:** System deployers deploy the the designed system on the defined hardware knots. They are responsible for the Deployment Model.

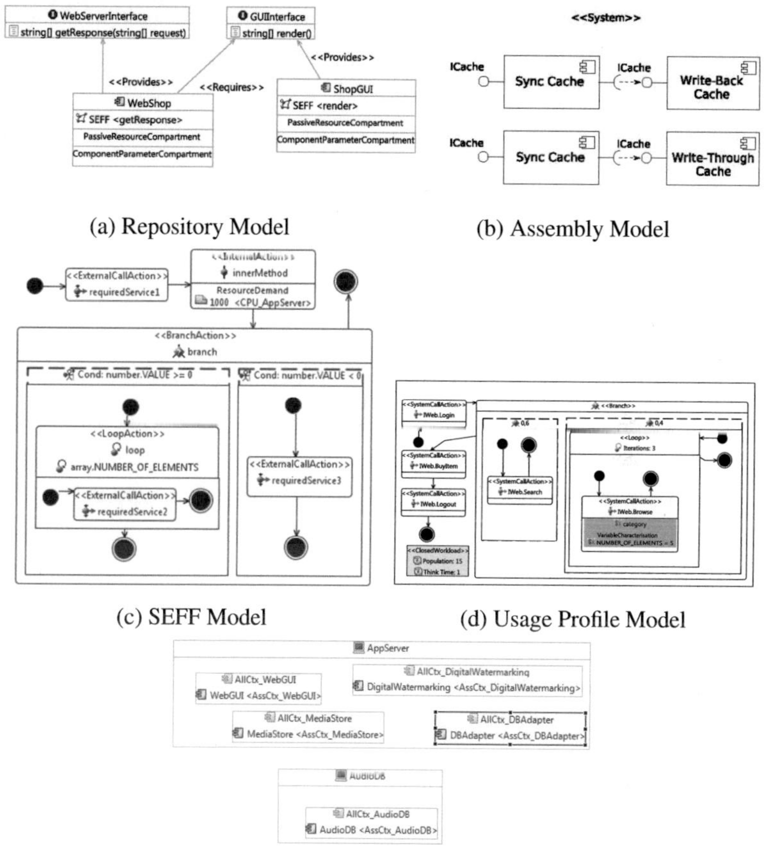

(a) Repository Model

(b) Assembly Model

(c) SEFF Model

(d) Usage Profile Model

(e) Deployment Model

Figure 2.13.: PCM Model Views [152, 154]

- **Business domain expert:** Business domain experts define usage scenarios of the system. They are responsible for the Usage Profile Model and its parametrisation.

There is no requirements engineer role defined for the PCM, because the requirements view is only implicitly present in PCM (through requirements on performance and reliability). However, the existence of this role or its substitute is assumed by PCM. The requirements engineer is responsible for elicitation of PC-relevant quality requirements and evaluation of PCM system evaluation results.

The AM3D approach uses PCM as architectural modelling approach for capture of design decisions connected to design pattern application. In particular, the approach uses the PCM System Model (UML-like Component Model, see Figure 2.13: (b) System Model). While design patterns are specified in their own repository, similar to the Repository Model concept of the PCM approach, they can be instantiated in the PCM system models. The instantiation required at least one component to be assigned to represent the design pattern in the design model. The instantiated components in PCM are called AssemblyContext, and connections between components are represented through AssemblyConnectors between an OperationProvidedRole of a component and an OperationRequiredRole of other component. The AssemblyContext is than annotated with information an instance of a design pattern is assigned to it.

The PCM approach was selected for the AM3D approach as an architectural modelling notation because PCM supports quality evaluation of system design at the architectural level. Thus, it is not only an architectural representation of system design (architectural model documentation), but can also be used for design-time evaluation of expected quality of the design. Such design-time evaluation provides a quick feedback into the decision making process. It allows for a lightweight modification of problematic system parts, which would otherwise be connected with higher costs, once system is implemented. Overall, it contributes to better evaluated design decisions, which is one of the goals of the approach.

2.5.2. Common Component Modelling Example (CoCoME)

CoCoME (Common Component Modelling Example) is an example business information management system, which was developed as an open source benchmark for component-based modelling approaches [155]. Besides the extensive documentation, which includes a complete requirement specification, use case definitions, architectural design models and textual descriptions, the functionality is implemented in Java as a component-based and as a SOA-based implementations. This allows CoCoME to be used as an example for a wide variety of modelling and quality prediction (performance and reliability) approaches. For example, it is used as an example by PCM [152], KLAPER [156], SOFA [157] and others. The implementations of the CoCoME can be deployed and run, thus allowing for measurements and comparison of the analysis prediction results.

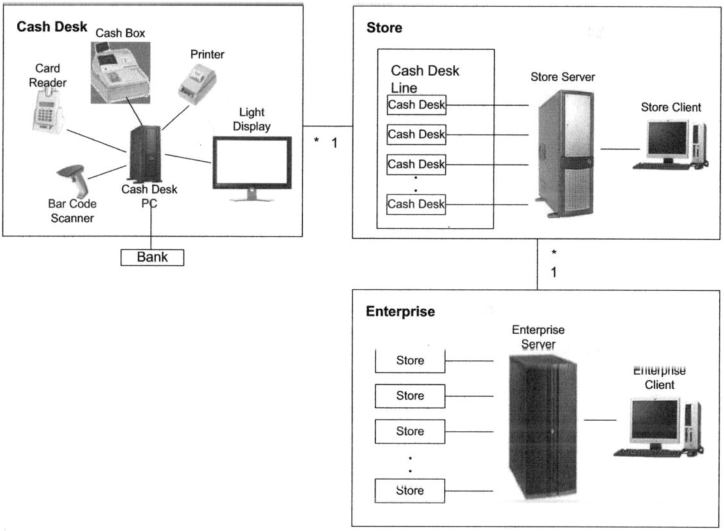

Figure 2.14.: Overview of the CoCoME System (Adopted from [155])

CoCoME is a trading system for management of goods at a supermarket, which can be a part of a supermarket chain. The system consists of three main parts: Cash desk, store subsystem and enterprise subsystem. The overview of the CoCoME is provided on Figure 2.14.

Each cash desk includes a card reader, a display, a bar code scanner, a printer and a cash box. Cash desk can built up a connection to bank for operations with the card. Store subsystem manages one particular supermarket, which can have multiple cash desks installed. Store subsystem has a client part, which has a reporting purpose, and a back-end part, which is responsible for management of the store database, inventory management support report generation, and other functionality related to a supermarket. Enterprise subsystem manages the whole chain of the supermarkets. It has a client part, responsible for reporting, and a back-end part, responsible for management of the store database, inventory management at the chain level, and other activities.

Customers come to the supermarket to buy goods. They fill in carts and proceed to the cash desks, where goods are scanned with a bar code scanner, the final sum is displayed on cash desk display and can be paid with card or a cash. Finally, customers receive a receipt. The goods can be re-ordered for a supermarket to fill in supplies via a request to an enterprise subsystem.

The CoCoME was selected as an example for demonstration of the applicability of the AM3D approach and its supporting artefacts later in this thesis. The reason why the CoCoME was preferred over other examples is that it represents a realistic system, which is complex enough to demonstrate the facets of the AM3D approach, but is still easy to understand and to follow. It is independent on the author of the thesis, and, therefore, provides a more objective demonstration of the AM3D approach. Moreover, the CoCoME is comparably well-known and recognised in the community.

The demonstration on the CoCoME example is based on the original CoCoME requirements and architectural models. The later are adapted to support an evolution scenario for the AM3D demonstration (the extension is described in Section 3.6), since the original CoCoME version does not define any evolution scenarios.

2.5.2.1. Requirements

An overview of the use cases of the CoCoME Trading System is presented on Figure 2.15 [155].

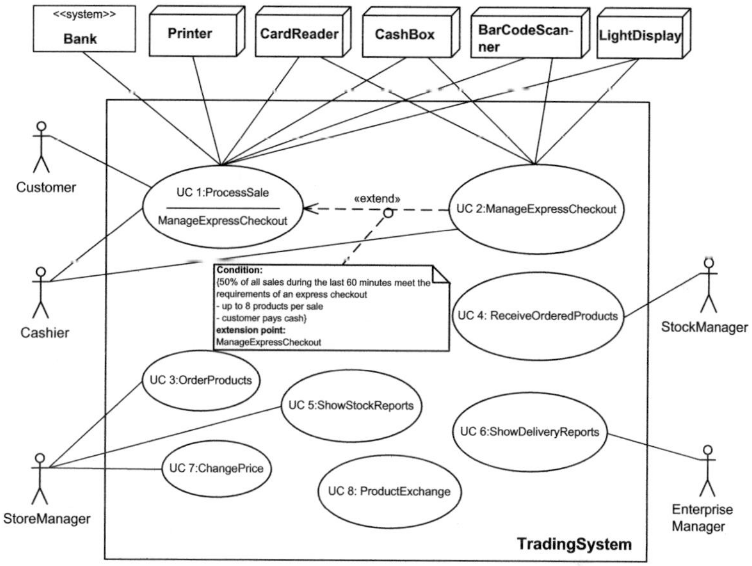

Figure 2.15.. An Overview of All Considered Use Cases of the CoCoME Trading System [155]

In the following, a brief description of the use cases is provided (text comes from [155]):

- **UC 1 - Process Sale:** At the Cash Desk the products that a Customer wants to buy are detected and the payment - either by credit card or cash - is performed.
- **UC 2 - Manage Express Checkout:** If some conditions are fulfilled a Cash Desk automatically switches into an express mode. The Cashier is able to switch back into normal mode by pressing a

button at his Cash Desk. To indicate the mode the Light Display shows different colours.

- **UC 3 - Order Products:** The Trading System provides the opportunity to order product items.
- **UC 4 - Receive Ordered Products:** Ordered products which arrive at the Store have to be checked for correctness and inventoried.
- **UC 5 - Show Stock Reports:** The possibility to generate stock-related reports is provided by the Trading System.
- **UC 6 - Show Delivery Reports:** The Trading System provides the possibility to calculate the average time that a delivery takes from each supplier to a considered enterprise store.
- **UC 7 - Change Price:** The System provides the possibility to change the sales price for a product.
- **UC 8 - Product Exchange Among Stores:** If a store runs out of a certain product (or a set of products; "required good"), it is possible to start a query to check whether those products are available at other Stores of the Enterprise ("providing Stores").
- **Extension on use case 8 - Remove Incoming Status:** If the first part of use case 8 (as described above) has passed, for moved products a quantity marked as incoming is added to the Inventory of the Store receiving the products. An extension allows for removing that incoming mark via a user interface at the Store Client if the moved products arrive at a Store.

2.5.2.2. Architecture

A component model of the CoCoME architecture in PCM System View is provided on Figure 2.16.

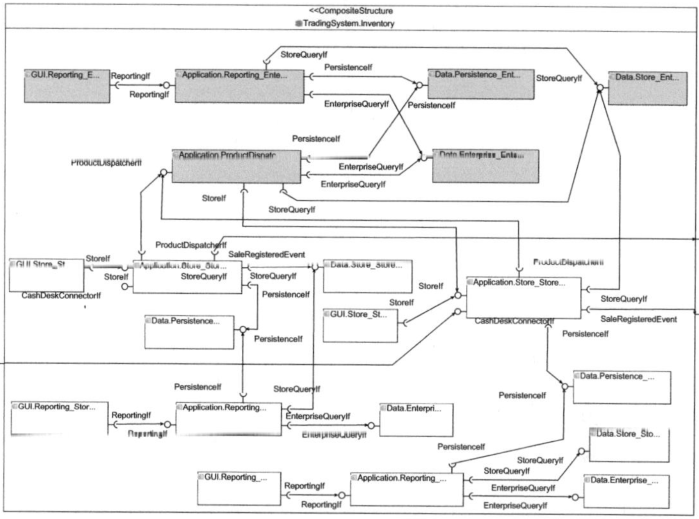

Figure 2.16.: Component Model of the CoCoME Architecture in PCM System View [158]

The application of the AM3D approach for the CoCoME as an example in this thesis is focused on the Enterprise subsystem, therefore, the related components are highlighted in grey on the Figure. The Enterprise subsystem consists of one component implementing the client (GUI of the reporting functionality), and of five components implementing the server (ProductDispatcher, Reporting, Persistence, Enterprise and Store).

The report on CoCoME [155] describes the functionality of the components as follows: The component ProductDispatcher updates the Enterprise Server database with the latest stock data of all Stores, which is extracted from their cache. It is also responsible for logistical calculations for good transportations from a number of Stores to the requesting Store. The reporting component process statistics by queering the database and generates reports about the enterprise. The reporting component in the GUI part is responsible for visualisation of various report types. Persistence component is the component responsible for management, storage and retrieval of the data. Enterprise component is the component responsible for synchronisation of the data between enterprise server and store servers. It manages the queries for the reporting and for the stores to verify of there are certain good left and to analyse if products shall be shipped from store to store. Another query type is a mean time to delivery considering all the stores.

A deployment model of the CoCoME architecture in PCM Allocation View is provided on Figure 2.17.

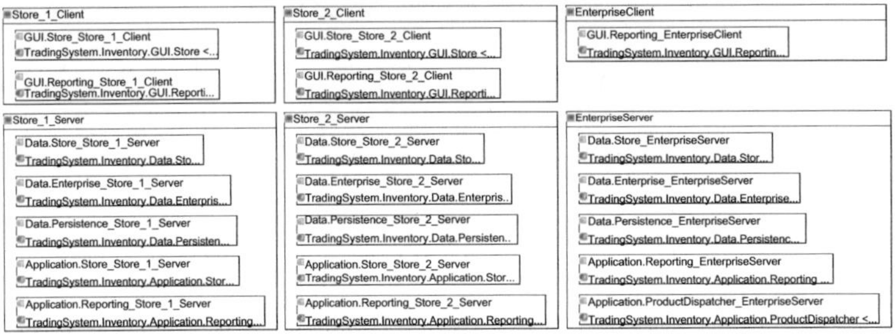

Figure 2.17.: Deployment Model of the CoCoME Architecture in PCM System View [158]

The main subsystems of the CoCoME are deployed each on separate hardware knots. The subsystems are the above described CashDesk (with devices), Store subsystem (consisting of the StoreClient and StoreServer), and Enterprise subsystem (consisting of EnterpriseClient and EnterpriseServer). Each of these subsystems is deployed on the own hardware. A CashDesk is deployed on a CashDesk hardware knot, a StoreClient on a StoreClient knot, and so on. A StoreServer is one per supermarket, to which many cash desks are connected. An Enterprise Server is one per supermarket chain, and StoreServers of different supermarkets in the chain connect to it. On the Figure 2.17, the modelled CoCoME system consists of two stores. The implementation of the system allows to deploy the subsystems on the same hardware knots or to replicate them to support higher usage load scenarios.

2.5.3. Controlled Natural Languages

This section is based on the information from a survey on controlled natural language (CNL) by Kuhn [159], a survey by Schwitter [160] and a technical draft by Sowa [161].

There is no generally agreed-upon definition for controlled natural languages and related terms, such as controlled language, constrained natural language, simplified language and controlled English [159]. Kuhn [159] defines controlled natural languages as "constructed languages that are based on a certain natural language, being more restrictive concerning lexicon, syntax and/or semantics while preserving most of their natural properties".

Definition 2.44 Controlled Natural Language [159]

A controlled natural language is a constructed language that is based on a certain natural language, being more restrictive concerning lexicon, syntax and/or semantics while preserving most of its natural properties.

The important difference to formal languages is that a controlled natural language can be intuitively and correctly understood by the speakers. However, it is an artificial language, which is constructed and defines strict rules on how the language is built up. The advantage of such languages is that while they are still understood by humans, they can be also better processed automatically. The controlled natural languages are naturally expressive and therefore are well-suited for knowledge representation [160].

Some of the examples of the controlled languages are Attempto Controlled English [162], Common Logic Controlled English [161] and SBVR Structured English [151]. These are just some of the examples, alone for the English controlled language there are over hundred of approaches [159]. For a survey of controlled natural languages please refer to Kuhn [159] and Schwitter [160]. Kuhn proposes a classification of controlled natural languages, for which he defines several criteria based on the followed goal (comprehensibility, translation or formal representation, including automatic execution), intent (language is intended to be written or spoken), origin of the language (academia, industry or a government), and if it was designed for a specific narrow domain.

The AM3D approach is interested in the written controlled languages which target improvement of comprehensibility and automatic execution. The AM3D approach uses the above mentioned properties of controlled natural languages (intuitive and correct understanding by the speakers) for the definitions of question annotations to design patterns. The definitions of the question annotations and the question styles concept described in Section 4.3.3 are based on the simplified version of the SBVR Structured English [151]. An example of SBVR Structured English is provided on Figure 2.18 (from [159]).

A rental **must** *be guaranteed by* a credit card *before* a car *is assigned to* the rental.
Rentals by Booking Mode *contains* the categories 'advance rental' **and** 'walk-in

Figure 2.18.: An Example of SBVR Structured English [159]

According to Kuhn [159] "the vocabulary of SBVR Structured English is extensible and consists of three types of sentence constituents: terms (i.e., concepts), names (i.e., individuals), verbs (i.e., relations), and keywords (e.g., fixed phrases, quantifiers, and determiners)". Some of the used keywords in the sentences have a precise meaning, other keywords are relaxed. The sentence structure can be partially ambiguous. Some structures are strictly defined (such as word or word groups members of the sentence), while others (such as order of them) are more flexible. The AM3D approach uses the idea of strict definition of word types and groups and of a rather loosely order of them in a question. It also uses two types of keywords – strictly defined in a vocabulary (described later in this section) and free-keywords that can be used by a user independently.

In addition to the simplified controlled English, the AM3D approach uses a so-called controlled vocabulary. Kuhn [159] (from ANSI/NISO 2005 [163]) defines controlled vocabularies as standardized collections of names and expressions, including "lists of controlled terms, synonym rings, taxonomies, and thesauri".

Definition 2.45 Controlled Vocabulary [159] from ANSI/NISO 2005 [163]
Controlled vocabularies are standardized collections of names and expressions, including lists of controlled terms, synonym rings, taxonomies, and thesauri.

The goal of the vocabulary is to limit the word choice for the sentences. It does not define rules on the language construction. Controlled languages, however, often define both the language construction rules and the vocabulary to be used. The AM3D approach uses such vocabulary, called glossary in the thesis, in order to limit choice of keywords used throughout artefacts, such as requirement specifications and question annotations.

3. Approach Overview

This is an introductory chapter to the AM3D approach. The goal of the chapter is to provide an overview of the approach, its parts and their interconnection, and to enable the reader to fit the following chapters into the overall picture of the approach. This chapter continues with the motivation line and structure presented in the introduction of Chapter 1. It highlights the main motivational aspects and aligns them to the technical details about the approach.

First, an overview of the AM3D approach is given in Section 3.1. The envisioned process is introduced in Section 3.2 together with the application scenarios. The process consists of multiple sub-processes for the application scenarios. Section 3.5 explains the difference between expert systems and the proposed approach. Section 3.3 describes the traceability support by the AM3D approach. Section 3.4 explains the contribution of the AM3D approach to the goal-oriented architecture-driven requirements elicitation. Finally, Section 3.6 introduces a CoCoME-based example and demonstrates the application of the AM3D approach on it.

3.1. Overview

This section gives an overview of the proposed approach called AM3D, it is partially based on previous publications, such as [1–4, 11, 15].

The approach focuses on architectural design patterns, as a class of recurring architectural design solutions. Such patterns are, for example, classical patterns by Gamma et al. [28] — Façade, Proxy, Adaptor, and others.

The goal of the approach is two-fold. First, it is to support the evaluation of pattern design solutions, thus supporting the decision to apply or not to apply a pattern, and contributing to a more goal-oriented requirements elicitation driven by the architectural design. Second, it is to support the lightweight documentation of the rationale of the decisions to apply or to discard a pattern, to support correct pattern application and to capture trace links between requirements, design decisions and architectural elements.

In order to achieve this goal, a new kind of a pattern catalogue is proposed. In this catalogue, design patterns are seen as a kind of recurring architectural design solution (solutions, which are known in advance and can be reused between projects) and are annotated with a set of solution-specific, but project-independent questions. The target users of the AM3D catalogue and of the AM3D approach based on it are software engineers and architects.

The catalogue is based on the idea that the goals and the properties of design patterns, as a type of architectural design solution, are well-known in advance. Thus, it is possible to prepare documentation stubs that describe goals and features of a pattern in advance and to store them in the catalogue together with the pattern description. These documentation stubs are stored in the form of questions to the desired properties of a pattern. Each question attached to the pattern in the catalogue is a fragment of a design rational, and a set of questions to each pattern forms a complete rationale for the pattern application. The questions in the set are divided into four groups – questions about the goal, advantages, consequences and variants of the pattern, and are used to generate documentation of a decision to use or to discard a design pattern.

Thus, the question annotations have two goals. First, they are a quick check-list to verify the suitability of the selected architectural design pattern for a given problem that the architect or engineer (the user of the approach) wants to solve. For this, the architect or engineer first does the transition between a question about the project-independent design pattern and a particular problem in the project-context. Second, answers to the check-lists are saved as a rationale for a decision to use or to discard the pattern. This lightweight rationale documentation can later be used during the system maintenance and evolution, for example to understand why the pattern was used, and to retrieve trace links to the triggering requirements or implementing architectural elements.

The structure of the question annotations and form of the questions is not an arbitrary choice, but the result of trial-and-error process and external reviews, partially explained in Heller [164].

An example of question annotations to a pattern catalogue entry is provided for the“Façade pattern”on Figure 3.1. In the example one can see three types of questions, which altogether define goals, intent and consequences that are properties of the Façade pattern. The fourth type is the questions to the variants of a pattern, available for some patterns.

Question Type	Questions
Goal	Would you like to provide an interface to some other object, resource, network connection, etc.?
Intent	Would you like to provide or to restrict the access to functionalities provided by another object or server?
	Would you like to provide an interface with some additional functionality, e.g. management of objects state, etc.?
	Would you like to provide a representative for an object in different address-space?
Consequence	You are not wishing to be able to extend the object's properties dynamically? (otherwise → Decorator)
	Is a potential performance bottleneck not a problem?
	Is a higher level of indirection not a problem?

Figure 3.1.: An Example Catalogue Entry: Façade Pattern Questions with Answers

Answers to the questions are limited to the “yes”, “no”, and “I don’t know” options, and can be accompanied with a comment. The answers to the questions are given by a user of the approach. The answer “yes” means that the feature (goal, intent, consequence or a variant feature) is important for the problem. The answer “no” means that the feature is important and cannot be met by the solution. The answer “I don’t know” means that either the feature is not important and can be neglected, or that the user has no information on this aspect. In the latter case, the user would need to acquire additional information by a requirements engineer or a project stakeholder directly. Answering the questions produces a kind of instantiation of the pre-saved fragments of design rationale for the pattern. If the questions cannot be answered by users based on the known requirements to the system, they may require elicitation of additional requirements or re-prioritization of the existing by requirements engineers. In this case, the requirements engineering is triggered by the system design.

The questions to the patterns have no uniform importance, as an issue pointed out by a question may have different values for different project problems. For example, the same consequence question can be replied "no" ("it is important, but the pattern does not support it") in two cases of pattern usage, but in one case the pattern can be still used and in the other it may be the reason to discard the pattern application. Thus, the pattern cannot be accepted or discarded automatically without the user's intervention.

Finally, once a decision to apply a pattern has been made, it shall be modelled in the architecture. The trace links are captured in parallel, to enable comprehension on which architectural elements implement each decision and what requirements have contributed to the decisions, and, vice versa, what decisions and why they are implemented with architectural elements.

As the structure of design patterns is well known in advance, design pattern entries in the catalogue are also annotated with architectural model stubs. These stubs support the user of the approach throughout the pattern modelling process. The purpose of the stubs is two-fold. First, they ease the modelling process, as a prepared modelling structure is made available through the catalogue entry. Second, the prepared structure allows one to define the constraints that can be used to check the correctness of the instantiated model and to notify the user in case of modelling mistakes. The modelling stubs, however, provide only the structural information and the logic of the pattern, and the relationship with the problem system has to be modelled and implemented by hand. The purpose of this manual step is the following. First, the connection to the context of the pattern application (such as other required and provided components and interface invocations) cannot be completely automated. Second, a complete automation would remove part of the creative work of the user. For example, the user may decide to instantiate a pattern in an already existing component. Therefore, the AM3D approach only offers structural architectural stubs for design pattern instances, and requires a manual assignment of design pattern roles and connectors to components and connectors in architectural models. Thus, the current implementation of the AM3D approach requires the user of the approach to decide manually which design pattern shall be implemented by which components in the architectural models. The AM3D approach guides the user and supports structural checks through the OCL constraints, however, it does not instantiate patterns on its own.

The AM3D approach works as outlined on Figure 3.2 (an older version of it was published in [1]).

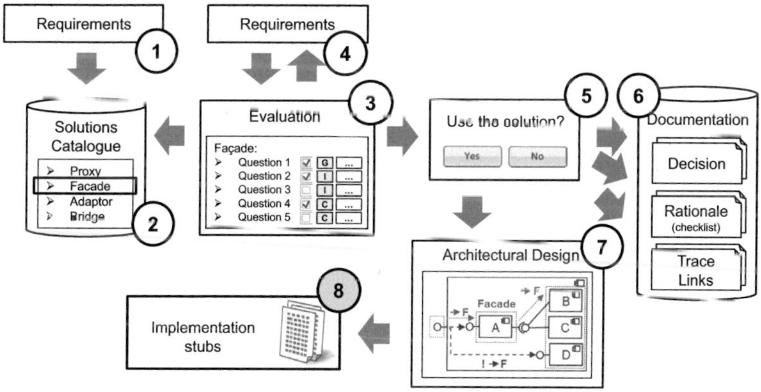

Figure 3.2.: Overview of the AM3D Approach (Adopted from [1])

In the first step, the user of the approach has an idea that a certain pattern could be suitable for solving his design problem (1). To select a pattern alternative they use either their own experience or other methods, such as expert systems, e.g. by Garbe et al. [73]. Once there is a potential pattern solution, the user proceeds to Step two. The design pattern is looked up in the pattern catalogue (2) and verified via the check-list (question annotations) attached to the pattern (3). If the information is not available to reply to the question annotations, a user may trigger elicitation of the additional requirements or re-prioritization of the existing ones (4). Such feedback from design to requirements engineering is called goal-oriented architecture-driven requirements engineering. In Step five, the user's decision to use or to discard the pattern (5) is recorded together with the provided answers and comments to the check-list (6). The trace links between requirements, design decisions are established. In the final sixth step, if the user decides to apply the pattern, the pattern can be instantiated in the architectural models (7), for example, in a composite diagram, using architectural model stubs saved in the catalogue. The trace links are accomplished with the information about the architectural elements implementing the decisions. Afterwards, it could be possible to generate implementation stubs (8) for the code implementation of a design pattern, the AM3D approach, however, focuses on the design level. The detailed process with the usage scenarios is presented is Section 3.2.

The results of the AM3D approach are: An evaluated and semi-automatically documented design decisions on accepted and discarded architectural design pattern , semi-automated captured rationale for the decisions, and trace links connecting design decisions to the triggering requirements and to the implementing architectural elements.

The proposed approach is not intended to be used as an expert system for pattern selection, but as a support for pattern validation and as lightweight documentation of the decisions about design patterns and rationale. The discussion of the relation of the proposed approach with expert systems is provided in Section 3.5. The AM3D approach is published most prominently in [1], [3], [2] and [4].

To summarize, the proposed catalogue of annotated design patterns is a new kind of design pattern catalogue, where patterns are pre-annotated with design rationales and architectural implementation details. Therefore, the proposed AM3D approach consists of three major parts: Pattern catalogue, question annotations and architectural stubs (architectural structure). Details on the pattern catalogue are provided in Section 4, question annotations are discussed in detail in Section 4.3. More details on answering the questions are given in Section 4.3.4.

3.2. Process to Use the Catalogue

The AM3D approach can be incorporated into any software development process having an explicit architectural design phase, for example, into the V-model [81, 82] or the RUP model [83]. This section describes the application scenarios of the AM3D catalogue of architectural design pattern and corresponding processes, starting from a general base process and detailing it for each of the application scenarios.

3.2.1. General Information on the Base Process

The AM3D approach is based on an incremental and iterative development process. Such a type of a process is schematically depicted on Figure 3.3. It consists of four recurring phases Requirements Engineering, Architectural Design, Implementation and Test. The AM3D approach concerns the requirements of the engineering and architectural design phases.
During the requirements engineering phase, information about the system, i.e., its goals, required functionality and environment conditions are collected. This information is received both, from external triggers, such as the customers, and internal triggers, such as technical and organisational constrains. This information is required to justify the design decisions and is the rationale for them. The AM3D approach makes use of this rationale,

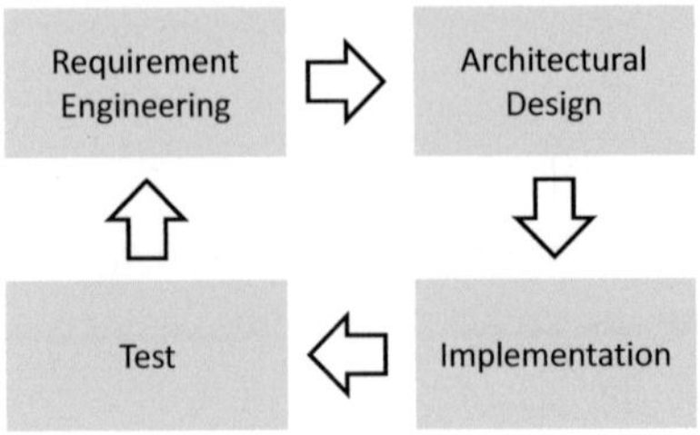

Figure 3.3.: Schematic Representation of an Iterative Incremental Software Development Process

in form of links to requirements and free text notes and explanations, if it is provided by the user.

During the architectural design phase, architects and engineers transform collected requirements into the architectural composition of the system. The transformation is done though design decisions, and the AM3D approach is used for recurring design solutions and decisions on such solutions. The iterative and incremental properties of a base process are important, as the AM3D approach assumes a feedback loop from its user to the design and requirements, and back.

3.2.2. Application Scenarios

This section describes the application scenarios of the proposed AM3D approach, based on the annotated pattern catalogue. The application scenarios are summarized in the use case diagram on Figure 3.4.
The supported usage scenarios for the AM3D approach are:

- Gaining general information about a design pattern
- Choosing between similar patterns
- Pattern application with evaluation and semi-automated rationale documentation
- Elicitation and prioritization of requirements on-demand

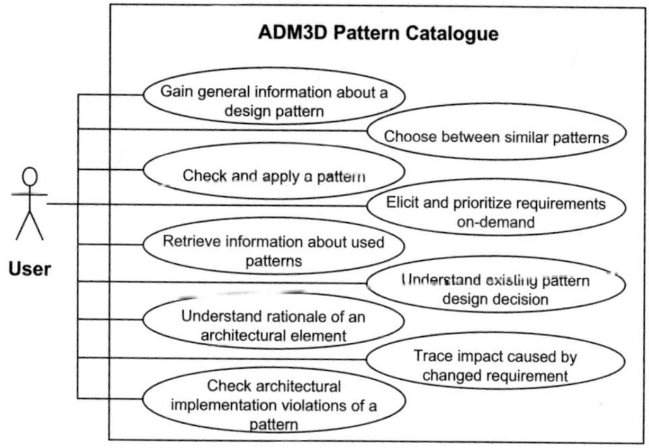

Figure 3.4.: Use Case Diagram of the Pattern Catalogue Application Scenarios

- System evolution: Retrieving information about used patterns
- System evolution: Understanding pattern design decision
- Tracing impact caused by changed requirements during maintenance
- Understanding the rationale of architectural elements through trace links to requirements
- Checking architectural implementation violations of a pattern

These scenarios are parts of the main approach process and are explicitly supported by the developed meta-model. While some of the application scenarios require a complete application of the AM3D approach with all the process steps and artefacts, others require only a partial application of the AM3D approach and its artefacts. In the following the scenarios and involved artefacts are explained in more detail:

- **Gaining information about a design pattern:** In addition to the question annotations, the AM3D pattern catalogue contains pattern descriptions from the classical pattern sources, such as Gamma et al. [28] or Buschmann et al. [29]. Thus, the catalogue supports a standard use as a pattern catalogue, as depicted on Figure 3.5, whereby a user can look up information about a pattern in the catalogue during the architectural design, evolution or just for general information on a pattern.

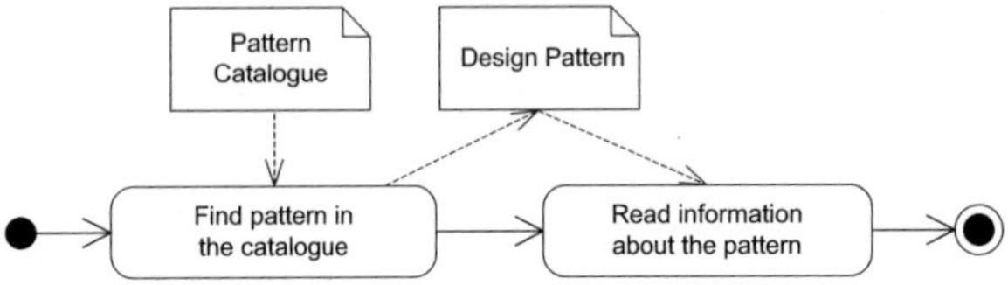

Figure 3.5.: Activity Diagram for Gaining Information About Pattern Use Case

In this case, the user opens the catalogue, navigates in it to find the desired pattern and reads the contained information about the pattern.

- **Pattern Application with Evaluation and Documentation:** The catalogue's main purpose is to support the user at design pattern application, providing checklists to evaluate a pattern and semi-automatically support documentation of the decision on it together with its rationale. This process is depicted on Figure 3.6.

  During architectural design or evolution, a user encounters a particular problem stated in one or several requirements. This problem can be potentially solved by an architectural design pattern. The initial idea on which pattern may be suitable to solve the problem can be based on a suggestion of an expert or of an expert system, on his own experience or on his own intuition. Once there is a pattern candidate to solve the given design problem, the user can answer the questions to the pattern provided by the AM3D catalogue in order to evaluate if the pattern is indeed the right solution. While answering the questions, the user may also link requirements and provide free text notes and explanations to each of the question or to the whole pattern, as

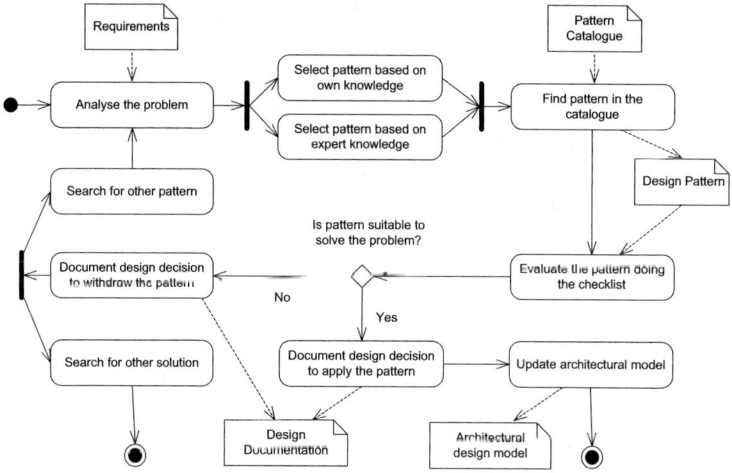

Figure 3.6.: Activity Diagram of Pattern Application Use Case

a rationale for his answers and decisions. The decision to use or to discard the pattern is then documented by the tool support together with the user's answers, and if provided, with links to requirements and free text explanations and notes. If the pattern is used, the architectural model stubs in the catalogue can be added to the architectural model of the system.

- **Choosing between similar patterns for pattern application:** In some cases, there are several pattern candidates potentially suitable to solve the given design problem. This case is depicted on Figure 3.7.

  During architectural design or evolution, a user encounters a particular problem stated in one or several requirements. This problem can be potentially solved by two or more seemingly similar architectural design patterns. The user can compare the patterns using questions from the pattern catalogue, and see if they are really suitable as a solution for the given problem and then decide which of the patterns is the most appropriate. The design decision is then captured together

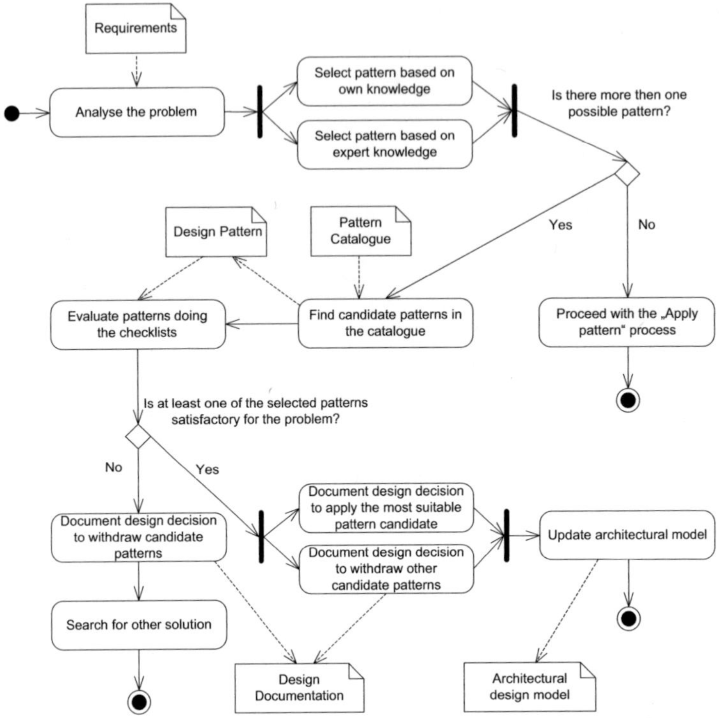

Figure 3.7.: Activity Diagram of Select Between Similar Patterns Use Case

with its rationale (answers to questions and, if applicable, links to requirements) and decisions to discard the alternatives. In case of a positive decision, the selected pattern candidate is then modelled using provided architectural modelling stubs.

- **Goal-oriented requirements elicitation:** The questions in the catalogue refer to explicitly asked details required for making a decision on a pattern application. If the information is insufficient or if the requirements contradict each other (for example, a conflict between functional and quality requirements), requirements elicitation and prioritization is triggered. Such requirements engineering is goal-oriented and is driven through the system design and its architecture. This use case is depicted on Figure 3.8.

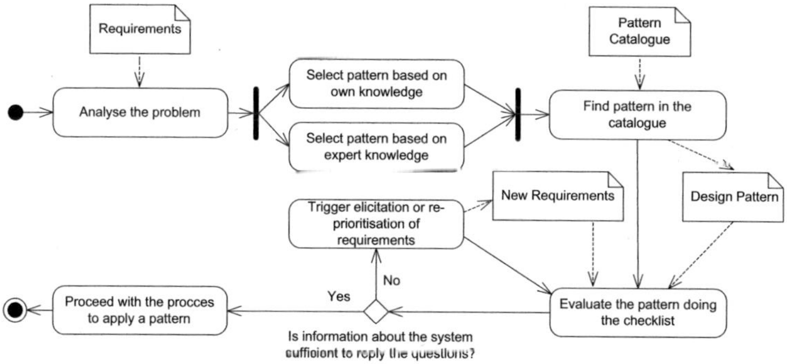

Figure 3.8.: Activity Diagram of Requirements Elicitation and prioritization Use Case

If during the analysis of an architectural solution requirements are insufficient to make a decision, or their prioritization requires a review, the help of a requirements engineer may be inquired. The requirements engineer then either answers the question himself, or inquires a stakeholder to obtain additional information about the system. Once there is enough information to make decisions, the user may proceed with the process to apply or to withdraw a pattern. The design decisions on pattern application or withdrawal are semi-automatically documented together with the rationale.

- **System evolution: Retrieving information about used patterns:** After the system was designed using the proposed approach, there is a set of documentations available on completed pattern design decisions. This documentation can be used to gain information on which patterns were applied in the system design. The process to this use case is depicted on Figure 3.9.

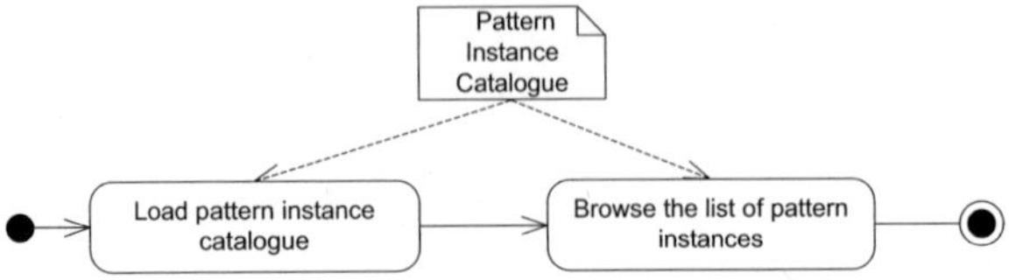

Figure 3.9.: Activity Diagram of Retrieve Information About Used Patterns Use Case

During the evolution the user needs to add or to remove functionality. This change may affect existing design decisions, and in particular a decision to apply a design pattern. Using the documentation of decisions on pattern application, a user can retrieve information about patterns used in the system and architectural elements that implement the patterns. This documentation is a result of usage of the proposed pattern catalogue during the system design.

As decisions are documented, the user can be warned if he is violating and causing inconsistencies in an existing design. In particular, sometimes there are a few structural differences between pattern architectural implementations. For example, a Proxy [28] and a Facade [28] patterns may look the same in an architectural model. The user may understand which pattern is actually used by using the produced documentation.

- **System evolution: Understanding pattern design decision:** If a system was designed using the AM3D approach, design decisions of pattern applications are documented together with their rationale. In this case, it is possible to retrieve the rationale for each pattern design decision, as depicted on Figure 3.10. This information is helpful to understand exactly which pattern is used, why it is used, what requirements triggered the decision to use the pattern and where it is implemented.

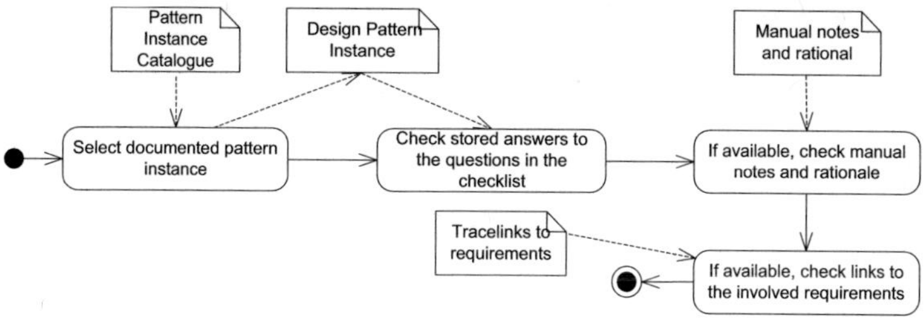

Figure 3.10.: Activity Diagram of Understanding Pattern Design Decision Use Case

To evolve the system the user requires an understanding of why a design pattern was used. Using the documentation of a decision on pattern application with the AM3D approach, the user can retrieve design rationale for the pattern application. This rationale consists of answers to questions, and if provided, links to requirements and free text explanations and notes. Checking the answers, the user can understand which assumptions were made for the pattern application and which features of the pattern were the most important in deciding to apply it.

- **Tracing impact caused by changed requirements during maintenance:** If requirements change, the decisions triggered by such requirements or decisions based on such requirements can be found through the trace links captured as a result of the AM3D approach. Further on, the architectural elements that implement these decisions can be traced as well. The process for this use case is depicted on Figure 3.11.

  The rationale for the decisions stored together with the decisions may then be verified and a decision may be re-evaluated. The rationale consists of the answers to the questions from the AM3D catalogue and may also contain textual explanations and links to requirements.

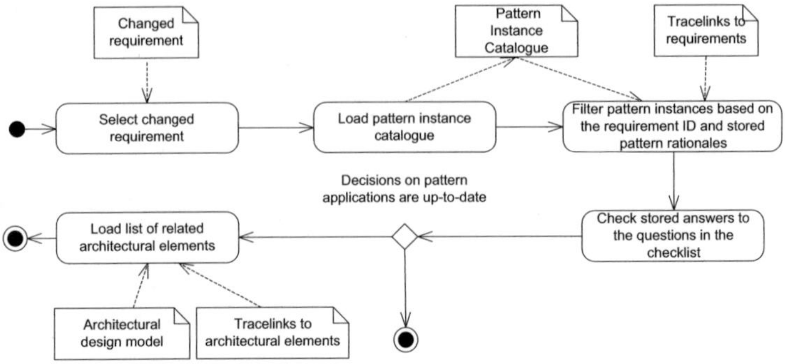

Figure 3.11.: Activity Diagram of Tracing Impact Caused by Changed Requirements Use Case

- **Understanding the rationale of architectural elements through trace links to requirements:** Captured trace links between requirements, design decisions and architectural elements allow retrieving of the decisions behind the architectural elements. The decisions are captured together with the rationale. Thus, it is possible to retrieve the rationale for each architectural element used in the model. The process for this use case is depicted on Figure 3.12.

  This is especially helpful during the system evolution, when the system undergoes changes and comprehension is important for its success. To evolve the system the user needs to understand why the architectural elements are used, and what dependencies they have. By using the documentation of decisions connected to the architectural elements, the user can retrieve such design rationale.

- **Checking architectural implementation violations of a pattern:** The AM3D catalogue contains structural information about the patterns for their implementation in architectural diagrams. This information is expressed through roles, connectors, and constrains. Such structural information not only allows the dynamic instantiation of

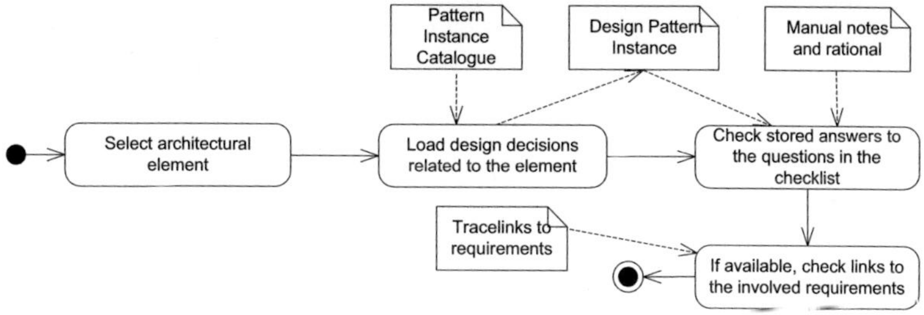

Figure 3.12.: Activity Diagram of Understanding of Rationale of Architectural Elements Use Case

patterns in architectural models, but also allows automated checks on design violation and inconsistencies. The process for this use case is depicted on Figure 3.13.

For example, the user selects a basic variant of the Model View Control (MVC) pattern [28], where Views collaborate with the Model through a Controller. However, by mistake or misunderstanding, the user applies another variant of MVC, where View collaborates directly with the Model, thus omitting the Controller in the communication path between the Model and View(s). Predefined constraints saved in the catalogue allow the user to check such pattern structure violation and to warn the user about it at design time.

3.3. Traceability Support

One of the contributions of the AM3D approach is a semi-automated documentation of trace links between requirements, architectural decisions and architectural elements. This section explains the traceability support.

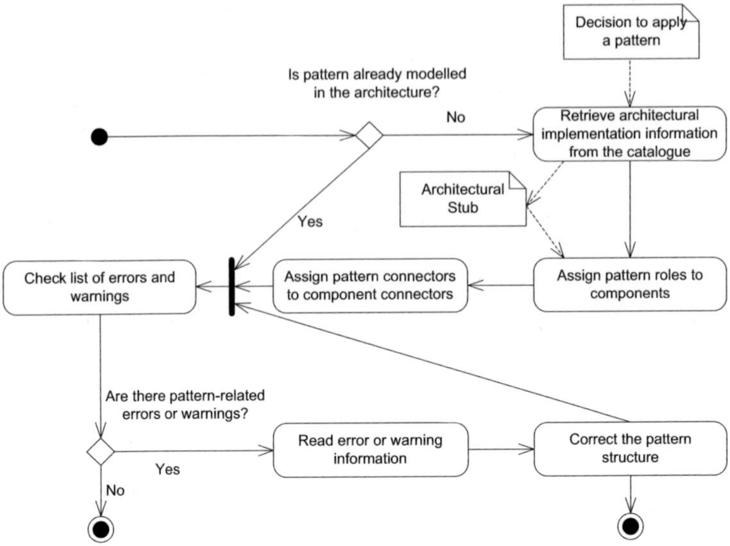

Figure 3.13.: Activity Diagram of Check Architectural Implementation Violations Use Case

At the step (6) of the process presented on Figure 3.2, trace links are captured together with design decisions and their rationale. This step is schematically depicted on Figure 3.14.

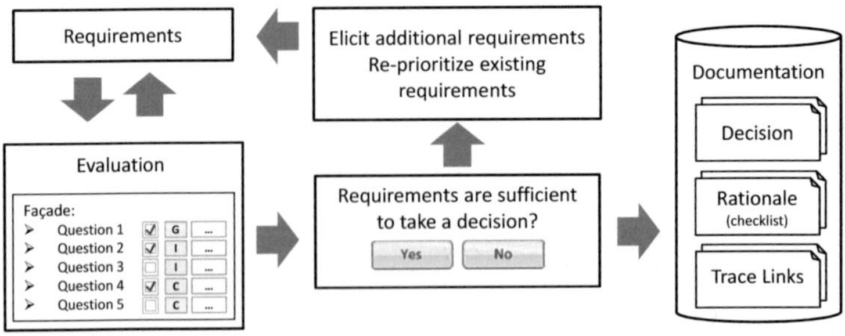

Figure 3.14.: Schematic Representation of Process to Document Trace Links

As can be seen on the Figure, the documentation of rationale, decisions and trace links are the result of the evaluation of design patterns with the help of question annotations to the patterns. When users reply to the questions, they base their answers on the requirements to the system and establish a link to the most relevant requirements which justify their answers. If the requirements are insufficient to be able to reply to a question or if there are ambiguities in the prioritization of requirements, the users may need to contact the requirements engineers to elicit additional requirements or to re-prioritize the existing ones.

The result of this process is a semi-automated documentation of decision together with the rationale and trace links. It is schematically depicted on Figure 3.15. Hereby, the rationale for the decision is generated from the responses to the questions and notes to the responses, eventually provided by the user. As the responses are based on the requirements to the systems, the links between requirements and decisions are established. Moreover, if a decision to apply a pattern is made, a trace link to the architectural instance of the pattern can be established too. The meta-model, which is described in detail in Section 4.6, supports this process and allows its automation. The documentation is called "semi-automated", because the users reply to the questions and provide links to the requirements.

Such traceability support demands several properties from the used requirements model. First, the requirements model shall support unique identification of requirements, such as requirements IDs or something similar. Second, it shall be possible to make a reference to these IDs during the pattern evaluation. Elicitation, capture, prioritization and management of requirements may succeed with the help of any of the exiting requirements engineering methods, which support the two above-mentioned properties. The requirements may be captured with the help of natural languages or in a formal way.

During the evolution of the system, requirements may change and design decisions may become obsolete. Trace links help to identify such potentially obsolete design decisions, as they capture a link from requirements to decisions. They also support identification of affected components in the architectural models. If a decisions is changed, trace links are updated with e.g. information about a new decision implementation. If a decisions is withdrawn, trace links are removed together with the corresponding architectural implementation. However, if documentation of design decisions is not updated during the system evolution, trace links naturally become obsolete.

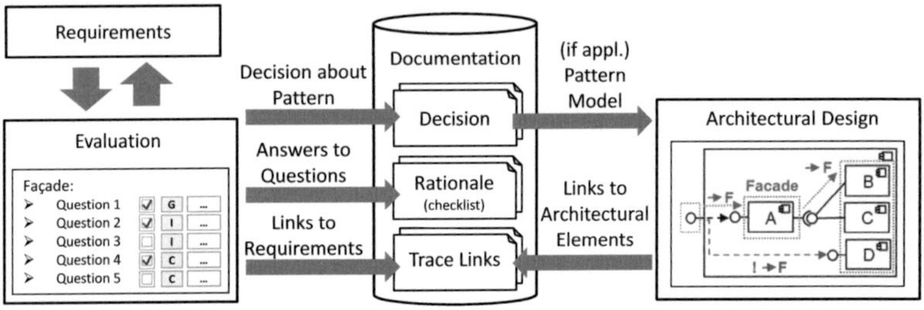

Figure 3.15.: Schematic Representation of Information Sources for Trace Link Documentation

3.4. Goal-Oriented Architecture-Driven Requirements Elicitation

System development typically starts from a requirement specification followed by stepwise refinement of available requirements while transferring them into the system architecture though design decisions made [11]. This classical approach is schematically depicted on Figure 3.16.

In such an approach, the granularity and the amount of requirements to be elicited for a successful architectural design are not well understood [11]. Moreover, there may be different priorities in the requirements for different system parts. This is particularly true for the quality requirements, which sometimes need to be re-prioritized for certain design decisions. While this

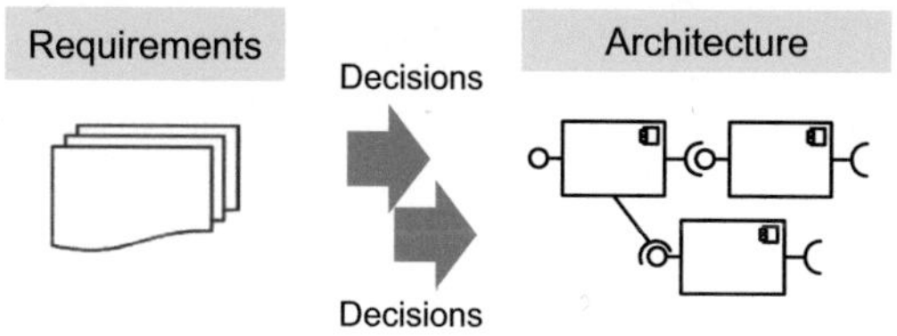

Figure 3.16.: Transfer of Requirements into Architectural Design via Design Decisions

usually happens for the local decision making, it is more of a result of an unauthorised and unconscious process.

The AM3D approach supports a goal-oriented elicitation and prioritization of requirements. The elicitation and prioritization happen on-demand and are directly connected to the current design decisions. They are in fact triggered during the design by the question annotations to design patterns. When available information about the system in the form of requirements to the system is not sufficient to reply certain questions, a user may need to contact stakeholders and requirements engineers in order to be provided additional information. In this case, the elicitation of requirements directly related to the current design state is triggered. The information is elicited on demand and its granularity is suited for the design question. Such on demand requirements elicitation and prioritization forms a goal-oriented architecture-driven requirements engineering.

It is schematically depicted on Figure 3.17.On the figure, not only requirements contribute to the architectural design, but also architectural design contributes to the requirements engineering. New requirements and re-prioritization of existing requirements are marked with a star (*), as architectural design does not provide new requirements or priorities directly. In fact, architectural design triggers requirements engineer to elicit new relevant requirements or to re-prioritize relevant existing requirements. Thus, architectural design creates a necessity for requirements engineering, rather than directly contributing new requirements and priorities itself.

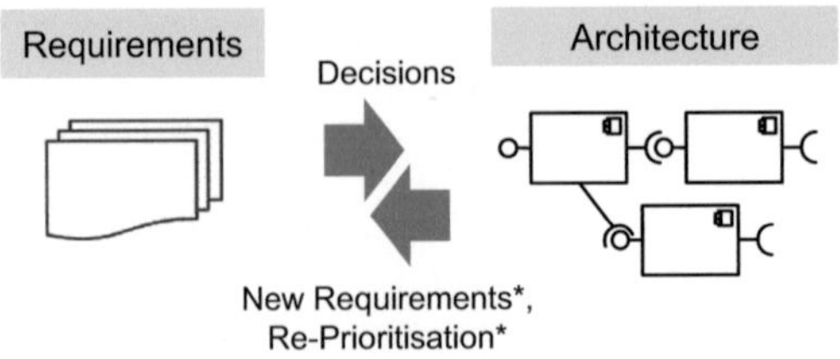

Figure 3.17.: Both-way Connection Between Requirements and Architectural Design

For example, Concrete Table Inheritance, Single Table Inheritance and Class Table Inheritance patterns solve the same problem of mapping from objects to relational database tables as they do not support inheritance [58] (this example was previously partially published in [11]). While answering the questions to these patterns, a user discovers a question "Are there few changes to the objects (classes) expected?" to the Concrete Table Inheritance pattern. In this case, a new elicited requirement could be the following: "The system must support a regular introduction of new object types or modification of existing object types", or an explicit constraint requirement would be formulated "New object types or modification of existing object types is not supported by the system". This part of the AM3D approach was published in [11] and in [3].

3.5. Difference between Expert Systems and AM3D Approach

This thesis provides its own definition of an Expert System, as definitions found in the literature did not sufficiently detail properties of an expert system. According to this thesis, an expert system is "a question-based system that guides the user with the help of questions in a top-down approach to a possible solution. The questions are of different granularity levels, stating from more generic questions in the beginning of the process, and up to low level questions at the end of the process. Answer to each question determines which set of questions will be shown in the next step, thus narrowing the solution space".

Definition 3.1 Expert System

A question-based system that guides the user with the help of questions in a top-down approach to a possible solution. The questions are of different granularity levels, stating from more generic questions in the beginning of the process, and up to low level questions at the end of the process. Answer to each question determines which set of questions will be shown in the next step, thus narrowing the solution space.

Thus, the purpose of expert systems is to help to retrieve a solution for a given problem. The user is guided through the solution space with the help of a question, until a final list of prioritized solutions is being produced. For an overview of expert systems for pattern selection refer to Section 7.

The goal of the AM3D approach is to help the user to evaluate and document a given solution candidate. Thus, the AM3D approach is complimentary to the expert systems. The AM3D approach uses a solution proposed by such a system, and supports the user in its evaluation, and in documentation of decision to apply or whether to discard the given solution. This relation between the AM3D approach and expert systems in terms of a process is presented on Figure 3.18.

An expert system produces a list of suitable pattern solutions. However, decisions to use these solutions cannot be automated, as the solution list may be imprecise. As the user is guided through the solution space with the help of questions, the answer to each question narrows down the final result list. A wrong answer to one or several questions, leads to the distortion of the final result list. The earlier such a mistake happens, the higher the risk that an actual right solution will be either low prioritized or even completely excluded from the final result list. Even though, some expert systems use a probabilistic approach to prioritize the solution list, this does not significantly reduce this risk of a wrong solution being mistakenly higher prioritized due to the wrong answers from the user. The AM3D approach is used to evaluate such solution candidates of an expert system or solution candidates based on the intuition of the user.

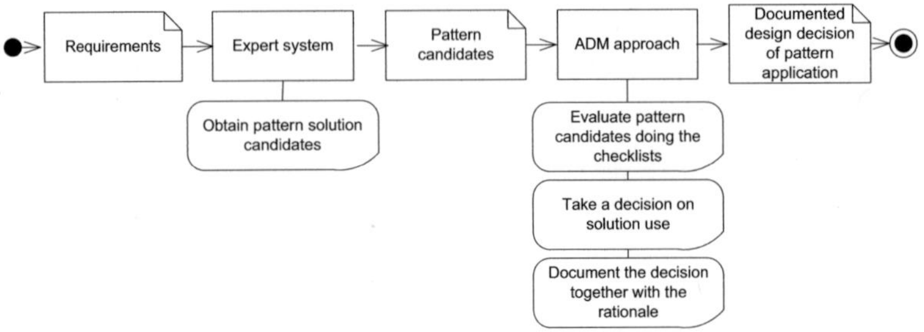

Figure 3.18.: Relation of an Expert System and the AM3D Approach in a Design Process

Property	Expert System	AM3D Approach
Search for a suitable solution, when a solution is unknown	✔	✘
Search for a suitable solution, when a solution is known, but other potential solutions are not known	✔	✔
Evaluate given candidate solution	✘	✔
Compare multiple given candidate solutions	✘	✔
Document a solution with a decision rationale	✘	✔

Table 3.1.: Expert system and the AM3D approach: Use case comparison

Comparison of the use cases of a pattern expert system and of an AM3D approach is provided in Table 3.1. The goal of an expert system is to provide suitable solutions, while the goal of the AM3D approach is to evaluate these solutions. Thus, an expert system is used to search for the possible solutions, while the AM3D approach is used to evaluate the results produced by the expert system (or any other approach) and to document the decision about the use of the solutions.

3.6. Example Application

This section describes the application of the AM3D approach on example to demonstrate the idea of the approach. The example is also used throughout the next chapters to demonstrate concepts of the proposed AM3D approach, and was partially published as a part of the [2] publication. Please note that this example is different from the example that used in the empirical study, described in Section 6.5.

Number	Requirement
NFR01	Support 700 stores
NFR02	Response time of UC3 is equal or less than 3 seconds.
NFR03	Response time of UC5 is equal or less than 5 seconds.
NFR04	Response time of UC7 is equal or less than 3 seconds.
NFR05	Maintain independence and low coupling between subsystems to enable easier exchange of the subsystems for technology changes.

Table 3.2.: Additional Non-functional (Quality) Requirements to the Hexxon CoCoME System

The example is based on the Common Component Modelling Example (CoCoME) [155], introduced in Section 2.5.2. The context of the example is the evolution of two systems following the merge of two petrol station groups: Hexxon and Nobil. The Hexxon petrol station group uses a CoCoME system to sell and manage goods at the cash desks of their petrol stations. The Hexxon CoCoME system was developed with the AM3D approach. The Hexxon CoCoME design decisions and design models are documented, including the pattern design decisions documented together with their rationale, trace links to requirements and design models, according to the AM3D approach. The functional requirements for the Hexxon CoCoME system remain the same as those for the original CoCoMe system, described in [155].

The non-functional requirements as well remain the same (listed in the description [155]), with the addition of the requirements provided in Table 3.2. An example of the NFR02 requirement entry in the AM3D meta-model instance is provided on Figure 3.19 (the AM3D meta-model is explained in detail in Section 4.6).

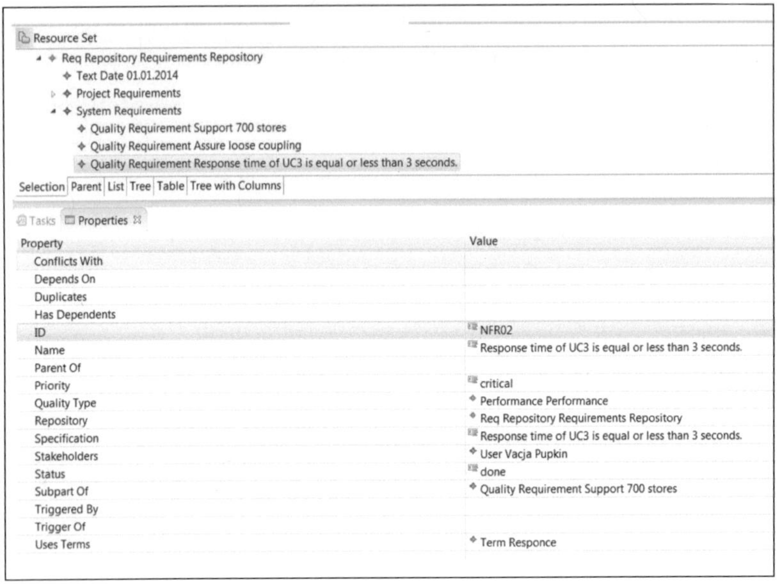

Figure 3.19.: NFR02 Requirement Entry in the AM3D Meta-Model Instance

3.6.1. Design

The components and deployment overview of the original CoCoMe is presented on Figure 3.20. The architecture consists of five logical parts: Enterprise Server, Enterprise Client, Store Server, Store Client and Cash Desk PC with devices connected to it.

The CoCoME enterprise server was adapted for the Hexxon CoCoME running example (it was also published in [2]), and its architecture is presented on Figure 3.21. The original architecture of the CoCoME can be seen on Figure 2.16 n PCM System View.

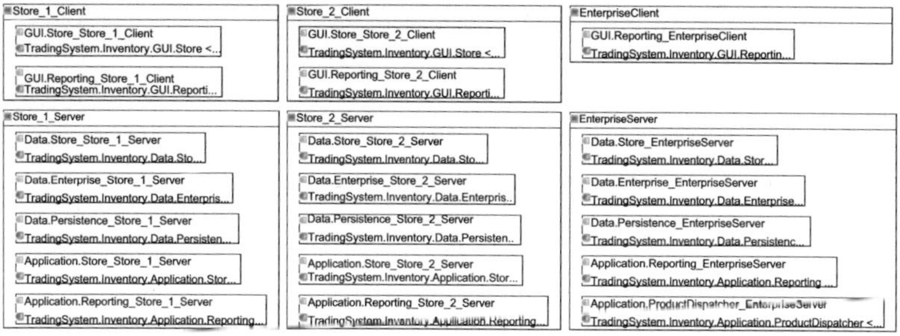

Figure 3.20.: Deployment Model of the CoCoME Architecture in PCM System View [158] (Repetition from Section 2.5.2)

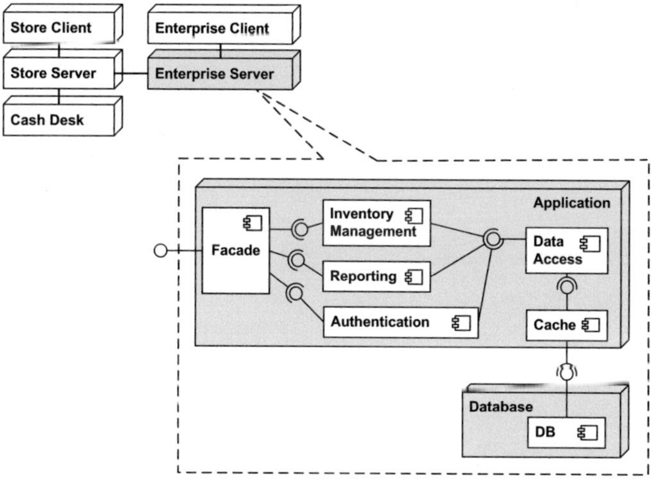

Figure 3.21.: Hexxon CoCoMe Architecture of the Enterprise Server (Adopted from [2])

The adopted Hexxon CoCoME enterprise server consists of the following components:

- **Inventory Management:** A component responsible for the management of the stock items. It is responsible for the use cases U3 "Order Products" and U7 "Change Price".

- **Reporting:** A component implementing the reporting functionality of the use case U5 "Show stock reports".
- **Authentication:** A component implementing the login-in features of the enterprise server.
- **Data Access:** A component implementing operations on the database.
- **Cache:** A component caching data acquired from the database for performance optimisation.
- **Database:** Database system, deployed on a separate node.
- **Façade:** A component responsible for the abstraction of the subsystem and separation of the calls to the subsystem through a unified interface. This component does not implement any additional functionality. Its duty is to forward invocations from the outside world to the abstracted subsystem and back.

It is assumed that the system was developed following the AM3D approach. Thus, the design decisions and their rationale are documented together with the trace links from requirements through decisions to the architectural elements. An example of a trace link connecting requirements NFR01 and NFR02, decision on Façade application and architectural elements implementing the decision is presented on Figure 3.22.

Architectural element implementing the decision on the Figure 3.22 is called "Pattern Architecture Instance". It is an instance of Façade pattern solution that is linked to the elements in the PCM System model. An example of the PCM System Model with the Façade design pattern instantiated in it and links to the PCM elements is presented on Figure 3.23.

With the help of the trace links, it is possible to track which requirements triggered which decisions and requirements, and which architectural elements implement which design decisions. Several design decisions relevant for the example are provided in Table 3.3 and Table 3.4 together with the rationale based on the catalogue questions. The answers marked with (*) are relevant for the evolution scenario described in the next section.

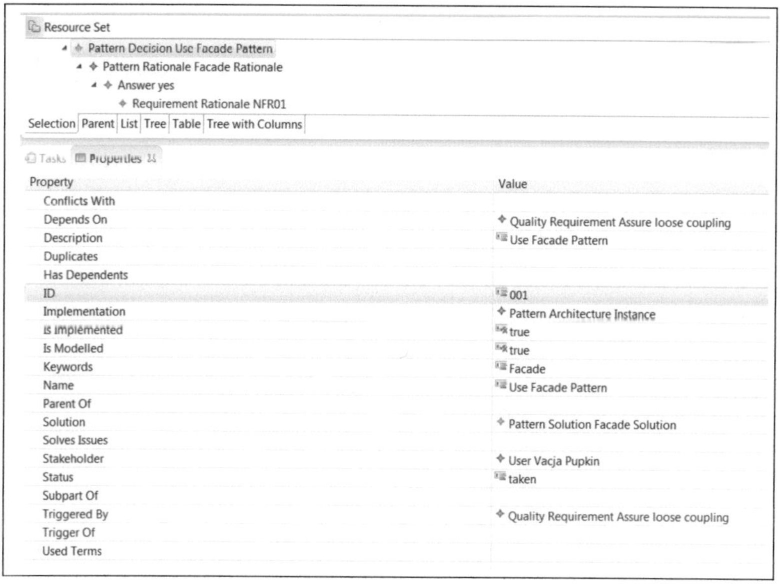

Figure 3.22.: An Example of Trace Link Between Requirements NFR01 and NFR01, Façade Decision and Façade Architectural Implementation

3.6.2. Evolution Scenario

In order to demonstrate the proposed AM3D approach, an evolution scenario for the Hexxon CoCoME system is defined. In this evolution scenario the Hexxon and Nobil petrol station groups merge. The Hexxon CoCoME system thus needs to support not only the Hexxon petrol stations, but also the Nobil petrol stations with their stores.

As a result, the existing non-functional requirements are modified. In particular, the requirement NFR01 is changed, as due to the expanded installation the system needs to support 1400 petrol stations instead of 700 (change request CR01). Because of the saved trace links, also dependent

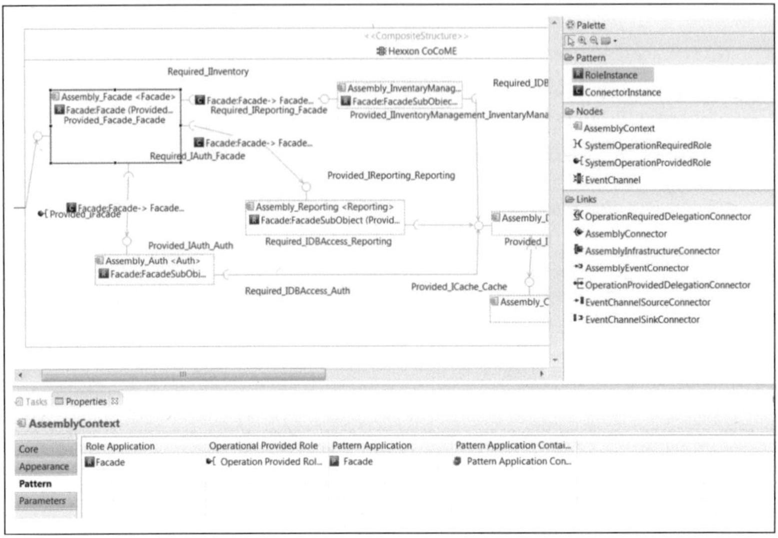

Figure 3.23.: Instantiation of the Façade Pattern in a PCM System Model

requirements NFR02, NFR03 and NFR04 can be identified and their fulfilment in the system can be verified using a performance analysis. During their verification the finding is that these requirements are indeed violated. Thus, the architecture of the enterprise server has to be redesigned in order to improve the performance of the system.

As to our publication in Konersmann et al. [2], there will be the following steps involved. Software architects may identify the following possible modification of the architecture: Adding a new component "Load Balancer", Replication of the enterprise Server part, deployment on additional hardware knots, and eventually reconfiguration of Hibernate. Such modified architecture of the Hexxon CoCoMe enterprise server is presented on Figure 3.24 (adapted from our publication in [2]).

The implementation of a new component Load Balancer would require its connection before the Façade component. As the Façade component might be a potential bottleneck, software architects would want to re-

Design decision DD01		
Façade application	Isolate the components of the Enterprise Server from the direct access of the rest of the Hexxon CoCoME system.	
QT	**Questions**	**Answer**
G	Would you like to provide a unified interface to a set of interfaces in a subsystem?	✔
I	Would you like to minimize the communication and dependencies between subsystems?	✔
	An additional functionality wrapped into the unified interface is not your intent? (otherwise → Proxy)	✔(*)
	Is a stateless unified interface your intent? (otherwise → Proxy)	– (*)
	Is it desired that subsystem classes know nothing about the Façade object(s)? (otherwise → Mediator)	–
	A new interface for an object is not your intent? (otherwise → Adaptor)	✔
C	You are not wishing to be able to extend the object's properties dynamically? (otherwise → Decorator)	✔
	Is a potential performance bottleneck not an issue?	✔

Table 3.3.: Extract from Design Decisions to the Hexxon CoCoME System, 1

evaluate the decision to use a Façade using the AM3D approach. They can check the rationale saved for the decision – answers to the questions from the solution catalogue, which are provided in the Table 3.3 and Table 3.4. In fact, the application of the Façade component is based on several assumptions which are based on the previous requirements. A question "An additional functionality wrapped into the unified interface is not your intent? (otherwise use Proxy)" is answered as being relevant for the decision. However, it contradicts the implementation of a Load Balancer, as the application component will be replicated and the Façade component would need to implement additional functionality in order to manage the sessions. The AM3D pattern catalogue suggests a Proxy pattern is such a case.

Architects can evaluate the Proxy pattern for its suitability for the given problem. The main requirement here is to keep on satisfying the relevant requirements (NFR01-NFR05) and to allow the adjustment of the functionality according to the requirements changes (CR01). The answers to the evaluation of the Proxy pattern as a solution are provided in Table 3.5.

Design decision DD02		
Concrete Table Inheritance application	Select a Concrete Table Inheritance strategy as a configuration option of the Hibernate (Data Access Component).	
QT	**Questions**	**Answer**
G	Would you like to present an inheritance hierarchy of classes in relational database?	✔
I	Shall one database table be used for each concrete class in the hierarchy and no tables for abstract classes?	✔
	Would you like to spread the request load between the tables?	✔
	Would you like the Database to be used by other applications that are not using (or do not know) objects?	–
C	Are there few changes to the objects (classes) expected?	✔(*)
	Is data collection (retrieval) from all of the tables seldom demanded in your application? (otherwise → Single Table Inheritance)	✔(*)

Table 3.4.: Extract from Design Decisions to the Hexxon CoCoME System, 2

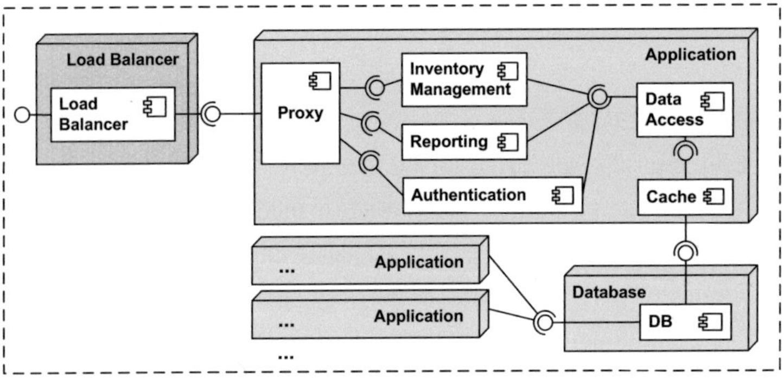

Figure 3.24.: Modified Hexxon CoCoMe Architecture of the Enterprise Server (Adopted from [2])

While from the functional point of view, the Proxy pattern seems to be suitable, there are two non-functional properties that require clarification.

In this case architects would need to evaluate if a Proxy pattern could be a performance bottleneck and cause additional indirection, for example with the help of the Palladio approach described in Section 2.5.1. If it is not, the question is clarified. If it is, architects would need to ask requirements engineers to prioritize requirements related to performance and requirements

Design decision DD03 (Replaces DD01)		
Proxy application	Provide a substitute in order to isolate the components of the Enterprise Server from the direct access of the rest of the Hexxon CoCoME system and adding a sessions control.	
QT	**Questions**	**Answer**
G	Would you like to provide an interface to some other object, resource, network connection, etc.?	✔
I	Would you like to provide or to restrict the access to functionalities provided by another object or server?	✔
	Would you like to provide an interface with some additional functionality, e.g, management of objects state, etc.?	✔
	Would you like to provide a representative for an object in different address-space?	–
C	You do not plan to extend the object's properties dynamically? (otherwise → Decorator)	–
	Is a potential performance bottleneck not a problem?	?✗→✔
	Is a higher level of indirection not a problem?	?✗→✔

Table 3.5.: Evaluation of the Proxy Pattern Applicability

related to the system's flexibility (NR01-NR04 vs. NR05). In this case, either potential performance problems or the flexibility may be neglected for the subsystem part.

If assumed that the questions were clarified and a decision is made to apply a Proxy, this decision is semi-automatically documented together with the rationale and trace links to the new involved requirements. Thus, not only an outdated decision about Façade was identified, replacing decisions about the application of the Proxy pattern was not spontaneous, but were a result of a systematic design and requirements engineering approach.

There is a second way to discover that the Façade design decision is deprecated [2]. Software architects could have started analysing the requirements to the system. They would have discovered the requirements contributing to the Façade pattern application decision. These requirements would be outdated due to the change request CR01. Based on the outdated requirements, software architects could obtain a list of design decisions, where the deprecated requirements triggered the decisions or were used as a rationale for them.

Further on, the next decision linked through requirements is a Hibernate mapping configuration strategy – Concrete Table Inheritance application. The rationale for it is provided in Table 3.3 and 3.4. Re-evaluation of these decisions also discovers a flaw due to the change of requirements. First, there are multiple expected changes to the objects (classes) due to the merge of the two petrol station chains. This contradicts a previous assumption in the data model's stability. Moreover, due to the change of requirement NFR01 caused by the change request CR01, there is a significant increase in reporting, and thus, a significant increase in data collection (retrieval) from all of the data tables. The AM3D catalogue proposed trying a Single Table Inheritance pattern in such a case.

Architects can evaluate the Single Table Inheritance pattern for its suitability as a new mapping strategy configuration. The answers to the evaluation of the Single Table Inheritance to the questions from the AM3D catalogue are provided in Table 3.6.

Design decision DD04 (Replaces DD02)		
Single Table Inheritance application	Select a Single Table Inheritance strategy as a configuration option of the Hibernate (Data Access Component) instead of Concrete Table Inheritance strategy due to the increased number of reporting inquires and expected frequent data object changes	
QT	**Questions**	**Answer**
G	Would you like to present an inheritance hierarchy of classes in relational database?	✔
I	Would you like to keep all data in a single table? (otherwise → Class Table Inheritance or Concrete Table Inheritance)	–
	It is important to avoid joins in retrieving data?	?✗→ ✔
C	Frequent locks on one table are not an issue?	✔
	A non-straightforward relationship between database and domain model is not a problem?	✔
	Is it not your intent for the Database to be used by other applications that are not using (or do not know) objects? (otherwise → Concrete Table Inheritance)	? → ✔

Table 3.6.: Evaluation of the Single Table Inheritance Pattern Applicability

Once again, there are open questions that require additional input and trigger systematic design and requirements engineering processes. First, the architects need to evaluate if it is important to avoid joins in retrieving data. This would require an application of a performance analysis tool. Second, there is an open question if the database has to be used by other applications that are not using (or do not know) objects. Here, architects would require help from the requirements engineers to elicit additional requirements about use case scenarios of the existing database outside of the Hexxon CoCoME system. When questions are clarified and there is a decision to apply a new strategy or to keep the old one, this decision is semi-automatically documented together with the rationale and trace links to the involved requirements and architectural elements.

4. Pattern Catalogue and Approach Details

This chapter provides a detailed explanation of the AM3D pattern catalogue as a core of the AM3D approach, and details on the AM3D approach formalization based on the developed meta-models. The purpose of the subparts of the AM3D approach are listed together with the information on structure and process to create the catalogue and to create the question annotations for it.

First, the purpose of the AM3D pattern catalogue is explained in Section 4.1. Then, Section 4.2 provides details of the structure of the catalogue, including blocks on general information about pattern, question annotations and architectural implementation. Section 4.3 explains the pattern catalogue questions, their structure, ways of formulation the questions and answers to the questions. It also provides a process to add questions to patterns. The process to create an AM3D pattern catalogue is defined in Section 4.4. The types of the patterns supported by the approach are listed in Section 4.5. Approach formalization based on the developed meta-models is presented and explained in detail in Section 4.6. Finally, Section 4.7 provides the summary of the approach and concludes the chapter.

4.1. Purpose of the Catalogue

While the general information about patterns, such as goal, properties and structure is available in different sources, e.g. [28] or [29], all this information is typically described in a free-text form. Such form requires time for reading and understanding. From the one side, such pattern catalogues are good for gaining fundamental understanding and knowledge about the subject. From the other side, they are less suitable as a short reference material. They cannot be used to quickly check a feature or to check pattern structure violations.

Meta-models and ontologies have been proposed to structure the pattern information in a better-accessible way (see Section 7 for more information). They have several advantages. First, they are easily supported by tolls and allow for automated tool-generation. They can be used to generate documentation of model elements, such as design documentation and their rationale, and to document trace links between various artefacts, such as requirements, design decisions, and architectural elements. Moreover, automated checks can be run on the instances of the meta-models. For example, the structure of the pattern in a model can be, thus, automatically checked for correctness.

However, meta-models usually concentrate only on one of the two aspects. Either it is descriptive information about the pattern, such as the pattern goal and advantages, or they focus on implementation details, such as UML class-diagrams and code. Such approaches are more information sources thanguidance for pattern selection, application and documentation.

The purpose of the proposed pattern catalogue is to join these aspects into one approach. The goals can be summarised as following:

- **Structure available information about patterns and present it in a quick assessable way:** The AM3D catalogue shall structure the available information about patterns. This information is taken from the common catalogue sources and is structured with the help of the meta-model. It shall provide a quick overview about a pattern, its properties, advantages, disadvantages, structure, and related patterns. However, it is not full-text information from the catalogues, but rather an essence with the goal to give an overview.

- **Support evaluation of patterns suitability for the given design problems:** The catalogue supports the evaluation of a pattern's suitability for the given design problems. The user is able to check what properties of the pattern satisfies the given requirements, and what properties are in the contradiction. Moreover, the consequences of a pattern application are made clear. The user is still responsible for the final decisions, but the catalogue supports him during the decision making process. The important part is to make the support quick and lightweight, avoiding the drawback of long textual descriptions.

- **Support semi-automated documentation of the use of design pattern as a solution for the problem together with the rationale for the pattern selection, and documentation of trace links between requirements, decisions and architectural elements:** Based on the support for pattern evaluation, the user is also supported at documentation of the pattern decisions and trace links between artefacts. Thus, the catalogue supports semi-automated documentation of design pattern as a solution for the problem. The rationale collected during the evaluation of the design pattern is saved together with the decisions to use or to discard the pattern for later software evolution. The focus here is on a lightweight documentation of not only decisions to use or to discard a pattern, but also on a lightweight documentation of the rationale for this decision.

- **Support goal-oriented architecture-driven requirements engineering:** While evaluation design patterns as solution candidates, the user may require additional information to be able to make a decision. This information may be either an elicitation of new requirements to the system or re-prioritization of the existing requirements.

- **Support pattern modelling formalization in order to simplify modelling and to allow checks for modelling violations:** Once there is a decision to use a pattern, the catalogue supports instantiation and checks of the patterns structure. Thus, the catalogue supports pattern modelling formalization in order to simplify modelling and to allow automatised checks for structure modelling violations.

The purpose of the proposed pattern catalogue is to (1) structure the information, which is already available in other catalogues, in a better accessible way; and (2) integrate support for evaluation of design patterns for their application, documentation together with the rationale and modelling.

4.2. Structure of the Catalogue

This section provides details on the AM3D pattern catalogues structure. The overview is schematically presented on Figure 4.1.

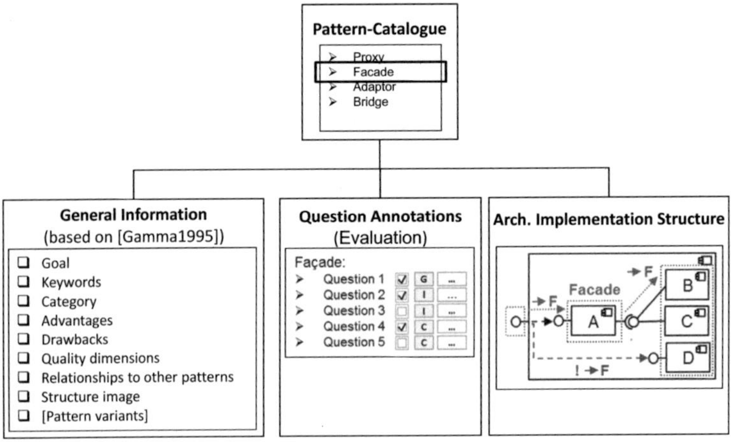

Figure 4.1.: Overview of the Catalogue Structure

Each pattern description is based on the AM3D pattern description template which consists of three building blocks:

- General information about a pattern
- Question annotations for pattern evaluation and documentation

- Architectural implementation structure (pattern structural information for UML-alike system diagrams and constraints).

They are explained in detail in the following subsections.

4.2.1. General Information About Patterns

General information block of the AM3D pattern description template comprises the pattern name, goal, keywords, type (e.g., object-oriented or security), category (e.g., structural or behavioural), identification number (ID), short description, advantages, drawbacks, influence on quality dimensions, structural image, information source, and, if existent, variants of a pattern and relations to other patterns, inspired by [28, 29].

These blocks are summarised on the left of the Figure 4.1 and are explained in the following:

- **Name:** A common name of a pattern, as defined in pattern catalogues. For example, a pattern name is a"Model View Controller", and a common known shortening of it is "MVC". An example, for the Name of a Model View Controller pattern is listed on Figure 4.2.

General Information Block		
Type: Architectural pattern	Category: Structural pattern	ID: AP001
Short Description: The pattern isolates "domain logic" (the application logic for the user) from the user inter-face (input and presentation), enabling independent development, testing and maintenance of each of them (separation of concerns).		
Goal of the Pattern: – Decouple user-interface aspects of a system from its functional core. – Interaction is limited to calling an update procedure.		

Figure 4.2.: An example of Name, ID, Type, Category, Goal and Short Description of an AM3D Catalogue Entry for Model View Controller Pattern

- **Type:** A type of a pattern, as defined in pattern catalogues. Usually pattern catalogues are dedicated to one of the types, for example to object-oriented patterns, security patterns or to patterns of distributed computing. This type is then listed in the AM3D pattern catalogue in the "Type" field. An example, for the Type of a Model View Controller pattern is listed on Figure 4.2.

- **Category:** A category of a pattern, as defined in pattern catalogues. Usually, the authors of a pattern catalogue define several categories for the listed patterns. For example, Gamma et al. [28] define the following categories for the object-oriented patterns: Structural, Creational, Behavioral and Concurrency patterns. This category is then listed in the AM3D pattern catalogue in the "Category" field. An example for the Category of a Model View Controller pattern is listed on Figure 4.2.

- **Information source:** A source from which the pattern information is adapted from. The source can be single or multiple. If multiple information sources are listed, it means that the information about a pattern in the pattern catalogue was merged from several information sources. An example for the Information source of a Model View Controller pattern is listed on Figure 4.2.

- **Identification number:** A unique identification number assigned to the pattern in the AM3D catalogue. This number is used to search information about patterns, and to reference patterns while describing the relationships between patterns in the AM3D catalogue. An example for the Identification number of a Model View Controller pattern is listed on Figure 4.2.

- **Goal:** A goal of a pattern. The goal describes an intent behind a pattern application, for example a high-level description of a problem that can be solved by a pattern. A goal can be divided into several small sub-goals, forming the main pattern application scenario. An example for the Goal is listed on Figure 4.2.

- **Short description:** A short description of a pattern. While a goal is a short description of the main application scenario of a pattern, a short description provides a summary of pattern properties. It shall provide a short introduction on pattern usage, which can be used as an alternative to a long-text description in other catalogues. The short description should also include the main characteristics of the pattern. If a pattern is unknown to a user, such a description might not be sufficient to understand all the features of a pattern. However, together with the other bits of information of the AM3D description template for the patterns, this description shall provide enough information to be able to structure the properties of a pattern for the user. Understanding of a pattern based on it shall be then enough to quickly access relation of a pattern and of a given problem. An example for the Short description of a Model View Controller pattern is listed on Figure 4.2.

- **Advantages:** Advantages of a pattern. A pattern application may bring a set of advantages for the reason why a user decides to select and to apply a pattern. For example, an advantage of the pattern Model View Control [28] can be a strict separation of a model from views, and thus exchangeability of the views without influence on a model. Usually, there is a set of advantages a pattern application brings. However, these advantages are intended advantages of a pattern. The final properties of a pattern depend on many factors. Some of these factors are an actual suitability of a pattern for the given problem, correct application of a pattern in the architectural design, correct implementation of a pattern in the system code and documentation of pattern application and of the rationale for it. Especially the given problem and the problem context influence the actual advantages of a pattern a lot. Sometimes, they do limit applicability of a pattern a lot and turn its advantages into drawbacks.

Therefore, the listed advantages shall be treated with care. They shall be seen and treated as a potential of a pattern, properties that a correct pattern application may bring and shall not be blindly relied on. And as these advantages are envisioned properties of the final implementation, and, therefore, they shall be controlled and re-evaluated in the final implementation in the code.

Finally, the advantages of a pattern are a subject of change over time, point of view or with the technology advance. For instance, some of the patterns that were considered to be useful in the past, are revised and considered to be anti-patterns nowadays. Some examples of this reconsideration are Visitor and Listener patterns. Another example are the patterns that can be considered useful or harmful depending on the point of view. For example, a Façade pattern [29] can be considered useful and its advantages valuable. However, in some cases this pattern is a clear anti-pattern and is a bottle-neck or can be seen as a god-class. In these cases, the advantages of the Façade pattern are actually its drawbacks. An example for the Advantages of a Model View Controller pattern is listed on Figure 4.3.

Advantages:	Drawbacks:
- Multiple views on the same model	- Increased complexity
- Strict model separation from view	- Potential for excessive number of updates
- Synchronized views	- Intimate connection between view and controller
- Pluggable views and controllers	- Close coupling of views and controller to a model
- Exchangeability of "look and feel"	- Efficiency of data access in view
- Framework potential	- Inevitability of change to view and controller when porting
	- Difficulty of using MVC with high-level GUIs

Figure 4.3.: An Example of Advantages and Drawbacks of an AM3D Pattern Catalogue Entry for Model View Controller Pattern

- **Potential Drawbacks:** Drawbacks are disadvantages of a pattern. Similar to the facts, that a pattern application follows a goal and brings a set of advantages, it also brings a set of drawbacks and problems. As patterns are considered to be standardized and well-approbed solutions, many users applying the patterns are actually not aware of the drawbacks of a pattern application. These drawbacks can be either light and reversible (can be avoided with some precautionary measures), or severe and unavoidable.

  Drawbacks of a pattern are the reason why a user decides to discard his idea to apply a pattern. For example, a drawback of the pattern Model View Control [28] can be an increased complexity of its implementation, and a higher number of bugs connected to it.

  Similar to the advantages, usually, there is a set of drawbacks a pattern application brings. These drawbacks are intended disadvantages of a pattern. Also here, the final properties of a pattern depend on many of the factors, such as its application in the architectural design, its implementation in the system code, problem and problem context. Especially the given problem and the problem context influence the actual advantages of a pattern a lot.

  The listed drawbacks shall be also treated with care. They shall be seen and treated as a potential threat of a pattern, negative properties that a pattern application may bring. Depending on a problem and its context, some of the drawbacks may never occur. However, also depending on a problem and its context, there may be additional drawbacks, which are not listed in the catalogue.

  As a set of drawbacks is known in advance, the user shall make use out of it. The measures to avoid or to minimise the negative pattern influence shall be taken during design, propagated into the implementation and monitored during later evolution of the system.

Finally, the drawbacks of a pattern are also a subject to change with the time, point of view or with the technology advance. In some cases, a technology and hardware advances can eliminate the drawback's feasibility. For example, in a Model View Controller pattern a potentially longer updates of the views can become infeasible because of a more powerful hardware. An example for the Drawbacks of a Model View Controller pattern is listed on Figure 4.3.

- **Keywords:** Keywords characterizing a pattern. A set of keywords reflecting the main properties of a pattern and its goal. Keywords can be used for a search for a pattern, for structuring a pattern in the pattern catalogue, for aligning a pattern in relationships to other patterns, and for a brief overview of pattern properties. An example for the Keywords of a Model View Controller is listed on Figure 4.4.

Keywords:	Quality Attributes:
- views	- Performance 0
- data display	- Scalability +
- independent presentation	- Reliability 0
- various data presentation	- Understandability +
- separation logic and presentation	- Flexibility +
- multiple user groups	
- interactivity	

Figure 4.4.: An Example of a Keywords and Influence on Quality Dimensions of an AM3D Pattern Catalogue Entry for Model View Controller Pattern

- **Potential impact on quality dimensions:** Influence on quality dimensions of a pattern. The influence on quality dimensions describes the expected influence of a pattern on non-functional (quality) attributes of a system, such as performance, reliability, scalability, maintainability, security, understandability and flexibility. The influence can be positive, neutral, negative or not available.

A positive influence "+" means that a pattern is expected to improve this quality dimension. A neutral influence "0" means that a pattern is expected neither to improve nor to decrease the quality in this dimension. Negative influence "–" means that a pattern is expected to decrease the quality in this dimension. Not available means that influence on a quality property cannot be evaluated for the pattern and that it may have a positive, neutral or negative influence on the given quality dimension depending on the architectural design, implementation and a problem context. In this case, the influence is indicated as an "n/a" against this quality attribute.

For example, the *Proxy* pattern [28] contributes to the separation of concerns (scalability "+"), but may negatively influence the response time (performance "–"). Influence of Proxy pattern on security cannot be estimated without evolution of architectural design, and surrounding components. Therefore, for the security the influence is indicated as "n/a".

However, a quality influence of a pattern cannot be predicted in advance. Thus, the influence on quality dimensions category of the pattern description template is only an indicator. It is possible to predict quality level for some quality attributes at the design time, for example for performance or reliability. Therefore, it is possible to analyse the pattern's influence on one of these quality dimensions at the design time. Nevertheless, actual quality influence of a pattern on the to be developed system can only be precisely evaluated when the implementation is complete and can differ depending on context and implementation details. Therefore, these descriptors only specify the influence type, but serve only for information purposes.

Another aspect is quantification of the quality influence. For some quality attributes, such as above mentioned performance and reliability, it is possible to derive a quantified influence of a pattern from a design time architecture-based prediction. However, for the other quality attributes a precise quantification at the architectural level is not possible. There are methods helping to obtain an evaluation for some of these quality dimensions, such as ATAM [165] for maintainability or security attack tree analysis for security [166] (based on [167]), however, they do not provide a precise quantified result. In general, they are highly dependent on a person or a group of persons performing the analysis.

It becomes even more complex at the implementation level. To be able to measure an actual influence of a pattern application, two system implementation variants are required – with and without a design pattern. However, it is hardly feasible and practicable in practice. Moreover, measurement does not work for most of the quality dimensions. The two exclusions are again performance or reliability influence, which can be measured in a running system. Thus, at the architectural level, a precise evaluation of a pattern's influence on a quality dimension is not possible at the architectural level.

In overall, a quantification of a pattern's influence on a quality dimension is not possible in a generic pattern catalogue. Therefore, a selected form of an influence is simplified to the 4 above mentioned categories. It serves only as an indicator, whereby the actual influence values depend on actual design and implementation of the system where a pattern is used. An example for the Influence on quality dimensions of a Model View Controller pattern is listed on Figure 4.4.

- **Variants of a pattern:** Variants of a pattern capture variants of a pattern known by the same name. Variants of a pattern have a similar goal as the base pattern, but they differ in some properties, as well as in advantages and drawbacks, on the structural level (in roles and connectors between them) and/or in the semantics. For example, a Façade pattern [28] can be implemented using either a single or multiple Façade objects. Or in the base variant of the Model View Controller pattern [28] a direct communication between the Views and the Model is not possible, however, it is possible in its variant, where a Controller can be omitted in the communication. In this case, some of the properties of the Model View Controller pattern change. So, the potential drawback of a controller becoming a performance bottleneck in the system is relaxed, as the load on the Controller is reduced through the allowed direct communication between the Views and the Model. An example for the Variants of a pattern of a Model View Controller pattern is listed on Figure 4.5.

Variants:
- Variant 1: The view is directly connected to the Model
- Variant 2: Mixed form of base variant and Variant 1. The view is connected to the model through a controller but in some case has a direct access to the model.

Figure 4.5.: An Example of Variants of an AM3D Pattern Catalogue Entry for Model View Controller Pattern

- **Relations to other patterns:** Relationships of a pattern to other patterns. There are several types of relationships between patterns.

  First, some of the patterns target similar problems, thus having similar goals and some of the properties, advantages and drawbacks. In this case, the patterns are related between each other as similar patterns and form a "similar to" relationship. It is important to notify a user about other patterns with similar goals and to support the user at the selection between these similar patterns. For example, the Single Table Inheritance pattern [30] is similar to the Class Table Inheritance pattern [30]. They follow the same goal, share most of the properties, and differ only in some fine details. These details are highlighted in the AM3D catalogue with the help of catalogue question annotations discussed later.

Second, some of the patterns are (often) used together. In this case, they form a "used with" relationship. For example, a Model-View-Controller and Observer patterns [28] are often used together, where an Observer is used to notify the Controllers in the Model View Controller about changes to a View or to a Model.

Third, patterns may exclude the application of some other patterns. Thus, if a decision is made to apply a pattern, a user shall be clear that certain other patterns, and thus goals in their face, cannot be applied any more in that subsystem. An example for the Relationships of a Model View Controller pattern is listed on Figure 4.6.

Relationships:

Recommended Co-Patterns:
–Observer
–Command processor pattern

Similar Patterns/Solutions:
–Presentation Abstraction Control
–Locks on data
–Offline user communication

Excluded patterns:
- Not listed.

Architectural Structure Image:

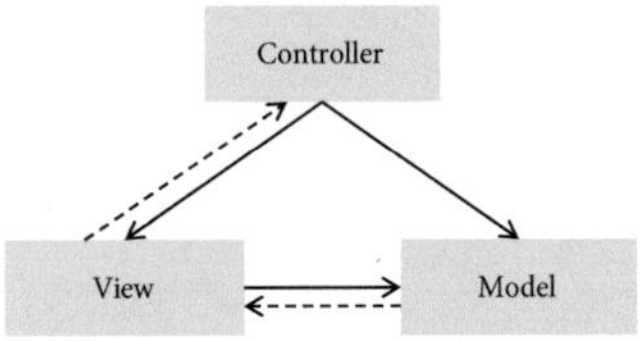

Figure 5.1.: Structure of Model View Controller

Figure 4.6.: An Example of Relationships and a Structural Image of an AM3D Pattern Catalogue Entry for Model View Controller Pattern

- **Structural image:** Structural image of a pattern. An image depicting a structure of a pattern in a UML notation [168, 169]. It provides a quick graphical overview of the main structural elements of a pattern, such as roles and connectors between roles (structural elements of a pattern are explained in detail in Section 4.2.3), interconnections between them (directions of connectors, relations between roles and connectors), involved structural elements of a system where pattern is applied to (e.g., invoked components, system subsystems, etc.), and of interconnection between pattern elements and elements of a system. Typically, the structure is depicted as a UML class diagram [168, 169] or a UML component diagram [169]. An example, for the Structural image of a Model View Controller pattern is listed on Figure 4.6.

4.2.2. Question Annotations

The question annotations block of the AM3D pattern description template is the main difference of the proposed pattern catalogue to other catalogues, such as catalogues by Gamma et al. [28], Buschmann et al. [31] or Fowler [30].

The goal of the question annotations block is first to support the catalogue user at evaluation if a selected design pattern is really appropriate to solve a problem the user has. Secondly, it is to semi-automatically support documentation of the user's decisions to apply or withdraw a pattern together with the rationale for the decision. The rationale is captured based on the answers to the questions, and can also contain links to the involved requirements, if these were provided.

Thus, the question annotations are design rationale fragments, captured in form of a checklist in the catalogue. Their attachment to the patterns has two goals. The first goal is to verify if the selected design pattern is indeed a suitable solution for the given problem in a given context. Here, the user of the AM3D catalogue does the transition between a question to the project-independent design pattern in the catalogue and a particular problem in the project-context. Secondly, answers to the checklist questions are saved as a rationale for a decision to use or to discard the pattern. The rationale is formed based on the questions in the checklist and answers to them. This rationale can be later used during the system maintenance and evolution, for example to understand why the pattern was used.

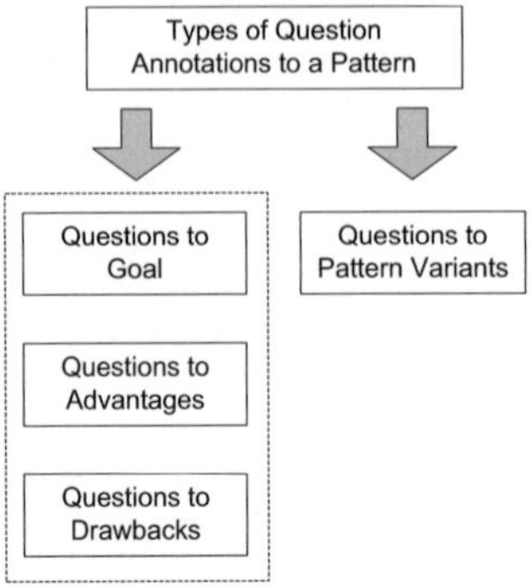

Figure 4.7.: Types of Question Annotations and Their Relation to a Pattern

There are four types of question annotations in the catalogue: Questions to the goal of a pattern, questions to the advantages of a pattern, questions to the drawbacks of a pattern and, if available, questions to the variants of a pattern. These types and their relation to the pattern are schematically depicted on Figure 4.7.

While the first three groups of question annotations form a question block to a particular pattern and are always available in this setting in the catalogue, the fourth group of question annotations – questions to the variants, is present only if variants are available and is independent on the first question annotation block. Some of its questions may repeat the questions from the first block, but the goal of them is to support the user at distinguishing between pattern variants. These four types are selected because they are capable of covering of all types of questions. In some cases, the question types may overlap, for example a goal question can be also an intent question. Such overlaps are allowed by the AM3D approach.

Answers to the questions can be "yes", "no", and "I don't know". A free-text comment and links to requirements can be provided as an explanation. The answers to the questions in the checklist are given by a user of the approach. Answer on a question depends on a particular problem, and may be different for the same patterns applied multiple times in the system. An example of the question annotations block of a pattern catalogue for the Model View Controller pattern entry is presented on Figure 4.8.

Question Annotations Information Block	
Goal	Would you like to present the same information in different ways e.g., through multiple views?
Intent	Would you like to enable to change the GUI (views) at run-time?
	Do you plan to exchange the underlying data model or the views representing this data? (design time)
Consequence	Is it acceptable to have potential delays by the view updates when larger amounts of data are transferred?
	The data in the model (e.g. DB) is not changed directly though the views (but though a controller), and will this be an issue in the future?

Figure 4.8.: Example of Question Annotations for Model View Controller Pattern

Section 4.3 provides detailed information on question annotations, types of questions, answers to the question, a process to annotate pattern with the questions and a discussion on questions form and structure.

4.2.3. Architectural Implementation Structure

The architectural implementation structure block of the AM3D pattern description template contains information on the pattern implementation in UML system diagrams. In the catalogue presented in this thesis, the architectural implementation details are schematically represented with the help of textual template which is explained later on.

4.2.3.1. Goals of the Architectural Implementation Block

The goal of the architectural implementation details block is threefold. First, it is to provide information on the architectural implementation of a design pattern. For this, the user can see the details of the pattern structure and on the structure of its variants, including the differences to the base pattern. The user can see how the structural parts of a pattern are connected between each other and how they are connected to the surrounding system.

Secondly, it is to support the user at modelling of a pattern. Once the user meets a decision to apply a pattern, the structure of a pattern or of its variant can be automatically instantiated (see details on the two-step instantiation of a pattern in Section 4.6.11. Such semi-automated instantiation helps to avoid structural mistakes while modelling a pattern. An example of a Façade design pattern instantiated in the PCM system model is presented on Figure 4.9 (repetition from Section 3).

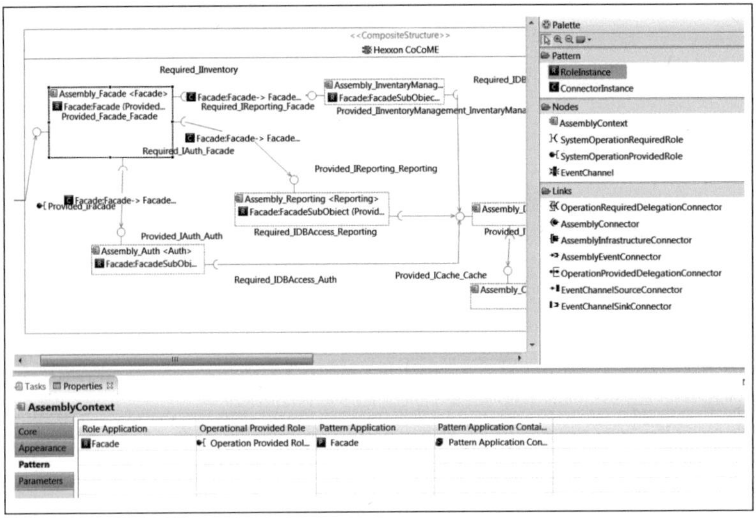

Figure 4.9.: An Example of Instantiation of the Façade Pattern in a PCM System Model (Repetition from Section 3)

Third, the structural information in the catalogue is enriched with constraints (OCL constraints, see Section 2.4.2), and implementation-based constraints). These constraints can be checked at the model level to notify the user if certain parts of a pattern are missing, if the connections between pattern parts are missing, and if the connections of the pattern parts to each other or to the rest of the system are structurally wrong. An example of such a check on a PCM model is presented on Figure 4.10.

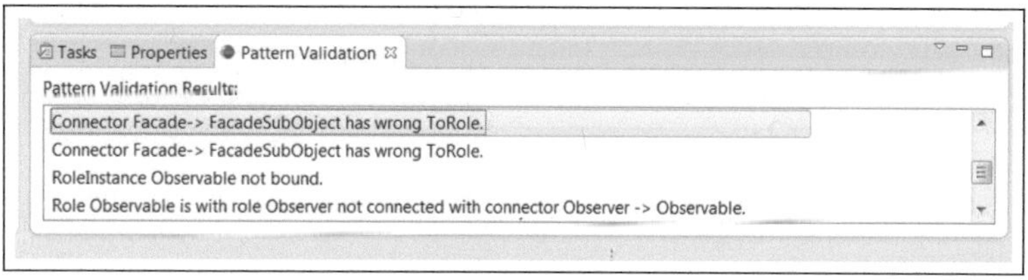

Figure 4.10.: An Example of Structural Check of the Façade Pattern in a PCM System Model

Moreover, once a pattern is modelled in the architecture, a check on the model level can be performed later to verify if a pattern was unintentionally modified during other design activities. For example, a part of a pattern may be accidentally deleted, or connections between parts may be changed. Such kind of check also goes beyond the pattern structure. It is capable of notifying the user if two contradicting patters are accidentally used together or if a required co-pattern is missing. For more information on relationships between patterns please refer to Section 4.2.1 and to Section 4.6.11.

4.2.3.2. Roles and Connectors Representation

There are multiple ways to model a pattern structure, for an overview of possible approaches please refer to Section 7.2. For this thesis the roles and connectors approach was selected to capture the architectural implementation details of a pattern in theAM3D catalogue. The roles and connectors approach, explained in [62], provides an ADL-independent way of capturing patterns structure as a set of roles and connectors between them. It supports modelling of all AM3D -relevant design patterns types (see Section 4.5 for the pattern types supported by the AM3D approach). Moreover, not only can they be represented with the same modelling formalism, but also at the same level of granularity and abstraction.

The level of abstraction is particularly important for the AM3D catalogue. A highly-detailed architectural representation of a pattern may be good for pattern comprehension, however, it is quite heavy-weight and requires a lot of time and effort for comprehension. An overly detailed description is actually often skipped by a user or misunderstood because of not enough time to deal with all of the provided details.

The goal of the AM3D pattern catalogue is to provide an easy and quick reference to a pattern, and to support the user at its evaluation for applicability and documentation. Therefore, a not over-detailed structural modelling of pattern is of high importance. The roles and connectors approach is detailed enough to be able to achieve all of the architectural implementation details block goals, including the constraint check possibility. However, it is still high-level enough to provide a quick reference for the pattern structure. The roles and connectors approach is sufficient for the mapping of pattern structure to the UML system components and system diagrams (please refer to Section 7.2.2 for other approaches on pattern modelling in architectural diagrams, such as UML). For the implementation in code a user can still consult the detailed architectural structure of a pattern from classical catalogues.

The idea behind the roles and connectors approach is that main actors in a pattern can be represented as roles and the relationships and actions between the roles can be represented as connectors. This concept is similar to the concept of a component diagram where the main acting units are components, and where the relationships between components are defined as component connectors. An example of the roles and connectors structure of a pattern is presented on Figure 4.11 for the Model View Controller design pattern.

The Model View Controller pattern consists of three roles: Model, View and Controller. Each of these roles can be implemented through several components or classes, however, structurally these classes form only three roles to be distinguished. Further on, there are three connectors: View →

Controller, View → Model and Controller → Model. The connectors are directed and mean that roles has an interaction with other roles in the given order. For the Model View Controller, the connector View → Controller (View to Controller) means that a View knows the controller and invokes it, whereby the controller cannot directly invoke the View. The Model role has no invocations to the other roles of the pattern, while it can be invoked by the View and by the Controller.

This structural representation clearly reflects the nature of the Model View Controller pattern. The Model does not know anything about the Views and Controllers. However, the View of course knows data of which Model it is reflecting. On the user's actions, the View would notify the Controller that some changes need to be implemented to a Model. However, the View cannot directly implement these changes. This is the limitation of the roles and connectors representation – although, it displays which roles of a pattern interact with which other roles, it does not reflect the behavioural details. So looking at the structural representation, a user cannot know what kind of interactions a View can undertake with the Model. However, this limitation is also true for the other modelling approaches to a patterns, unless for the very detailed ones. To overcome this limitation, a constraint on the action type can be stored in the pattern catalogue to notify the user about possible interactions between roles of a pattern.

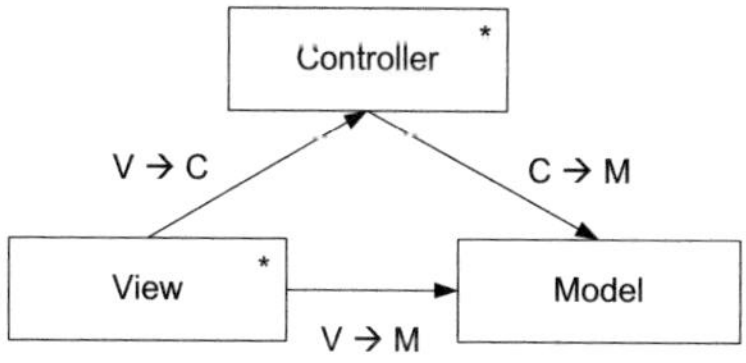

Figure 4.11.: An Example of Roles and Connectors Representation for the Model View Controller pattern

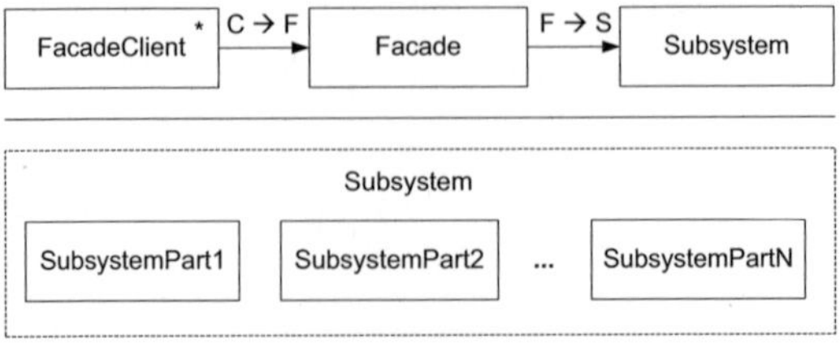

Figure 4.12.: An Example of Roles and Connectors Representation for the Façade Pattern

Another example of a roles and controllers notation is presented on Figure 4.12 for the Façade pattern. The Façade pattern consists of three roles: a Façade Client, a Façade itself and a Subsystem. The notable difference between the roles of the Model View Controller and the roles of Façade, is that the roles of the later involve the surrounding system, while the Model View Controller is independent from it. So, the Façade Client is the Client communicating to the Subsystem. Subsystem consists of multiple interconnected parts, which are abstracted under a single Subsystem pattern role. A Façade role is the actual design pattern Façade whose role is to decouple a subsystem from the invoking clients.

Façade pattern has two connectors: Façade Client → Façade and Façade → Subsystem. The Façade Client knows the Façade, but does not know the Subsystem, as it communicates with the Subsystem only through the Façade role. Façade role forwards the requests to the Subsystem role and returns its replies. The Façade pattern in the AM3D catalogue is annotated with the corresponding constraints, and if the user mistakenly models communication between the Façade Client and the Subsystem, a corresponding warning is produced[1] In this case the user is aware of the pattern violation. However, the final decision if the violation of the pattern structure is acceptable or not is left to the user and is on purpose not automated by the

[1] Unless, the user actually selected to use a non-strict variant of the Façade pattern, where such a direct communication is allowed.

AM3D approach. The AM3D approach supports informed decision making on design patterns, but on the contrary to the expert systems, does not take over the decision making from the user of the approach.

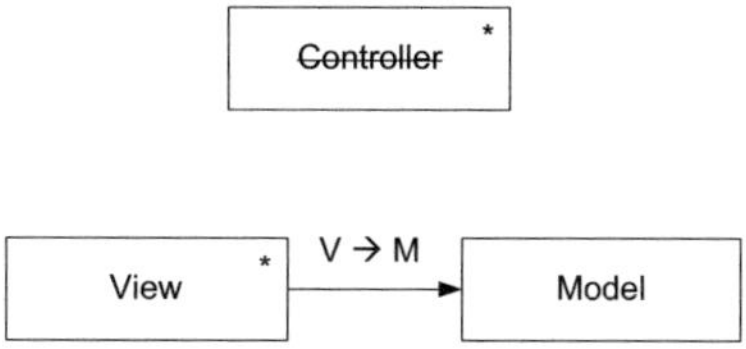

Figure 4.13.: An Example of Roles and Connectors Representation for the Variant of Model View Controller Pattern

If a pattern has a variant, its representation as roles and connectors may be different from the base pattern. Figure 4.13 depicts representation for the variant of the Model View Controller pattern, where View roles can communicate directly with the Model, and the Connector role is deprecated. Representation for variant of the Façade pattern is depicted on Figure 4.14. Here Client roles can communicate with the Subsystem both through the Façade or directly.

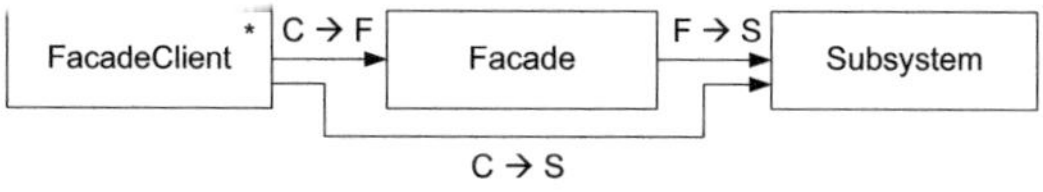

Figure 4.14.: An Example of Roles and Connectors Representation for the Variant of Façade Pattern

4.2.3.3. Textual Notation of the Roles and Connectors Representation

This section introduces a textual notation for the roles and connectors. The textual representation consists of two subparts: Roles and connectors. The roles of a pattern are listed as a list in the roles subsection of the description template in alphabetic order. The connectors of a pattern are listed in the connector's subsection of the description template in alphabetic order. The connectors have the following notation: Role1 → Role2. It means that the Role1 of a pattern has a directed interaction with the Role2 of a pattern. Unless a connector Role2 → Role1 is also present in the list, this interaction will be only mono directional, meaning that Role2 does not know about the Role1 invoking it.

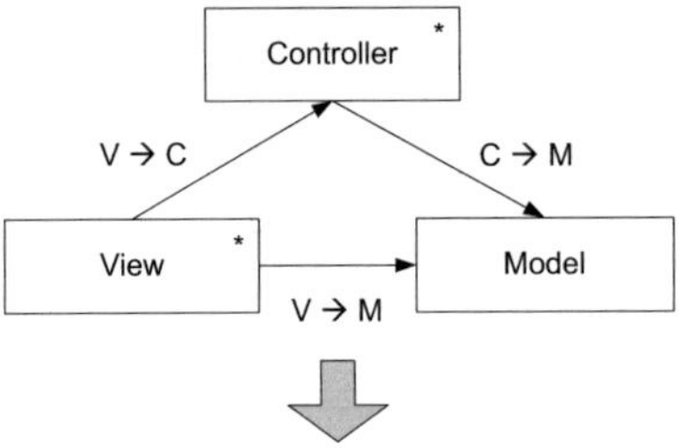

Architectural structure:	
Roles:	**Connectors:**
- Controller - Model - View	- Controller → Model - View → Controller - View → Model

Figure 4.15.: An Example of a Textual Representation for the Model View Controller Pattern

An example of such textual representation for the Model View Controller pattern is presented on Figure 4.15. An example of the textual representation for the Model View Controller variant is presented on Figure 4.16. List of Roles contains three Role of the Model View Controller pattern, and list of Connectors contains three Connectors of the Model View Controller pattern. In the example, Controller → Model Connector means that the Controller can access the Model, while as there is no opposite Connector, the Model does not know about the Connector directly and cannot access it. In the variant, the crossed-through items of the Roles and Connectors lists mean the deprecated Roles and Connectors of the base pattern.

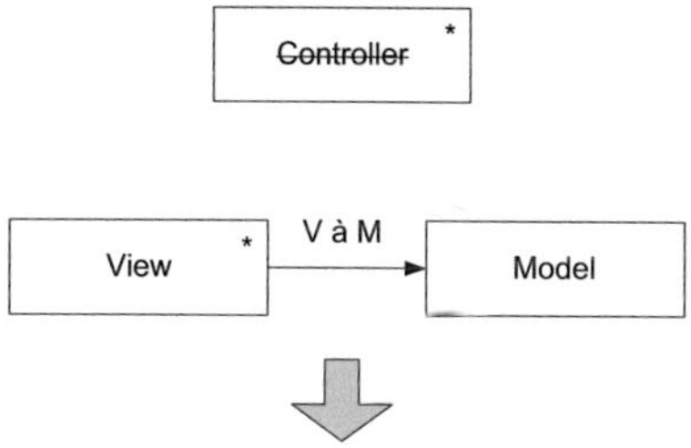

Structure variant: Variant 1	
Roles:	**Connectors:**
- ~~Controller~~ - Model - View	~~- Controller → Model~~ ~~- Controller → View~~ - Model → View - View → Model ~~- View → Controller~~

Figure 4.16.: An Example of a Textual Representation for the Model View Controller Pattern Variant

A complete example of the architectural structure information block of a pattern catalogue entry for the Model View Controller pattern entry is presented on Figure 4.17. A Model View Controller pattern is saved together with its two variants in the catalogue. Therefore, on Figure 4.17 the pattern has one subsection dedicated to its base structure, and two subsections dedicated to the structure of its variants. The differences between the variants are highlighted with the stroke through deprecated Roles and Connectors in the variants.

4.3. Pattern Catalogue Questions

This section explains the concept of pattern question annotations in detail. First, the purpose of the question annotation is explained in Section 4.3.1. Afterwards, an overview of possible ways to formulate a question to a pattern is given in Section 4.3.2. Section 4.3.3 explains types of question annotations, and Section 4.3.3 provides details on answers to question annotations. Finally, a process to add a question to the AM3D pattern is listed in Section 4.3.5. This process was used to annotate patterns in the sample AM3D pattern catalogue provided in Section 5.

Architectural Structure Information Block	
Structure:	
Roles: - Model - View - Controller	Connectors: - View → Controller - Controller → Model - View → Model
Structure variant: Variant 1	
Roles: - Model - View - ~~Controller~~	Connectors: - ~~Controller → Model~~ - ~~Controller → View~~ - Model → View - View → Model - ~~View → Controller~~
Structure variant: Variant 2	
Roles: - Model - View - Controller	Connectors: - Controller → View - Controller → Model - Model → View - View → Model - View → Controller

Figure 4.17.: Example of Complete Architectural Structure Information Block

4.3.1. Purpose

Pattern catalogue questions annotations are check-lists containing sets of questions that summarize the core features of a pattern, such as its goal, its intent or consequence of its application.

Pattern question annotations support the overall goal of the AM3D approach to lightweight support pattern evaluation and documentation for the decision on pattern application. The questions support critical evaluation of the applicability of the selected pattern from different points of view. These points include the main goal of a pattern, its positive features (advantages), its negative features (drawbacks) and its variants.

Often, the user is aware of the pattern goal and of some of its advantages. Very common the drawbacks of a pattern are forgotten or neglected, as a user does not expect a pattern to have any. This is due to the establish image of the design patterns as common and approved solutions for design problems. Another common problem with design patterns is that they are often misunderstood or only partially understood. So, the important features of a pattern may remain hidden to the user. These features can be both positive and negative. Finally, users are often unaware of pattern variants. Therefore, questions pointing out the features of pattern's variants are not to be forgotten by an all-round pattern description. Thus, the goal of the AM3D question annotations to a pattern is to make the user aware of all of the above mentioned features.

While answering the questions, the users receive hints about patterns and their aspects that they might have forgotten or might not have considered otherwise. The answers to these questions reflect the most important factors contributing to the selection or to discard of a pattern. If captured, these answers can serve as a rationale behind the decision to apply or to the discarding of a pattern and as a documentation for the pattern application.

An important feature is that question annotations are generic and project-independent. Answers to the questions are, however, project- and problem-specific. A user of the catalogues does the translation from a generic project-independent question to a project-specific question application in a context of the given problem of a particular project. For the same pattern in the catalogue, a potential application in different parts of the same project may bring different answers to the questions in the question checklists. This is because at various parts of the project various pattern features matter in different ways. Thus, what in one place may be an important drawback, in another place in the system may be neglected or may even become an advantage.

In general, the generic description of pattern features through the question annotations provides only hints on the potential properties if a pattern is applied. The real and final properties of a pattern depend on how the pattern is applied in the existing architecture of a system, and how it is implemented in its code implementation. Thus, the expected benefits of a pattern become benefits only if a pattern is correctly placed and modelled in a system, and then also correctly implemented in the code.

To summarise, the pattern question annotations have the following goals:

- **Support users at understanding the features of the pattern:** The users become aware of what features a pattern has, including goals of a pattern, advantages of a patterns, drawbacks of a pattern and variants of a pattern. Especially, the drawbacks and variants of a pattern are often omitted by the users, and with the help of AM3D catalogue questions it is assured that the users received hints also to these pattern properties.
- **Support users at understanding whether they really want to apply a pattern or if a pattern is an over-engineered solution with too many drawbacks to their problem:** The users are faced with a brief but comprehensive list of pattern features. Seeing all features at a glance, the users can re-evaluate their initial estimation on the appropriateness of a pattern for a particular problem. Seeing a pattern's drawbacks directly together with the advantages supports a better-balanced evaluation of a pattern. Sometimes, a pattern may be a fairly good solution to a particular problem a user has, however, a correct implementation of a pattern with sight on preventing its drawback would require so much effort, that a solution without pattern would be more appropriate. The AM3D catalogue questions may help a user to realize this situation.
- **Prevent quick decisions of users on pattern application:** Answering questions from the question annotations check-lists prevents

users from a quick decision to apply a pattern. The users are faced with properties of a pattern and are thus forced to spend some time evaluating their decisions.

- **Support users at generating documentation with the rationale for their decision about pattern:** As question annotations contain a general description of pattern's features, answers to the question highlight the relation between general features of a pattern and a particular context of a problem in the project. Answers to the question form a rationale for a decision to apply or to discard a pattern. A decision of a user can be thus semi-automatically saved together with the rationale generated while answering the questions. This documentation together with the rationale improves later software evolution.

Please note, that the question annotations are not intended to help with the initial selection of a possible pattern, in the meaning that the AM3D pattern catalogue is not intended to be used as an expert system. For a detailed discussion on this topic please refer to Sections 3.5.

The question annotation concept differentiates the AM3D pattern catalogue approach from other related approaches. In the following sections, ways of formulating questions in question annotations and types of the questions are described. They are followed by several examples of such questions and an explanation of the process that was used to add questions to the sample AM3D catalogue.

4.3.2. Ways of Formulating a Question

There are multiple ways of formulating a question to a pattern. The ways to formulate a question differ in the level of abstraction and level of granularity. The higher are these levels, the higher level of reuse between question to patterns can be achieved. Lover levels of abstraction allow for a better understanding of a question, as there are more details included into a question. However, fine-granular questions to a pattern also require a deeper knowledge of a pattern from the user.

For this thesis, two of the possible approaches were designed, analysed and compared with the help of examples and by independent reviewers as a part of a diploma thesis by Heller [164]:

- **Two-step question annotations:** The first approach to formulate a question consists of two-step question annotations – of generic questions and of fine-grained questions. The fine-grained questions describe and summarize the properties of a pattern in detail. They include the pattern's intent and important interactions among roles of a pattern. Thus, a fine-grained question annotations set consists of questions to intent and to interactions between pattern's roles. Each of these fine-grained questions is linked to a generic question. Such generic questions describe recurring properties of patterns and are formulated based on a set of keywords, generated from pattern descriptions related to the software development process (e.g. communication, separation of concerns or creator).

  The results are a pair of questions, where a generic question describes a problem to be solved, and a fine-grained question describes how this problem is solved by a particular pattern (which feature of a pattern solves this problem). These pair of questions requires from the user a more detailed knowledge and understanding of a pattern in order to be able to understand the questions. An example of such question pairs is represented on Figure 4.18.

  The focus here lies in the reusability of questions between patterns. The fine-grained question to pattern properties are not limited and are extended through additional information in form of generic questions. The generic questions are added to a question repository on demand, meaning that if a suitable generic question was not found in the repository, it can be created, otherwise an existing question

Model-View-Controller 2.3.3 [BMR+96][BHS07a][Fow02]

No.	general question	pattern refinement
1	Separate the user interface from the underlying logic and/or data.	Divide an interactive application into three parts: the *Model* contains data and domain logic, the *View* displays the information contained in the *Model*, the Controller processes input of the user.
2	Support a *loose coupling* between *Model* and user interface.	Use an *OBSERVER* to propagate updates of the *Model* towards the user interface (Controller and *View*). *NFR: "+" Portability*
3 opt.	Support a *loose coupling* between *View* and *Controller*.	When building *thin-client* web applications a strong separation of *Controller* and *View* occurs when the *View* runs on the client and the *Controller* on the server [TMQ+03]. Implement e.g. the *Controller* using a *PAGE CONTROLLER* when building simpler web applications or use a *FRONT CONTROLLER* for more complex ones.

Figure 4.18.: An Example a Question Pair: Generic Question and Fine-grained Question for Model View Controller Pattern [164]

is reused. The basis for generic questions is a keyword repository – a glossary (keywords are highlighted in italic in the example Figure 4.18). These keywords in the glossary allow for relating generic questions solving the similar problems between each other. Further on, the fine-grained questions can be also related, in this case based on their relation to the generic question and keywords used in the generic questions.

- **Four-types question annotations:** The second approach is to formulate rather fine-grained questions to a pattern omitting a generic question, but structuring the fine-grained questions into sets of four question types. In this approach, a question is linked directly to a pattern. Each question corresponds to a certain property of a pattern (positive or negative) or to a property of pattern variants. The possible types of a question are questions to: Goal, advantages (pattern's intent), drawbacks (pattern's consequences) and variants. These types are explained in the following Section 4.3.3. An example of questions formulated using this second approach is presented of Figure 4.8. The roles of a pattern are not considered by the questions, as it would make questions too specific and detailed.

> For the second approach to formulate questions, a coarse-grained understanding of a pattern is sufficient for the user to be able to understand the question. This was also confirmed as a part of evaluation conducted for the AM3D approach and is described in detail in Section 6.4.

For the details on the comparison of these two approaches with corresponding examples please refer to the diploma thesis by Heller [164].

The second approach to formulate the questions was selected based on the results of the conducted comparison and on the opinion of independent reviewers, to whom both variants of questions were presented to. The reviewers considered it as comprehensive and sufficient for the AM3D catalogue's goal, especially for the cases when there is few knowledge about a design pattern available in advance.

Besides the structure of question annotation sets, another issue is the formulation of the text of the question itself. It is clearly a creative step, which is comparable to architectural design itself. However, it is possible to use predefined question templates, as some kinds of questions are more suitable than the other.

Examples of such question templates are: "Would you like to ... through ... ?", "Are potential ... acceptable in ...?", "Is ... probable in the future?". Ultimate question forms are avoided, as they might be always replied with "yes". For example, "Would you like to improve the ABC's maintainability?" will likely be always answered with "yes". Also the disadvantages shall never be named directly, as such questions will be likely always replied with "no". For example, "Do you want to reduce the throughput of the ABC?" will likely be always answered with "no".

The question templates actually differ depending on the type of question annotation (goal, intent, consequence or variants). To assure the understandability it is important to ask questions in the same style for each section of question annotations. Moreover, as sometimes a user might be inconsistent in the answers (e.g., mentioning that a potential increase in performance can be tolerated, however, that the performance of the system shall be increased at the same time), there are pairs of questions matched to identify when such inconsistencies among answers appear. The styles and pairs are explained in detail the following Section 4.3.3 together with the question types.

Clearly, the approach and the style which was chosen to formulate the questions is not the only approach possible. This topic falls under the subpart of Computational linguistics – Structural Approaches research area (see a survey of controlled natural languages by Kuhn [159]). The approach to and the rules to formulate pattern questions can be further refined and are part of the future work described in Section 8.3.

4.3.3. Question Types and Corresponding Styles

Several ways to formulate the questions to validate hypotheses on the appropriate use of patterns were investigated. An initial idea of two question types of question annotations for the AM3D approach was proposed in [4]. The idea was evolved into two approaches analysed and compared in Heller [164], where two types of questions were proposed and compared on an example from Buschmann et al. [31]. Based on the comparison and on the reviews by researchers of the initial catalogue entries, it was concluded to distinguish in total four types of questions to validate hypotheses on the appropriate use of patterns: General questions, Intent questions, Consequences questions and Variant questions.

As described in the previous Section, a style to formulate questions to a pattern depends on its belonging to one of these types. These styles are semi-formal and allow for a question's understandability and a similar level of abstraction in the formulation. They allow for standardized question annotations throughout the pattern catalogue. The styles idea is inspired by the SBVR Structured English [151] (for more information on controlled natural languages please refer to Section 2.5.3).

The AM3D approach does not require a special role to be defined to formulate questions to patterns in the catalogue and to use the styles for this purpose. Questions to design patterns may be created by an expert in the area of architectural design patterns or other architectural solutions that are planned to be added to the catalogue.

In the following, the types and the styles are described in detail:

- **General questions**. General questions deal with the main goal of the pattern. Their goal is to help to distinguish if the general idea of a pattern is intact with the main idea of the problem the user wants to solve with this pattern. For example, general questions help to distinguish between groups of patterns, such as structural and behavioural patterns, or point out infrastructure constraints that would limit possible pattern application, such as service-oriented systems or embedded systems.

  Usually there is only one general question to a pattern in the question annotations set, as patterns usually follow just one main goal.

  The semi-formal style template to formulate the general questions uses the "Would you like to G-VERB (improve, separate, map, etc.) ... G-OBJECT (presentation, subsystem, etc.) ... OPTIONAL ... ?" question form. Where: G-VERB is a compulsory verb stored in the glossary as a verb-keyword and describing an action that shall happen in the system; G-OBJECT is a compulsory object stored in the glossary as an object-keyword and describing an object to which the action shall happen; OPTIONAL are other verbs and objects, which are not necessarily stored in the glossary and usually refine the details on action or on the object. An example of a question to a goal is presented in Table 4.1.

  In the example the main purpose of the Model View Controller pattern is formulated as a "Would you like to ... ?" types of question. The G-VERB from the glossary is "to present" and the G-OBJECT

<table>
<tr><th>ID</th><th>Pattern catalogue question</th><th>Type</th></tr>
<tr><td>01</td><td>Would you like to present the same information in different ways e.g., through multiple views?</td><td>G</td></tr>
<tr><th colspan="3">Analysis of the template style:</th></tr>
<tr><td colspan="3">| "Would you like to" | PRESENT | the same | INFORMATION | in different ways e.g., through MULTIPLE VIEWS | "?" |</td></tr>
</table>

Table 4.1.: Example of a Goal Question for Model View Controller Pattern

from the glossary is "information". The additional OPTIONs specify what kind of information is presented and how – through "multiple views", where"views" and "multiple" is also a keyword pair from the glossary. The expected answer to the question is "yes".

- **Intent questions**. Intent questions clarify the intent of a pattern. They provide hints on the intended features and properties of the pattern. Usually these features and properties can be seen as positive and desired, basically, as the advantages of a pattern.

  Usually there is a set of intent questions to a pattern. Such questions help to distinguish between patterns inside of one target group. For example, Model View Controller and Presentation Abstract Control belong to the same structural patterns group and have the same goal question: However, the features and properties are partially different and intent questions can be used for the differentiation.

  The semi-formal style template to formulate intent questions uses the "Would you like to G-VERB (improve, map, etc.) ... G-OBJECT (presentation, subsystem, etc.) ... OPTIONAL ... ?" question form. Where: G-VERB is a compulsory verb stored in the glossary as a verb-keyword and describing an action that shall happen in the system; G-OBJECT is a compulsory object stored in the glossary as an object-keyword and describing an object to which the action shall apply; OPTIONAL are other verbs and objects, which are not necessary stored in the glossary and usually refine the details on action or on the object. An example is presented in Table 4.2.

ID	Pattern catalogue question	Type
02	Would you like to add at run-time new views or delete existing views?	I
03	Do you plan to exchange underlying data model or views representing this data? (Design Time)	I
Analysis of the template style:		
I "Would you like to" I ADD I at run-time new I VIEWS I or I DELETEI existing IVIEWS I "?"		
I "Do you plan to" I EXCHANGE I underlying I DATA MODELS I or I VIEWS I representing this data I "?" I (DESIGN TIME) I		

Table 4.2.: Example of a Intent Question for Model View Controller Pattern

In the example the two described features of the Model View Controller pattern are formulated as "Would you like to . . . ?" and "Do you plan to . . . ?" questions. The G-VERBs from the glossary are "to add", "to delete" and "to exchange". The G-OBJECTs from the glossary are "views" and "data model". There are no additional OPTIONs specified. The expected answers to the questions are "yes".

- **Consequence questions**. Consequence questions clarify possible consequences of the pattern. This consequences can be side-effects and negative features that might be undesired in a system. Consequence questions often reflect possible negative impact on non-functional properties, e.g. decrease of maintainability or performance. However, these possible consequences are only hints, and final maintainability or performance of the system depends on how the pattern is actually implemented. Still, provided hints on the possible pattern drawbacks, the user gets a chance to neutralize potential negative influence or even might decide not to apply the pattern as one of the drawbacks in not compatible with the desired system properties. Usually there is a set of consequences questions to a pattern, as a pattern may have several potential drawbacks.

  The semi-formal style template to formulate consequences questions uses the "Can you G-VERB (neglect, accept, map, etc.) . . . G-

OBJECT (delays, changes, etc.) ...OPTIONAL ...?" question form. Where: G-VERB is a compulsory verb stored in the glossary as a verb-keyword and describing an action that shall happen in the system; G-OBJECT is a compulsory object stored in the glossary as an object-keyword and describing an object to which the action shall happen; OPTIONAL are other verbs and objects, which are not necessary stored in the glossary and usually refine the details on action or on the object. An example of questions to consequences is presented in Table 4.3.

ID	Pattern catalogue question	Type
04	Can you accept potential delays by the view updates because of larger amounts of data?	C
05	Can you neglect changes of the data in the model though the views now and also in the future?	C
Analysis of the template style:		
I "Can you "I ACCEPT I potential I DELAYS I by the I VIEW UPDATES I because of larger amounts of I DATA I "?" I		
I "Can you "I NEGLECT I CHANGES I of the I DATA I though the I VIEWS I now and also in the future I "?" I		

Table 4.3.: Example of a Consequence Question for Model View Controller Pattern

In the example the two described features of the Model View Controller pattern are formulated as "Can you ...?" questions. The G-VERBs from the glossary are "to accept", "to neglect". The G-OBJECTs from the glossary are "delays" and "data changes". The additional OPTIONs specified are "view updates" and "views". The expected answers to the questions are "yes". If the consequence question is relied as "no", it does not mean that the pattern will be discarded. Some of the drawbacks can be prevented by the contra-measures. In this case, an answer of "no" means that a drawback is considerably important, however, it can be neglected because of the planned measures against it.

- **Variant questions**. Variant questions deal with the properties of variants of a pattern. For example, a classical Model View Controller pattern (a base pattern) differs in some properties to the variant where the Controller role is omitted.

  Base patterns and their variants have the same general goal, and similar intent and consequences that can be generalized to the most common pattern variant called base variant. However, some of the intents of a variant are different, and also some of the consequences differ from the base pattern. Moreover, some of the advantages may even become drawbacks and vice versa, some of the drawbacks may become advantages. The goal of the pattern variant questions is to help to identify the most suitable pattern variant, and to inform the user about its possible advantages or disadvantages. Usually there is a set of variant questions to a pattern.

  The semi-formal style template to formulate variants questions uses the "Would you like to G-VERB (improve, add, etc.) ... G-OBJECT (delays, data, etc.) ... negative G-VERB* (reducing, skipping, etc.) ... G-OBJECT* (changeability, performance, etc.) ... paired with ... G-OBJECT** (data model, subsystem, etc.) ... OPTIONAL?" question form. Where: G-VERB is a compulsory verb stored in the glossary as a verb-keyword and describing a positive (an improvement) action that shall happen in the system; G-OBJECT is a compulsory object stored in the glossary as an object-keyword and describing an object to which the action shall happen; G-VERB* is a compulsory verb stored in the glossary as a verb-keyword and describing a negative (a decrease) action that shall happen in the system; G-OBJECT* is a compulsory object stored in the glossary as an object-keyword and describing an influence of the action by the G-VERB*; G-OBJECT** is a compulsory object stored in the glossary as an object-keyword and describing an object pair to the G-

OBJECT* to which the action by the G-VERB* shall happen; OPTIONAL are other verbs and objects, which are not necessary stored in the glossary and usually refine the details on action or on the object. An example of questions to variants is presented in Table 4.4.

ID	Pattern catalogue question	Type
06	Would you like to improve delays in the view updates reducing the changeability of underlying data model?	V
07	Would you like to add data manipulation through view reducing the changeability of underlying data model?	V
Analysis of the template style:		
I "Would you like to" I IMPROVE I DELAYS I in the view updates I REDUCING I the I CHANGEABILITY I of underlying I DATA MODEL I "?" I		
I Would you like to" I ADD I DATA MANIPULATION I through a view I REDUCING I the I CHANGEABILITY I of underlying I DATA MODELI "?" I		

Table 4.4.: Example of a Variant Question for Model View Controller Pattern

In the example the two described variant features of the Model View Controller pattern are "Would you like to ... ?" questions. The positive G-VERBs from the glossary are "to improve" and "to add". The negative G-VERB* from the glossary is "to reduce". The G-OBJECTs from the glossary is "delays" and "data manipulation". The G-OBJECT* from the glossary are "changeability". The paired G-OBJECT* from the glossary is "data model". There are no additional OPTIONs specified. The expected answers to the questions are "yes", in order to favour a pattern variant over a base pattern.

The question styles presented here can be further formalized through a more strict formalisms, such as those described in the survey by Kuhn [159]. Please refer to the Section 8.3 for a discussion about it.

4.3.4. Answers to Questions

There are several ways how to formulate a question, and therefore several possible answer types, and finally several ways to interpret the answers.

To simplify this multi-dimensional answer space, the AM3D approach formulates questions in a way to allow only four types of answers. These types of answers were considered as the most suitable for the purpose of the approach. These four preferred answers to the questions are: Relevant property (a question replied as "yes"), irrelevant property (a question replied as "no"), unknown property (a question replied as "I don't know") and empty property (a question left without an answer). In the following they are explained in detail:

- **Answer "Yes":** An answer "yes" on a question to a pattern indicates that the feature described by a question is actively desired and is important for the target system. Questions replied to with "yes" therefore indicate the most important features and properties that contributed to the decision to apply the pattern. This does not imply that the other features are undesired or wrong. Answering "yes" solely indicates that the selected features were the ones to contribute to the decision.

- **Answer "No":** An answer of "no" on a question to a pattern indicates that the feature described by a question is undesired in the target system. Questions replied with a "no" therefore indicate the most important features and properties that contributed to the decision to discard the pattern. Similar to the answer "yes", answer "no" solely indicates that the selected features were the ones to contribute to the decision, but does not imply that other features are correct or wrong.

- **Answer "I don't know":** An answer of "I don't know" on a question to a pattern indicates that the feature described by a question is either unclear or that there are insufficient requirements to a system known in order to be able to answer the question. In that case, the requirements are insufficient, and a user may inquire a requirement engineer to elicit additional requirements. The "I don't know" answer may be linked to an event in the requirement engineering process in the tool chain. However, such events are beyond the scope of the AM3D approach and are not reviewed here. In any case, the answer "I don't know" is saved as a part of rationale for the decision to apply or discard a pattern. Usually, a question with such an answer is neither positively nor negatively contributing to the decision, however, it explains the circumstances under which the decision was taken. For example, later during the system evolution, a decision can be reviewed and discarded, if it was mistakenly taken due to the insufficient information about a problem or a context.

- **No answer:** If no answer to a question was provided, it indicates that the feature described by a question is irrelevant for the given problem and its context. The question remains unanswered, when the user sees no value in the feature and simply ignores it. In this case, the question is not included into rationale generation, unless a comment to a question was provided by the user. A comment can be a short explanation why the feature is not important or is not considered for the decision making. In this case, it is of course important to save the rational for the future evolution of a system.

The questions to the patterns and answers to them are aligned to requirements to the system. To be able to answer the questions, a user requires either to know the corresponding requirements to the system, or to be able to ask a requirements engineer to provide additional information on the subject. If currently available requirements are not sufficient to answer the pattern questions, the requirements engineer may elicit new additional requirements that are needed at the current stage of the project. In this case, requirements elicitation is driven through the architectural design process and is called an architecture-driven requirements engineering.

4.3.5. Process to Add Questions to a Pattern

This section describes a process to use in order to add question annotations to a pattern in the catalogue.

Adding questions to a pattern in the catalogue is a creative process. Moreover, all the questions are formulated in a semi-formal but still natural language, and the risk of inconsistencies in their form and organisation is fairly high. If the catalogue contains information in various forms, which is not comparable between its entries, its usability is likely to be reduced. Such a catalogue is then likely to become confusing and misleading mean, instead of a support for an improved system design and evolution.

A defined process reduces such a risk, because a user follows the same process for all the catalogue entries, and is more likely to produce similar result. Thus, the goal of the process is to assure that all the patterns in the catalogue are treated in a similar way and that the provided question sets are unified and homogenous between the patterns.

The process defined for the AM3D approach is depicted on Figure 4.19. This process was used to annotate patterns with questions for the sample AM3D catalogue provided in this thesis. In the following its steps are explained in detail:

1. **Excerpt pattern's summary:** Excerpt pattern's summary out of the pattern description in the source. Source can be a description of a design pattern, e.g. a book or a conference article. The so-collected pattern summary may be long. Another passage through it helps to reduce the length. This step can be omitted, if a description of a pattern in the source is short and well-structured.

2. **Divide the summary into facts:** Divide the summary into facts, where each fact of the pattern summary is a single item. Ideally, the fact list shall form a list of short sentences briefly describing the main features of a pattern. An example excerpt of such a fact list summary for the Model View Controller pattern is presented on Figure 4.20.

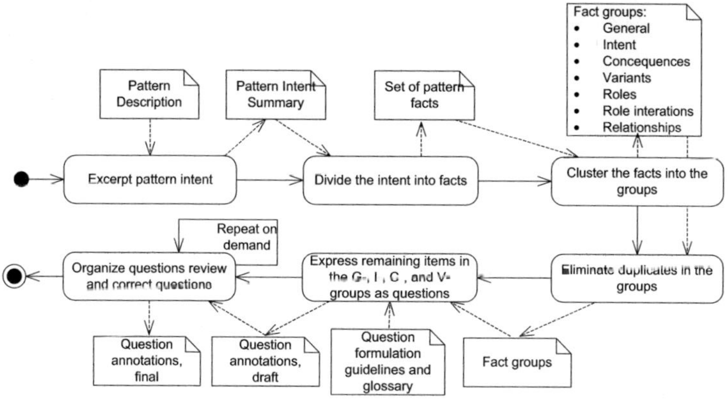

Figure 4.19.: A Process to Add Questions to a Pattern

Summary:

- Isolates domain logic from the user interface
- Decouple user interface
- Multiple views on the same data
- Strict data and presentation separation
- Exchangeability of data model
- Interaction with data through a controller
- Requires an Observer pattern
- Strict model separation from view
- Synchronized views
- Potential performance problems
- Controller potentially a bottleneck
- Improved flexibility through exchangeable views
- Improved support of multiple platforms
- Potential data time-out
- Potential data consistency
- A version where Controller can be omitted
- A version where communication both through and without Controller
- Has View, Model, Controller roles
- Controller communication with View and Model
- Model does not know about View and Controller
- ...

Figure 4.20.: An Excerpt of a Fact List for the Model View Controller Pattern

3. **Cluster the facts into groups:** Cluster the exacted items into the following groups:

    a) General goal or idea: General Goal or idea can be shared between several patterns.

    b) Intent: What can be achieved through pattern application, e.g. improved changeability of the GUI or reduced number of joints for the tables.

c) Consequences: Potential drawbacks of pattern application, e.g. decreased performance of the subsystem.

d) Variants: Design and implementation variants of a pattern. Variants follow the same goal as a base pattern, however, their positive and negative properties differ.

e) Pattern roles and connectors: Main actors of a pattern and interactions between them., e.g. a Controller role in the Model View Controller is interacting both with Model and with Views.

f) Relationships: Relationships between pattern and other patterns, including similar patterns, patters that shall be used together and patterns that cannot be used together.

An example excerpt of a fact list clustered by groups for the Model View Controller pattern is presented on Figure 4.21. Content of questions to design patterns may require questions to various patterns properties. This information is not only relevant for creation of questions to design patterns, but also to fill in the general information block of a design pattern in the AM3D catalogue.

4. **Eliminate fact duplicates:** After the facts are clustered into groups, eliminate duplicated or synonym items. Merge similar facts if they provide details on the same pattern property.

5. **Express facts as questions:** Express the facts in the four Groups – Goal, Intent, Consequences and Variants – in a question form. This is a creative step, which is comparable to architectural design itself. However, it is possible to use a predefined question template to warranty structural and logical similarity in question and expected answers to them. Examples of such question templates are: "Would you like to ... though ... ?", "Do you plan to ... by ... ?" or "Can you accept ... ?". A semi-formal version of the "Would you like to ... ?" Question is: "Would you like to G-VERB (improve,

separate, map, etc.) ...G-OBJECT (presentation, subsystem, etc.) ...OPTIONAL ...?". Avoid ultimate questions, such as "Do you want to ..." etc., as such questions might be always replied with "yes". Also avoid naming disadvantages directly, as such questions will be most likely always replied with "no". The styles to formulate questions are described in detail in Section 4.3.3. An example formulated questions for the Model View Controller pattern is presented on Figure 4.22.

Groups:

Goal

- Isolates domain logic from the user interface

Intent

- Decouple user interface
- Multiple views on the same data
- Strict data and presentation separation
- Exchangeability of data model
- Strict model separation from view
- Synchronized views
- Improved flexibility through exchangeable views
- Improved support of multiple platforms
- ...

Consequences

- Potential performance problems
- Potential data consistency problem
- Potential data time-out
- Controller potentially a bottleneck
- ...

Variants

- A version where Controller can be omitted
- A version where communication both through and without Controller

...

Relationships

- Requires an Observer pattern
- ...

Roles and Connectors

- Has View, Model, Controller roles
- Controller communication with View and Model
- Model does not know about View and Controller
- Interaction with data through a controller
- ...

Figure 4.21.: An Excerpt of Fact Groups for the Model View Controller Pattern

Questions:

- Would you like to present the same information in different ways e.g., through multiple views? (G)
- Would you like to add at run-time new views or delete existing views? (I)
- Can you accept potential delays by the view updates because of larger amounts of data? (C)
- Would you like to improve delays in the view updates reducing the changeability of underlying data model? (V)
- ...

Figure 4.22.: An Excerpt of Questions for the Model View Controller Pattern

6. **Perform a review:** Perform a review of the draft of the question annotations. It is better to have several patterns with question an-

notations collected for the review, in order to minimize the review process. The goals of the review are:

- To check the understandability of formulated questions to an independent reviewer (an independent user)
- To check the precision of a pattern description through the questions, and in particular, if provided questions are sufficient to uniquely characterise a pattern and to correctly distinguish it from the other patterns, and especially from the similar patterns following a similar goal
- To check if the generic questions can be translated to the concrete problems and desired properties in a sample project
- To check correctness of the language
- To check the level of abstraction used to describe pattern properties in the questions
- To check the completeness of pattern properties described in question annotations
- To check if all described pattern properties indeed belong to the pattern
- To check if provided technical details are sufficient, but not overwhelming in the question annotations

The potential reviewers are available software engineers, developers or any other third party experts having sufficient knowledge in the area. In case of project specific solutions that were selected to include into the pattern catalogue, select an expert involved into the project to perform the review. After the review, correct the questions according to the review results.

Some liabilities of the questions that may be encountered during the review are: Low precision of the formulations of question annotations, too technical question annotations, too abstract question annotations, unclear definition of properties, irrelevance for the real pattern application as compared to known theory about a pattern, relevant questions (propertied of a pattern) missing, or pattern core intent cannot be definitely concluded from the question annotations.

7. **Repeat the review:** Repeat the review with another reviewer and after the review, correct the questions according to the review results. If again many liabilities of the questions annotations were found, one more review round is required. The experience collected during creation of the AM3D sample pattern catalogue showed that in most cases two reviews were sufficient to reach more than 95% understandability rate by the question (also see the Survey results in Section 6.4.5 for more details on the understandability of questions). Although, the reviews are effort-demanding, they assure the objectivity of the question annotations and reduce the personal influence of the original catalogue author.

Despite following this defined process to add question annotations to a pattern, definition of question annotations is still a creative task. However, the architectural design is also a highly creative, subjective and, thus, often an error prone task. Systematic reviewers of question annotations help to reduce this negative side and to assure the quality of questions and their comparability between each other.

4.4. Process to Fill in Catalogue

This section describes a process to add patterns to the catalogue. The definition of this process follows similar goals as the definition of the process to add questions to a patter, described in Section 4.3.5. The information about a pattern is formulated in free-text natural language. Even though it follows a description template (see Section 4.2), the risk of inconsistencies in the description and organisation is high without a defined process. If the catalogue contains information that is not comparable between its entries, its usability is likely to be reduced. A defined process forces a user to follows the same steps while filling in the catalogue with patterns. Thus, the goal of the process is to assure that all the pattern in the catalogue are treated in a similar way, follow the same description template and are thus homogenous.

The process to add a pattern to the catalogue defined for the AM3D approach is depicted on Figure 4.23. This process was used to add patterns to the sample AM3D catalogue provided in this thesis. The process consists of the following steps:

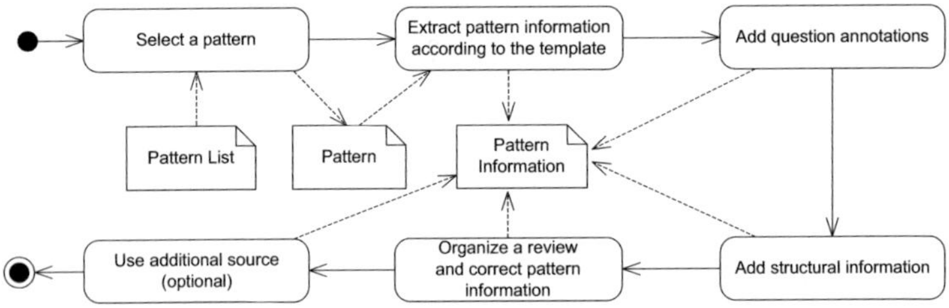

Figure 4.23.: Process to Add Patterns to a Catalogue

1. **Prepare a list of patterns:** Prepare a list of patterns to add to the catalogue. Such a list can be obtained based on the project area or particular project demand. A list of sample patterns for the sample AM3D pattern catalogue was obtained based on the results of survey of most common used and famous patterns. The survey was based on the results from the Internet, from the related work and from the available lecture slides. The list was updated with the patterns, which were mentioned in the relationships of the initially selected patterns (similar patterns and co-usable patterns).

2. **Select a pattern to add:** Pick up a pattern from the list. Usually a group of similar patterns is processed one by one in a row, as it allows for easier cross-references and questions between their descriptions.

3. **Extract general pattern information according to the template:** Extract the information available in the literature source filling up the pattern description template. In this step, fill in the general information block of the description template. Please note that the process to add questions to a pattern, described in Section 4.3.5, only deals with the properties relevant for the questions. The general information block, however, contains more properties than the questions describe. Therefore, in this process the current and the following steps are separated, unlike the corresponding steps of the process described in Section 4.3.5

4. **Add question annotations:** Add question annotations to the pattern. For this, use the before collected general information in order to generate a pattern's summary. Then follow the process to add question annotations to a pattern, as described in Section 4.3.5.

5. **Add structural information:** Add structural information to fill in the architectural implementation details block of the description template. This information contains roles of a pattern, and interactions between them – connectors.

6. **Organize a review:** Review the filled in pattern template. In order to optimise the review process, it is better to have a set of several patterns ready for the review. Especially similar patterns shall be reviewed together, to assure that the fine differences between them are highlighted clearly and sufficiently.

   The potential reviewers are available software engineers, developers or any other third party experts having sufficient knowledge in the area. If the catalogue contains project-specific design patterns, select an expert involved into the project to perform the review.

7. **Correct pattern information:** Correct the information about a pattern based on the review results.

8. **Use additional source (optional):** Depending on the review results, use additional information source. Sometimes, a merge of information from several literature sources is required in order to obtain enough information about a pattern and to be able to distinguish properties of similar patterns.

This process may seem simple. Nevertheless, one must ensure that the same steps are followed for each pattern, and that the same pattern template and its parts are filled in with the information about a pattern. Quality and completeness of question annotations and structural information of a pattern depend on how well the general information about a pattern was understood and captured. Thus, filling in the template in a different order may lead to inconsistencies in the description, and to the low quality of it.

4.5. Types of Patterns in Catalogue

The AM3D approach was developed for the architectural design patterns. Under architectural design patterns in the AM3D approach are understood the patterns defined by Taylor at al. as:

Definition 4.1 Architectural design pattern [115]

An architectural pattern is a named collection of architectural design decisions that are applicable to a recurring design problem, parametrized to account for different software development contexts in which that problem appears

The AM3D approach does not distinguish between architectural design patterns and design patterns explicitly, as do some literature sources. In this thesis, the term "design pattern" is used as a synonym for the term "architectural design pattern".

In other words, all patterns that are visible at the architectural level, are of interest for the AM3D pattern catalogue. Whereby, the visibility implies one of the following properties:

- A pattern can be presented in at least one of the supported architectural diagram types
- A pattern cannot be presented in the supported diagram types, but its influence is visible on the architectural level
- A pattern can be presented in at least one of the supported architectural diagram types and its influence is visible on the architectural level

If a pattern satisfies one of these properties, it is considered to be an architectural design pattern in terms of the AM3D approach. Such pattern can be captured and used following the AM3D approach.

Despite that this thesis focuses on the architectural design patterns, it does not exclude support of other pattern types or support of other architectural design solutions. Moreover, the AM3D approach can be also extended to support design solutions that are invisible at or cross-cutting to the system architecture. For the discussion about possible extensions of the AM3D approach to support further solutions please refer to Section 8.3.

4.6. Approach Formalization with Meta-Models

This section presents the formalization of the design patterns, decisions and connected project contexts with the help of a developed meta-model of the AM3D approach. The meta-model is based on state of the art, such as works by Kruchten [130], Tang et al. [133], Wang et al. [55], and others. For more information on related meta-models refer to Sections 7.3.3 and 7.2.3. The meta-model was developed in several stages. M. Heller [164], A. Khakulov [142] and S. Werfel [170] have contributed to its development during their diploma theses, executed under my supervision.

The goal of the meta-model is to formalize architectural design patterns with question annotations and design decisions connected to them together with the involved project context. The project context involves requirements, issues, design solutions with the design patterns as a sub-part, solution implementation, glossary, effects, relations and users.

Usage of the meta-model has the advantage of an easy tool-support, as it allows for automated tool-generation. Also the documentation of model elements can be documented with the help of a meta-model. Meta-model allows for automated checks on the meta-model instances. Thus, the structure of the pattern in an architectural model can be automatically checked on its correctness.

The meta-model is directly involved in the support of the all-but-one usage scenarios, described in detail in Section 3.2.2: Systematic capture of information about design patterns to allow to gain information about patterns, select a pattern or to select between similar patterns, and to check architectural implementation violations of a pattern; and documentation of decisions on design pattern application to allow to retrieve information and rationale for the used patterns, trace changes from requirements to architectural models, and understand rationale of architectural elements. The meta-model also supports "elicitation and prioritization of requirements" usage scenario, however, it does this indirectly through the formalization of question annotations to design patterns. The instances of the questions, in their turn, facilitate elicitation and prioritization of requirements. To summarise, the meta-model is an important support of the AM3D approach, allowing formalization, and systematic modelling of all the relevant concepts, and in particular, of design patterns and question annotations to them. Moreover, the developed meta-model allows to generate a tool to support all of the processes described in Section 3.2.2, as it also formalizes the relevant project context artefacts and required interactions and dependencies between them. These artefacts include requirements, architectural solutions, actors (users), decisions and decision-making process, and relations between these. Hereby, design patterns are a sub-type of possible architectural solutions.

The developed meta-model is divided into several packages; the general structure is presented on Figure 4.24.

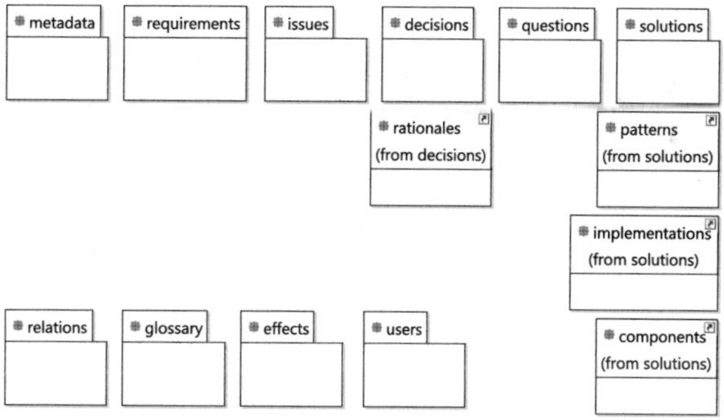

Figure 4.24.: Overview of Meta-model Packages

The packages are:

- **Metadata:** Metadata package contains classes to abstract the recurring information about the model elements, such as Name,ID and to manage the dates of their creation and modification.
- **Effects:** Effects package describes effects, such as quality or general effects, which can be produced by other meta-model elements, such as decisions or design patterns.
- **Users:** Users package describes users of the approach, such as stakeholders of requirements, solutions or decisions.

- **Glossary:** Glossary package classes are responsible for presentation of glossary and of terms that are used to formulate requirements, text of the rationale, keywords or questions to a pattern.

- **Requirements:** Requirements package describes the requirements space, types of requirements and relationships between them.

- **Issues:** Issues package formalizes the concept of issues, which are triggered by the requirements and require a solution in term of the AM3D approach.

- **Solutions:** Solutions package describes the concept of a solution in the AM3D approach, including possible alternatives and types of solutions. It contains Patterns, Components and Implementations packages.

- **Patterns:** Patterns package is a subpackage of Solutions, and describes architectural design patterns as a subclass of architectural design solutions. It formalizes the AM3D pattern catalogue.

- **Questions:** Questions package is a package describing the questions concept of the AM3D approach in a generic way, to enable application not only with design patterns, but also with other solution subclasses.

- **Components:** Components package is a subpackage of solutions and describes reusable components (COTs) as a subclass of architectural design solutions.

- **Implementations:** Implementations package is a subpackage of solutions and describes implementation of solutions, such as patterns and components, in architecture and in code. As the AM3D approach is focused on architecture, the code implementation is kept as an abstract class and can be extended with the help of other approaches.

- **Decisions:** Decisions package formalizes the decisions concept of the AM3D approach, where decisions on patterns and components can be re-evaluated and documented together with the rationale.
- **Rationale:** Rationale package is a subpackage of Decisions package and describes rationale of design decisions, which can be text, requirements or answers to the AM3D approach questions.
- **Relations:** Relations package is a help package that contains formalization of relations between various approach concepts, such as decisions, requirements, patterns or issues, with the focus of relations between one or similar concepts.

The meta-model is developed and structured in a modular way to facilitate its extension and reuse. Most of the packages are stand-alone meta-models, which can be easily extracted for a separate use. The concepts in the meta-model are formalized in a way to allow easy editing and addition of new subtypes and subsolutions, without the need to restructure depending or connected meta-models.

In the following, the meta-model packages are explained in detail. The sections are sorted starting from the most basic packages, which have no dependencies on other packages, and continuing to the more complex packages requiring understand of the basic packages. For example, package issues are explained after the requirements package, as understanding of requirements package concepts is required to follow on the issues concept.

4.6.1. Metadata

The Metadata meta-model is presented on Figure 4.25. The goal of the meta-model is to abstract the recurring information about the model elements, such as Name, ID and to manage the dates of their creation and modification. The meta-model contains the following classes:

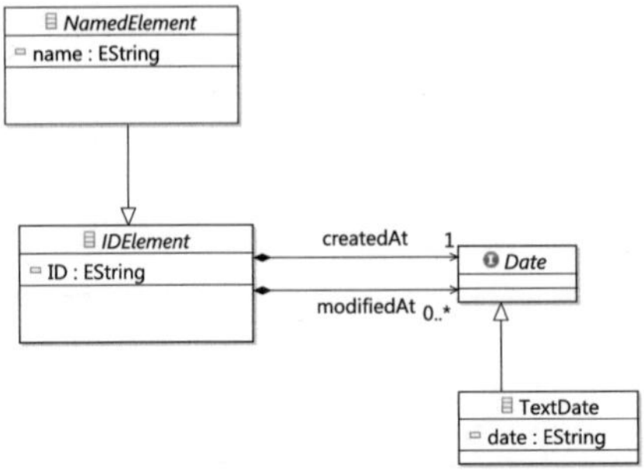

Figure 4.25.: Metadata Meta-Model Package

- **IDElement:** `IDElement` describes an element of the meta-model having an `ID`. Together with the `ID`; it also always has a `CreatedAt` date, and can optionally have one or multiple `ModifiedAt` date.
- **Date:** `Date` is an interface that can be implemented by other meta-model classes accordingly on demand.
- **TextDate:** `TextDate` is the date option implemented by the AM3D meta-model to define `CreatedAt` and `ModifiedAt` dates.
- **NamedElement:** `IDElement` describes an element of the meta-model that has a Name in addition to the `ID` and `CreatedAt` and `ModifiedAt` dates.

Most of the other meta-model elements inherit from the Metadata classes `IDElement` and `NamedElement`, therefore they have a `ID`, `CreatedAt` and `ModiefiedAt` dates and a `Name`.

4.6.2. Effects

The Effects meta-model is presented on Figure 4.26. The goal of the Effects package is to describe effects that can be produced by other meta-model elements, such as decisions or design patterns. The meta-model contains the following elements:

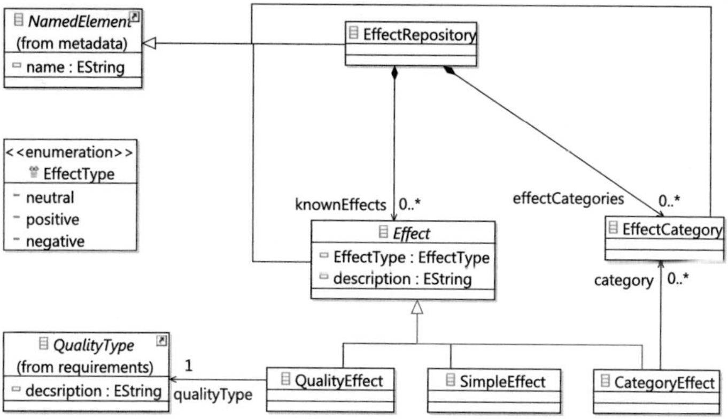

Figure 4.26.: Effects Meta-Model Package

- **EffectRepository:** EffectRepository is the root repository contains all effects known in the context of the project. The repository can be reused between projects, once it is defined.

- **EffectCategory:** EffectCategory is a class to define a manual category during the project. The category can then be referenced from an Effect of type of CategoryEffects.

- **Effect:** Effect class describes all known effects of other meta-model classes. It is an abstract class and needs to be defined trough one of the provisioned Effect types. An example of an effect is a solution that may have a quality effect on the system if it is decided for, or a decision that may have a restrictive technology effect on other decisions. Effect has an EffectType, which is "neutral" by default, but otherwise can be "positive" or "negative".

- **SimpleEffect:** SimpleEffect is one of the provisioned Effect type classes. It describes a simple textual Effect.

- **QualityEffect:** QualityEffect is one of the provisioned Effect type classes. It describes a quality effect of a decision, solution, etc., and is connected to one of the known QualityTypes from the Requirements meta-model.

- **CategoryEffect:** CategoryEffect is one of the provisioned Effect type classes. It describes a complex effect of a type that is defined by a user of the approach with the help of the EffectCategory.

- **EffectType:** EffectType is an enumeration describing known types of effects, such as "neutral", "positive" or "negative". New types of effects can be easily added to the enumeration on demand.

The effects are an important part of the decision making, usually involving trade-offs between quality requirements to the system. They are also an important part of the rationale behind decisions and solutions, and a part of description of issues.

4.6.3. Users

The Users meta-model is presented on Figure 4.27. The goal of the Users package is to describe users of the approach, such as stakeholders of requirements, solutions or decisions. The meta-model contains the following classes:

- **UserRepository:** UserRepository is the root repository that contains the users known in the context of the project. The repository can be reused between projects, once it is defined.

- **User:** User is a class to define users in the project. The user may have different roles defined by RoleType, and be stakeholders of several elements of the model, such as requirements, decisions or solutions.

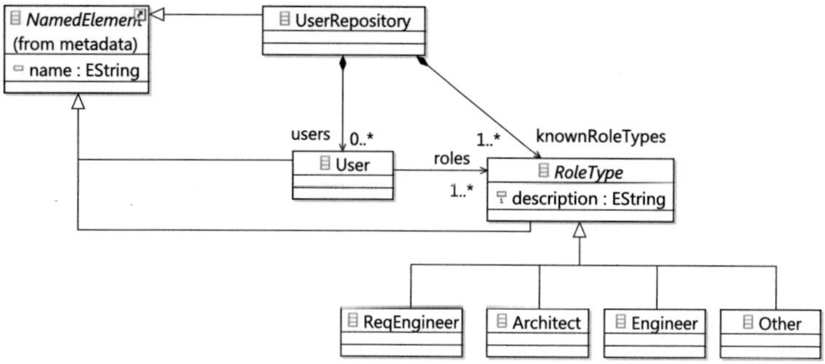

Figure 4.27.: Users Meta-Model Package

- **RoleType:** RoleType is a class to define the role of a user in a project. It is an abstract class and is specified by several defined role possibilities, such as an architect or an engineer.
- **ReqEngineer:** ReqEngineer is one of the provisioned role type classes and specifies a requirement engineer role in a project.
- **Architect:** Architect is one of the provisioned role type classes and specifies an architect role in a project.
- **Engineer:** Engineer is one of the provisioned role type classes and specifies a regular software engineer role in a project.
- **Other:** Other is one of the provisioned role type classes and specifies an option to add a project-specific role to a project.

Once role types are defined for the project and stored in the user repository, the users can be added and roles can be assigned to them. The Users meta-model is kept simple, as it is a help concept to the approach. The meta-model can be easily extended to support more complex user environments and descriptions.

4.6.4. Glossary

The Glossary meta-model is presented on Figure 4.28. The goals of the meta-model are to present the glossary and terms that are used to formulate requirements, text of the rationale, keywords or questions to a pattern.

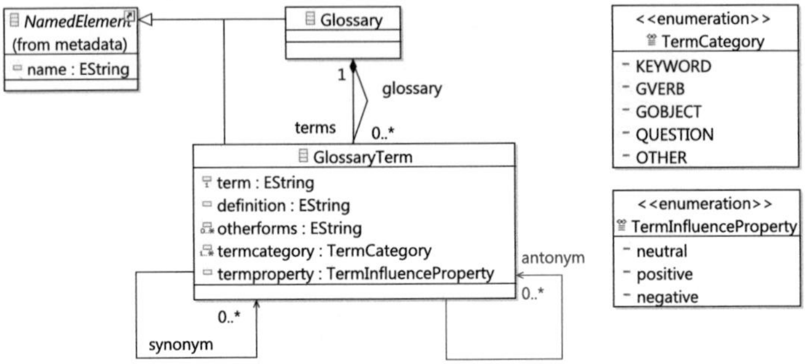

Figure 4.28.: Glossary Meta-Model Package

The meta-model contains the following elements:

- **Glossary:** Glossary is a class presenting the concept of the term collection for reuse, it is a repository of terms.
- **GlossaryTerm:** GlossaryTerm is a term that can be used to build questions, rationales, and other textual descriptions. Terms can have antonyms and synonyms, which can be linked to each other. Each term has a category and an influence property.
- **TermCategory:** TermCategory enumeration describes possible types of terms. The default type is a “keyword”. Other types, such as “gobejct”, “gverb” and “question”, describe term types used in question annotations, as detailed in Section 4.2.2.
- **TermInfluenceProperty:** TermInfluenceProperty is an enumeration describing types of influence of a term, such as “neutral”, “positive” or “negative”. The default state of a term influence is “neutral”.

Terms may be used to formulate questions and requirements, and to be referenced to from various textual descriptions. The main purpose of glossary is to use a limited subset terms, whereby terms do not comprise a sentence completely. The term are used as main subjects and objects recognisable and reusable between such descriptions, while details and joins can be expressed also with terms that are not contained in the glossary. Thus, all textual descriptions are combinations of terms from glossary and freely selected terms that are not included into the glossary.

4.6.5. Requirements

The Requirements meta-model is presented on Figure 4.29. The goal of the meta-model is to describe the requirements space, types of requirements and relationships between them. The meta-model contains the following elements:

- **ReqRepository:** ReqRepository is the root repository that contains the requirements known in the context of the project. The repository can be partially reused between projects, once defined, in particular when a project is related to a previously built system. The repository is divided into three types of the requirements: system requirements, process requirements and project requirements, according to the classification by Glinz [104].
- **SystemRequirements:** SystemRequirements is one of the provisioned types of the requirements and contains system requirements.
- **ProcessRequirements:** ProcessRequirements is one of the provisioned types of the requirements and contains process requirements.
- **ProjectRequirements:** ProjectRequirements is one of the provisioned types of the requirements and contains the requirements of a project.

- **Requirement:** Requirement is a class to define requirements in a project. It is an abstract class, and can be instantiated with defined types – system requirement, process requirement or project requirement. Each requirement has at least one stakeholder (a user) responsible for it. A text of a requirement is build using terms from the project glossary. Requirements have defined status, e.g. "accepted", and a priority, e.g. "medium".

- **SystemRequirement:** SystemRequirement class is the provisioned type of the requirements class and describes a system requirement of a project. SystemRequirement is contained in the SystemRequirements repository. It is an abstract class and can be redefined as a quality requirement, functional requirement or constraint, following the classification by Glinz [104].

- **ProcessRequirement:** ProcessRequirement class is the provisioned type of the requirements class and describes a process requirement of a project. ProcessRequirement is contained in the ProcessRequirements repository.

- **ProjectRequirement:** ProjectRequirement class is the provisioned type of the requirements class and describes a project requirement of a project. ProjectRequirement is contained in the ProjectRequirements repository.

- **QualityRequirement:** QualityRequirement class is the provisioned type of the system requirements class and describes a quality requirement of a project. Quality requirements has a reference to a quality type, defining which quality attributes defined in a project are related to the requirement. For example, a quality requirement may refer to maintainability and performance quality attributes.

- **FunctionalRequirement:** FunctionalRequirement class is the provisioned type of the system requirements class and describes a functional requirement of a project.
- **Constraint:** Constraint class is the provisioned type of the system requirements class and describes a constraint of a project.
- **QualityTypeRepository:** QualityTypeRepository is a repository that contains the definitions of quality types known in the context of the project. The repository can be partially reused between projects. There are several quality types already predefined by the AM3D meta-model, such as performance, reliability, security, usability and maintainability.
- **QualityType:** QualityType is a class to define known types of quality dimensions in a project. It is an abstract class, and has a set of predefined quality dimensions, according to Glinz [104].
- **Performance:** Performance class is the provisioned type of the QualityType class and defines the performance quality dimension of a project.
- **Reliability:** Reliability class is the provisioned type of the QualityType class and defines the reliability quality dimension of a project.
- **Security:** Security class is the provisioned type of the QualityType class and defines the security quality dimension of a project.
- **Usability:** Usability class is the provisioned type of the QualityType class and defines the usability quality dimension of a project.
- **Maintainability:** Maintainability class is the provisioned type of the QualityType class and defines the maintainability quality dimension of a project.

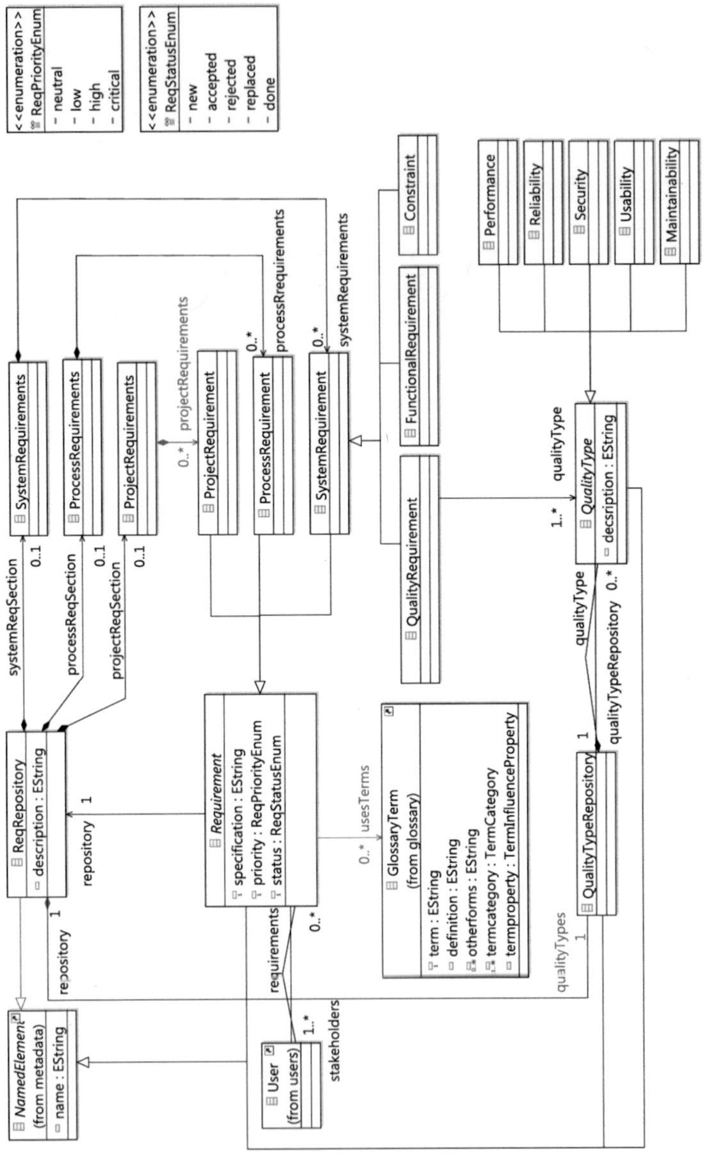

Figure 4.29.: Requirements Meta-Model Package

- **ReqPriorityEnum:** ReqPriorityEnum is an enumeration describing a priority of a requirement, and can be "neutral", "low", "medium" or "high", as according to Glinz [104].
- **ReqStatusEmun:** ReqStatusEmun is an enumeration describing a status of a requirement, and can be "new", "accepted", "rejected", "replaced" or "done".

Types of the requirements are explained in detail in Section 2.2. The requirements are not only triggers of decisions making process, but are one of the main rationales for taken design decisions and shall be linked, if possible, as a rationale for the decisions.

4.6.6. Issues

The Issues meta-model is presented on Figure 4.30. The goal of the meta-model is to formalize the concept of issues, which are triggered by the requirements and require a solution in term of the AM3D approach. The meta-model contains the following elements:

- **IssueRepository:** IssueRepository is the root repository that contains issues known in the context of the project. The repository can be partially reused between projects, once defined, in particular when a project is related to a previously built system.
- **Issue:** Issue is a class to define issues in a project. It is an abstract class and can be instantiated with pre-defined types – text issues and requirement issues. Each issue has a status, which can be e.g. "accepted" or "resolved". Issues have at least one stakeholder defined by though the link to stakeholders of the user repository. Issues have a trigger, which is an interface which can be implemented through various model elements of the AM3D meta-model.
- **TextIssue:** TextIssue is one of the provisioned types of issues and defines a simple text issue.

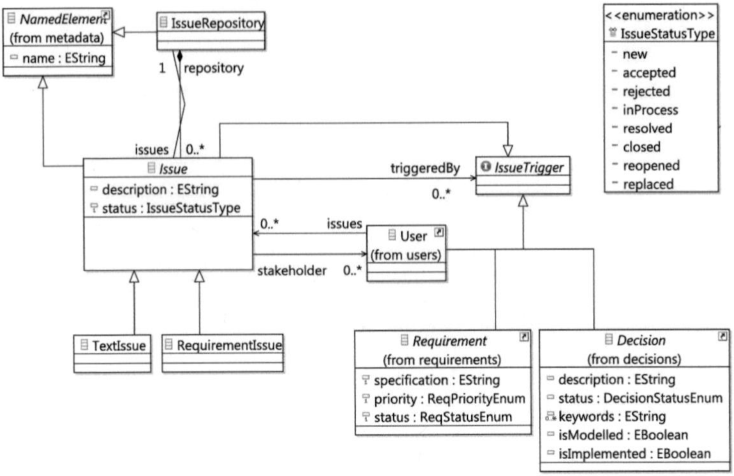

Figure 4.30.: Issues Meta-Model Package

- **RequirementIssue:** RequirementIssue is one of the provisioned types of issues and defines a requirement issue, which is triggered by a requirement.
- **IssueTrigger:** IssueTrigger is an interface that can be implemented by various elements of the AM3D meta-model. Issue trigger describes a trigger of the issue, such as the requirements or a decision.
- **IssueStatusEnum:** IssueStatusEnum is an enumeration describing a status of an issue, and can be "new", "accepted", "rejected", "inProcess", "resolved", "closed", "reopened" or "replaced".

4.6.7. Solutions

The Solutions meta-model is presented on Figure 4.31. The goal of the meta-model is to formalize the concept of a solution in terms of the AM3D approach, including possible alternatives and types of solutions. The meta-model contains the following classes:

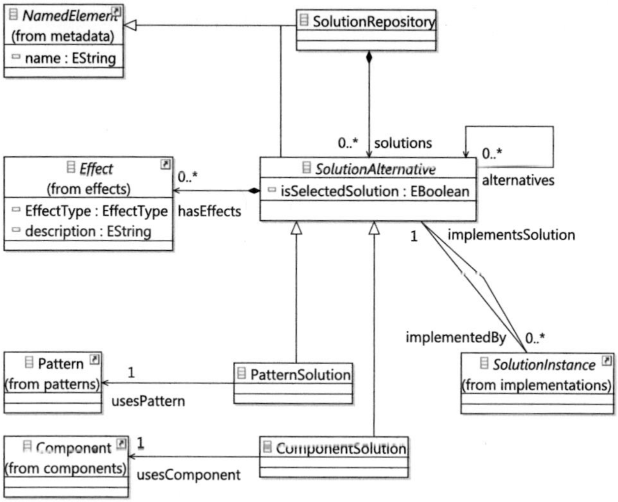

Figure 4.31.: Solutions Meta-Model Package

- **SolutionRepository:** SolutionRepository is the root repository that contains potential and selected solutions of the project. The repository can be partially reused between projects, once defined, in particular when a project is related to a previously built system.

- **SolutionAlternative:** SolutionAlternative is an abstract class to define solution alternatives of a project. As an abstract class it can be instantiated with pre-defined types – architectural design pattern and reusable component solutions. An alternative solution may become a selected solution, once a decision on its behalf is taken. An alternative solution is aware of other alternative solutions to a given problem through an "alternatives" reference link. Each solution alternative may have certain effects, defined in the Effects repository of the project, for example an effect on one of the quality dimensions. Once a solution is selected, it may be implemented through a SolutionInstance, which is defined in the Implementations repository.

- **PatternSolution:** PatternSolution is one of the provisioned types of the solution alternatives in the AM3D approach. It links design patterns defined in the pattern catalogue as potential solution alternatives to the problem.

- **ComponentSolution:** ComponentSolution is one of the provisioned types of the solution alternatives in the AM3D approach. It links reusable components defined in the component repository as potential solution alternatives to the problem.

The Solutions meta-model is describes a generic solution concept and contains Patterns, Components and Implementations subpackages.

4.6.8. Patterns

The Patterns meta-model is presented on Figure 4.32. The goal of the meta-model is to describe architectural design patterns as a subclass of architectural design solutions. It formalizes the AM3D pattern catalogue. The meta-model contains the following elements:

- **PatternCatalogue:** PatternCatalogue is the root repository that contains patterns defined in the catalogue and potentially useful for the project. The catalogue can be reused between projects, once defined. It is one of the core concepts of the AM3D approach.

- **Pattern:** Pattern is a core class and formalized pattern description in term of the AM3D approach. The details on pattern description are explained in Section 4.2. The pattern formalization with the help of the meta-model follows the pattern catalogue structure described in the section. Pattern has a Name, an ID, creation and modification dates, domain type, a category and three additional blocks of description – general description, question annotations and architectural structure description. Patterns may be involved into pattern-specific relationships, such as being similar to a pattern, exclusion of a pattern, and co-usage with a pattern, defined through an abstract class PatternRelations of the Patterns meta-model package. If a pattern has a variant, the variant can be defined using the same description template as a pattern under a pattern type PatternVariant. Pattern variant is in a relation to its base pattern, and vice versa, allowing for navigation and a comparison between them. Besides quality effects, a design pattern as a subtype of a solution may have some general effects defined in the Effect repository.

- **PatternVariant:** PatternVariant class defines a variant of a pattern. It is formalized with the same structure, as its base pattern, however carries a type of a pattern variant. It has a reference to its base pattern, and its base pattern has a reference to all of its variants.

- **GeneralPatternDescription:** GeneralPatternDescription is an abstract class, and defines general description information block of the description template. It contains various properties of a pattern, links to the information sources and diagrams, and a short description.

- **Property:** Property class describes general pattern properties for the general information block of the pattern description template. Properties are goals of a pattern, its keywords, potential advantages, drawbacks and quality influence. Each property description can be linked to the known terms of the glossary.

- **Goal:** Goal is one of the provisioned types of the pattern property. It describes goals of a pattern.

- **Keyword:** Keyword is one of the provisioned types of the pattern property. It describes keywords characterising a pattern.

- **Advantage:** Advantage is one of the provisioned types of the pattern property. It describes potential advantages of a pattern application.

- **Drawback:** Drawback is one of the provisioned types of the pattern property. It describes potential drawbacks of a pattern application.
- **QualityInfluence:** QualityInfluence is one of the provisioned types of the pattern property. It describes potential quality influence of a pattern and is linked to the quality effects of the Effects repository.
- **QuestionAnnotations:** QuestionAnnotations is an abstract class, which refers question annotations to a pattern. It contains links to questions from the question repository. These questions are used for pattern evaluation as a possible design solution, and for a decision documentation to use or to withdraw a pattern as a solution candidate. Questions in the repository have a back reference to a pattern to be able to track and find out which pattern uses similar questions and to propose alternative pattern candidates based on the answers to questions. The reference "noCaseCandidates" refers to the candidate patterns, which shall eb proposed in case of an answer "no" to a question.
- **ArchitecturalStructure:** ArchitecturalStructure is an abstract class, and defines architectural structure information block of the description template. It consists of the Role and Connector classes.
- **Role:** Role class defines roles of a pattern explained in Section 4.2.
- **Connector:** Connector class defines connectors between pattern roles, as explained in Section 4.2.
- **PatternRelations:** PatternRelations class defines possible relations between patterns. It is an abstract class, which can be specified with the following types of relations: Similar, Exclusion and CoUsage.
- **Similar:** Similar class is one of the provisioned types of the relationships between patterns. It links similar patterns to each other. Similar

patterns can be then proposed as solution candidates instead of the currently actively selected pattern solution, based on the answers to the questions to a pattern.

- **Exclusion:** Exclusion class is one of the provisioned types of the relationships between patterns. It links patterns that cannot be used together. This relationship is useful to detect potential violations, when user attempts to use to excluding patterns together in a subpart of a system design.
- **CoUsage:** CoUsage class is one of the provisioned types of the relationships between patterns. It links patterns that can be used together, in the meaning of help patterns. Such co-patterns can be then proposed to a user, once a decision to apply a pattern is made. An example of co-used patterns is a Model View Controller pattern or an Observer pattern.
- **DomainType:** DomainType is a class describing known domain types of a pattern, such as architectural patterns or security patterns. Known types are contained in the pattern catalogue, and can be referenced to from patterns.
- **Category:** Category is a class describing known domain categories of a pattern, such as creational or structural patterns. Known categories are contained in the pattern catalogue and can be referenced to from patterns.

The Pattern Meta-Model is one of the core concepts of the AM3D approach. It formalizes the pattern application in a way to be used for the benefits, such as decisions evaluation and documentation to together with the rationale. The Pattern Meta-Model is a subpackage of the Solutions Meta-Model package, as architectural design patterns are a subclass of reusable architectural design solutions.

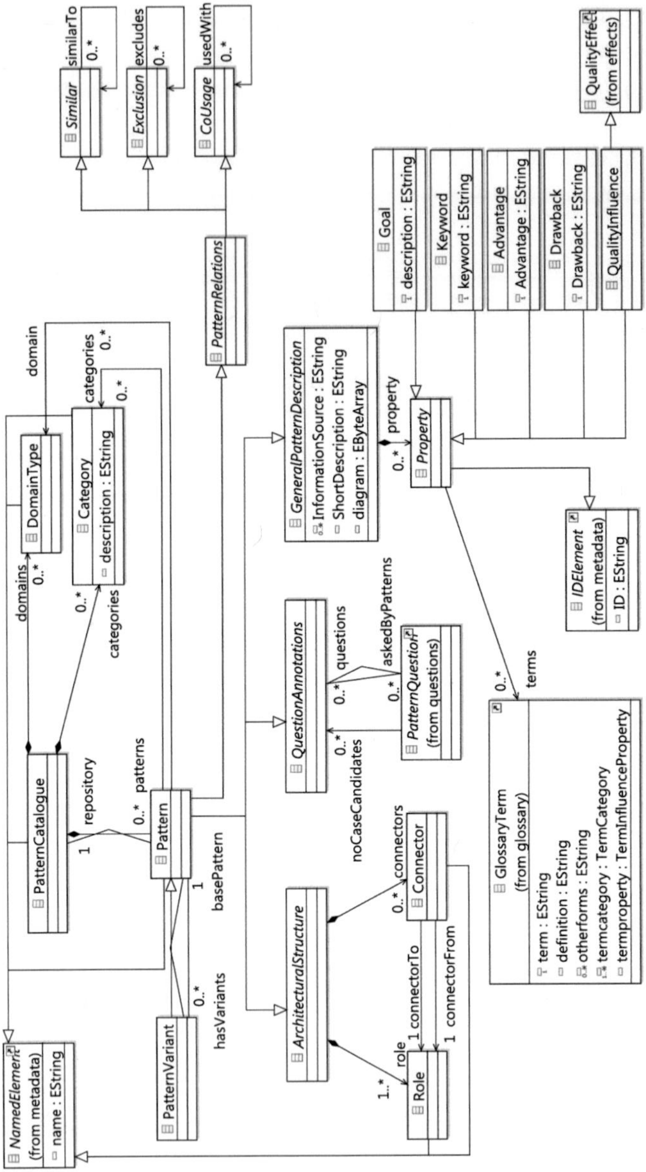

Figure 4.32.: Patterns Meta-Model Package

4.6.9. Questions

The Questions meta-model is presented on Figure 4.33. It formalizes the questions concept of the AM3D approach in a generic way, to enable application not only with design patterns, but also with other solution subclasses. The meta-model contains the following classes:

- **QuestionRepository:** QuestionRepository is the root repository that contains all defined questions for question annotations of solutions. The repository can be reused between projects. Question repository contains definitions of known AnswerTypes.
- **Question:** Question is an abstract class to define questions to solutions. Questions are used for solution evaluation and documentation of decisions to apply or to discard a solution together with the rationale for decision. It is an abstract class, and can be instantiated with pre-defined types – the AM3D meta-model currently pre-defines PatternQuestion and ComponentQuestion as a type. A question text refers to the defined glossary terms and their types, such as “gverb”, “gobject” or “keyword”.
- **PatternQuestion:** PatternQuestion is a provisioned type of the questions and defines pattern question annotations. It is an abstract class and can be specified as a goal question, intent question, consequence question and a variant question. Pattern question has a defined AnswerType – PatternAnswerType, picked up from the defined AnswerTypes of the QuestionRepository. For a detailed information on pattern question annotations and their types refer to Section 4.3.
- **GoalQuestion:** GoalQuestion is a provisioned type of the pattern questions and defines goal pattern question annotations. It describes questions to the goals of a pattern. Refer to Section 4.3 for more information on question to pattern goals.

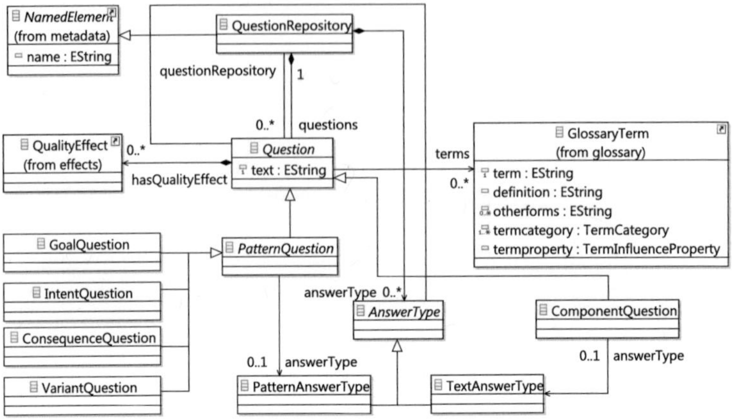

Figure 4.33.: Questions Meta-Model Package

- **IntentQuestion:** IntentQuestion is a provisioned type of the pattern questions and defines intent pattern question annotations. It describes questions to the (potential) intent of a pattern. Refer to Section 4.3 for more information on question to pattern intent.

- **ConsequenceQuestion:** ConsequenceQuestion is a provisioned type of the pattern questions and defines consequence pattern question annotations. It describes questions to the consequences of a pattern. Refer to Section 4.3 for more information on pattern consequences.

- **VariantQuestion:** VariantQuestion is a provisioned type of the pattern questions and defines variant pattern question annotations. It describes questions to the variants of a pattern. Refer to Section 4.3 for more information on questions about pattern variants.

- **ComponentQuestion:** ComponentQuestion is a provisioned type of the questions and defines component question annotations. A Component question has a defined AnswerType – TextAnswerType, picked up from the defined AnswerTypes of the QuestionRepository.

- **AnswerType:** AnswerType is an abstract class to define the supported answer type by a question. It can be specified to pre-defined PatternAnswerType and TextAnswerType.

- **PatternAnswerType:** PatternAnswerType is one of the provisioned types of the answers to the question annotations. It defines that a question can be answered as "yes", "no", "I do not know" and "no answer". For detailed information on answers to pattern question annotations refer to Section 4.3.4.

- **TextAnswerType:** TextAnswerType is one of the provisioned types of the answers to the question annotations. It defines that a question can be answered as a free-text question.

Each architectural design pattern can have multiple questions annotated to it and stored in the generic question repository for reuse. Questions can be reused between patterns. During pattern instantiation, questions are mapped to requirements through the answers to the questions. Question annotations are one of the core concepts of the AM3D approach.

4.6.10. Components

The Components meta-model is presented on Figure 4.34. The goal of the meta-model is to and describes reusable components (COTs) as a subclass of architectural design solutions. The meta-model contains the following classes:

- **ComponentRepository:** ComponentRepository is the root repository that contains all components defined as solutions for the project. The repository can be reused between projects, once defined.

- **Component:** Component is a class describing reusable and third-party component solutions. Component has a Name, an ID, creation and modification dates. Components as a subtype of a solution may have effects defined in the Effect repository, and question annotations in terms of the AM3D approach, for a component evaluation as of a solution candidate and its documentation with the rationale.

The Component Meta-Model is a subpackage of the Solutions Meta-Model package, as reusable and third-party components are a subclass of reusable architectural design solutions.

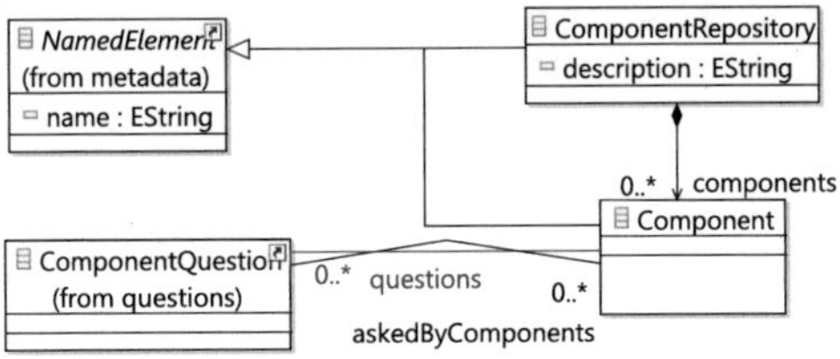

Figure 4.34.: Components Meta-Model Package

4.6.11. Implementations

The Implementations meta-model is presented on Figure 4.35. The goal of the meta-model is to describe implementation of solutions, such as of patterns and components, in architecture and in code. The meta-model contains the following classes:

- **ImplementationRepository:** ImplementationRepository is the root repository that contains the implementations of the selected solutions of the project. The repository has two subtypes – a pattern instance repository and a component instance repository. The supported types of implementation are architectural and code implementations, whereby the focus is on the architectural ones.
- **SolutionInstance:** SolutionInstance is an abstract class defining implementation instances of the selected solutions, which can be either architectural or in code.

- **ArchitectureInstance:** ArchitectureInstance is one of the provisioned types of the SolutionInstance implementation types and describes an architectural implementation of a selected solution.
- **CodeInstance:** CodeInstance is one of the provisioned types of the SolutionInstance implementation types and describes a code implementation of a selected solution.
- **PatternInstanceRepository:** PatternInstanceRepository is one of the provisioned types of the ImplementationRepository and contains implementations of selected architectural design pattern solutions – pattern instances.
- **PatternInstance:** PatternInstance is one of the provisioned types of the SolutionInstance and describes an implementation of a selected architectural design pattern solution.
- **PatternArchitectureInstance:** PatternArchitectureInstance is one of the provisioned types of the ArchitectureInstance and describes an architectural implementation of a selected architectural design pattern solution. PatternArchitectureInstance contains role and connector instances of a pattern's roles and connectors.
- **RoleInstance:** RoleInstance is a class describing instance of a pattern role in architecture or in code.
- **ConnectorInstance:** ConnectorInstance is a class describing instance of a pattern connector between roles in architecture or in code.
- **PCMRole:** PCMRole is an abstract class describing how an architectural instance of a role is implemented in terms of a PCM architectural model; it contains its references to the classes AssemblyContext and OperationProvidedRole of the PCM meta-model.

- **PCMConnector:** PCMConnector is an abstract class describing how an architectural instance of a connector is implemented in terms of a PCM architectural model; it contains its references to the Assembly-Connector class of the PCM meta-model.

- **ComponentInstanceRepository:** ComponentInstanceRepository is one of the provisioned types of the ImplementationRepository and contains implementations of selected reusable component solutions – third-party (COT) component instances.

- **ComponentInstance:** ComponentInstance is one of the provisioned types of the SolutionInstance and describes an implementation of a selected component solution.

- **ComponentArchitectureInstance:** ComponentArchitectureInstance is one of the provisioned types of the ArchitectureInstance and describes an implementation of a selected component solution.

- **Component:** Component is a class describing instance of a reusable component in an architecture or in code.

- **PCMComponent:** PCMComponent is an abstract class describing how an architectural instance of a component is implemented in terms of a PCM architectural model, it contains its references to the classes AssemblyContext and OperationProvidedRole of the PCM meta-model.

As the AM3D approach is focused on architecture, the code implementation is kept as an abstract class, which can be extended with the help of other approaches. The implementations package focuses on implementation of patterns and components in architectural models.

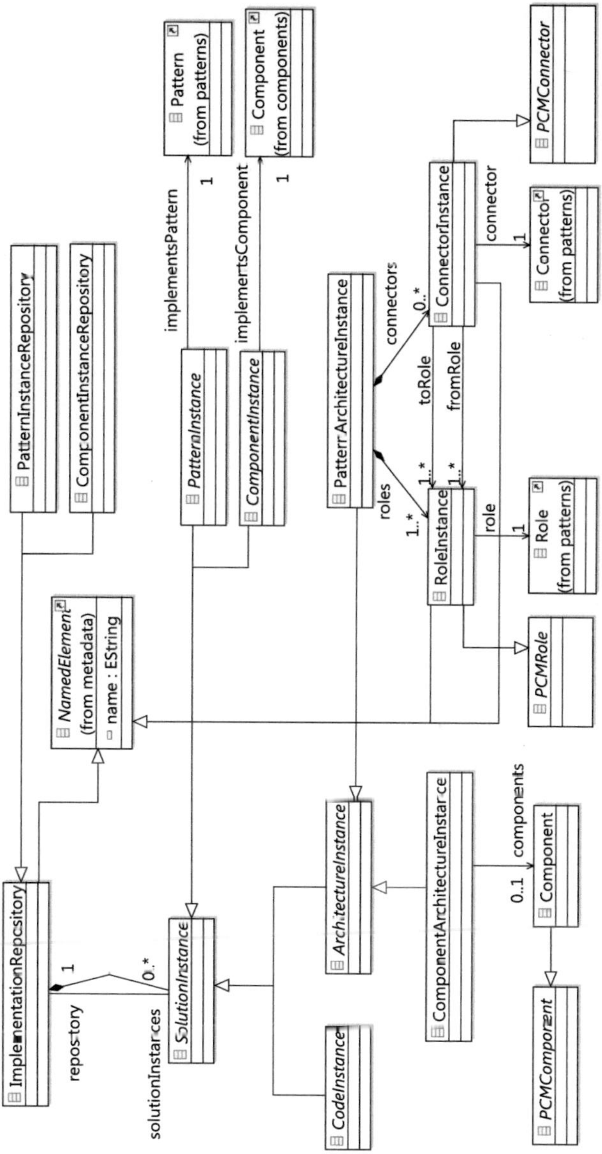

Figure 4.35.: Implementations Meta-Model Package

The Implementations meta-model represents a concept of a two-step instantiation of solutions in the AM3D approach. This concept is based on the idea that a solution is first described and captured in a solution catalogue. At this level, it is a generic and reusable solution. It can be used multiple times in one project and in different projects. In this case a solution is instantiated in the first step in the catalogue. Then, a solution is instantiated in an architectural model or in code via the implementations repository. At this level, it is a project and problem specific solution, as it is assigned to e.g. components in a model, or to classes in code implementing it. This is the second step of the solution instantiation, this time in an implementations repository. The Implementations meta-model is a subpackage of Solutions Meta-Model package.

4.6.12. Decisions

The Decisions meta-model is presented on Figure 4.36. The goal of the meta-model is to formalize the decisions concept of the AM3D approach, where decisions on patterns and components can be re-evaluated and documented together with the rationale. The meta-model contains the following elements:

- **DecisionRepository:** DecisionRepository is the root repository that contains decisions met during the project.
- **Decision:** Decision is an abstract class formalizing the concept of a decision of a project. It can be instantiated with pre-defined types – pattern decisions, deployments decisions, component decisions and constraint decisions. Each decision has a Name, ID, a description and a status, for example an "obsolete" decisions. A decision may be characterised with a set of defined keywords. Keywords and decision description can use terms from the project Glossary of terms. Decisions have two flags – "isModelled" and "isImplemented", identifying the status of a decision, if it was modelled in the architecture

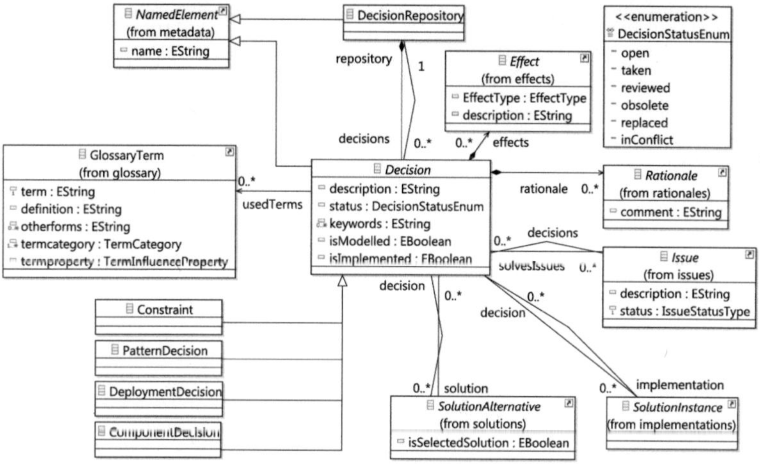

Figure 4.36.: Decisions Meta-Model Package

model and if it has a code implementation. Each decisions has a trigger and typically solved an issue with a referenced selected architectural solution, and referred to discarded architectural solutions. If a decision is modelled or is implemented, it also has a reference to its architectural and code implementations from the Implementation package. Finally, each decision has a rationale. Rationale is based on the Rationale meta-model package of the AM3D meta-model. It can be a simple text rationale, or in case of patterns and components it can be a rationale based on the answers to the pattern or components question annotations. Answers to the questions are saved together with the decisions about a pattern or a component.

- **Constraint:** Constraint is one of the provisioned types of the decisions and defines a constraint in a project.

- **PatternDecision:** PatternDecision is one of the provisioned types of the decisions and defines a pattern decision of a project (a positive or negative decision about a pattern application).

- **DeploymentDecision:** DeploymentDecision is one of the provisioned types of the decisions and defines a deployments in a project.
- **ComponentDecision:** ComponentDecision is one of the provisioned types of the decisions and defines a component decision of a project.
- **DecisionStatusEnum:** DecisionStatusEnum is an enumeration describing a status of a decision, and can be "open", "taken", "reviewed", "obsolete", "replaced" or "inConflict".

The Decisions meta-model links selected or discarded solutions through issues to requirements of a project. If a pattern or a component was selected or discarded while answering questions in the annotations, answers to the questions are saved together with taken decisions and are a kind of semi-automated generated rationale for the decisions enabling a lightweight documentation of latter.

4.6.13. Rationales

The Rationales meta-model is presented on Figure 4.37. The goal of the meta-model is to formalize rationale of design decisions, which can be text, requirements or answers to the AM3D approach questions. The meta-model contains the following elements:

- **Rationale:** Rationale is an abstract class formalizing the concept of a decision rationale. It can be instantiated with pre-defined types – pattern decision rationale, requirement decision rationale and text decision rationale. The rationale can be question-based, depending on its type.
- **RequirementRationale:** RequirementRationale is one of the provisioned types of the decision rationale and defines a rationale mainly based on a requirement. This rationale is linked to existing requirements of a project.

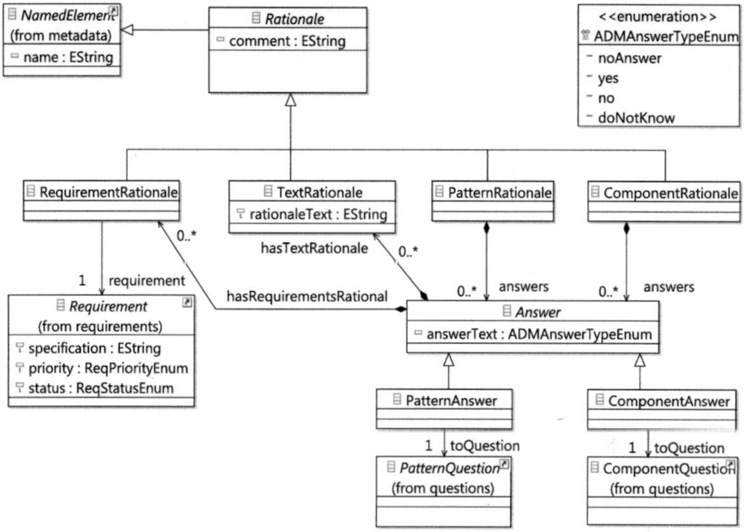

Figure 4.37.: Rationales Meta-Model Package

- **TextRationale:** TextRationale is one of the provisioned types of the decision rationale and defines a rationale based solely on a textual explanation.

- **PatternRationale:** PatternRationale is one of the provisioned types of the decision rationale and defines a rationale based on answers to provided question annotations to a solution. The solution is a design pattern defined in the pattern catalogue.

- **ComponentRationale:** ComponentRationale is one of the provisioned types of the decision rationale and defines a rationale based on answers to provided question annotations to a solution. In this case, solution is a reusable component.

- **Answer:** Answer is an abstract class formalizing the concept of an answer as of a part of a decision rationale. Answer has an answer text specified with the ADMAnswerTypeEnum, which is specific for the AM3D approach. Answer can also have a rationale, which can be based on requirements to the system or can be provided as text. If a user wants to provide a detailed explanation to the question answer, a requirement or a text rationale can be attached to it.

- **PatternAnswer:** PatternAnswer is one of the provisioned types of the answers and defines an answer to the pattern question annotations. It is linked to the question in question repository.
- **ComponentAnswer:** ComponentAnswer is one of the provisioned types of the answers and defines an answer to the component question annotations. It is linked to the question in question repository.
- **ADMAnswerTypeEnum:** ADMAnswerTypeEnum is an enumeration describing possible answers to the question annotations in terms of the AM3D approach. The answer can be "no answer", "yes", "no" or "I do not know". Answers to the AM3D questions are described in detail in Section 4.3.4.

The Rationales Meta-Model is a subpackage of the Decisions Meta-Model package and is one of the core concepts of the AM3D approach. This formalization allows for a semi-automated documentation of answers to the solution questions serving as a rationale for the taken decisions.

4.6.14. Relations

The Relations meta-model is presented on Figure 4.38. Its goal is to formalize relations between various approach concepts, such as decisions, requirements, patterns or issues, with the focus of relations between one or similar concepts. The meta-model contains the following classes:

- **RelationsModel:** RelationsModel is the root repository that contains possible types of relations between elements of the AM3D meta-model and references to known relations between the objects. The repository can be reused between projects.

- **RelationType:** RelationType is a class describing a type of a relationship between objects. Relation reference to the relation types contained in the relations model.

- **Relation:** Relation is a class defining relations that can be implemented by various objects of the AM3D meta-model. A relation can be bidirectional (to and from) and has a type defined by the RelationType. Relation is a generic relationship, awarding flexibility to the participating objects to define their own relationships at run-time.

- **RelationObject:** RelationObject is an abstract class defining objects involved in the relationship. A RelationObject can be an Issue, a Requirement, a Decision and a GlossaryTerm. Some of these objects also contain additional pre-defined relationships as specified by the Relations meta-model.

- **AllRelations:** AllRelations is an abstract class defining all additional pre-defined relationships specified by the Relations meta-model. It is implemented for a convince purpose, as most of the RelationObjects implement all of the pre-defined relationships.

- **Trigger:** Trigger is one of the provisioned types of the additional pre-defined relationships and defines a "trigger" relationship between the objects, where one of the involved objects is a trigger of the other(s).

- **Dependency:** Dependency is one of the provisioned types of the additional pre-defined relationships and defines a "dependency" relationship between the objects, where one of the involved objects is dependent the other(s).

- **Duplication:** Duplication is one of the provisioned types of the additional pre-defined relationships and defines a "duplication" relationship between the objects, where one of the involved objects is a duplicate of the other(s).

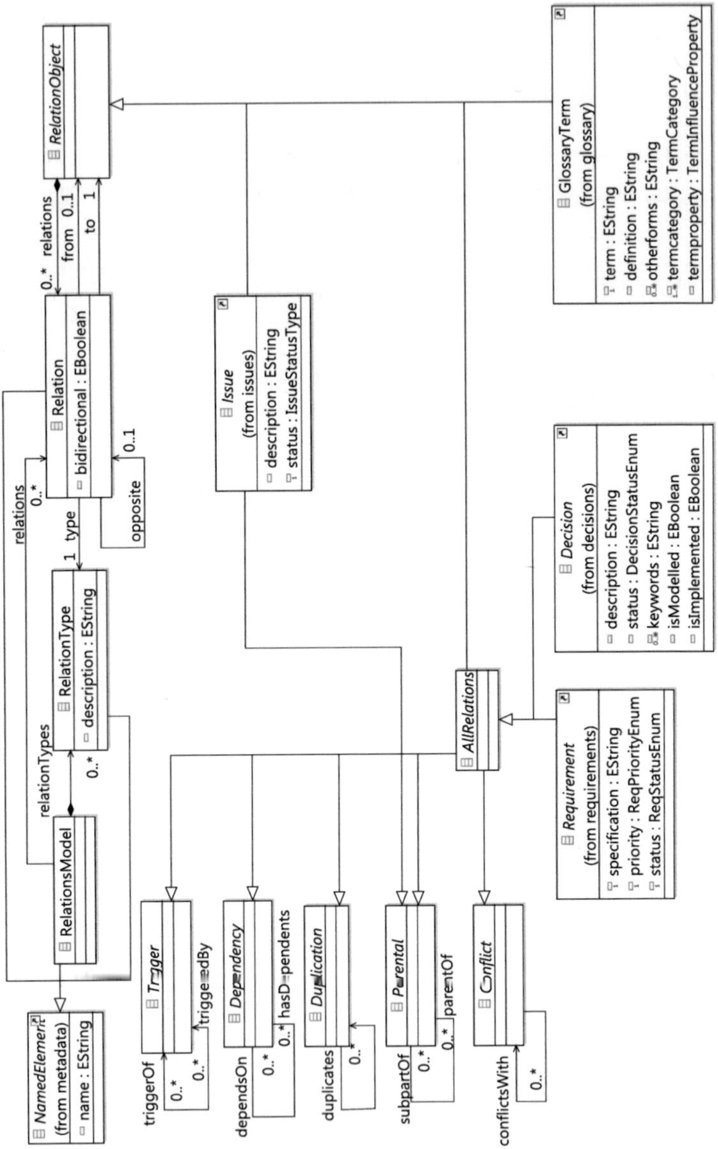

Figure 4.38.: Relations Meta-Model Package

- **Parental:** Parental is one of the provisioned types of the additional pre-defined relationships and defines a “parental” relationship between the objects, where one of the involved objects is a parent of the other(s), while other are children of the parent(s).

- **Conflict:** Conflict is one of the provisioned types of the additional pre-defined relationships and defines a “conflict” relationship between the objects, where one of the involved objects is in a conflict with the other(s).

The Relations meta-model is a help meta-model, its purpose is to abstract and to structure the relationships between various objects in a package.

4.7. Summary

In this chapter, the AM3D pattern catalogue, which is a core of the AM3D approach, was explained in detail.

The goal of the AM3D pattern catalogue is to structure available information about patterns and to present it in a quick and assessable way. At the same time, the catalogue supports evaluation of patterns suitability for the given design problems together with the support of semi-automated documentation of design patterns, as of solutions for design problems together with the rationale for the pattern selection. Moreover, pattern modelling formalisation is co-saved in the catalogue and allows to simplify modelling and to allow checks for architectural modelling violations.

The pattern description in the catalogue is structured with the help of the defined pattern template. The template consists of three building blocks: General information about patterns, question annotations and architectural structure of a pattern. The description template is explained in Section 4.2.

The goal of the question annotations to a pattern is to support the overall goal of the AM3D approach for a lightweight pattern evaluation and documentation together with the rationale for the decision on pattern application. Question annotations support users at understanding the features of the pattern and whether they really want to apply a pattern, as a pattern may have too many drawbacks, as compared to the won advantages of its application. They support users at generating documentation with the rationale for the decisions about patterns. For these purposes, the question annotations are of four types: Goals questions, intent questions, consequence questions and variant questions. They are formulated following the rules defined in Section 4.3.3. Answers to the questions are given by a user and are rationale for the decision to apply or to withdraw a pattern.

The AM3D approach is supported by the formalisation of the pattern catalogue of this new type, design decisions on pattern application and of connected project contexts. The formalisation results through a developed meta-model, explained in detail in Section 4.6. The meta-model supports systematic approach to capture and management of patterns, decisions on pattern application and other relevant project context artefacts and elements. It also allows automated tool-generation, documentation of model elements and automated checks on the meta-model instances (e.g. to verify structural correctness of a pattern instance in an architectural model). Thus, the meta-model structurally and conceptually supports the application scenarios of the AM3D approach (defined in Section 3.2.2), and provides a tool support for them. The target user of the meta-model and its instances is the same as the target use of the AM3D approach (a software engineer or a system architect). It can be also used by a requirements engineer.

The next Section 5 provides a version of a pattern catalogue filled in with pattern instances as an example of the AM3D pattern catalogue. The sample patterns in the catalogue are described with the developed description template, and following the process defined in the current chapter. Also the questions annotations to the sample patterns follow the here-defined guidelines. The catalogue was used for the approach evaluation in the conducted survey and during the empirical study. For more details on validation of the approach please refer to Section 6.

5. Pattern Catalogue Example Entries

This chapter contains entries of the AM3D pattern catalogue. It is a sample pattern solution catalogue developed following the AM3D approach. Each of the pattern entries in the catalogue is provided with question annotations in terms of the AM3D approach. The entries of the catalogue were used in the validation of the AM3D approach – for the survey and for the controlled experiment, as described in Section 6. The description of the AM3D catalogue entries used for the survey and the experiment was shortened down to a short description and question annotations sections.

These entries are a combination of a set of well-known design patterns from Gamma et al. [28] and Buschmann et al. [29], together with a set of lesser known and more complex patterns of enterprise architectures by Fowler [30]. The goal of the combination of various patterns was to demonstrate that the AM3D pattern catalogue can be used to describe all patterns in an easy and comprehensible way, so that the users of the pattern catalogue can successfully understand both pattern sets, patterns that are well-known to them, and patterns that they have never applied or have even never heard about.

There are currently 12 patterns described: Model View Controller in Section 5.1, Client-Server style in Section 5.2, Multi-Tier style in Section 5.3, Fat Client in Section 5.4, Thin Client in Section 5.5, Proxy in Section 5.6, Façade in Section 5.7, Adaptor in Section 5.8, Singleton in Section 5.9, Class Table Inheritance in Section 5.10, Single Table Inheritance in Section 5.11, and Concrete Table Inheritance in Section 5.12.

5.1. Model View Controller

Model View Controller pattern entry of the AM3D catalogue described using the description template:

<table>
<tr><th colspan="3">General Information Block</th></tr>
<tr><td>Type: Architectural pattern</td><td>Category: Structural pattern</td><td>ID: AP001</td></tr>
<tr><td colspan="3">Short Description:
The pattern isolates “domain logic” (the application logic for the user) from the user interface (input and presentation), enabling independent development, testing and maintenance of each of them (separation of concerns).</td></tr>
<tr><td colspan="3">Goal of the Pattern:
– Decouple user-interface aspects of a system from its functional core
– Interaction is limited to calling an update procedure</td></tr>
<tr><td>Potential Advantages:
– Multiple views on the same model
– Strict model separation from view
– Synchronized views
– Pluggable views and controllers
– Exchangeability of “look and feel”
– Framework potential</td><td colspan="2">Potential Drawbacks:
– Increased complexity
– Potential for excessive number of updates
– Close coupling of views and controller to a model
– Low efficiency of data access in view
– Inevitability of change to view and controller when porting
– Difficulty of using MVC with high-level GUIs</td></tr>
<tr><td colspan="3">Information Source:
Pattern-oriented software architecture, Buschmann et al., 1996 [29].</td></tr>
</table>

Recommended Co-Patterns/Solutions:

– Observer

– Command processor pattern

Similar Patterns/Solutions:

– Presentation Abstraction Control

– Locks on data

– Offline user communication

Excluded Patterns/Solutions:

– Not listed

Variants:

– Variant 1: The view is directly connected to the Model.

– Variant 2: Mixed form of base variant and Variant 1. The view is connected to the model through a controller but in some cases has a direct access to the model.

Question Annotations Information Block	
Goal	Would you like to present the same information in different ways e.g., through multiple views?
Intent	Would you like to enable to change the GUI (views) at run-time?
	Do you plan to exchange the underlying data model or the views representing this data? (design time)
Conse-quence	Is it acceptable to have potential delays by the view updates when larger amounts of data are transferred?
	The data in the model (e.g. DB) is not changed directly through the views (but through a controller), and will this be an issue in the future?

5.2. Client-Server Style

Client-Server Style pattern entry of the AM3D catalogue described using the description template:

<table>
<tr><th colspan="3">General Information Block</th></tr>
<tr><td>Type: Architectural pattern</td><td>Category: Structural pattern</td><td>ID: AP002</td></tr>
<tr><td colspan="3">Short Description:
The pattern structures the system into servers (centralized systems) and clients referring to that system and using its resources through a connecting network.</td></tr>
<tr><td colspan="3">Goal of the Pattern:
– Structure the system as a distributed system with independent clients and servers and a connecting network between them
– Provide a centralized source to store the data and centralized access to it</td></tr>
<tr><td>Potential Advantages:
– Higher security
– Centralized data access
– Ease of maintenance
– Light (Thin) clients possible
– Support of multiple clients and client types
– Centralized data management, storage, and backup</td><td colspan="2">Potential Drawbacks:
– High coupling
– Reliability of server
– Performance bottlenecks
– Central target of security attacks
– High dependency on connectivity
– Data consistency problems</td></tr>
<tr><td colspan="3">Information Source:
Wikipedia, design articles and Microsoft MSDN.
"Software Architecture and Design" [171].</td></tr>
<tr><td colspan="3">Recommended Co-Patterns/Solutions:
– Redundancy
– Client-side Caching
Similar Patterns/Solutions:
– Multi-Tier Style
Excluded Patterns/Solutions:
– Not listed</td></tr>
</table>

Variants:

- Variant 1: Client-Queue-Client, where clients communicate with other clients through a server-based queue. Clients can read data from and send data to a server that acts simply as a queue to store the data. This allows clients to distribute and synchronize files and information [171].
- Variant 2: Peer-to-Peer (P2P), where client and server swap their roles in order to distribute and synchronize files and information across multiple clients. It extends the Client-Server style through multiple responses to requests, shared data, resource discovery, and resilience to removal of peers [171].
- Variant 3: Application server-based style, where the server hosts and executes applications and services that a thin client accesses through a browser or specialized client installed software [171].

Question Annotations Information Block

Goal	Would you like to design a distributed system with independent servers (capture resources), clients (demand resources), and a network connection between them?
Intent	Would you like to have central data storage and a centralized access to the system data?
	Is a better control over security essential for your system?
	Would you like multiple clients to have access to the data?
	Would you like to support different client types or different devices?
Consequence	Is dependency on connectivity acceptable in your application?
	Are investments in server redundancy and data consistency manageable in your project?

5.3. Multi-Tier Style

Multi-Tier Style pattern entry of the AM3D catalogue described using the description template:

General Information Block		
Type: Architectural pattern	**Category:** Structural pattern	**ID:** AP003

Short Description:

The pattern defines a Client-Server architecture, in which presentation, application processing and data management functions are logically separated.

Goal of the Pattern:

- Logically separate functions so that specific layers can be added or modified, instead of reworking the entire application
- Separate system according to physical structure of an infrastructure

Potential Advantages:	Potential Drawbacks:
– Higher maintainability and scalability of components through lower coupling – Flexibility via independent tier management – Higher overall availability	– One tier may become a bottleneck for the entire application – Security flaws in one tier may endanger complete application – Increased management complexity – Backups and updates need to be synchronised – Different evolution cycles of used technologies

Information Source:

Pattern-oriented software architecture, Buschmann et al., 1996 [29].
"Software Architecture and Design" [171].

Recommended Co-Patterns/Solutions:

- Not listed

Similar Patterns/Solutions:

- Presentation-Abstraction-Controller
- Client-Server Style

Excluded Patterns/Solutions:

- Not listed

Variants:

- Variants are variations in the number of tiers, starting from the classical 3-Tier application with business, presentation and data access tiers.

Question Annotations Information Block	
Goal	Would you like to be able to add or modify specific components instead of reworking the whole application?
Intent	Would you like to structure the system according to the underlying physical infrastructure?
	Would you like to prevent the client from accessing the data directly?
	Would you like to have a linear communication model in your system, a strong linear hierarchy of communication?
Consequence	Are you aware that all communication will run through a middle tier, which can become a bottleneck?
	Is potential involvement of multiple communication protocols with different evolution cycles not an issue in the future?

5.4. Fat Client

Fat Client pattern entry of the AM3D catalogue described using the description template:

General Information Block		
Type: Architectural pattern	**Category:** Structural pattern	**ID:** AP004
Short Description: The pattern describes a computer (client) in a client-server architecture that provides rich functionality independent of the central server.		
Goal of the Pattern: – Provide (partial) independence of the client from the server – Assure the ability to work offline (at least partially) – Improve performance of complex computations on the client side		

Potential Advantages:	**Potential Drawbacks:**
– Reduced dependency on connectivity to the server – Reduced server and network load – Lower server requirements – Possibility to work offline – Offloading costs on the client-side	– Maintainability of the clients – Slower application start-up – Higher requirements to client resources – Data security problems due to decentralized storage – Data consistency and back up problems

Information Source:

Wikipedia, design articles.

Recommended Co-Patterns/Solutions:

– Not listed

Similar Patterns/Solutions:

– Thin Client

Excluded Patterns/Solutions:

– Not listed

Variants:

– Not listed

Question Annotations Information Block

Goal	Would you like a client to be able to perform the functionality in circumstances of potential disconnection to the main server?
Intent	Would you like to reduce the load on your main server or network offloading the processing and capacity demands to the client devices?
	Is working offline essential for your application?
Consequence	Will the application be running on powerful devices and porting to low-performance devices can be excluded in the future? (otherwise – Thin Client)
	Is your infrastructure standardized with little software heterogeneity, and will it stay like this in the future? (otherwise → Thin Client)
	Is potential slower start-up of the application acceptable?

5.5. Thin Client

Thin Client pattern entry of the AM3D catalogue described using the description template:

General Information Block		
Type: Architectural pattern	**Category:** Structural pattern	**ID:** AP005
Short Description: The pattern describes a computer (client) in client-server architecture that heavily depends on the functionality provided by a central server.		
Goal of the Pattern: – Put role responsibilities on the server (e.g. computation, persistence, or even GUI rendering) – Keep updates centralized and simplify the maintenance of computational services		
Potential Advantages: – Centralized updates – Higher data consistency – Reliable backups – Fast application start-ups – Low load on the client resources – Easier maintainability of clients – Usage data available on company site – Reduced dependencies on OSs	**Potential Drawbacks:** – Increased network load – High server load – Data availability depends on the network – Higher requirements to the server, higher server costs – Dependency on network connection	
Information Source: Pattern-oriented software architecture, Buschmann et al., 1996 [29].		
Recommended Co-Patterns/Solutions: – Not listed **Similar Patterns/Solutions:** – Fat client **Excluded Patterns/Solutions:** – Not listed		

Variants: – Not listed	
Question Annotations Information Block	
Goal	Would you like to put responsibility for data computation, persistence, etc. on the server side?
Intent	Would you like to keep SW updates centralized?
	Is your infrastructure heterogeneous?
	Would you like to support low-performance devices?
Consequence	Is working offline not essential for your application? (otherwise → Fat Client)
	Are main changes (SW updates) expected to be on the server side? (otherwise → Fat Client)

5.6. Proxy

Proxy pattern entry of the AM3D catalogue described using the description template:

General Information Block		
Type: Architectural pattern	**Category:** Structural pattern	**ID:** AP006
Short Description: The pattern provides a representative (a place-holder) for another object to control access to it.		
Goal of the Pattern: – Provide an interface to some other object, resource, network connection, etc.		

Potential Advantages:	**Potential Drawbacks:**
– Hide real object, recourse, etc., and its address – Add additional functionalities to an object, resource or network connection – Restrict or manage access to an object, resource or network connection – State-full object, resource, etc., access possible	– Only statical extensions possible – Decreased performance via access to an additional object – Higher level of indirection – Increased complexity

Information Source:

Design Patterns. Elements of Reusable Object-Oriented Software, Gamma et al., 1995 [28].

Recommended Co-Patterns/Solutions:

– Not listed

Similar Patterns/Solutions:

– Façade
– Mediator
– Adaptor

Excluded Patterns/Solutions:

– Not listed

Variants:

– Variant 1: Remote proxy provides a local representative for an object in a different address space.
– Variant 2: Virtual proxy creates expensive objects on demand
– Variant 3: Protection proxy controls access to the original object.

Question Annotations Information Block	
Goal	Would you like to provide an interface to some other object, resource, network connection, etc.?
Intent	Would you like to provide or restrict the access to functionalities provided by another object or server?
	Would you like to provide an interface with some additional functionality (management of objects state, etc.)?
	Would you like to provide a representative for an object in different address-space?
Consequence	Are you not planning to be able to extend the object's properties dynamically? (otherwise → Decorator)
	Is a potential performance bottleneck not a problem?
	Is a higher level of indirection not a problem?

5.7. Façade

Façade pattern entry of the AM3D catalogue described using the description template:

General Information Block		
Type: Architectural pattern	**Category:** Structural pattern	**ID:** AP007
Short Description: The pattern provides a unified interface to a set of interfaces in a subsystem.		
Goal of the Pattern: – Minimize the communication and dependencies between subsystems – Simplify a number of complicated interfaces with a subsystem into a single interface		

Potential Advantages:	Potential Drawbacks:
– Unified access to the subsystem – Reduced communication between subsystems – Reduced cohesion – Hide subsystem implementation details	– Performance bottleneck – Only stateless access possible – Only static access – No modification of functionality – No additional interface implementation

Information Source:

Design Patterns. Elements of Reusable Object-Oriented Software, Gamma et al., 1995 [28].

Recommended Co-Patterns/Solutions:

– Not listed

Similar Patterns/Solutions:

– Proxy
– Mediator
– Adaptor

Excluded Patterns/Solutions:

– Not listed

Variants:

– Variant 1: Singleton Façade (implemented through singleton pattern)
– Variant 2: Multiple Façade objects provide the same interfaces to the same set of subsystems
– Variant 3: Multiple Façades provide different interfaces to the same set of subsystems

Question Annotations Information Block	
Goal	Would you like to provide a unified interface to a set of interfaces in a subsystem?
Intent	Would you like to minimize the communication and dependencies between subsystems?
	An additional functionality wrapped into the unified interface is not your intent? (otherwise → Proxy)
	Is a stateless unified interface your intent? (otherwise → Proxy)
	Is it desired that subsystem classes know nothing about the Façade object(s)? (otherwise → Mediator)
	A new interface for an object is not your intent? (otherwise → Adaptor)
Consequence	Are you not wishing to be able to extend the object's properties dynamically? (otherwise → Decorator)
	Is a potential performance bottleneck not an issue?

5.8. Adaptor

Adaptor pattern entry of the AM3D catalogue described using the description template:

General Information Block		
Type: Architectural pattern	**Category:** Structural pattern	**ID:** AP008

Short Description:
The pattern converts an interface of a class into another interface that clients expect.

Goal of the Pattern:
- Convert the interface of a class into another interface that clients expect
- Adapter lets classes work together, that could not otherwise, because of incompatible interfaces

Potential Advantages:	**Potential Drawbacks:**
– Add additional interface without direct object modification – Improve interoperability of classes	– Decreased maintainability – Increased code complexity

Information Source:

Design Patterns. Elements of Reusable Object-Oriented Software, Gamma et al., 1995 [28].

Recommended Co-Patterns/Solutions:

– Not listed

Similar Patterns/Solutions:

– Façade

– Mediator

– Proxy

Excluded Patterns/Solutions:

– Not listed

Variants:

– Variant 1: Object Adaptor, contains an instance of class it wraps and makes calls into the instance of wrapped object.

– Variant 2: Class Adapter, includes multiple polymorphic interfaces by implementing or inheriting both the interface that is expected and the interface that is pre-existing.

Question Annotations Information Block

Goal	Would you like to convert an interface of a class (or an object) into another interface that clients expect?
Intent	Would you like to make interfaces of incompatible classes compatible?
	Would you like to change the interface of an existing object (a new interface design for an object)? (otherwise → Proxy or Decorator)
Conseq.	Are you aware of the size of the code you have to write and maintain to adapt the class?

5.9. Singleton

Singleton pattern entry of the AM3D catalogue described using the description template:

General Information Block		
Type: Architectural pattern	**Category:** Structural pattern	**ID:** AP009

Short Description:

The pattern restricts the instantiation of a class to one object.

Goal of the Pattern:

– Ensure a class only has one instance

– Provide a global point of access to it

Potential Advantages:	Potential Drawbacks:
– Global access to an object possible – Restricted data modification	– Decreased maintainability – Security issues – Limited parallelization of application – Limited multi-thread capability

Information Source:

Design Patterns. Elements of Reusable Object-Oriented Software, Gamma et al., 1995 [28].

Recommended Co-Patterns/Solutions:

– Not listed

Similar Patterns/Solutions:

– Not listed

Excluded Patterns/Solutions:

– Not listed

Variants:

– Variant 1: Singleton permits a number of its instances; the number can be configured in the Class.

Question Annotations Information Block	
Goal	Would you like to ensure that a class has only one instance?
Intent	Would you like to make class instance easily accessible (globally)?
Conse-quence	If you are developing a distributed application, is it not an issue that the data stored in the instance can not change too often?
	Having global access to the class instance is not a potential threat to the application?
	You are not developing a multi-thread application, respectively have you extended singleton for this case?

5.10. Class Table Inheritance

Class Table Inheritance pattern entry of the AM3D catalogue described using the description template:

General Information Block		
Type: Architectural pattern	**Category:** Object-Relational Pattern	**ID:** OP001
Short Description: The pattern represents an inheritance hierarchy of classes with one table for each class. Database structure maps clearly to objects and allows links anywhere in the inheritance structure.		
Goal of the Pattern: – Map fields in inheritance hierarchy to a relational database – Straightforward relationship between database and domain model – Tables are easy to understand and don't waste space		
Potential Advantages: – Compact data structure – Lower complexity of domain model relationship	**Potential Drawbacks:** – Lower data-base application interoperability – Low extendibility – Reduced performance because of frequent joins	

Information Source: Patterns of Enterprise Application Architecture, Fowler, 2005 [30].

Recommended Co-Patterns/Solutions: – Not listed **Similar Patterns/Solutions:** – Single Table Inheritance – Concrete Table Inheritance **Excluded Patterns/Solutions:** – Not listed

Variants: – Not listed

Question Annotations Information Block	
Goal	Would you like to represent an inheritance hierarchy of classes in relational database?
Intent	Would you like a straightforward relationship between the database and the domain model to achieve easier understanding of the Database?
Conse-quence	Is it not a problem that the majority of requests can be satisfied only with performance expensive joins?
	Is it not your intent for the Database to be used by other applications that are not using (or do not know) objects? (otherwise → Concrete Table Inheritance)
	Is the final number of tables in the database structure limited (small) and is it unlikely to change in the future?

5.11. Single Table Inheritance

Single Table Inheritance pattern entry of the AM3D catalogue described using the description template:

General Information Block		
Type: Architectural pattern	**Category:** Object-Relational Pattern	**ID:** OP002

Short Description: The pattern represents an inheritance hierarchy of classes in a relational database as a single table that has columns for all the fields of the various classes. It maps all fields of all classes of an inheritance structure into a single table. Each class stores relevant data to it in one single row. .
Goal of the Pattern: – Map fields in inheritance hierarchy to a relational database – Minimization of joins

Potential Advantages:	**Potential Drawbacks:**
– Centralized data storage – Minimisation of joins – Control of individual class extensions	– Lower scalability of larger tables – Frequent lock on the table – Higher complexity of domain model relationship – Lower data-base application inter-operability

Information Source: Patterns of Enterprise Application Architecture, Fowler, 2005 [30].
Recommended Co-Patterns/Solutions: – Not listed **Similar Patterns/Solutions:** – Class Table Inheritance Concrete Table Inheritance **Excluded Patterns/Solutions:** – Not listed
Variants: – Not listed

Question Annotations Information Block	
Goal	Would you like to represent an inheritance hierarchy of classes in relational database?
Intent	Would you like to keep all data in a single table? (otherwise → Class Table Inheritance or Concrete Table Inheritance)
	Is it important to avoid joins in retrieving data?
Conse-quence	Frequent locks on one table are not an issue?
	A non-straightforward relationship between database and domain model is not a problem?
	Is it not your intent for the Database to be used by other applications that are not using (or do not know) objects? (otherwise → Concrete Table Inheritance)

5.12. Concrete Table Inheritance

Concrete Table Inheritance pattern entry of the AM3D catalogue described using the description template:

General Information Block		
Type: Architectural pattern	**Category:** Object-Relational Pattern	**ID:** OP003
Short Description: The pattern represents an inheritance hierarchy of classes in a relational database with one table for each concrete class. Database structure maps clearly to objects and allows links anywhere in the inheritance structure.		
Goal of the Pattern: – Map fields in inheritance hierarchy to a relational database – Spread the load between tables – Assure that Database can be used by other applications that are not using the objects – Assure each table is self-contained and has no irrelevant fields		

Potential Advantages:	**Potential Drawbacks:**
– Improved data-base application interoperability – Improved request load between the tables	– Low modifiability – Reduced extendibility – Reduced performance through expensive joins

Information Source:
Patterns of Enterprise Application Architecture, Fowler, 2005 [30].

Recommended Co-Patterns/Solutions:
– Not listed
Similar Patterns/Solutions:
– Single Table Inheritance – Class Table Inheritance
Excluded Patterns/Solutions:
– Not listed

Variants:
– Not listed

Question Annotations Information Block	
Goal	Would you like to represent an inheritance hierarchy of classes in relational database?
Intent	Shall one database table be used for each concrete class in the hierarchy and no tables for abstract classes?
	Would you like to spread the request load between the tables?
	Would you like the Database to be used by other applications that are not using (or do not know) objects?
Conse-quence	Are there few changes to the objects (classes) expected?
	Is data collection (retrieval) from all of the tables seldom demanded in your application? (otherwise → Single Table Inheritance)

5.13. Collected Experience

The experiences collected during the creation of the example catalogue are also summarized under the steps of the processes to add questions to a pattern in Section 4.3.5 and to fill in the catalogue in Section 4.4.

First of all, creation of such a catalogue is a time-demanding task. It requires an expert who would go through the common design pattern descriptions and would extract the required information out of those descriptions. The expert is then responsible to structure the extracted information according to the defined AM3D pattern description. Afterwards, the entries shall be sequentially reviewed by two independent reviewers. Such a process assures a high understandability of the catalogue entries, as demonstrated by the conducted AM3D approach validations, where the example catalogue was used for the approach's validation (see Chapter 6 for details).

Second, the meta-model used for the approach's formalization and the process supported by it could be applied to describe patterns in the example catalogue without limitations. The descriptions could also be used for the application on the CoCoME example, described in Section 3.6.

Finally, the descriptions of some design patterns may vary from source to source. Such ambiguities have to be solved by an expert in the area – an expert in architectural design patterns or an expert in other solutions that are to be described in the catalogue.

6. Validation

This chapter describes the validation of the AM3D approach. The AM3D approach improves ease and feasibility of application of architectural design patterns, and supports architects and software engineers in documentation of corresponding design decisions, together with their rationale and trace links between design decisions, patterns as design solutions, requirements and architecture, thus improving maintainability of the system architecture during system evolution.

To describe and to classify the validation, four types of empirical validation in architectural knowledge management area were defined together with validation goals, subjects, objects, artefacts and effort estimations. The validation types are based on the common types for the model-based performance prediction methods from [85] and [86]. The types include: Feasibility (Type 0), Appropriateness (Type I), Applicability (Type II) and Cost-Benefit (Type III).

The validation of the AM3D approach consists of three parts: (1) A survey, (2) application on a common example, and (3) an empirical study based on a controlled experiment.

The goal of the survey is to evaluate the feasibility of the motivation of the approach and to evaluate the feasibility of the proposed annotated pattern catalogue as of a potential solution for the problems with design pattern use and documentation (Type 0 validation: Feasibility). The survey research method is structured interviews, which is a qualitative research method. It is described in detail in Section 6.4.

The goal of the application on a common example is to demonstrate applicability of the AM3D approach, including the applicability of its artefacts and the process (Type I validation: Appropriateness). It is described in detail in Section 4.

The goal of the empirical study is to validate the claimed benefits of the approach (Type II validation: Applicability). The empirical study validates if design patterns annotated according to the AM3D approach can be better understood and applied more correctly as compared to the design pattern catalogue based on the standard approach. Further-on, it is validated if a system architecture, which is documented according to the AM3D approach and, thus, is the result of development of the system using the AM3D approach, can be better maintained compared to the system documented according to the standard catalogue approach. The empirical study research method is controlled experiment, which is a quantitative research method. The experiment is described in detail in Section 6.5.

This chapter is structured as follows. Section 6.1 introduces types of validation and explains them. It presents our developed validation type classification for the area of the design decisions research. Section 6.2 describes the validation goals together with the kinds of validation, which were conducted for the AM3D approach. Section 6.3 introduces the Goal Question Metric approach by Basili [172], which is used to define the research goals and questions for the survey and the experiment. Section 6.4 explains in detail the conducted survey, its research questions, its method, and its design, including the context, subjects, process and materials. It explains test of the method, provides information on participants and the analysis of the results, together with the discussion of the treats to validity and summary of the survey results. Section 6.5 explains in detail the conducted experiment, its research questions, its method, and its design, including the context, subjects, process and materials. It explains test of the method, provides information on participants and the analysis of the results, together with the discussion of the treats to validity and summary of the experiment results. Finally, Section 6.6 concludes the chapter.

6.1. Types of Validation

An overview of validation and verification methods in knowledge engineering research area is provided by Preece in [173]. It is an overview for the whole area and is not detailed enough for our approach. Koziolek proposed three types of empirical evaluations for the model-based performance prediction methods in [86]. They are sketched on Figure 6.1.

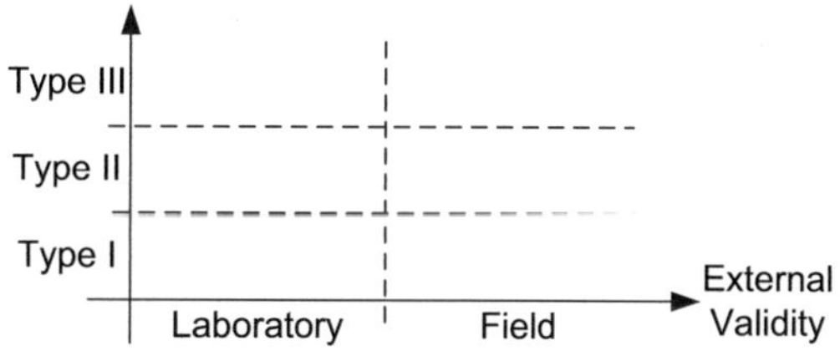

Figure 6.1.: Types of Empirical Validation [86]

We adopt these three types by Koziolek [86] to the area of the design decisions research, and define four types of the empirical evaluations for the area. The empirical evaluations type summary is provided in Table 6.1.

In the following we explain the design decisions area empirical evaluations types:

- **Type 0 (Feasibility):** The entry level evaluation of the application feasibility of design decision capture and management approaches. Authors of an approach develop means to capture and manage design decisions (e.g., meta-models, models, text templates, etc.) and instantiate them with several example decisions. The goal is to demonstrate that a developed template or a model can be used for this goal.

Type	Goal	Who	How	Tools	Example	Effort
Type 0 (Feasibility)	Demonstrate feasibility	Authors	Models, Meta-Models, Text description templates, Text applied on an example though a comparison to the “no-approach” situation or though a survey with users	No tool, Research prototype	Research example	+
Type I (Appropriateness)	Demonstrate applicability in a system context	Authors	Type 0 artefacts + Requirements model, Trace links, Architectural model applied on an example	Research prototype	Research example in a context	+ / ++
Type II (Applicability)	Demonstrate applicability by extern users in a system context	Authors, Extern users	Type I artefacts + and real-world-alike artefacts applied on an example	Stable research prototype, Tool support	Real-world example	++
Type III (Cost-Benefit)	Demonstrate benefit-over-cost applicability by extern users in a real-life system context	Authors, (Independent) Extern users	Type II artefacts + applied in a real-world-alike context over a longer period of time or on a project executed twice, with and without the method and analysed in a longer time perspective	Mature tool support	Real-world system	+++

Table 6.1.: Types of Empirical Evaluations in the Design Decision Area

In such evaluation a comparison is done to a no-approach situation, where e.g. undocumented design decisions are compared to documented design decisions. The authors either use no example, or use a simple self-invented example to place the provided decisions into some context. The authors sketch a usage process for the proposed approach. A tool-support for the approach, if any, is a research prototype. Usually it is a pure research evaluation with no industrial context application. Typo 0 evaluation is a low-effort evaluation.

- **Type I (Appropriateness):** The evaluation of the appropriateness of design decision capture and management approaches. The goal is to demonstrate that developed artefacts can be used to capture and manage design decisions and other relevant context information, such as requirements, which are part of a decision rationale, architectural models where decisions are implemented, trace links between various artefacts, documentation, etc. A reference approach for the comparison by such evaluation is usually a no-approach situation, where e.g. undocumented design decisions are compared to a possibility to document design decisions with the proposed approach. The authors use a self-invented example to demonstrate the approach and have a process (often informal) about how the approach shall be applied. A tool-support for the approach is a research prototype. In some cases of Type I evaluation authors ask subjects to anticipate and to speculate about a potential approach application and to fill in their opinion in a questionnaire. In this case evaluation is performed as interviews, which are usually based on the (fixed) questionnaires.

  If the Type I evaluation is a comparison-based evolution, it requires a comparably low effort. In case of a survey, especially with industrially-employed participants, a Type I evaluation involves a moderate effort.

- **Type II (Applicability):** Type-II studies evaluate (or actually validate) the applicability of a method, when it is used by the targeted users of an approach instead of the authors of the method [86]. Target users are usually software architects, engineers, developers, testers or students. The evaluation subjects are often students, whose suitability for the computer science area is discussed by Tichy in [174]. The developed approach is put into a real-world-alike context and demonstrated with the help of a stable research prototype tool used by the subjects. The type II evaluation compares the proposed approach and its artefacts and tool-support to an approach common for the research area, such as e.g. no documentation of design decisions or pure textual documentation of them. Type II evaluation is effort and cost prone.

- **Type III (Cost-Benefit):** This form of evaluation (actually, of validation) is a cost-benefit analysis [86], and relies on a mature tool support, capable of handling real world problems in hands of extern users. Documentation of design decisions, their rationale, involved requirements and architectural elements, and implementation of trace links between these artefacts causes high initial costs. It is not clear if these costs pay off during the later system life-cycle phases. Type III evaluation compares the later maintenance costs and their reduction (if any) with the initial investments connected to the approach introduction and usage. As to Koziolek [86], ideally, the improvement claim shall be checked by conducting the same software project at least twice; once without applying the approach and accepting the costs for late life-cycle maintenance, and once applying the approach thereby investing higher upfront costs. Comparing the respective costs for both projects enables assessing the benefit of a prediction method in terms of a business value. However, such evaluation is extremely cost and effort intense. To our best knowledge, this type of evaluation cannot be found in the design decisions research field.

Evaluation and validation in the area of knowledge management is highly time and cost consuming in general. Thus, approach evaluations seldom go beyond the Type II validation. The most common evaluations are of Type I and Type II, which is a well known and accepted fact in the community. Type III evaluation is almost never used (to our best knowledge, it have been never used up to now), as it requires a stable connection to an industrial context over a long period of time (usually, for several years). Thus, the majority of the related work approaches (see Section 7) is limited to the Type 0, Typo I and Type II validations.

6.2. What is Validated?

We have evaluated our approach using Type 0, Type I and Type II evaluation types. A summary of the AM3D approach validation, artefacts and description sources is listed in Table 6.2. In the following, we provide details on the conducted validation, which consisted of three parts:

- **Type 0 (Feasibility):** Type I validation is carried out on the survey. In this type of the evaluation, we designed and conducted a survey based on the structured interviews, which is a qualitative research method. The goals of the survey are to evaluate the feasibility of the motivation of the approach, and to evaluate the feasibility of the proposed annotated AM3D pattern catalogue as a potential solution for some problems with design pattern application. The survey goals, design and analysis of the results are provided in Section 6.4.
- **Type I (Appropriateness):** Type I evaluation was carried out with the help of meta-models described in Section 4.6, and meta-model instances in the form of a the AM3D pattern catalogue, provided in Section 5. In this type of evaluation, the proposed AM3D approach was applied on an example CoCoME-based system to demonstrated

Evaluation Type	How	What	Explained in
Type 0 (Feasibility)	Survey based on structured interviews with 25 participants	– Justified motivation of the approach. – Feasibility of the applicability of the proposed annotated pattern catalogue evaluated by independent subjects.	Section 6.4
Type I (Appropriateness)	AM3D approach artefacts and process,	– Support of capture and management of pattern design decisions and related artefacts in a context of a system.	Section 3
Type II (Applicability)	A case study based on the controlled experiment with 20 participants	– Improvement of understandability and correctness of pattern application in a system design using AM3D compared to the standard approach. – Improvement of maintainability of the system architecture documented with AM3D compared to the standard approach.	Section 6.5

Table 6.2.: The AM3D Validation Summary

the applicability of the proposed AM3D approach. The application on example is described in Section 3.

- **Type II (Applicability):** Type II validation is an empirical study based on the controlled experiment. Controlled experiment is a quantitative research method. In the empirical study, we validate the claimed benefits of the AM3D approach. We validate if design patterns annotated according to the AM3D approach can be better understood and applied more correctly, as compared to the design pattern catalogue based on the classical approach (well-established book-catalogues, such as books by Buschmann2007b et al. [31] or Gamma et al. [28]). Further-on, we validate if a system architecture documented according to the AM3D approach, as the result of development following the AM3D approach, can be better maintained compared to the system documented according to the classical catalogue approach. The empirical study goals, design and analysis of results are provided in Section 6.5.

Table 6.3 presents the relations between the validation types and the AM3D approach application scenarios and benefits. A positive relation (✔) means that the application scenario or benefit was one of the goals of the validation. Correspondingly, a negative relation (✘) means that the validation of the application scenario or benefit was not one of the goals.

Scenario	**Type 0**	**Type I**	**Type II**
Gaining general information about a design pattern	✔	✘	✔
Choosing between similar patterns	✔	✘	✔
Pattern application with evaluation and semi-automated rationale documentation	✔	✔	✘
Elicitation and prioritisation of requirements on-demand	✘	✔	✘
System evolution: Retrieving information about used patterns	✔	✔	✔
System evolution: Understanding pattern design decision	✔	✘	✔
Tracing impact caused by changed requirements during maintenance	✔	✘	✘
Understanding the rationale of architectural elements through trace links to requirements	✘	✔	✔
Checking architectural implementation violations of a pattern	✔	✔	✘
Benefit	**Type 0**	**Type I**	**Type II**
Documented rationale of design decisions on the pattern application	✔	✔	✔
Semi-automated documentation of trace links between requirements, decisions and architectural elements	✘	✔	✘
A more appropriate use of design patterns and design pattern variants	✔	✘	✔
Goal-oriented architecture-driven requirements engineering	✘	✔	✘

Table 6.3.: Relations Between Covered Validation Types and Scenarios and Benefits

As explained in Section 6.1, Type III validation is, in fact, impossible for the problem area. It is a recognized practice in the community, and Type 0 to Type II evaluations are considered to be sufficient.

6.3. The Goal Question Metric Approach (GQM)

In this section we briefly explain the Goal Question Metric approach that is used to derive the validation plans for the survey and the experiment.

The Goal Question Metric approach was proposed by Basili et al. [172] and aims to improve the measureability of results. The result of the application of the Goal Question Metric approach is the "specification of a measurement system targeting a particular set of issues and a set of rules for the interpretation of the measurement data" [172]. The approach builds upon so-called measurement model that consists of three levels: Conceptual level ("Goal"), Operational level ("Question") and Quantitative level ("Metric"). These levels built a hierarchical structure of the approach and are depicted on Figure 6.2.

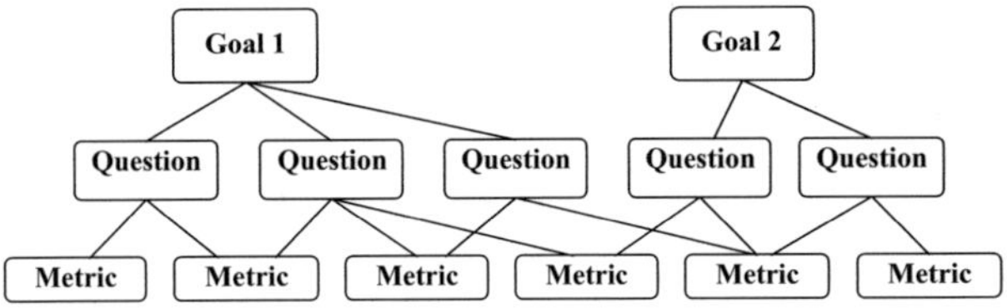

Figure 6.2.: Hierarchical Structure of the Goal Question Metric Approach [172]

Basili et al. [172] describe these levels as follows (direct text citation):

- **Goal:** A goal is the purpose of the measurement in respect to the object for which the measurement is conducted. This object can be a product, a production object, a process, an activity or a resource. Goal defines the viewpoint from which the measure is taken and the reason for it.

- **Question:** A question specifies how the goal can be measurably achieved. The purpose of the question is to characterise the goal from the quality perspective, and to specify the quality issue. Usually the goal is refined into several questions – a set of questions.

- **Metric:** A metric characterises an answer to a question in a quantitative way. A metric can measure time, performance and any other measurable and comparable attribute. Each question usually refined into several metrics – a set of metrics. The same metric can be used in order to answer different questions under the same goal. And several goals can reuse questions and metrics. However, clearly no metrics can be defined in a case where the evaluation of the goal is done in a non-quantitative way. A set of metrics is therefore an optional characteristic of the Goal Question Metric approach and shall be defined only when meaningfully applicable.

Goal # ...	
Purpose	[The purpose of the measurement]
Issue	[a property to be validated]
Object (Process)	[object, which property shall be validated]
Viewpoint	[target user of the object that is measured]
Comparison object (optional)	[comparison object for the measurement]

Table 6.4.: A Sample Table to Describe a Goal Question Metric Plan (Adopted from Basili et al. [172])

A classical way to describe Goal Question Metric plans is to use a table, such as a sample Table 6.4 (adopted from Basili et al. [172]). An example of such a table usage is presented on Figure 6.3. Here the goal "Improve the timeliness of change request processing from the project manager's viewpoint" is first defined using the sample table, and then it is refined into questions. Questions are supplied with the defined metrics in order to measure the achievement of the goal. For more details about the Goal Question Metric approach please refer to [172].

Goal	Purpose Issue Object (process) Viewpoint	Improve the timeliness of change request processing from the project manager's viewpoint
Question	Q1	What is the current change request processing speed?
Metrics	M1 M2 M3	Average cycle time Standard deviation % cases outside of the upper limit
Question	Q2	Is the (documented) change request process actually performed?
Metrics	M4 M5	Subjective rating by the project manager % of exceptions identified during reviews
Question	Q3	What is the deviation of the actual change request processing time from the estimated one?
Metrics	M6 M7	$\frac{\text{Current average cycle time - Estimated average cycle time}}{\text{Current average cycle time}} * 100$ Subjective evaluation by the project manager
Question	Q4	Is the performance of the process improving?
Metrics	M8	$\frac{\text{Current average cycle time}}{\text{Baseline average cycle time}} * 100$
Question	Q5	Is the current performance satisfactory from the viewpoint of the project manager?
Metrics	M7	Subjective evaluation by the project manager
Question	Q6	Is the performance visibly improving?
Metrics	M8	$\frac{\text{Current average cycle time}}{\text{Baseline average cycle time}} * 100$

Figure 6.3.: An Example of a Goal Question Metric Plan [172]

6.4. Survey

This section provides details on the conducted survey with 25 doctoral researchers and developers. The survey is one of the validation methods of the AM3D approach. The survey followed two goals: Firstly, to elicit an opinion on design patterns and their application as a check of the motivation of the AM3D approach. Secondly, to validate the applicability of the proposed pattern catalogue and of the pattern question annotations on example of three sample pattern catalogue entries.

The conducted survey is exploratory and is based on structured interviews, which is a qualitative research method. Its aim is the collection of descriptive statistics and not an evaluation of hypotheses. The applicability of the proposed pattern catalogue and of the pattern question annotations is validated based on the opinions of the survey participants.

The survey was conducted with participants both from academia and industry, whereby 25 valid questionnaires were collected[1]. The obtained questionnaires have an approximately equal distribution of academia and industry. The feasibility and representability of the survey together with other threats to validity is discussed in Section 6.4.6.

This section is structured as follows. Section 6.4.1 defines the goals and research questions of the survey. Section 6.4.2 describes the research method. Survey design is explained in Section 6.4.3, and testing of the method in Section 6.4.4. Survey results are analysed and presented in Section 6.4.5, whereby the data is structured according to the defined research questions. Section 6.4.6 discusses internal and external threats to validity. Finally, Section 6.4.7 concludes with the summary of the evaluation.

6.4.1. Research Questions

The goal of the survey is to qualitatively evaluate the motivation of the AM3D approach, and the appropriateness of the proposed pattern catalogue and of the pattern question annotations on example of three sample pattern catalogue entries.

First, it surveys the extent of the widespread of the design pattern usage, general perception of engineers towards the design patterns and problems potentially faced during pattern application and during the evolution of systems with applied patterns.

[1] The survey results were published in [1]. The paper reports the analysis of the results for 21 obtained questionnaire. The questionnaire was since still available online, and we have obtained four more valid questionnaires.

Second, the survey investigates the potential impact of the AM3D pattern catalogue on the problems with the design pattern application, implementation of the new functionality with the help of design patterns, as well as impact on the modification of the system during its evolution.

Finally, it researches the understandability of the AM3D question annotations for the persons who were not involved into the question annotation creation. The understandability is researched on example of three sample catalogue entries selected based on their usage wide-spread (very common, moderate known, and likely unknown).

To plan the survey we have implemented a Goal Question Metric plan for the validation, which is described in the following. As the survey is a qualitative research method, and thus it collects descriptive statistics instead of hypotheses evaluation, the Goal Question Metric approach is implemented only up to the question definition. The definition of the hypotheses and of the corresponding metrics is omitted.

6.4.1.1. Goals

We define the goal of our experiment using the Goal-Question-Metric approach [172], explained in Section 6.3. The six goals of the Goal Question Metric plan defined for the survey are provided in Table 6.5 in the usual Goal Question Metric form. These goals were chosen for the survey due to the survey target audience, who were participants from the industry. Questions to these goals, in our estimation, could be more meaningfully answered by such participants then questions to the design tasks requiring direct catalogue application and training. Moreover, the correctness of the assumed motivation of the AM3D approach based on the scientific publications had to be evaluated before conducting the controlled experiment. These goals are:

- **Goal I:** The first goal is to qualitatively evaluate the motivation of the AM3D approach from the point of view of software engineers or architects. The goal evaluates if design patterns are used on practice, and if there are problems with selection and application of patterns.

- **Goal II:** The second goal is to qualitatively evaluate the positive impact of the AM3D pattern catalogue on the pattern application from the point of view of software engineers or architects.
- **Goal III:** The third goal is to qualitatively evaluate the positive impact of the AM3D pattern catalogue on system evolution in case of implementation of new or change of the existing functionality with the help of design patterns from the point of view of software engineers or architects.
- **Goal IV:** The fourth goal is to qualitatively evaluate the positive impact of the AM3D pattern catalogue on system evolution in case an applied pattern is outdated due to the requirement changes from the point of view of software engineers or architects.
- **Goal V:** The fifth goal is to qualitatively evaluate the understandability of the question annotations by software engineers or architects who were not involved in the catalogue development.
- **Goal VI:** The sixth goal is to qualitatively evaluate if the question annotations are sufficient to describe a pattern from the point of view of software engineers or of architects.

The next step of the Goal Question Metric approach is to derive the research questions to the defined goals. These questions are listed in the Section 6.5.1.2.

6.4.1.2. Questions and Metrics

The research questions to the goals were defined following the Goal Question Metric approach. The questions are divided into two groups: (1) General research questions about patterns, and (2) pattern catalogue research

Goal I	
Purpose	Qualitatively evaluate
Issue	the feasibility
Object	of the motivation of the AM3D approach
Viewpoint	from the point of view of software engineers or architects.
Goal II	
Purpose	Qualitatively evaluate
Issue	the positive impact of the AM3D pattern catalogue
Object	on the pattern application
Viewpoint	from the point of view of software engineers or architects.
Goal III	
Purpose	Qualitatively evaluate
Issue	the positive impact of the AM3D pattern catalogue
Object	on system evolution in case of implementation of new or change of the existing functionality with the help of design patterns
Viewpoint	from the point of view of software engineers or architects.
Goal IV	
Purpose	Qualitatively evaluate
Issue	the positive impact of the AM3D pattern catalogue
Object	on system evolution in case of evaluation whether an applied pattern is outdated due to the requirement changes
Viewpoint	from the point of view of software engineers or architects.
Goal V	
Purpose	Qualitatively evaluate
Issue	the understandability
Object	of the question annotations
Viewpoint	from the point of view of software engineers or architects who were not involved into the catalogue development.
Goal VI	
Purpose	Qualitatively evaluate
Issue	if the question annotations are sufficient
Object	to describe a pattern
Viewpoint	from the point of view of software engineers or architects.

Table 6.5.: Goals of the GQM Plan of the Survey

questions. Please note that goals and questions do not have a one-to-one relation. According to Basili [172], the same question can be used for evaluation of several goals. The general research questions about patterns are:

- **Q1. Are patterns used in practice, and to what extent?** This question evaluates if the patterns are indeed common solutions that are applied on practice, of if the patterns are rather theoretical solutions and are only seldom used in real life projects. Further on, this question evaluated to which extent the design patterns are used – if the usage is limited only to a few patterns or if a wide variety of patterns is applied. Question I is related to Goal I.

- **Q2. What is the attitude towards patterns, and are they considered worthwhile and helpful?** This question evaluates the attitude towards design patterns. If the attitude towards design patterns is rather negative, the proposed AM3D approach will be most likely rejected by the participants, since the design patterns are already evaluated as useless. Question II is related to Goal I.

- **Q3. Are there any problems with application or documentation of patterns?** This question evaluates if there are any problems connected to pattern selection, application and modification of already applied design patterns in order to evaluate the feasibility of the motivation of the pattern catalogue. Question III is related to Goal I.

The pattern catalogue research questions are:

- **Q4. Can the proposed catalogue of patterns be helpful during the pattern application?** This question evaluates if the proposed pattern catalogue could potentially solve some of the problems with design patterns, if there are any. Question IV is related to Goal II.

- **Q5. Can the usage of pattern catalogue ease system evolution, in case of (a) the implementation of new or change of the existing functionality and (b) evaluation whether an applied pattern becomes outdated due to the requirement change?** This question evaluates the use of the catalogue for two scenarios: Implementation of the new functionality, and modification of the existing functionality on the example of estimation if a pattern becomes outdated in a course of changes or not. Question V is related to Goals III and IV.

- **Q6. Are the catalogue questions understandable to persons who were not involved into the catalogue development and do they reflect the pattern intent?** This question evaluates if the catalogue questions actually characterise the pattern and if the questions can be understood by the persons, who did not participate in the catalogue creation. The understandability of the questions to the external users is an important point, since the questions are generic enough to be reused between different projects, but they also need to be well understood to be translated into the project's context. Question VI is related to Goals V and VI.

6.4.2. Research Method

This section describes the applied research method. The research method is a survey, as defined by Definition 6.1. The aim of the survey is to develop generalized conclusions about the AM3D approach motivation and its potential usage.

Definition 6.1 Survey [175] from [176]

A survey is a system for collecting information from or about people to describe, compare or explain their knowledge, attitudes and behaviour. The primary means of gathering qualitative or quantitative data are interviews or questionnaires.

For the evaluation of the AM3D approach, we chose structured interview (see Definition 6.2) as a method of gathering the data in the survey.

Definition 6.2 Structured Interviews [176]

A structured interview is a quantitative research method, which ensures that each interview consists of exactly the same questions.

Though the structured interviews are typically a quantitative research method, they can be also used for the qualitative evaluations [176]. Thus, we have used structures interviews to perform the qualitative evaluation of the defined research questions.

The structured interviews were held with the help of a developed questionnaire, as in [177]. The questionnaire was available in two forms – as an online document in Google Docs, and as an offline Word document. The questionnaire can be found in Appendix A of this thesis.

As mentioned by Wohlin [176], the surveys may be tedious for respondents to fill out, and the data quality may consequently decline. However, the goal is to provide a broad overview, and not a detailed matter understanding [176].

6.4.3. Survey Design

This section provides details on the survey design. It describes the survey context, object and subjects of the survey, and the survey materials – questionnaire.

6.4.3.1. Survey Context, Object and Subjects

The survey took part during a three week period, in which the invitations to participate in the survey were distributed, and the replies were collected.

The survey object is the questionnaire with general questions about the pattern application, and specific questions about the AM3D pattern catalogue and its question annotations, as well as with questions collecting the information about participants. The questionnaire is described in detail in the following Section 6.4.3.2.

The subjects of the survey were software engineers, software architects and doctoral researchers (doctoral researchers). The analysis of the data collected during the survey resulted in an approximately equal distribution between participants having an industrial and academia experience

In particular, developers from andrena objects AG and developers from Wincor Nixdorf AG were asked to participate. Other ways of promoting the survey included SDQ mailing list, Facebook and VKontakte announcements. The participation was anonymous; therefore, there is no information on which of the ways was the most efficient.

While some of the participants from academia knew the authors personally, the participants from industry did not. Nevertheless, as survey was anonymous, fair replies are assumed. This threat to validity is discussed in Section 6.4.6.

6.4.3.2. Survey Materials: Questionnaire

As mentioned above, a questionnaire was developed following Punch [177] to support the structured interviews. The questionnaire was available online as a Google Docs form, and offline as a Word document. The questionnaire can be found in Appendix A of this thesis.

The questionnaire consists of four parts and an introduction. Most of the questions are multiple choice and check-box questions, with a few free-text questions. The questions in the questionnaire are only one of the possibilities to investigate the earlier defined research questions. However, these questions seemed more appropriate for the target audience of survey. They define a perspective on the survey. The questions were reviewed and tested by two people each, as described in the following Section 6.4.4.

In the introduction, information on the proposed approach was provided, together with the survey goal and instructions on how to fill in the questionnaire. The purpose of the introduction was to clarify the goals of the survey, to explain the approach in focus and to instruct the participants on data safety and anonymity.

In the first part of the questionnaire, the participants were pre-screened on their knowledge of patterns. It focuses on the investigation of the general research questions of the survey. The second part is divided into the sections dedicated to the three sample AM3D catalogue patterns and five question annotations to each. Due to the time constraint, only three catalogue entries could be included into the survey.

The included patterns were Model View Controller, Fat Client and Single Table Inheritance. They were intentionally selected to be different on their level of renomination and specificity to provide a better demonstration of the AM3D catalogue. The Model View Controller pattern is expected to be well known to the participants. In this case, the participants were able to evaluate if the question annotations of the AM3D pattern catalogue match with the perception and understanding of the pattern. The Fat Client pattern is less known, however, it is easy to understand. In this case, the participants have a chance to rely on their knowledge and common understanding of the topic. The Single Table Inheritance pattern is usually rather unknown, and few of the participants were expected to be aware of it and its details. In this case, the participants were expected to rely solely on understanding of the question annotations and on their software engineering knowledge. Such different patterns were selected with the goal to provide a simulation of three various scenarios for the usage of the catalogue.

A question to check if the pattern is known to the participant was included into the questionnaire, together with the questions to evaluate catalogue question annotations on their relevance and clarity. The participants had four options to evaluate the catalogue questions: Relevant, somewhat relevant, irrelevant or unclear, and an option "I don't know", if they did not know if the feature captured in the question belongs to the pattern. The "I don't know" answer option is, in fact, important, as it prevents the participants from a random selection of some other answer option, and thus, it increases the reliability of the results. An example was provided to assure that the participants understand how to reply to the questions.

In the third part, questions to evaluate if the proposed catalogue of patterns could be helpful during the pattern application from the participants perspectives were asked. The participants were also asked to evaluate potential usefulness of the catalogue for two given evolution scenarios. The first scenario was the implementation of the new functionality with the help of a pattern. The second scenario was modification of the existing functionality on the example of estimation if a pattern becomes outdated because of requirements changes.

Finally, in the fourth part, the questions concerning the background of the participants were asked, e.g. about education and practical experience. The questionnaires took about 20 minutes to complete.

6.4.4. Testing the Method

The pattern catalogue entries underwent a review process by two external reviewers. To test the survey, reviews of the questionnaire and test interviews were organized. The review of questionnaire was performed by two external persons. The first reviewer was an expert in the research method, and the second reviewer was a doctoral researcher in the computer science area. The test interviews were performed with two computer science doctoral researchers. The questionnaire was improved first based on the review results, and then based on the results from the test interviews.

In addition, a feedback was collected while performing the survey to be used during the data evaluation and for the further experiment development.

6.4.5. Survey Results

This section presents the results of the survey aligned to the research questions formulated in Section 6.4.1. The results summarize the data from the 25 valid questionnaires that were collected during the survey.

First, the outline removal is described in Section 6.4.5.1, followed by the information about the participants in Section 6.4.5.2. The data on general research questions about patterns is presented in Section 6.4.5.3, and the data on the pattern catalogue research questions is presented in Section 6.4.5.4. Feedback and analysis of other questions is provided in Section 6.4.5.5. Threats to validity are discussed in Section 6.4.6. Finally, Section 6.4.7 concludes the survey description.

6.4.5.1. Data Validation and Outlier Removal

Some of the questionnaires were removed before the data analysis, since they were incomplete (abandoned before the questionnaire was completed). In the next step, the data in the questionnaires was analysed and one more of the questionnaires had to be removed from the data set, due to the unserious answers provided to it. At the end, a set of 25 valid questionnaires were left and used for the data analysis.

6.4.5.2. Background of the Participants

The questionnaires were distributed between people with different levels of experience and academic background, but all of the participants were related to software engineering in their occupation. Table 6.6 displays the data summary about the survey participants.

From the table it follows that 24% of the survey participants stated to be employed solely in industry, 28% in industry and academia mixed, and 48% were involved in academia.

About 40% have worked in industry for about one to five years, 20% participated in industrial projects, 12% have worked in industry for more than five years, 8% worked in industry for less than one year, and 16% had industrial practice during their studies. None of the participants selected the option "No experience". One participant selected "Other", and stated to "programmed over 7 years within a small project as a side job", and to have participated in a practice during the studies.

This data shows balanced proportions between industry and academic participants, all having industrial experience. The comparison of opinions of three persons with over five years of experience and of participants who collected their doing a practice during their studies is of particular interest,

1. Industrial experience	**#**	**%**
I have worked in industry for about 1 – 5 years	10	40
I participated in industrial projects	5	20
Practice during my studies	4	16
I have worked in industry for more than 5 years	3	12
I have worked in industry for about a year	2	8
No experience	0	0
Other	1	4
2. Current academic degree	**#**	**%**
Graduate (Master /Diplom)	17	68
Doctoral researchers	4	16
Graduate (Bachelor)	3	12
Other	1	4
Undergraduate	0	0
No academic degree	0	0
3. Occupation	**#**	**%**
Doctoral researcher	8	32
Both academia and industry mixed	7	28
Industry	6	24
Student	3	12
Post-Doctoral researcher	1	4
Research division of a company	0	0
Professor	0	0

Table 6.6.: Information about Survey Participants

as these are two extremities in the industrial experience. The amount of the questionnaires is not sufficient to draw statistically significant conclusions, however, they provide valuable insight on their opinions and give directions to the main validation experiment described in Section 6.5.

The most common academic degree was graduate (master or diploma) in 68% of cases, 16% held a doctoral degree, 12% held a Bachelor degree, and one participant selected "Other"as the degree mentioning to have almost completed the Diploma graduate degree. This data means that all of the participants must have received at least a theoretical training in architectural design pattern , and are familiar with the survey main topic.

Table 6.7 provides data on the amount of the experience in applying the design patterns of the survey participants. About 40% of the participants applied design patterns from time to time during their work. About 24%

Experience	#	%
Very low (I have not applied any)	0	0
Low (I have applied patterns during one or two test or study projects)	6	24
Medium (From time to time I am applying patterns during my work)	10	40
High (I am regularly applying design patterns)	6	24
Very high (My work is connected to design patterns, I am proficient in application of design patterns, I regularly apply design pattern from different domains)	3	12

Table 6.7.: Experience in Applying Design Patterns

applied patterns regularly and in 12% of the cases, the participants stated to be proficient in application of design patterns and to regularly apply design pattern from different domains. Thus, the majority of the participants had real experience in design pattern application and their opinion can be considered particularly valuable for the goals of the evaluation. Another target group is participants who have applied patterns during one or two test or study projects (24%). These participants might profit the most from the AM3D pattern catalogue, as do not apply pattern on a regular basis and are more likely to forget the precise specification of a design pattern.

6.4.5.3. General Research Questions About Patterns

The data connected to the general research questions about design patterns is analysed in this section. The section is structured according to the research questions:

- **Q1. Are patterns used in practice, and to what extent?**

  The majority of the participants stated to apply design patterns at least from time to time in their work, and many apply patterns regularly, as well, as also 12% of the participants apply design patterns very often (see Table 6.7). A number of regularly used design patterns is rather low – it is about 14 patterns on average per participant. Despite the moderate number of survey participants, this is an interesting data indicating that the design patterns are used on practice.

However, these numbers cannot be fully anticipated, as some of the participants stated to have high experience in design pattern application, but apply regularly relatively few patterns (about 10). While some of the participants stated to have medium experience, but have regularly applied more than 20 design patterns. Clearly, self perception is highly subjective. However, this data can be also interpreted in terms of a security feeling during the design pattern application.

No definite conclusion about the connection between participant's education degree or occupation and the extend of design pattern application could be drawn from the data, besides that the student participants and the participants with the bachelor degrees have low experience in applying design patterns and have applied only few of them. This means that the amount of practical experience during the studies is rather low and that the main experience in design pattern application is collected during the employment, both in academia and in industry. All of the participants with a year and more of industrial experience stated that they at least apply design patterns from time to time during their work. And two of three participants with more than five years of experience apply patterns very often during their work.

From this data, the conclusion is drawn that the design patterns are commonly applied in practice, and that the participants are mostly experienced with the pattern application.

- **Q2. What is the attitude towards patterns, are they considered worthwhile and helpful?**

  As provided in the Table 6.8, none of the participants discarded the idea of patterns and only one participant considered the usefulness of patterns for better quality of software (e.g., maintainability, non-functional properties, extendibility) as low. In general, design patterns are estimated as highly useful by 40% of the participants and as absolutely useful (very high) by 28% of them. About 28% consider patterns as average useful for the software quality.

Usefulness	#	%
Very low	0	0
Low	1	4
Medium	7	28
High	10	40
Very high	7	28

Table 6.8.: Usefulness of Design Patterns for Quality of Software

Hereby, four from six participants occupied in industry specified that the design patterns are absolutely useful, while students were moderately convinced in the usefulness of the design pattern application. Interestingly, the only low consideration came from the participant occupied in research. No other definite conclusions about the connection between participants' education degrees, ages of experience or occupation and the attitude towards design patterns could be drawn from the data. The general attitude towards the design patterns can be summarized as positive or even as highly positive.

- **Q3. Are there any problems with application or documentation of patterns?**

  This question was inspired by an empirical study by Vocac et al. [32], uncovering pattern application problems. Our results on this question are provided in the first section of Table 6.9.

  Only two participants have not encountered any problems while applying or working with design patterns. However, almost half of the participants (44%) have not witnessed any inappropriate use or documentation of pattern in the projects they have worked in. From whom, however, only one of the participants had no problem with pattern application personally. This interesting result may be explained by two factors. First, pattern application is not obvious, and

Problems with Application (multiple choice)	#	%
Yes, I was unsure which pattern (of several appropriate patterns I knew) was the most suitable for the problem	15	60
Yes, I did not know which pattern could be used to solve my problem	13	52
Yes, the implementation of the pattern was unclear	9	36
Yes, the structure of the pattern was unclear	7	28
Yes, it happened to me to overlook some properties of a pattern or some consequences of a pattern application and then to discover that the choice was non optimal	6	24
Yes, while modifying the system or code I have not noticed that there was a pattern applied, and modified its structure	5	20
No, never	2	8
Other	1	4
Problems with Maintenance	**#**	**%**
Yes	13	52
No	11	44
Other	1	4

Table 6.9.: Problems with Application, Documentation or Maintenance of Design Patterns

can be easily overseen unless it is explicitly documented. Second, the participants may have had higher trust in the pattern application by other persons, as compared to their own pattern application. Considering that the majority of the participants had some problems with pattern application personally, most probably, also other pattern applicants were similarly troubled. In addition, people with longer industrial experience seem more likely to have experienced problems with the patterns application and documentation. This corresponds to the previous observation that the employed persons are more likely to practically apply design patterns then the students.

The variety of problem types is rather large. The majority of the participants (60%) had experienced problems to decide which pattern (of several appropriate patterns known) was the most suitable for the given problem. About 52% of them did not know which pattern may be suitable to solve their problem. The structure and the implementation of the pattern were unclear to 36% and to 28% of the participants. About 24% of the participants happened to overlook some properties or consequences of a pattern application, and then to discovered that the choice was non optimal. About 20% of the participants have not noticed that there was a pattern applied, while modifying the system or code, and have occasionally modified its structure. One of the participants had problems using the pre-existing pattern in an API. Even participants with large experience had problems to select one of the similar patterns they knew, or to find a pattern suitable to solve the problem.

Moreover, the participants provided an estimation that the inappropriate use of patterns was encountered by them in 40% percent of projects and inappropriate documentation in 54% of the projects.

This data shows that despite of numerous related work and tools, the problems with pattern selection and application are not yet eliminated in practice and there are still problems with pattern application that the majority of the engineers meet. This observation is most probably valid also for other design techniques, since they are usually highly vulnerable to the subject's experience with design in general.

The classification of mentioned reasons for the encountered problems with the pattern application is presented in Table 6.10.

Reasons (multiple choice)	**#**	**%**
... few experience with patterns	16	64
... insufficient understanding of requirements to the system	6	24
Other	2	8
No problems	2	8
... low experience in programming in general	1	4

Table 6.10.: Reasons for the Problems with Pattern Application

Little experience with patterns was the main reason for the encountered problems named by 62% of the participants, while 24% named insufficient understanding of requirements to the system. This is a remarkable finding, as according to the information the participants have provided on their background, all of the participants were experienced engineers. It seems that one cannot conclude the experience with patterns from the general experience. Additionally, two participants named an existing pattern API implementation and insufficient documentation as reasons (comments to the option “Other”).

The participants had a possibility to provide free-text comments on the topic. Part of the comments was concerned with the quality of teaching of the design patterns at universities. For example[2], “In education, there is too few time spent on teaching and especially on applying patterns, although it is very important. In the lecture it was said, that you must practice it at home. It should be more in the focus on mandatory exercises.”, “At university and also in literature, one only learns the theory of patterns and a selection of patterns. Yet, it takes much more time and *practice* to get the necessary know-how for everyday work.”, “Not enough real world examples in handbooks/lectures. It would be useful to show a problem solved with a pattern and without it, in order to learn the advantages of pattern use.” and “large amount of patterns, unclear how to implement, few training during studies”.

Some other comments were[3]: “Experience in abstract reasoning about design and architecture is hard to obtain”, “”Some patterns are mainstream knowledge and therefore easy to apply because you have often seen them and were taught often in different lectures”, “large amount of known patterns, interesting application domains of different patterns, different interpretations of the same pattern by different persons”, “depends on the difficulty and complexity of the pattern especially if several patterns are mixed”, and “I only apply

[2] Some of these comments are translated from German into English

[3] Some of these comments are translated from German into English

patterns with which I'm already familiar with. I almost never search for unknown patterns to solve a problem I encounter. I think the appliance of patterns should be encouraged in projects and the developers trained. An application of a pattern should be documented properly. Especially if it is a rather unknown and complex pattern". These are interesting insights into the pattern application problems. All of them can be generalized to the need to improve practical education on design patterns.

To summarise, the results are: The knowledge on patterns and on documentation of patterns remains a big problem in development projects. It is assumed that the inappropriate documentation of patterns can be one of the major contributors to the resulted high percent of problems with the maintenance connected to the patterns.

6.4.5.4. Pattern Catalogue Research Questions

The data connected to the pattern-specific research questions is analysed in this section. The section is structured according to the research questions:

- **Q4. Can the proposed catalogue of patterns be helpful during the pattern application?**

  The results of the survey to this question are listed in the Table 6.11.

Usage scenario (multiple choice)	#	%
It might help clarifying properties and consequences of a pattern	17	68
It might help to select the most suitable pattern between several candidate patterns	15	60
It might solve documentation problem, if answers to the questions are automatically documented	14	56
It might help to find a pattern that the person does not know	13	52
It might help to better apply a pattern, through explicit hits to the pattern's structure or implementation	11	44
It will not solve any problems connected to the pattern application	2	8
Other	2	8

Table 6.11.: Potential Use of the Pattern Catalogue

The majority of the participants (68%) indeed believe that such a pattern catalogue with questions to patterns might help to clarify properties and consequences of a pattern, and 56% supported that it might solve documentation problems, if answers to the questions are automatically documented. About 60% of the participants believe that the pattern catalogue might also help to select the most suitable pattern between several candidate patterns, thus supporting the evaluation of the pattern candidates.

This is an encouraging result, supporting the motivation of the AM3D approach, as one of the goals of the survey evaluation. Only two participants remained sceptical and said that the catalogue will not solve any problems connected to the pattern application. These participants also selected "Low improvement" for the usefulness of the AM3D pattern catalogue in both of the evolution scenarios. One of these participants is employed as a doctoral researcher, and another in a combination of academic research and industry. However, in general, no definite conclusion about the connection between participants' education degrees or occupations and their views on the pattern catalogue usage could be done.

An interesting point is, that although the proposed catalogue is not intended to be used as an expert system, 52% of the participants believe that the pattern catalogue could be used to find a pattern that the person does not know, which is a task of expert systems.

Based on the obtained answers, the focus of the second empirical study (described in Section 6.5) was laid on the validation of the here top-mentioned expected benefits: Clarification of properties and consequences of a pattern, selection of the most suitable pattern between several candidate patterns and documentation of pattern application together with the rationale, based on answers to the questions.

- **Q5. Can the usage of pattern catalogue ease system evolution, in case of (a) the implementation of new or change of the existing functionality and (b) decision whether an applied pattern is outdated or not due to the requirement change?**

  The participants were asked to estimate two given evolution scenarios considering usefulness of the AM3D pattern catalogue to support them. In particular, they were asked to estimate to what degree such a catalogue of patterns with questions could improve software evolution if the requirements have changed or a new functionality would need to be added. Clearly, a quantitative answer cannot be given without a concrete project. However, the goal of the survey was to elicit opinions for the further research and validation directions, and not to statistically validate the AM3D approach.

  The proposed condition for the evaluation tasks was that the system was previously developed following the AM3D approach. Thus, the questions for the patterns and provided answers to the question annotations were documented in an accessible form together with the applied patterns. The results are summarised in Table 6.12.

Task A. Finding a location to change functionality	#	%
Low (No improvement)	9	36
Medium (Some improvement)	13	52
High (Noticeable Improvement)	3	12
Task B. Deciding whether an applied pattern is outdated due to the requirement changes	**#**	**%**
Low (No improvement)	3	12
Medium (Some improvement)	12	48
High (Noticeable Improvement)	10	40

Table 6.12.: Potential Use of the Pattern Catalogue in Evolution

For the Task A "Find a location where functionality needs to be changed" (the first section of the Table), 36% of the participants supposed that the catalogue would bring no improvement (9 participants, three from whom were employed in academia and industry, and one solely in academia, thus about 44% actively present in industry). Some improvement was expected by 52% participants (13 participants, four of whom were employed in industry, and three in academia and industry, thus about 62% actively present in industry), and only 12% of the participants expected some noticeable improvement. No definite conclusion about the connection between participants' education degrees or occupations and their views on the pattern catalogue usage in evolution could be done.

For the Task B "Decide whether an applied pattern is outdated or not due to the requirement change" (the second section of the Table), the participants were rather positive and about 40% of them expected the AM3D catalogue to bring a noticeable improvement (30% of participants are employed in industry or related), and about 48% of the participants (67% of whom are employed in industry or related) expected at least some improvement. This time, only 12% of the participants expected no improvement at all (all of the participants employed in industry or related). Here, the observation is that the participants from academia tended to estimate the catalogue improvement higher than the participants from the industry. This observation can be disputed from two points of view. The first one, is that the participants from industry have more of the practice-related experience and tend to better realise the real needs of the projects. The second view is that the participants from industry might not value the documentation of design and investments into its update, since it does not directly contribute to the project's value (so-called "Waste" concept).

Thus, according to the participants, the main benefit of the AM3D approach during the evolution can be expected from the pattern decision documentation, e.g. to detect outdated pattern decisions.

- **Q6. Are the catalogue questions understandable to persons who were not involved in the catalogue development and do they reflect the pattern intent?**

  This research question was evaluated on three sample catalogue patterns, that gradually varied in their complexity and usage. The familiarity of sample design patterns to the participants is summarised in Table 6.12.

Model View Controller	#	%
No	0	0
Somewhat (I have read about it)	7	28
Yes (I have applied it several times)	18	72
Fat Client	#	%
No	3	12
Somewhat (I have read about it)	12	48
Yes (I have applied it several times)	10	40
Single Table Inheritance	#	%
No	10	40
Somewhat (I have read about it)	11	44
Yes (I have applied it several times)	4	16

Table 6.13.: Familiarity with Sample Patterns

While the majority not only knew about the Model View Controller pattern, but had also applied it on practice several times, the Fat Client pattern was lesser known and was less applied. The Single Table Inheritance pattern was even lesser known, as was assumed, as only four participants have applied it directly.

This information is taken into account while evaluating the understandability and correctness of the AM3D pattern catalogue questions. While the understandability of question annotations can be evaluated by all participants, the correctness of pattern question annotations may be evaluated only by those, who have applied the patterns in question on practice or at least know about them. The results to the question annotations understandability are presented in the Table 6.14, in accordance to the above mentioned distinction. Values marked with "*" in the table are calculated for all of the participants.

For all of the above mentioned patterns, the understandability was evaluated as high. So, for the Model View Controller pattern, the understandability of questions was between zero and one fails, besides the factor number four, which was not understood by four of the participants. The understandability is even better for the Fat Client pattern, where only last two questions had received each one negative score. For the Single Table Inheritance, the understandability is in average 93%, whereby the question number two having six negative scores. Such overall high understandability can be explained through the careful review process, which pattern question annotations underwent before the survey. Even participants who were not familiar with patterns could understand the questions, according to the answers they have provided. This data shows good understandability of the questions for the participants, who have never seen the catalogue questions before.

Further on, the collected data lets to evaluate how the participants estimated the relevance of the question annotations, taking into the account how well the participants were familiar with the patterns.

For the Model View Controller pattern, question number five was evaluated as either "irrelevant" or " somewhat relevant", even by the participants with experience who were familiar with the pattern. However, this question actually describes a serious drawback of the pattern, which can have a significant negative influence on the performance quality attribute (a potential quality influence).

The question two describes another potential negative consequence of the pattern application and is also negatively evaluated. For the Fat Client, the data shows similar results. Questions (four and five) describing potential negative consequences for maintainability and performance were evaluated as low relevant. For the Single Table Inheritance, question number three, describing the potential negative extendibility influence, was rated as irrelevant. Other questions, however, were evaluated to be relevant or somewhat relevant.

Pattern	Factors					
Model View Controller	**1**	**2**	**3**	**4**	**5**	
Irrelevant	1	10	3	3	15	#
	4	40	12	12	60	%
Somewhat relevant	3	5	13	11	4	#
	12	20	52	44	16	%
Relevant	21	4	6	8	2	#
	84	16	24	32	8	%
I don't know	0	2	3	2	3	#
	0	8	12	8	12	%
I haven't understood the factor*	0	4	0	1	1	#
	0	16	0	4	4	%
Fat Client	**1**	**2**	**3**	**4**	**5**	
Irrelevant	1	3	0	10	1	#
	5	14	0	45	5	%
Somewhat relevant	2	6	4	6	14	#
	9	27	18	27	64	%
Relevant	19	11	18	2	5	#
	86	50	82	9	23	%
I don't know	0	2	0	3	1	#
	0	9	0	14	5	%
I haven't understood the factor*	0	0	0	1	1	#
	0	0	0	4	4	%
Single Table Inheritance	**1**	**2**	**3**	**4**	**5**	
Irrelevant	1	2	6	3	2	#
	7	13	40	20	13	%
Somewhat relevant	0	4	5	4	4	#
	0	27	33	27	27	%
Relevant	13	1	1	4	5	#
	87	7	7	27	33	%
I don't know	0	5	3	4	4	#
	0	33	20	27	27	%
I haven't understood the factor*	1	6	0	0	2	#
	4	24	0	0	8	%

Table 6.14.: Understandability of Questions to Patterns (* for All Participants)

The following conclusion can be drawn from the obtained samples (further validation is, however, required): The evaluation of pattern questions follows two trends. First, the more well-known the pattern is, the higher seem to be the perception of its general positive influence on the system. Hereby, the potential negative consequences of a pattern seem to be discarded and considered as low relevant. Second, the less pattern is known, the more persons rely on the expert knowledge provided in the catalogue, and are more eager to accept potential negative properties of a pattern. Of course, only three sample patterns available for the evaluation, and the amount of data points is not significant. This conclusion clearly requires further validation.

The participants were also asked to provide information on potentially under-represented pattern qualities described by the questions. As a result, three participants provided comments for each, the Model View Controller and for the Fat Client patterns. Interestingly, the factors provided by the participants were also formulated as questions.

To summarize, the understandability of the questions to the sample pattern has shown to be high by the persons who were not participating in the creation of the catalogue. The perception of the relevance of the question annotations seem to depend on how self-confident the person is, but in general, the potential negative influence of patterns seems to be neglected.

6.4.5.5. Feedback

The participants were asked to provide feedback on the suitability of the questionnaire for the goals of the survey, and, if desired, to provide comments and suggestions.

Only two of the participants commented on this question. Both of them stated that they did not know, if the questionnaire was suitable or not. These few comments can be considered a result of the mistake in the questionnaire design, because the question was marked as optional. The participants probably did not take time to think on the topic, especially, as this question was the last in the questionnaire.

6.4.6. Threats to Validity, Limitations of the Evaluation

This section provides discussion on threats to validity, divided into internal and external validity. For the description of threats to validity we use the classification by Yin [178] via Wohlin [176], and the definitions of types of threats by Wohlin [176].

According to them, there are four types of validity: Construct validity, internal validity, external validity, and reliability. The construct validity reflects to what extent the operational measures that are studied really represent what the researcher has in mind and what is investigated according to the research questions 6.3. Internal validity reflects if causal relations are examined 6.4. External validity is concerned with to what extent it is possible to generalize the findings, and to what extent the findings are of interest to other people outside the investigated case 6.5. Finally, reliability is concerned with to what extent the data and the analysis are dependent on the specific researchers 6.6.

Definition 6.3 Construct Validity [176, 178]

Construct validity reflects to what extent the operational measures that are studied really represent what the researcher has in mind and what is investigated according to the research questions.

Definition 6.4 Internal Validity [176, 178]

Internal validity reflects if causal relations are examined. When the researcher is investigating whether one factor affects an investigated factor there is a risk that the investigated factor is also affected by a third factor.

Definition 6.5 External Validity [176, 178]

External validity is concerned with to what extent it is possible to generalize the findings, and to what extent the findings are of interest to other people outside the investigated case. During analysis of external validity, the researcher tries to analyse to what extent the findings are of relevance for other cases.

Definition 6.6 Reliability Validity [176, 178]

Reliability is concerned with to what extent the data and the analysis are dependent on the specific researchers. Hypothetically, if another researcher later on conducted the same study, the result should be the same.

The next sections deal with the above mentioned threats to validity types for the conducted survey evaluation.

6.4.6.1. Construct Validity

The participants were aware of the topic of the survey and it might have influenced their answers. They could have become more sensitive to the problems with pattern application and documentation. It is a natural threat and is common to surveys and experiments involving humans as subjects.

The participants, obviously, could have also guessed the desired outcome of the survey, and modified their answers in accordance to their attitude to the survey. However, the participants took part in the survey on their free will, and thus should have not had any significant predisposition about the survey. Part of the participants from academia personally knew the survey authors. However, the survey was anonymous and fair replies are assumed (the participants were explicitly asked to be objective).

Some participants might have "improved" their stated experience with the design pattern application, in order to look more professional. The perception of own experience is usually rather subjective. This is a common threat, and one can only rely on honesty of the provided data.

6.4.6.2. Internal Validity

The main survey was held in August. It clearly influenced the number of the participants in the survey. It might have also influenced the results of the survey, since it was a vacation time in Germany and the participants might have been not completely concentrated on the survey. Once again, since the participation was voluntary, we assume that only the motivated participants took part in it.

The survey used three sample patterns from the AM3D pattern catalogue. The number and the selection of these design patterns for the survey might have influenced the results. In order to minimize this threat, the sample patterns were selected from different domains and with different levels of complexity and renomination. Although the survey indicates potential usefulness of the approach for the pattern applicability and documentation of pattern application, an empirical study with more AM3D catalogue entries is required to validate if the catalogue questions and answers to these questions indeed ease the system evolution.

The questions in the survey were formulated in a natural language. A common problem is that the questions might be misinterpreted or become so-called leading questions. To minimize this threat, the survey design was relied on recommendations of acknowledged literature on empirical research, such as [177]. The participants had a possibility to select "I don't know" option where appropriate to avoid being lead by a question. Finally, a survey review was held also by an expert in the research method and the recommendations were implemented.

The selection of the participants, who have participated in the survey, might have influenced the results. However, the selection was accidental (based on their own will). It might have been influenced through the choice of mailing lists and companies, where the questionnaires were distributed. However, we did not really had choice, as only few companies are ready to spend time of their engineers on participation in a survey. Similarly, not every mailing list can be used to distribute the invitations with a confidence to get serious and trustworthy replies.

Several participants did drop out from the survey (did not complete the survey). All this data points were removed.

6.4.6.3. External Validity

The data of the survey is based on the opinion of 25 participants, and therefore reflects their opinions on design patterns, the proposed AM3D pattern catalogue and the questions. This perception does not necessarily reflect the actual situation with design patters in the projects.

Answers to the questions in the questionnaire are subjective and reflect personal opinions. For example, even if the experience with design patterns is stated to be high, it does not mean that the experience of two participants can be compared between each other.

Part of the participants from academia personally knew the survey author. However, the survey was anonymous and fair replies are assumed.

The survey was conducted on a sample selection from the catalogue, presented in a form suitable for the survey. The participants might have replied differently, if they had a real instance of the AM3D catalogue at hand. Unfortunately, it was not possible due to the strict time constraints.

The amount of the participants is not enough to draw statistically significant conclusions. Moreover, as stated above, the survey does not substitute an empirical study for the AM3D catalogue's validation. Nevertheless, the survey results provide a valuable indication on the potential usefulness of such a catalogue.

6.4.6.4. Reliability and Conclusion Validity

The data sample is too small to make any definite statements in the evaluation. It, however, reflects the possible trends in the data and clarifies direction for further evaluation.

In general, percentages are not always the appropriate way to present the data. But since the survey statistics is of a descriptive nature, it is acceptable in this case. Reliability of the survey can only be checked with an increased number of participants. Since the questionnaire can be used independently of the survey designers, we would expect the results similar to those we have collected. All the material is available online in a free access and the survey can be repeated any time, by anybody, following the description of the process provided in this thesis.

6.4.7. Summary of the Results

The goals of the survey were (1) to elicit an opinion on design patterns and their application as a check of the feasibility of the motivation of the approach, and (2) to validate the applicability of the proposed pattern catalogue and of the question annotations on example of three sample pattern catalogue entries. These goals were refined into six research goals described in Section 6.4.1.1. All of the evaluation goals were achieved.

Both, academia and industry were represented approximately equally in the survey, with all of the participants having industrial experience. Moreover, all of the participants have received at least a theoretical training in architectural design patterns, and are familiar with the survey main topic.

Based on the survey data, it can be concluded that the design patterns are indeed commonly applied in practice, and that the participants are mostly experienced with the pattern application. The attitude towards design pattern was shown to be positive, as only one of the 25 participants considered patterns as not useful to improve the quality of software (e.g., maintainability, non-functional properties, extendeability).

Most of the participants (90%) have encountered problems both with the application of patterns in their work and with the already applied patterns, as well as their documentation. Moreover, the participants provided an estimation that the inappropriate use of patterns was encountered by them in 40% percent of projects and inappropriate documentation of patterns in 54% of the projects. Only two of the participants have never faced problems applying patterns, one of whom, however, commented that he/she could not select the right pattern for the design problem he/she has had.

It seems that when patterns are applied by other persons, the participants seem to be more confident in the pattern application and to consider the patterns to be more appropriately applied in such a case, then when they apply patterns themselves. 44% of the participants said to have not witnessed any inappropriate use or documentation of pattern in the projects they have worked in. However, from these 44% only one of the participants had no problem with pattern application personally. Even participants with larger experience had problems to select one of the similar patterns they knew, or to find a pattern suitable to solve the problem.

Little experience with patterns was the major reason for the encountered problems, named by 62% of the participants, while 24% named insufficient understanding of requirements to the system. However, according to the information the participants have provided on their background, all of the participants were experienced software engineers. It seems that one cannot conclude the experience with patterns from the general experience. In addition, participants commented on the need to improve especially practical education on design patterns. These results show that the knowledge of patterns and on documentation of patterns remains a big problem in the development projects despite numerous related work and tool support in the area. This data supports the motivation of the AM3D approach, as there are still open research questions in the area to be solved.

Another goal of the survey was to evaluate the idea of the AM3D pattern catalogue and some of its entries. The catalogue idea was in general perceived positively, with 68% of the participants expecting such a pattern catalogue with question annotations to help clarify properties and consequences of a pattern, and with 56% of the participants expecting it to solve the documentation problems, if answers to the questions are automatically documented. About 60% of the participants also supposed that the AM3D pattern catalogue might help to select the most suitable pattern between several candidates patterns, thus supporting the evaluation of the pattern candidates.

From the evolution tasks, the catalogue was estimated to be useful to clarify which patterns are outdated due to the requirement changes, and only 12% of the participants expected no improvement at all in this area. The AM3D catalogue was estimated to be less useful for the task of finding a location where functionality needs to be changed, with 36% of the participants expecting no improvement in this area.

For all of the sample patterns, the understandability of the questions was estimated as very high. Thus, even people who did not participate in creation of the catalogue do understand the question annotations. Such overall high understandability can be explained through the careful review process, which pattern question annotations had undergone.

The positive opinion on the benefits of the AM3D approach and the high understandability of the question annotations are encouraging results, empirically supporting the main expected benefits of the AM3D approach, as one of the goals of the survey evaluation. Based on the obtained results, the focus of the second empirical study (described in Section 6.5) is laid on the validation of the here top-mentioned expected benefits: Clarification of properties and consequences of a pattern, selection of the most suitable pattern between several candidate patterns and documentation of a pattern application together with the rationale, based on answers to the question annotations in the AM3D catalogue.

Even though the collected data sample is too small to draw statistically significant conclusions and reflects personal opinions of 25 professionals, still the survey provides valuable insights into the situation with the design pattern application and on the potential usefulness of the catalogue.

6.5. Controlled Experiment

This section provides details of the empirical study conducted to validate two of the claimed benefits of the approach. First, it validates if design patterns annotated according to the AM3D approach can be better understood and applied more correctly as compared to the pattern catalogue based on the standard approach. Second, it validates if system architecture documented with the AM3D approach can be better maintained compared to the system documented with the standard approach. The study is based on the controlled experiment, combined with a quantitative research method.

The experiment was executed during a half-year long software development practical course (PSE course) at Karlsruhe Institute of Technology (KIT). The experiment subjects were 20 students enrolled in the course. The feasibility and representability of the students as experiment subjects are discussed later on. The experiment object was a user management system called PSE system, which was used by the students for their implementations during the practical course. The AM3D study was one of three overall experiments conducted during the course, and some of the practical materials and training were shared with other experiment designers.

This section is structured as follows. Section 6.5.1 describes the evaluation goals according to the Goal Question Metric plan. It lists goals, questions to the goals and metrics to measure the goals. Finally, it lists the so derived hypotheses for the empirical study. In Section 6.5.3 we present the design of the empirical study, including the experiment context, object, subjects, experiment process and materials. Section 6.5.4 explains how the research method was tested. Participant information is summarized in Section 6.5.5.2. The results of the experiment are analysed and presented in Section 6.5.5, including information on the participants, description of the statistical method used to analyse the results, and analyses of the research questions. The threats to validity and limitations of the evaluation are discussed in Section 6.5.6. Finally, Section 6.5.7 concludes the survey description.

6.5.1. Research Questions

The goal of the empirical study is to empirically validate if the proposed AM3D pattern catalogue can improve applicability and documentation of design patterns.

First, it tests whether design patterns annotated according to the AM3D approach can be better understood and applied more correctly as compared to the design pattern catalogue based on the standard approach. Second, it tests whether system architecture documented with the AM3D approach can be better maintained compared to the system documented with the standard approach. Hereby, it is evaluated if the effort to use the AM3D pattern catalogue is at least comparable to that to use the standard approach.

To plan the study, a Goal Question Metric plan for the validation was implemented, and is described in detail in the following section.

6.5.1.1. Goals

This section describes the goals of the experiment using the Goal-Question-Metric approach [172], explained in Section 6.3. First, two higher-order goals for the generalized AM3D approach were derived to enable an overview of the validation plan. An overview of the Goal Question Metric plan in the usual Goal Question Metric form is provided in Table 6.15.

The first goal is to empirically validate if the AM3D pattern catalogue can improve applicability and documentation of patterns from the software engineer's or architect's point of view. The second goal is to empirically validate if documented patterns can support maintenance from the soft-

Goal I	
Purpose	Empirically validate
Issue	if the AM3D pattern catalogue can improve applicability and documentation
Object	of patterns
Viewpoint	from the software engineer's or architect's point of view
Goal II	
Purpose	Empirically validate
Issue	if design patterns documented in terms of the AM3D approach can support
Object	maintenance
Viewpoint	from the software engineer's or architect's point of view

Table 6.15.: High-order Goals of the Goal Question Metric Plan for the AM3D Approach

ware engineer's or architect's point of view. These goals are defined for the AM3D approach.

The refinement of the general Goal Question Metric goals of the validation is presented in Table 6.16. The refinement details the high-level goals. It also adds a third cross-cutting goal related to the potential overhead cause by the approach throughout design and maintenance (relevant for both previous goals). In the following these goals are explained in detail:

- **Goal I:** The first goal is to empirically validate the more appropriate applicability of annotated patterns from the software engineer's or architect's point of view compared to regular pattern catalogue. The AM3D approach claims that question annotations support evaluation of design solutions for a specific problem. The first validation goal targets this claim. If users of a catalogue with patterns annotated with such questions make more correct choices of the patterns than users of a standard catalogue, the question annotations are helpful for the pattern evaluation and lead to less mistakes during the design phase.

- **Goal II:** The second goal is to empirically validate the positive impact of the better documented patterns on the software evolution (list tasks) from the software engineer's or architect's point of view.

Goal I	
Purpose	Empirically validate
Issue	the more appropriate applicability
Object	of annotated patterns
Viewpoint	from the software engineer's or architect's point of view
Comp. obj.	compared to regular pattern catalogue
Goal II	
Purpose	Empirically validate
Issue	the positive impact of the better documented patterns
Object	on the software evolution (list tasks)
Viewpoint	from the software engineer's or architect's point of view
Goal III	
Purpose	Empirically validate
Issue	no significant additional overhead caused by
Object	the semi-automatic documentation of the appropriate application of annotated patterns
Viewpoint	from the software engineer's or architect's point of view

Table 6.16.: Detailed Goals of the GQM Plan of the Experiment for the Annotated Design Pattern Catalogue

The AM3D approach claims that a decision to use a pattern can be semi-automatically documented with the help of answers provided to question annotations, and this documentation can be than used to re-evaluate decisions in face of changes during system evolution. Thus, the maintainers of the system documented using the AM3D approach have can more accurately evaluate if the used pattern is still optimal for the specific problem, than the maintainers of a system documented with the standard approach.

- **Goal III:** The third goal is to empirically validate that no significant additional overhead is caused by the semi-automatic documentation of the application of annotated patterns from the software engineer's or architect's point of view. This goal has a similar idea to that of the Type III evaluation type (quantitative cost-benefit evaluation). Here the usage of the approach for the solution of the task is qualitatively evaluated during the experiment.

The next step of the Goal Question Metric approach is to derive the research questions to the defined goals. These questions are listed in the Section 6.5.1.2.

6.5.1.2. Questions and Metrics

The following research questions were formulated to follow on the the goals of the experiment validation:

- **QI. Can annotated patterns be more appropriately selected and re-evaluated if documented with the proposed approach than without it?**

  This question evaluates if there is a difference in common usage scenarios of design patterns of the approaches for cases described by questions II and III (for design and for maintenance). Question I is related to Goals I and II.

- **QII. Can annotated patterns be more appropriately selected if documented with the proposed approach than without it?**

  This question validates the suitability of a limited pre-selected choice of pattern solutions though the catalogue questions. Its goal is to measure the influence of the annotation of patterns with questions on the pattern selection. This validation is based on the question annotations to the patterns stored with each pattern in the AM3D catalogue. Question II is related to Goal I.

- **QIII. Can the outdated patterns (decisions to use a pattern) be more easily found if documented with the proposed approach than without it?**

  This question validates the re-evaluation of saved outdated patterns though the catalogue questions. Its goal is to measure the influence of the annotation of patterns on recovering the rationale of the decisions to use these patterns. Question III is related to Goal II.

Question	Metric
Question I (Quantitative)	
Can annotated patterns be more appropriately selected and re-evaluated if documented with the proposed approach than without it?	Metric 1.1 Number of correct patterns Metric 1.2 Number of incorrect patterns Metric 1.3 Number of undecided
Question II (Quantitative)	
Can annotated patterns be more appropriately selected if documented with the proposed approach than without it?	Metric 2.1 Number of correct patterns Metric 2.2 Number of incorrect patterns Metric 2.3 Number of undecided
Question III (Quantitative)	
Can the outdated patterns (decisions to use a pattern) be more easily found if documented with the proposed approach than without it?	Metric 3.1 Number of correct patterns Metric 3.2 Number of incorrect patterns Metric 3.3 Number of undecided
Question IV (Qualitative)	
Is the annotated pattern catalogue easier to use as compared to the standard design pattern catalogue?	Metric 4.1 Easiness to select a pattern measured on a 4 point scale Metric 4.2 Easiness to re-evaluate a pattern measured on a 4 point scale Metric 4.3 Usability of the catalogue to select a pattern measured on a 6 point scale Metric 4.4 Usability of the catalogue to re-evaluate a pattern measured on a 6 point scale

Table 6.17.: Summary of Questions and Corresponding Metrics

- **QIV. Is the annotated pattern catalogue easier to use as compared to the standard design pattern catalogue?**

  This question evaluates if there is a difference in usability of the approaches for cases described by questions I, II and III (for design and for the maintenance). Question IV is related to Goal IV.

For each of these questions, metrics are defined in order to be able to measure the goal achievement. The metrics are summarized in Table 6.17. For questions I, II and III the number of cases where patterns were selected correctly, the number of cases where patterns were selected incorrectly, and the number of cases where a pattern could not be selected is measured. These metrics are quantitative. For the question IV anticipated easiness of catalogue usage on a four-point scale, and the usability of the catalogue to perform the tasks on a six-point scale for both of the cases is measured.

6.5.1.3. The Experiment Hypotheses

In order to be able to evaluate the data collected for the defined metrics, the analysis hypotheses has to be defined. The hypotheses are defined for each of the question's metrics. The defined hypotheses are presented in Table 6.18, where μ is the mean of the variable for the experiment. The defined hypotheses are so-called null hypotheses.

Definition 6.7 A null hypothesis [176]

The null hypothesis refers to a general or default position that there is no relationship between two measured phenomena, or that a potential treatment has no effect. Rejecting or disproving the null hypothesis means that there is a relationship between two phenomena or that a potential treatment has a measurable effect.

It means, there is an assumption that there is no difference between the number of correct, incorrect and "I do not know" answers for the tasks for the both of the approaches. Thus, for the Question I it is assumed that the experiment participants will have the same success in all tasks for both approaches. For the Question II it is assumed that the experiment participants will have the same success rate in selecting the right design pattern from the catalogue for both approaches, and that there will be a comparable number of participants who could not select the right pattern. For the question III it is assumed that the experiment participants will have the same success rate in finding the right design pattern to be changed for both approaches, and that there will be a comparable number of participants who could not find the right pattern.

Question I: Null Hypotheses	
$H_0^{1a} : \mu_c^a = \mu_c^b$	The AM3D approach group has the same number of the correct answers to the tasks, as the standard approach.
$H_0^{1b} : \mu_i^a = \mu_i^b$	The AM3D approach group has the same number of the incorrect answers to the tasks, as the standard approach.
$H_0^{1c} : \mu_{dn}^a = \mu_{dn}^b$	The AM3D approach group has the same number of the "I do not know" answers to the tasks, as the standard approach.
Question II: Null Hypotheses	
$H_0^{2a} : \mu_c^a = \mu_c^b$	The AM3D approach group has the same number of the correct answers to the tasks for Q I, as the standard approach.
$H_0^{2b} : \mu_i^a = \mu_i^b$	The AM3D approach group has the same number of the incorrect answers to the task for Q I, as the standard approach.
$H_0^{2c} : \mu_{dn}^a = \mu_{dn}^b$	The AM3D approach group has the same number of the "I do not know" answers to the task for Q I, as the standard approach.
Question III: Null Hypotheses	
$H_0^{3a} : \mu_c^a = \mu_c^b$	The AM3D approach group has the same number of the correct answers to the tasks for Q II, as the standard approach.
$H_0^{3b} : \mu_i^a = \mu_i^b$	The AM3D approach group has the same number of the incorrect answers to the task for Q II, as the standard approach.
$H_0^{3c} : \mu_{dn}^a = \mu_{dn}^b$	The AM3D approach group has the same number of "I don't know" answers to the task for Q II, as the standard approach.
Question IV: Null Hypotheses	
$H_0^{4a} : \mu_{es}^a = \mu_{es}^b$	The AM3D approach group requires the same effort to select the right pattern as the standard approach group.
$H_0^{4b} : \mu_{ef}^a = \mu_{ef}^b$	The AM3D approach group requires the same effort to re-evaluate the patterns as the standard approach group.
$H_0^{4c} : \mu_{us}^a = \mu_{us}^b$	The AM3D approach group receives the same support from the AM3D catalogue to select the right pattern as the standard approach group receives from the standard catalogue.
$H_0^{4d} : \mu_{us}^a = \mu_{us}^b$	The AM3D approach group receives the same support from the AM3D catalogue to re-evaluate patterns as the standard approach group receives from the standard catalogue.

Table 6.18.: Experiment Hypotheses for Statistical Analysis

Furthermore, it is assumed that both of the approaches are comparably easy to use and that they have a comparable effectiveness in guiding of the participants though the tasks. Thus, for the question IV it is assumed that it makes no difference whether to use an AM3D annotated pattern catalogue, or to use a standard pattern catalogue. These assumptions are validated based on the data collected from the experiment

6.5.2. Research Method

This section describes the research method. The research method of the empirical study is a subtype of a controlled experiment – a quasi-experiment, which a quantitative research method. For the definition of a controlled experiment see the Definition 6.8, for the definition of a quasi-experiment see the Definition 6.9. The subjects were assigned quasi-randomly to one of the treatments, as due to the differences in their performance we had to ensure a comparable proportion between very good and good students in each of the groups.

Definition 6.8 A controlled experiment [176]

A control experiment in software engineering is an empirical enquiry that manipulates one or several factors or variables of the studied setting.

Definition 6.9 A quasi-experiment [176]

A quasi-experiment is an empirical enquiry similar to an experiment, where the assignment of treatments to subjects cannot be based on randomization, but emerges from the characteristics of the subjects or objects themselves.

The experiment is a one factor with two treatments experiment, where subject's performance in the architectural tasks is compared between the AM3D approach (Group A, AM3D) and the standard approach (Group B, Book). For the definition of a one factor with two treatments experiment see the Definition 6.10.

Definition 6.10 A one factor with two treatments experiment [176]

A one factor with two treatments experiment compares the two treatments against each other. The most common is to compare the means of the dependent variable for each treatment.

The experiment design is balanced, as there is the same amount of subjects per each treatment. For the definition of a balanced experiment see the Definition 6.11.

Definition 6.11 A balanced experiment [176]

The treatments are assigned in a way so that each treatment has equal number of subjects in order to have a balanced design. Balancing simplifies and strengthens the statistical analysis of the data.

It is a multi-test study, as there is one object of study and a set of subjects performing actions with the object. For the definition of a balanced experiment see the Definition 6.12.

Definition 6.12 A Multi-test study [176]

A Multi-test study is a study that examines a single object across a set of subjects.

To summarize, the research method of the empirical study is a controlled multi-test balanced quasi-experiment with one factor with two treatments.

6.5.3. Experiment Design

This section provides details on the experiment design. It describes the experiment context, the experiment object, the experiment subjects, their group assignments, the experiment tasks and the experiment process and materials.

6.5.3.1. Experiment Context

The AM3D experiment took place during a half-a-year long software development practical course at Karlsruhe Institute of Technology (KIT) involving 20 bachelor students as subjects. In the practical course students had to

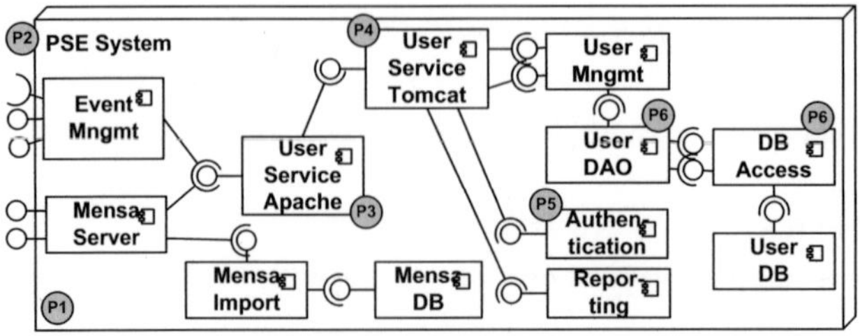

Figure 6.4.: System View of PSE Architecture with Marked Pattern Positions (P)

develop two mobile applications in four groups. All of these groups had to use a user-management system (PSE system) which was the subject of the experiment. Everybody received several trainings to the practical course topics and to the experiment topics to assure the required knowledge. In particular, training on design patterns and on the component-based software development was given, as these topics were required to manage the experiment.

The AM3D experiment was one of the three independent experiments that took place at the end of the course. Therefore, materials, such as PSE system design (experiment object), PSE system requirements and implementation, warm-up and cool-down tasks are a contribution of the complete experiment team. The trainings were held by each of the experiment designers to the own topic.

This thesis only reports the results of the experiment related to the AM3D approach.

6.5.3.2. Experiment Object

The experiment object is a user management system (a composite component) called PSE. The system view is presented on Figure 6.4. Grey circles with "P" mark components with implemented design patterns, which were subject of change during the experiment.

The PSE system was designed and implemented by practical course supervisors together with the experiment designers. The students received specification of the PSE system interface, PSE system documentation and PSE system implementation (running on the provided Web server) to be used for their mobile application implementations.

The goal of the PSE system is to manage the users of mobile applications. Besides the usual user information, such as name, gender or age, the users of the PSE system may have food and event preferences lists. Two main use-cases of the PSE system are (1) storing user votes and preferences for the menus and food options of the University canteen, and (2) storing user votes and preferences for the participation in events.

The experiment subjects had to use the PSE system to manage and authenticity users of the apps that were developed during the practical course. Therefore the subjects were familiar with the system functionality and provided and required interfaces, as they had to program towards them. They were, however, not familiar with the implementation details and the PSE system architecture was a black box for them.

During the experiment, the PSE architecture and detailed documentation were revealed to the subjects. The subjects were provided with time to get acquainted with the system: The first part of the experiment contained easy warm-up tasks to assure that each of the subjects knew about available artefacts, had an overview of them and of the PSE architecture in general. All of the subjects succeeded in these warm-up tasks.

6.5.3.3. Experiment Subjects and Assignment of Subjects to Experiment Groups

The subjects of the experiments were 20 bachelor students (mainly third year) taking part at the half-a-year long software development practical course at Karlsruhe Institute of Technology (KIT).

During the PSE course, a large difference in the participants knowledge was observed. Some of the participants have shown a very high motivation and skill levels, while some were moderate. Thus, it was not possible to assign the participants to the treatment and control groups completely randomly. The characteristics of the participants had to be taken into account, to avoid accidental concentration of the top participants in one of the groups.

Therefore, the following approach to assign the participants to the groups was used. The course supervisors have provided two lists of students to the experiment organisers – top students and other students. The randomisation was then performed on both of these lists. The result was four lists of participants – two lists with top participants, and two lists with the other participants. These lists were then merged into two, combining each top-participant list with one other-participants list. Even though the assignment to the groups is not completely random, the experiment designers did not influence assignment of students to one or other of the groups.

In the following, the treatment group will be called the Group A, and the control group will be called the Group B.

6.5.3.4. Process and Materials

At the beginning of the practical course, subjects received a list of requirements to the planned mobile apps, requirements to the PSE system, PSE system documentation and its implementation. Besides an introduction organised by the course supervisors, subjects received trainings, as explained in Section 6.5.3.1. The AM3D experiment took place at the end of the course together with one more experiment on the architectural decision views. Due to this topic similarity the introduction materials and warm-up and cool-down questionnaires were shared.

The plan of the experiment is outlined on Figure 6.5, and consisted of the following parts:

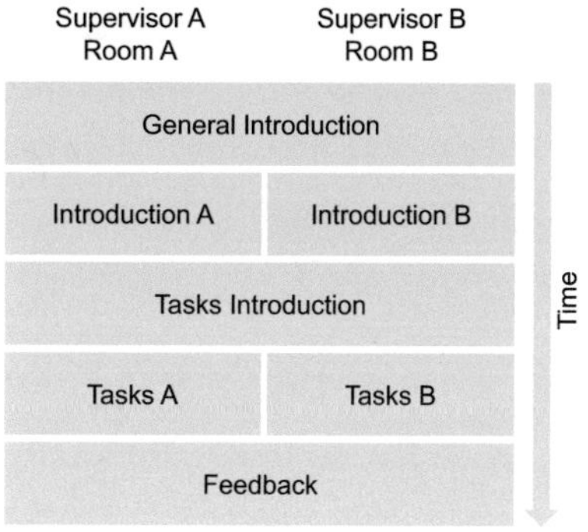

Figure 6.5.: Plan of the Experiment

- **General introduction:** General introduction contained a short reminder about key architectural terms required for the experiment, and introduction to the PSE system.

- **Group-specific introduction:** Group-specific introduction explained the corresponding approaches (the AM3D approach, and the standard approach), handled in experiment materials and their structure, and usage of them. . Both of the introductions were done according to the protocol for the reproducibility of the experiment. The introduction texts have the same structure and length, and differ only in the approach details.

- **Warm-up tasks:** After the introduction, both groups proceeded with the first questionnaire containing the warm-up tasks. The participants had a chance to get acquainted with each of the provided artefacts, such as lists of requirements, the reminder of the PSE system design, the PSE system architecture (was also explained in introduction), list of design decisions and the AM3D pattern catalogue or a book with excerpts from the pattern books. The participants had a paper version of the introductory presentations at their side, together with the transcript, for the case they would need a reference.

- **Design decision views tasks:** After 10 minutes the first questionnaire was collected, and the participants proceeded with the second one dedicated to the design decisions. This questionnaire is not related to the AM3D approach and, therefore, is not described here.

- **The AM3D tasks:** After 30 minutes, the second questionnaire was collected and the participants proceeded with the third one, dedicated to the AM3D approach. Time was captured once a participant was done with the questionnaire. The AM3D questionnaire consisted of two parts, each containing the main task and three feedback questions. The first task was to evaluate already met design decisions on design pattern taking into the account provided requirements changes. In this case, both groups had a list of design decisions to the PSE system, documents either with the AM3D approach or with the classical approach. The second task topics was to evaluate which of the given design pattern could solve the given design problems. The tasks are listed in the Appendix B.

  Each of the two tasks had a defined process to follow to solve the task, and an example with the solution. Each of these tasks had 4 data points – 4 patterns to decide on, or 4 problems to find a pattern for. All tasks were multiple choice.

  The feedback questions collected information on how easy the task was for the participants according to their own perception, an estimation if the AM3D catalogue (or the book for the Group B) was helpful to solve the task, and a chance to provide a free-text comment to the task. The participants had 30 minutes to complete the tasks.

- **Cool-down tasks:** Finally, the participants received the last fourth questionnaire, which collected the information on their background, their knowledge of programming, design and design patterns, comments to the understandability of the questionnaires, information on problems with the questionnaires and if the problems were solved or not, and a general comment to consider by the experiment organisers.

All materials including the experiment protocol can be found in Appendix B.

6.5.3.5. Tool-Supported vs. Questionnaire-Based Experiment

The empirical study about the AM3D design pattern catalogue was not tool-based. This decision was taken based on the following arguments:

- Too high risk to end up validating the tool instead of the idea of the AM3D pattern catalogue.
- A tool requires some time to get proficient with. It would either require an additional training to the students, or more time for the experiment, which was no option.
- In particular, a tool would be a research prototype and not a matured tool, and thus most likely would have not the best usability.
- A tool requires certain pre-installed technical environment. The experiment organisers, however, had only a limited influence on the lab computers. A risk on an unexpected Java-update or some other technical defect was too high, considering that there was only one time slot for the experiment with a rather tight schedule.

The drawback of the decision is that the tool support is not validated to the end. However, it was neither a contribution of the approach, nor the focus of a dissertation project. Another drawback is that the tool support would have enabled tracking of the participants actions, which was not possible with the paper questionnaires and catalogues. To tangle this drawback, a process was defined for the participants to follow during the task solution. This process ensured similarity of participant's actions and common understanding of the task between all of the participants. Moreover, the feedback questions were included into the tasks to collect information on the participant's actions.

At thc end, the decision not to use the tool during the experiment has proven to be right, as one of the experiment organizers indeed experienced technical problems with the lab computers, even despite the installations were tested in the lab before.

6.5.4. Testing the Method

The validity of the experiment design was assured in two ways. First, the experiment design was carried out in a team with regular meetings and discussions. Two of the meeting participants had grounded experience in empirical work, and have organized a controlled experiment before. The experience collected during the survey was also considered during the design, in particular during the questionnaire design. In overall, the design phase of the experiment lasted over half a year. During this half a year, the students were regularly provided with required artefacts and training, and the final experiment part was designed and reviewed.

Second, the experiment was pretested in three steps. In the first step, a review of the complete experiment was conducted and the collected comments were implemented in the design. In the second step, the experiment was simulated with two doctoral researchers, one of whom is an expert in the body of empirical work, with a detailed feedback session after they have completed the experiment. The doctoral researchers were assigned accordingly to the treatment and to the control groups. Once again, the collected feedback was implemented in the experiment design. Finally, in the third step, one more simulation of the experiment took place with three doctoral researchers. This time, one doctoral researcher student was assigned to the treatment group, and two to the control group. The collected feedback was implemented in the experiment design.

6.5.5. Experiment Results

This section presents the results of the experiment aligned to the research questions formulated in Section 6.5.1. The results summarize the data from the 20 valid questionnaires that were collected during the experiment.

First, the outline removal is described in Section 6.5.5.1, followed by the information about the participants in Section 6.5.5.2. Section 6.5.5.3 explains the method that was selected for the statistical evaluation. Section 6.5.5.4 analyses the data related to the pattern common tasks research question, Section 6.5.5.5 analyses the data related to the pattern selection task research question, Section 6.5.5.6 analyses the data related to the pattern re-evaluation task during the system evolution research question. Section 6.5.5.7 analyses the data related to the AM3D catalogue easiness of usage. Finally, Section 6.5.5.8 analyses all the data considering the comments, the participants have provided as a justification to their answers. Feedback is summarized in Section 6.5.5.9.

6.5.5.1. Data Validation and Outlier Removal

Before the data analysis, one of questionnaires from the Group B was removed, as the solution for the tasks was incomplete due to the external factors. This participant came too late and also changed the work station during the experiment, as the result, the task I was missing completely, and Task II was only partially solved. This participant also did not complete other questionnaires. In the next step, the data in the questionnaires was analysed for the outliers. No outliers were detected. At the end, a set of 20 valid questionnaires was left and used for the data analysis.

6.5.5.2. Participant Information

The experiment participants were students who voluntary enrolled into the half-a-year practical course on software development. The information on the participant's background is presented in Table 6.19.

Study semester	#
Third	14
Fifth	3
Seventh	1
No answer	2
Practical programming experience (multiple choice)	**#**
Yes, during studies	6
Yes, in addition to studies	6
Yes, software development for money	5
No	9
Practical architectural design experience (multiple choice)	**#**
Yes, during studies	1
Yes, in addition to studies	2
No	14
Knowledge of design patterns (multiple choice)	**#**
Yes, from lectures	14
Yes, self-education	5
Yes, applied on practice	7
No	0

Table 6.19.: Information on Experiment Participants

All of the participants were bachelor students. From 20 participants, 14 were in the third semester, three in the fifth semester and one in the 7th, and two students provided no information. From all the participants, 9 had no practical programming experience before the PSE course beyond the regular studies, while 5 had developed software for money. Some of the students provided no answer to the question. Similarly, 14 participants had no experience in system design before the PSE course. None of the participants selected "no knowledge of patterns", while 14 had collected the knowledge from the lectures, 5 have collected an additional knowledge from the personal research, and 7 have applied patterns on practice before.

6.5.5.3. Selected Statistical Test

To be able to select the right statistical test, we need to find out if the collected data forms a normally distributed population or not.

	Group A		Group B	
	Task I	Task II	Task I	Task II
Correct answers	(6,5,9,6)	(6,10,6,8)	(3,6,5,6)	(2,8,5,3)
Incorrect answers	(4,3,0,3)	(4,0,4,2)	(7,3,4,5)	(8,2,5,7)
“I don’t know” answers	(0,2,1,1)	(0,0,0,0)	(0,1,1,0)	(0,0,0,0)

Table 6.20.: Experiment Data

The data sets are presented in Table 6.20. To test if the datasets have the normal (Gaussian) distribution, the Shapiro-Wilk Test was selected. The results of the Shapiro-Wilk Test for the data sets are presented in Table 6.21. The dataset distribution is normal, when the results of the Shapiro-Wilk Test (`W`) exceed the critical value, characteristic for the data set sample size. The null hypothesis (H_0) here means the normal data distribution.

Numbers of “I don’t know” answers for the Group A in Task I and II, and for the Group B in Task II do not follow a normal distribution. Thus, for evaluation of the data, which is normally distributed, a two sample paired t-test [179] is used to evaluate the null hypotheses. Otherwise, a two sample paired Wilcoxon signed rank test [180] is used. The confidence level is 95% in both cases ($\alpha = 0.05$), which is a standard confidence level for the statistical evaluations.

The data is analysed with the help of the R Statistic program (The R Project for Statistical Computing) [181], which is a strict functional language and environment for statistical calculations.

6.5.5.4. Question I: Common Pattern Tasks

The results for the research Question I “Can annotated patterns be more appropriately selected and re-evaluated if documented with the proposed approach than without it?” are summarized in Table 6.22. Boxplots to the data in the table are presented on Figure 6.6.

According to the data, the first null hypothesis that the treatment Group A has the same number of correct answers to tasks as the control Group B is rejected. The treatment Group A has significantly more of correct answers

Gr.	Task	Data	Mean	St. Dev.	Var.	W	Crit. W (5% s.l.)	H_0
A	All	corr (6,5,9,6,6,10,6,8)	7.0	1.8	3.2	0.850	0.818	✔
B	All	corr (3,6,5,6,2,8,5,3)	4.8	2.0	4.0	0.948	0.818	✔
A	All	incorr (4,3,0,3,4,0,4,2)	2.5	1.7	2.9	0.814	0.818	✔
B	All	incorr (7,3,4,4,8,2,5,7)	5.0	2.1	4.6	0.938	0.818	✔
A	All	dntk (0,2,1,1,0,0,0,0)	0.5	0.8	0.6	0.724	0.818	✘
B	All	dntk (0,0,0,0,0,0,0,0)	0.0	0.0	0.0	n/a	0.818	✘
A	I	corr (6,5,9,6)	6.5	1.7	3.0	0.840	0.748	✔
A	II	corr (6,10,6,8)	7.5	1.9	3.7	0.863	0.748	✔
B	I	corr (3,6,5,6)	5.0	1.4	2.0	0.827	0.748	✔
B	II	corr (2,8,5,3)	4.5	2.7	7.0	0.946	0.748	✔
A	I	incorr (4,3,0,3)	2.5	1.7	3.0	0.840	0.748	✔
A	II	incorr (4,0,4,2)	2.5	1.9	3.7	0.863	0.748	✔
B	I	incorr (7,3,4,4)	4.5	1.7	3.0	0.840	0.748	✔
B	II	incorr (8,2,5,7)	5.5	2.7	7.0	0.946	0.748	✔
A	I	dntk (0,2,1,1)	1.0	0.8	0.7	0.945	0.748	✔
A	II	dntk (0,0,0,0)	0	0	0	n/a	0.748	✘
B	I	dntk (0,1,1,0)	0.5	0.6	0.3	0.729	0.748	✘
B	II	dntk (0,0,0,0)	0.0	0.0	0.0	n/a	0.748	✘

Table 6.21.: Shapiro-Wilk Test

Hypothesis	Mean Δ	p-value	H_0
$H_0^{1a} : \mu_c^a = \mu_c^b$	2.25	0.01994	✘
$H_0^{1b} : \mu_i^a = \mu_i^b$	-2.5	0.005266	✘
$H_0^{1c} : \mu_{dn}^a = \mu_{dn}^b$	0.25	0.1573	✔

Table 6.22.: Analysis of the Research Question I

than the Group B (p-value = 0.01994). The second null hypothesis that the treatment Group A has the same number of incorrect answers as the control Group B is also rejected.

The treatment Group A has significantly less of incorrect answers than the Group B (p-value = 0.005266). The third null hypothesis that the treatment Group A has the same number of "I do not know" answers to the pattern selection tasks as the control Group B can neither be rejected, nor confirmed. The p-value in this case is 0.1573, which might be an indicator that the treatment Group A in cases of uncertainty tends to select “I don’t know option” instead of a definite decision. This could be a positive effect by the AM3D approach, however, it requires further validation. For critical discussion of threats to validity please refer to Section 6.5.6.

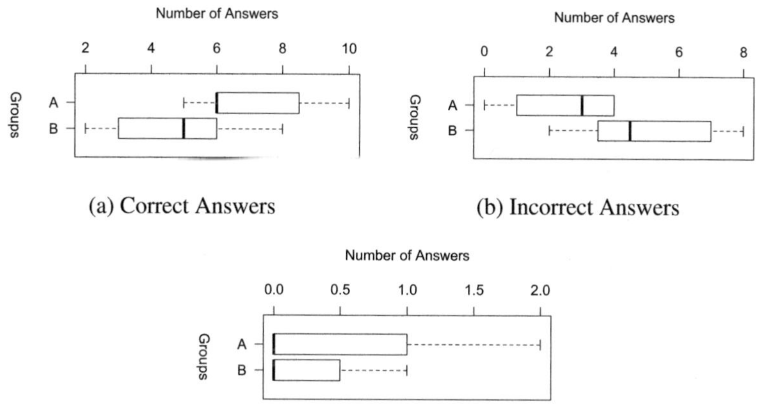

(a) Correct Answers

(b) Incorrect Answers

(c) “I don’t know” Answers

Figure 6.6.: Boxplots to Common Pattern Tasks

6.5.5.5. Question II: Pattern Selection

The results for the research Question II “Can annotated patterns be more appropriately selected if documented with the proposed approach than without it?” are summarized in Table 6.23 (the Question I evaluation is based on the Task II data, as questions were in a reversed order in the experiment). Boxplots to the data in the table are presented on Figure 6.7.

Hypothesis	Mean Δ	p-value	H_0
$H_0^{2a} : \mu_c^a = \mu_c^b$	3	0.04621	✘
$H_0^{2b} : \mu_i^a = \mu_i^b$	-3	0.04621	✘
$H_0^{2c} : \mu_{dn}^a = \mu_{dn}^b$	n/a	n/a	✔

Table 6.23.: Analysis of the Research Question II

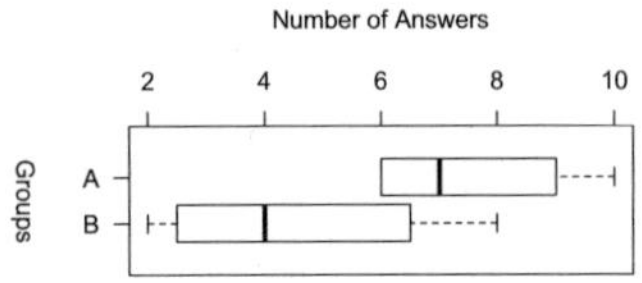

(a) Correct Answers

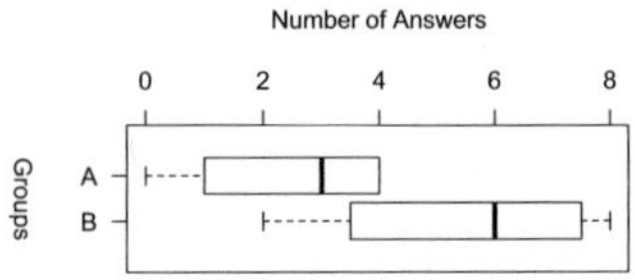

(b) Incorrect Answers

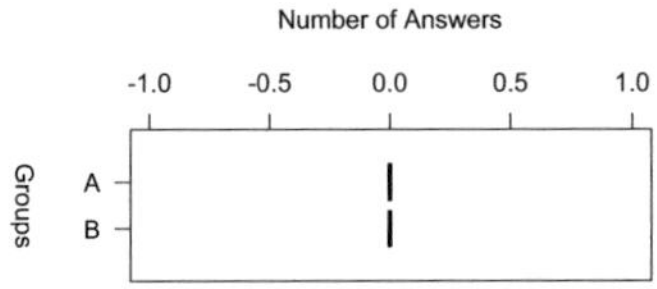

(c) "I don't know" Answers

Figure 6.7.: Boxplots to Pattern Selection

According to the data, the first null hypothesis that the treatment Group A has the same number of correct answers as the control Group B is rejected. The treatment Group A has significantly more of correct answers than the Group B (p-value = 0.04621).

The second null hypothesis that the treatment Group A has the same number of incorrect answers as the control Group B is also rejected. The treatment Group A has significantly less of incorrect answers than the Group B (p-value = 0.04621).

The third null hypothesis that the treatment Group A has the same number of "I do not know" answers as the control Group B is confirmed. In both cases there were no "I don't know" answers. For critical discussion of threats to validity please refer to Section 6.5.6.

6.5.5.6. Question III: Pattern Re-Evaluation

The results for the research Question III "Can the outdated patterns (decisions to use a pattern) be more easily found if documented with the proposed approach than without it?" are summarized in Table 6.24 (please note, that the Question III evaluation is based on the Task I data, as questions were in a reversed order in the experiment). Boxplots to the data in the table are presented on Figure 6.8.

Hypothesis	Mean Δ	p-value	H_0
$H_0^{3a} : \mu_c^a = \mu_c^b$	1.5	0.2967	✔
$H_0^{3b} : \mu_i^a = \mu_i^b$	-2	0.1162	✔
$H_0^{3c} : \mu_{dn}^a = \mu_{dn}^b$	0.5	0.1573	✔

Table 6.24.: Analysis of the Research Question III

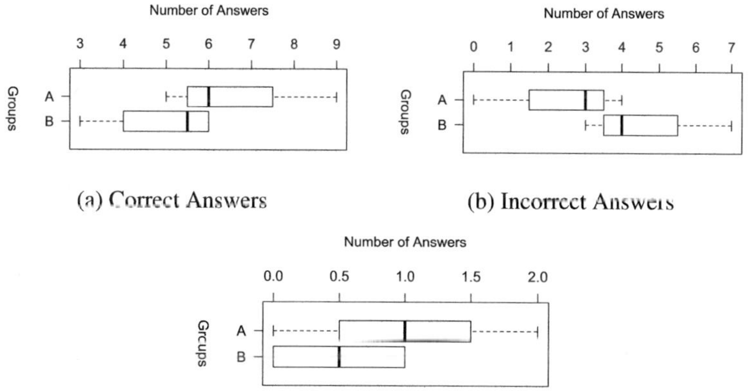

(a) Correct Answers

(b) Incorrect Answers

(c) "I don't know" Answers

Figure 6.8.: Boxplots to Pattern Re-Evaluation

According to the data, the first null hypothesis that the treatment Group A has the same number of correct answers as the control Group B cannot be rejected with statistical significance, as the p-value equals 0.2967. Even though the hypothesis cannot be rejected, the p-value = 0.2967 is still a good result. It means that in 70% of the cases, the treatment Group A will give correct answers, compared to the control Group B.

The second null hypothesis that the treatment Group A has the same number of incorrect answers as the control Group B. It also cannot be rejected with a statistical significance, as the p-value equals 0.1162. However, also in this case, the p-value = 0.1162 is a good result. It means that in 82% of the cases, the treatment Group A will give less incorrect answers, compared to the control Group B.

The third null hypothesis that the treatment Group A has the same number of "I do not know" as the control Group B cannot be rejected with a statistical significance, as the p-value equals 0.1573. Also here, the p-value = 0.1573 may be an indicator that the treatment Group A in cases of uncertainty tends to select "I don't know option" instead of a definite decision, which is positive effect for the evolution as it produces less mistakes through the too-quick decisions. For critical discussion of threats to validity please refer to Section 6.5.6.

6.5.5.7. Question IV: Easiness of Usage

The results for the research Question IV "Is the annotated pattern catalogue easier to use as compared to the standard design pattern catalogue?" are summarized in Table 6.25 and Table 6.26. The block diagrams to the data in the tables are presented on Figure 6.9. As the data scale is not ordinary in both questions (which is an experiment design mistake, but there are no perfect experiments in real world [174]), the hypothesis test based on statistics cannot be performed. Instead the results are evaluated descriptively and are compared with the help of block diagrams.

According to the diagrams (A) and (B), the treatment Group A seem to require less effort to select the right pattern and to re-evaluate the patterns as the control Group B . The participants of the treatment Group A also seem to have felt easier doing the tasks, than the participants from the Group B. This observation is based on the mostly positive comments provided about the perception of the easiness of the tasks on pattern selection.

	Group A		Group B	
	Task I	Task II	Task I	Task II
The answers to the questions from the catalogue saved together with the taken decisions were sufficient to solve the tasks	4	–	–	–
I felt myself supported by the catalogue / by the book	4	4	10	5
I felt myself supported by the catalogue / by the book , but I have had or had required additional materials	0	1	0	2
I could partially use the catalogue / the book to solve the tasks, but the information was in most of the cases insufficient	0	2	0	3
The catalogue / the book were useless to solve the tasks	1	1	0	0
The tasks were so simple that I did not need the catalogue / the book	0	1	0	0

Table 6.25.: Data to the Research Question IV: Support

	Group A		Group B	
	Task I	Task II	Task I	Task II
Right	2	3	4	3
Partially right	5	3	6	5
Partially wrong	2	2	0	2
Wrong	0	1	0	0

Table 6.26.: Data to the Research Question IV: Easiness

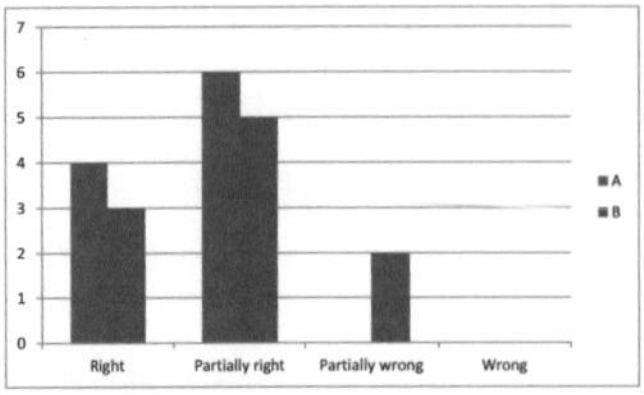

(a) Effort by Pattern Selection

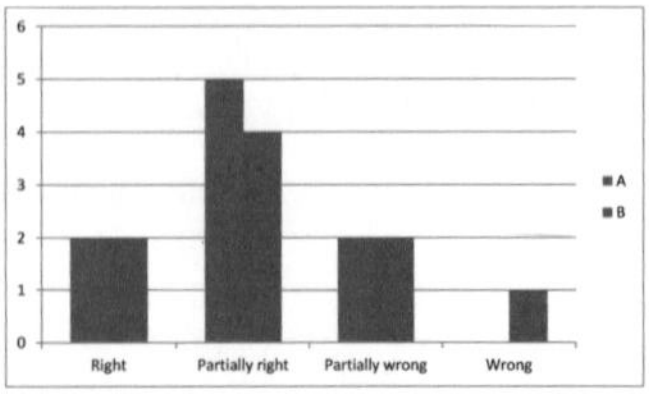

(b) Effort by Pattern Re-Evaluation

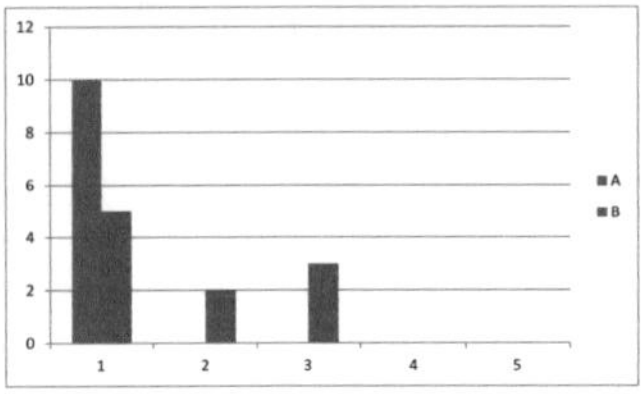

(c) Support by Pattern Selection, where: (1) I felt myself supported by the catalogue / by the book, (2) I felt myself supported by the catalogue / by the book , but I have had or had required additional materials, (3) I could partially use the catalogue / the book to solve the tasks, but the information was in most of the cases insufficient, (4) The catalogue / the book were useless to solve the tasks, and (5) The tasks were so simple that I did not need the catalogue / the book

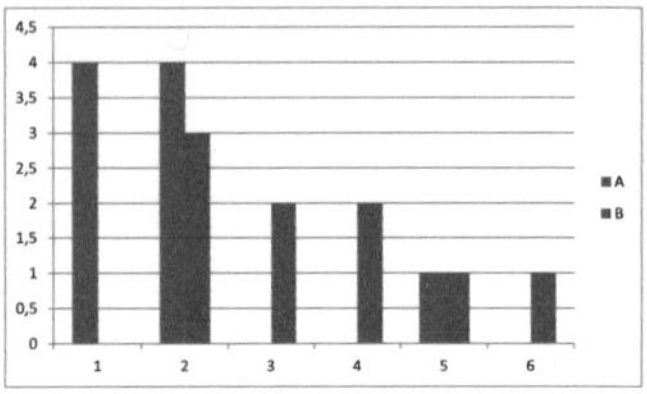

(d) Support by Pattern Re-Evaluation, where: (1) The answers to the questions from the catalogue saved together with the taken decisions were sufficient to solve the tasks, (2) I felt myself supported by the catalogue / by the book, (3) I felt myself supported by the catalogue / by the book , but I have had or had required additional materials, (4) I could partially use the catalogue / the book to solve the tasks, but the information was in most of the cases insufficient, (5) The catalogue / the book were useless to solve the tasks, and (6) The tasks were so simple that I did not need the catalogue / the book

Figure 6.9.: Boxplots to Easiness of Usage of the Catalogue

Furthermore, according to the diagrams (C) and (D), the treatment Group A received a better support from the AM3D catalogue to select the right pattern and to re-evaluate patterns as the control Group B by the book. Also here, the participants of the treatment Group A seem to have felt more supported by the AM3D catalogue doing the tasks, than the participants from the control Group B by the book. This observation is, as well, based on the mostly positive comments provided about the perception of the support by the catalogue to complete the tasks, both during the pattern selection and during the pattern re-evaluation.

We have also captured the time for the cases, when the participants finished the questionnaires quicker than the given time. However, unfortunately in few cases the participants have kept the questionnaire for themselves until they finished the part and did not notify the supervisors that the tasks were completed before time. Therefore, the time data cannot be used for the precise evaluation. The only valid observation is that in the Group A, the participants tended to finish the tasks quicker, than in the Group B. About half of the Group A participants have finished the tasks earlier then the given time, while in the Group B only two participants have completed the tasks earlier, to our best knowledge. For critical discussion of threats to validity please refer to Section 6.5.6.

6.5.5.8. Evaluation of Data Considering Comments

Up to now the answers to the tasks were evaluated solely based on what answer was selected. However, an actual correctness of the answer depends on how the subject understood the task and what reasoning was the subject following solving the task. This difference is due to the different assumptions the participants might have took while solving the tasks.

The participants were asked to provide comments to their answers, with an explanation why this or that answer was selected. These comments were used to evaluate the answers of the participants, considering if the tasks were indeed understood and done correctly. From this point of view, there are four classes of answers, which are presented in Table 6.27.

Type	Answer	Justification	Final Task Evaluation
AA	Correct	Correct justification	Answer is considered correct
AB	Correct	Incorrect justification	Answer is considered incorrect
BA	Incorrect	Correct justification	Answer is considered correct
BB	Incorrect	Incorrect justification	Answer is considered incorrect

Table 6.27.: Types of Answers According to Provided Justifications

All questionnaires were re-evaluated based on this classification. In cases, where the answer was correct, but had an incorrect explanation, the answer to the task was marked to be actually incorrect. Vice versa, if the answer to the task was initially incorrect, but the justification for the answer was correct, the answer was considered to be correct. For example, if a participant has selected that the Singleton decision shall be re-evaluated, because it may be used in the change request C001 due to the potential change of session-management in the authentication singleton component. Even though the answer is not correct in the context of the task, the reasoning behind the provided answer is correct. In this case, the answer to the task shall be considered as correct, since the participant's reasoning went beyond the task and a special case was analysed. This principle was, of course, equally applied to both, to the control and to the treatment group.

The results are summarised in Table 6.28 (the data was checked for normality of distributions to select the right tests), whereby the hypotheses to "I don't know" answers are excluded, as the answers did not change for these types of hypotheses. Boxplots to the data are presented on Figure 6.10.

The results of the task evaluation with comments are actually even better for the AM3D approach. So, the hypothesis $H_0^{3b*} : \mu_i^a = \mu_i^b$ can be rejected since the p-value in inside the accepted confidence interval. Also the

Hypothesis	Data	Mean Δ	p-value	H_0
$H_0^{1a*}: \mu_c^a = \mu_c^b$	A(7,7,9,8,6,10,9,8), B(3,7,5,5,2,8,5,3)	3.25	0.0006543	✘
$H_0^{1b*}: \mu_i^a = \mu_i^b$	A(3,1,0,1,4,0,1,2), B(7,2,4,5,8,2,5,7)	-3.5	0.0001305	✘
$H_0^{2a*}: \mu_c^a = \mu_c^b$	A(6,10,9,8), B(2,8,5,3)	3.75	0.009447	✘
$H_0^{2b*}: \mu_i^a = \mu_i^b$	A(4,0,1,2), B(8,2,5,7)	-3.75	0.009447	✘
$H_0^{3a*}: \mu_c^a = \mu_c^b$	A(7,7,9,8), B(3,7,5,5)	2.75	0.06222	✔
$H_0^{3b*}: \mu_i^a = \mu_i^b$	A(3,1,0,1), B(7,2,4,5)	-3.25	0.02267	✘

Table 6.28.: Analysis of the II and III Research Questions Considering Comments (* Hypothesis with Comments)

hypothesis $H_0^{3a*}: \mu_c^a = \mu_c^b$ has almost reached the 95% level. Other null hypotheses have been already rejected in evaluation without the comments. However, for all of the hypotheses the results have additionally improved.

The threat to validity is that this re-evaluation is subjective, and that not all of the participants have provided comments. In cases, where no comments were provided, the answer could not be checked. Therefore, the data provided in this section shall be taken with care. It solely shows the trend. In case of the experiment replication, the participants shall be checked better, to prevent the comment field left blank.

6.5.5.9. Feedback

The participants were asked to provide feedback to the tasks to patterns, and to the experiments in general.

In particular, the participants were asked to mention the artefacts and tasks that have caused some misunderstanding or confusions, and if the questions about those artefacts or tasks could be answered by the experiment supervisors. There were no understandability comments to the AM3D experiment. Those participants, who have stated that they had problems with some tasks or artefacts named only the AM3D experiment unrelated materials. The participants were also asked to provide a detailed feedback to each of the tasks of the AM3D experiment.

To the tasks on the pattern selection, the following comments were received from the Group A (translated from German into English): "Question to the patterns (Qxxx) have very well supported me during the selection of patterns, in particular the alternatives part was the most interesting", "The catalogue was helpful, however, the differences between the X Table Inheritance patterns could have been pointed out better", and "Trade-off decisions are most meaningful, when the priorities for the problems are set (performance, maintenance, security, simplicity)?".

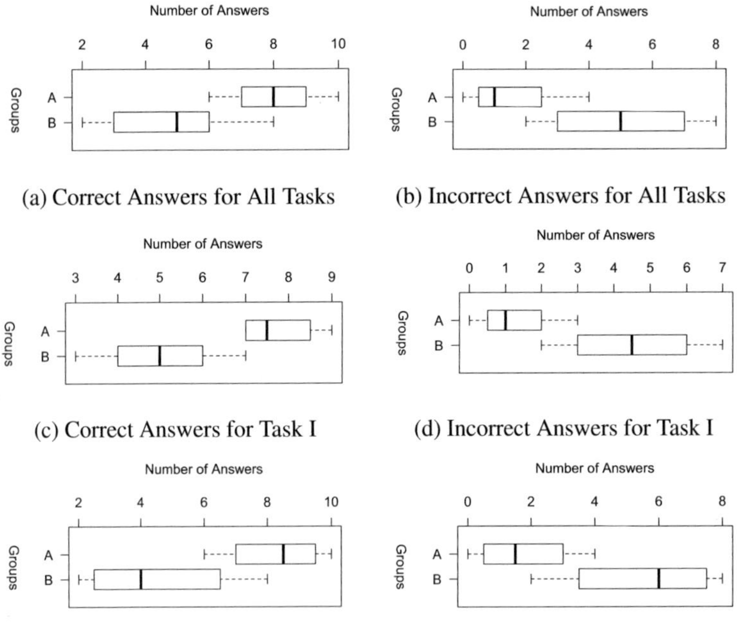

(a) Correct Answers for All Tasks

(b) Incorrect Answers for All Tasks

(c) Correct Answers for Task I

(d) Incorrect Answers for Task I

(e) Correct Answers for Task II

(f) Incorrect Answers for Task II

Figure 6.10.: Boxplots to Pattern Re-Evaluation

To the tasks on the pattern re-evaluation, the following comments were received from the Group A (translated from German into English): “The catalogue is good, I would have gladly had one privately”, and “Too few information on priorities”. As one of the participants commented on the understanding of the Table Inheritance patterns, the catalogue entries to them could be reviewed for additional questions.

In the Group B, the following comments were received to the tasks on the pattern selection (translated from German into English): “The client was not really explained well”, and “Long descriptions”. However, as for the Group B the information was taken from the common public catalogues, the organisers had no influence on the information quality and length.

The fact that the Group B provided little feedback can be explained by the fact that they were more under pressure than the participants of the Group A, as explained before.

6.5.6. Threats to Validity, Limitations of the Evaluation

This section provides discussion on threats to validity, using the same classification, as the classification of threats in Section 6.4.6, namely: Construct validity, internal validity, external validity, and reliability.

6.5.6.1. Construct Validity

The questionnaire design was not optimal for the measurement of the metrics for the research question IV “Is the annotated pattern catalogue easier to use as compared to the standard design pattern catalogue?”. The possible answer options to the questions about effort and about support were not forming an ordinary scale. As the result, the hypothesis test could not be performed. Even though it would be possible to assign nominal values to the answer option, e.g. “right” = 2, “partially right = 1”, “partially wrong = “-1” and “wrong = -2”, the distance between the answers actually cannot be precisely estimated. So such an assignment would rather be incorrect from the statistical point of view. Nevertheless, the collected data allowed for the descriptive statistics and data analysis.

Some of the students forgot to notify the experiment supervisors when they have completed their tasks before time. Therefore, no time metric could be collected with enough precision and we had to omit the time evaluation for the research question IV.

The participants were aware of the topic of the experiment and it might have influenced the answers. It is a natural threat and is common to surveys and experiments involving humans as subjects. However, the participants were unaware to which group they were assigned to and did not know what the difference to the other group was. Both groups took part in the experiment at the same time, and thus, they could not exchange information.

None of the participants knew the topic, the AM3D experiment designer was working on. Therefore, the participants could not have unlikely guessed the desired outcome of the experiment, and modified their answers in accordance to their attitude to the experiment and experiment object.

The participation in the experiment was on a semi-free will, and might have negatively affected the attitude towards the experiment and the motivation in the experiment. The following measures were taken to reduce this threat: The usage of the additional materials was multiple times explained during the trainings and course. We have tried to explain the benefit the participants would get from the experiment, such as additional experience in the design-related tasks, since the experience possibilities are rare during the University studies. The participants were also provided with snacks after the experiment and were in general in a good-mood and cooperative.

Some participants might have "improved" their stated experience with software design and development, however, this "improvement" had no influence on the correctness of their solutions to the tasks.

To reduce the threat of mono-operation bias, and to create more realistic conditions, the participants have received multiple artefacts they had to work with. The time was limited, so that participants could not spend as much time as they liked doing the tasks, since it is also not the case in the real-life work environment.

There might have been an interaction of testing and treatment, and the participants might have felt under pressure to produce the best possible results. To reduce the stress, the participants were informed that the results do not influence the PSE course mark and are anonymous. This fact might have actually influenced the participants towards the other direction, making them less motivated.

Another factor for motivation could potentially be the assignment to the control and treatment groups. However, as mentioned before, the participants were not aware about these divisions and did not know what the other alternatives were. Thus, the motivation shall have been rather personal and not related to the group assignments.

The PSE system might be not representative enough for the real-world problems. This treat was tangled in several ways. First, the system is complex and contains several architectural twists. Second, the participants have worked with the system code during the PSE course and were familiar with its functionality. This reflects a real-world scenario, where engineers work with parts of the system, however, do not necessary know how its structured and what decisions were taken in it. Then a change request arrives, which requires changing a part of the system the engineers actually know only through interfaces. Here, both, engineers and student participants face similar problem – they have to take design decisions and to modify existing design decisions, while trying to understand why the design is like it is and if the modifications would fit into it.

To avoid restricted generalizability across constructs, the research questions were defined with a goal to co-evaluate also the potential additional influence of the AM3D approach – namely the influence on the easiness to use. If the catalogue would help to achieve better results for the pattern application, it is important to know how high is the price for this improvement in terms of time, effort and comfort feeling.

The design of the tasks and questions in the questionnaire might have influenced the collected results. To reduce this threat, the experiment design was regularly reviewed in a group. Moreover, the tasks were modified by two of the reviewers, and also modified after the pre-tests based on the feedback of the test participants. The version of the tasks the students have received was, thus, hardly a reflection of a personal desire of the experiment designer, since all of the material underwent a critical review process. In particular, the own interest of the designer was to do the experiment as objective and real-life close as possible, and to avoid as many threats as possible, in order to obtain a valid and replicable data.

6.5.6.2. Internal Validity

The experiment took part after the course, and this could have potentially affected the motivation of participants to perform well in the experiment. If it was the case, the effect shall be random for both groups, since the distribution between groups was semi-random.

The experiment had only a limited number of patterns per task, all together 8 cases of pattern usage with four options per each usage. However, despite this, the statistically significant results could be achieved at least for parts of the hypotheses.

The tasks and questions in the questionnaire were formulated in a natural language. A common problem is that questions might be misinterpreted or become so-called leading question. To minimize this threat, the experiment design followed recommendations of literature on empirical research, such as Punch [177] and Wohlin [176], and underwent several reviews. This is a common threat for the experiments.

The selection of the participants, who have participated in the experiment, might have influenced the results. However, the selection was accidental, as the participants have enrolled into the course on their own will.

Since the participants performance was expected to be unequal (based on the experience during the course), the assignment to groups was semi-random. The participants were divided into two groups (high performance and normal performance), and then randomisation was carried out on both of these groups.

The experiment was based on the paper artefacts. The drawback is that tool support was not validated and the participant's actions could not be tracked. However, on the other side, the negative influence of inmature user interface and of inmature tool support was removed as a variable, as well as instability of software in the lab environment.

As already mentioned, the participants were not aware if they belong to the control or to the treatment group, and what kind of treatment they were receiving. This factor could not have influenced their replies.

The control group B provided fewer comments to the task answers, than the treatment group A. This can be explained through more time pressure on the group B, since their pattern catalogue contained longer descriptions. However, this actually can be seen as one more positive effect of the pattern catalogue. Its pattern entries are kept short on purpose, and the fact that the group B took longer to solve the tasks, and still did more mistakes, may be an indicator that the catalogue explains the material in a more compact way and still precisely enough to complete the tasks correctly.

6.5.6.3. External Validity

The data of the experiment is based on 20 student participants, and might not be suitable to apply the observations to the real-world projects with software developers. However, Tichy [174] describes cases, where the students are acceptable as subjects. As the participants of the experiment have been sufficiently trained, they at least are as well prepared, as the job beginners in the companies who are ex-students themselves. Moreover, the students are used to establish a trend [174] between usage of the AM3D approach and the usage of the classical approach. Since the results show a considerable difference, the arguments of Tichy [174] can be applied: "If one method has a clear relative advantage over the other with student subjects, then one can make the argument that there will be a difference in the same direction (although perhaps of a different magnitude) for professionals, provided the professionals use the methods in a similar fashion".

Answers to the questions on the effort and on the support amount in the questionnaire are subjective and reflect personal opinions of the participants. The comparison between the same option selected by several participants, therefore, is possible only with a descriptive statistic and is not statistically measurable.

Similarly to the survey, the experiment was conducted on a selection from the catalogue, presented in a form suitable for the experiment. The participants might have replied differently, if they had a real instance of the catalogue at hand. However, the sample selection contained 12 patterns, which is a realistic number. All of the tasks had each four pattern alternatives to choose from or to analyse in the task. The control group had up-to-date materials, which were based on the common catalogue books.

6.5.6.4. Reliability Validity

To assure the reliability validity of the experiment, all the materials were captured and are available in the Appendix B of this thesis.

All the trainings, and introductions to the experiment groups were transcribed and the introduction was done reading the script. This was done for several purposes. First, to assure both groups have received exactly the same introduction and have an equal chance in the experiment. Second, to be able to recheck what was explained during the introduction, in case there would be some problems with collected questionnaires. Finally, to enable replicability of the experiment.

6.5.7. Summary of the Results

The goals of the controlled experiment were to test whether (1) design patterns annotated according to the AM3D approach can be better understood and applied more correctly as compared to the classical pattern catalogue, and (2) system architecture documented with the AM3D approach can be better maintained compared to the system documented with the standard approach. The usage of the AM3D catalogue shall remain as easy as the usage of the classical catalogue. These goals were refined into three research goals followed on by four research questions, described in Sections 6.4.1.1 and 6.4.3.2. All of the evaluation goals were achieved.

The validation results of the experiment can be summarized as follows. The treatment Group A using the AM3D catalogue had significantly more correct answers when selecting between several patterns, than the Group B using the standard catalogue. The Group A also had significantly fewer mistakes than the Group B.

When re-evaluating the pattern decisions, the Group A outperformed the control Group B in number of correct answers, and also had fewer incorrect answers. However, the null hypotheses in both cases could neither be rejected nor accepted within the defined confidence level, as the p-value was 0.2967 and 0.1162 accordingly.

According to the data, there may be an indicator that the treatment Group A in cases of uncertainty tends to select "I don't know option" more often instead of a definite decision, than the control Group B. Is can be seen as a positive effect, as fewer mistakes are done because of quick decisions.

In general, if considering both tasks together, the treatment Group A clearly outperformed the control Group B, as shown by the statistically significant results.

The hypotheses on the ease of usage of the AM3D catalogue as compared to the classical catalogue could not be statistically evaluated due to the mistake in the experiment design, because the answers to the questions were not placed on an ordinary scale. Instead, a descriptive approach was used to compare the data. The treatment Group A seemed to require less effort to select the right pattern and to re-evaluate the patterns, as the control Group B. The participants of the treatment Group A seemed to have felt easier doing the tasks, than the participants from the control Group B. This observation is based on the mostly positive comments provided by the participants about the perception of the difficulty of the tasks connected to the pattern selection. Furthermore, the treatment Group A received a better support from the AM3D catalogue to select the right pattern and to re-evaluate patterns as the control Group B by the book. Also here, the participants of the treatment Group A seem to have felt more supported by the AM3D catalogue doing the tasks, than the participants from the control Group B by the book.

Since the time measurement was not mistake-free, the time data was not used for the statistical evaluation. The only valid observation made is that in the Group A the participants tended to finish the tasks quicker, than in the Group B. About half of the Group A participants have finished the tasks earlier then the given time, while in the Group B only two participants completed the tasks earlier, to our best knowledge.

Thus, to summarise, the treatment Group A achieved at least better, and in some cases, significantly better results doing pattern selection and decision re-evaluation compared to the control Group B. Hereby, the treatment Group A had less effort and felt more supported during the tasks by the AM3D catalogue, than the control Group B using the classical approach.

6.6. Validation Summary

In Section 6.2 we have described the goals and types of the validations of the AM3D approach. In this section, we summarise the obtained results of the validations. Table 6.29 presents the summary of what is validated and what results were obtained during the validation. For the relations between the validation types and the AM3D approach application scenarios and benefits, please refer to Table 6.3, presented earlier in the chapter.

The feasibility of the approach was demonstrated on the application of the AM3D developed artefacts on the CoCoMe-based system. All artefacts were successfully applied following the defined process, and are capable of supporting the AM3D approach.

The motivation of the AM3D approach was successfully evaluated during the conducted survey. Not only the design patterns are indeed often applied in practice, but also there is still a plenty of problems connected to their application, despite the extensive research and the established information sources in the area. Problems mentioned particularly often are selection between similar pattern alternatives, documentation of patterns, problems with understanding of structure and implementation of patterns, and also the search for a new/unknown pattern suitable for the problem.

The potential applicability of the AM3D approach was also positively evaluated. The participants suggested the AM3D approach can be beneficial for the selection between similar patterns, for pattern documentation, and also for the search of new pattern solution. Since number of survey participants was rather small, these results show the trends and shall not be treated as statistically significant results. Details on the survey, including the discussion of the threats to validity, are listed in Section 6.4.

In the next step, the AM3D approach was validated in the controlled experiment for the pattern selection and re-evaluation tasks. The treatment group using the AM3D approach showed significantly more of the correct answers, and significantly less mistakes when selecting the right pattern between several similar alternatives, then the control group using the classical book approach. For the re-evaluation of the taken pattern design decisions no statistically significant results were achieved. However, the treatment group had noticeably more of the correct answers (> 70%) and noticeably less of the incorrect answers to the tasks on the decision re-evaluation.

Eval. Type	How	What	Results	Section
Type 0 (Feasibility)	Survey based on the structured interviews with 25 participants	Feasibility of the motivation of the approach, and of the potential applicability of the proposed AM3D catalogue evaluated by independent subjects.	Motivation supported: Design patterns are commonly applied on practice, and only 10% of the participants did not experience problems with their application or documentation. Potential applicability supported: The majority of the participants positively evaluated applicability of the catalogue for clarification of properties and consequences of a pattern (68%), for selection between pattern alternatives (60%), and for improving documentation of pattern decisions (55%). Understandability to the extern users was evaluated as high.	Section 6.4
Type I (Appropriateness)	Approach artefacts and process	Support capture and management of pattern decisions and related artefacts a system context.	AM3D approach artefacts and process successfully used to support capture and management of the pattern decisions and related artefacts in system context.	Section 3
Type II (Applicability)	A case study based on controlled experiment with 20 participants	Improvement of understandability and correctness of pattern application in design using AM3D , and improvement of maintainability of the architecture documented with AM3D compared to the standard approach.	Statistically significant improvement of correctness of pattern selection (> 95%) and noticeable improvement of correctness of re-evaluation of pattern design decisions (> 70%). The AM3D catalogue users estimated to have spent less effort for pattern-selection and evaluation, and to be better supported by the AM3D catalogue at these tasks, then the users of the classical approach based on the common book cataogues.	Section 6.5

Table 6.29.: The AM3D Validation Summary

Even though the results for re-evaluation tasks did not reach the confidence level of 95 %, they can still be considered as positive. Moreover, the treatment group stated to feel better supported and to have spent less effort to do the tasks, then the control group. Details on the experiment, including the discussion of the threats to validity, are listed in Section 6.5.

7. Related Work

This chapter describes and analyses work related to the AM3D approach. The AM3D approach belongs to the area of software architecture knowledge management. The area is consists of a very large number of topics related to architecture, architectural design, its capture and management, and there are a lot of research activities going on in the area. Therefore, it is meaningful to narrow down the topic and to define criteria characterizing the AM3D approach in order to be able to select really relevant approaches in this large research field. Section 7.1 provides an overview of the criteria and introduces the classification scheme, based on which the related work is structured in the later sections.

Section 7.2 reviews related approaches on formalisation and documentation of design patterns. It is divided into three subsections, each describing a sub-area defined by the classification scheme. The subsections are: Textual approaches for formalisation and documentation of design patterns 7.2.1, visual approaches 7.2.2, and structural approaches 7.2.3.

Section 7.3 reviews related approaches on formalisation and documentation of design decisions and their rationale. It is divided into three subsections, each describing a sub-area defined by the classification scheme. The subsections are: Textual approaches for formalisation and documentation of design decisions 7.3.1, visual approaches 7.3.2, and structural approaches 7.3.3. Approaches dealing with documentation of decisions on design pattern application are also described in this section.

Section 7.4 discusses the approaches that support search for and selection of suitable pattern candidates. The approaches are divided into the approaches that support search for and selection of patterns based on quality attributes and category definitions, discussed in Section 7.4.1, and approaches based on guiding questions, discussed in Section 7.4.2.

Section 7.5 gives an overview the approaches in architecture-driven requirements engineering area. Finally, Section 7.6 concludes the chapter.

7.1. Classification Scheme

The software architecture knowledge management (SAKM) is a general topic spanning over multiple research directions. Its overview can be found in a book "Software Architecture Knowledge Management" by Babar at al. [182]. Tang et al. [183] compares five architectural knowledge management tools for the provided support in the architecture life-cycle (ADDSS [184], Archium [126], AREL [133], and The Knowledge architect [185], all of which are also reviewed in this chapter).

Since not all of the research directions of the SAKM are really related to the AM3D approach, this section defines criteria to characterise and to classify the AM3D approach in the field of the related work. The main topics of the AM3D approach from the SAKM research field are summarised in Table 7.1.

Topics of the AM3D approach
Design decision evaluation
Design decision documentation
Design decisions formalisation
Design decisions on design pattern application
Design pattern formalisation
Design pattern catalogues or repositories
Reasoning and selection of design patterns

Table 7.1.: Topics of the AM3D Approach from the SAKM Research Area

These topics are: Design decision evaluation, documentation, formalisation, design decisions on design pattern application, design pattern formalisation, design pattern catalogues or repositories, and reasoning and selection of design patterns. In addition, the AM3D approach also deals with goal-oriented requirements engineering, therefore this chapter also provides an overview of the approaches related to this area.

The topics in the SAKM area are divided between design decisions and design patterns, whereby they overlap considering decisions about design pattern application. Moreover, the related approaches on both of these topics (design decisions and design patterns) can be clustered in two dimensions – by their goal and by the formalisation method used. An overview of the usual goals for design pattern approaches is presented in Table 7.2.

Goals Followed by Design Pattern Approaches
Document information on existing patterns (Books, wikis, web-based repositories, etc.)
Formalise pattern description and application (Pattern languages , meta-models, pattern conflict detection, etc.)
Enable search for patterns (Wikis, web-based repositories, other electronic repositories)
Propose pattern candidates as solutions to a problem (Expert systems, search-based pattern repositories)
Document decisions on pattern application (Textual documents, web-decision repositories, etc.)
Design systems based on patterns (Pattern languages)
Pattern code generation (Support implementation of patterns in code)
Detection of patterns in code (Recover used patterns from code)
Visualize pattern application in architectural models

Table 7.2.: Goals of the Pattern Related Approaches

The typical goals are to: Document information on patterns, formalise pattern description and application, enable search for patterns, propose pattern candidates as solutions to a problem, document decisions on pattern application, design systems based on patterns, generate pattern code, detect patterns in code, and visualize patterns in architectural models.

An overview of the usual goals for decision pattern approaches is presented in Table 7.3.

Goals Followed by Design Decision Approaches
Formalize design decision description (Description templates, meta-models, etc.)
Document taken design decisions (Textual documents, wikis, web-repositories, etc.)
Trace requirements in design and code (Tracelinks between various artefacts)
Support decision-making process (Trade-off decisions, quality goals, etc.) Restore taken design decisions (Design recovery)
Document and restore decision rationale (Textual, semi-automated, etc.)
Visualize taken design decisions (Decision views, graphs, etc.)
Visualize change propagation (Impact views, graphs, etc.)
Comprise architectural design (Decisions as part of design, often implicit)

Table 7.3.: Goals of the Decision Related Approaches

The typical goals of design decision approaches are to: Formalize design decision description, document taken design decisions, trace requirements in design and code, support decision-making process, restore taken design decisions, document and restore decision rationale , visualize taken design decisions, visualize change propagation, and comprise architectural design.

Formalisation Methods
Textual
Ontology-based
Graph-based
Meta-model-based
ADL-based (including UML)
Code-based

Table 7.4.: Formalisation Methods in the Related Approaches

Finally, the approaches use different formalisation methods. An overview of the methods is presented in Table 7.4. The related work, therefore, can be classified either based on the followed goals or based on the formalisation method or based on the subtopics of the SAKM research are.

Based on this, the following related work classification for the AM3D approach is proposed: First, the approaches are structured based on their relation to one of the research subfields, such as design patterns formalisation and documentation, design decisions formalisation and documentation, reasoning about and selection of patterns, and architecture-driven requirements engineering. Further on, sections on documentation and formalisation are divided based on the formalisation methods, such as textual (textual description templates, wikis, etc.), visual (graphs, UML, etc.) and structural (meta-models, ontologies, etc.). The section on reasoning about and selection of patterns is structured based on the selection and reasoning methods, such as quality- and categories-based selection and question-based selection (expert systems).

Such classification scheme covers all of the main AM3D approach aspects and allows for comprehensive related work coverage. The dimensions of the classification scheme, however, allow some overlap in topics or formalisation methods of the related work classifications. This is due to the complex nature of the approaches, which usually follow multiple goals and combine multiple topics and formalisms. In such cases, approaches are described in detail in one section, while another section only gives a short reference to the approach.

An overview of approaches based on their belonging to the defined clusters can be found on Figure 7.1. These related work approaches are described in the next sections.

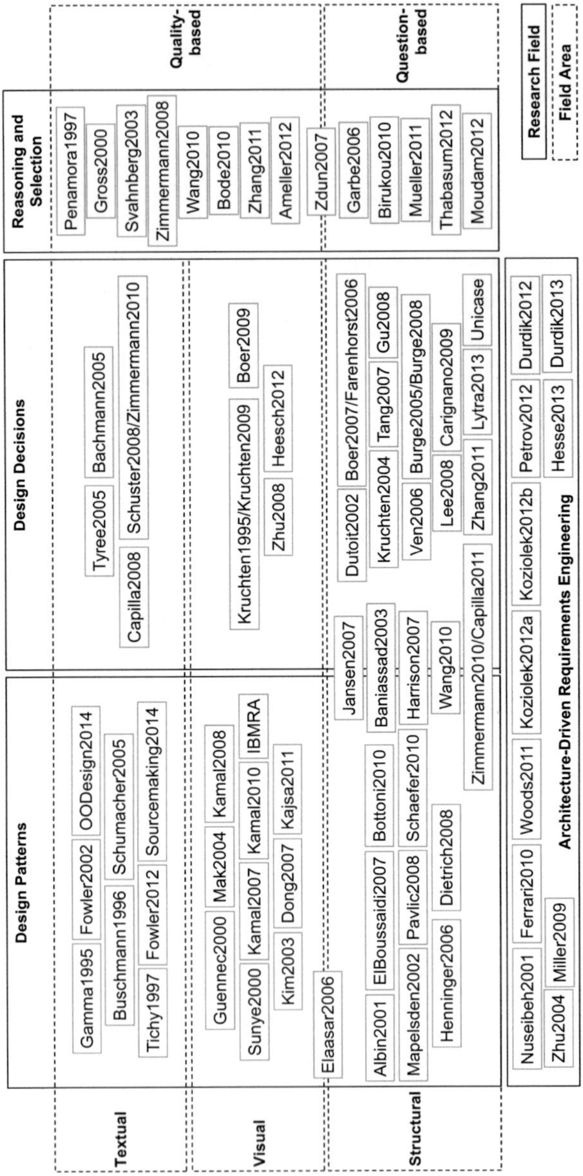

Figure 7.1.: Overview of the Related Approaches According to the Clusters

7.2. Formalisation and Documentation of Design Patterns

An extensive overview of pattern formalization techniques is provided by Taibi et al. [69]. This section focuses on the related work selected according to the previously defined classification – on the approaches for design pattern formalisation and documentation that are the most related to the AM3D approach. The strictly formal approaches typically engage into verification and formal composition checks of design pattern application. Therefore, they are omitted on purpose, since their goal and methods are very different from the AM3D approach.

Documentation of design patterns here means a collection of information on patterns (pattern catalogues, etc.), and not documentation of application of design patterns (decisions on pattern application). Related work on documentation of pattern application is provided in the next Section 7.3.3.

The idea of formalizing and documenting design patterns is not new. The documentation can be carried out with textual approaches, based on books and Wikis (various kinds of pattern catalogues), with structural approaches, based on ontologies and meta-models, with the visual approaches based on UML models and graphs, or in the code. Some of the approaches form so-called pattern languages, which define how to use pattern design solutions to form a complete and complex system design.

While textual approaches, such as books, provide comprehensive but long descriptions of patterns, the meta-models re-capture this information in a similar to book structure, or deal with pattern implementation in the architectural models or code. The majority of the approaches cover only a part of these aspects, such as documentation or implementation on UML diagrams. The AM3D approach, however, combines several of them, namely: Formalisation of design pattern documentation in a new type of pattern catalogue, design pattern application documentation, and design pattern modelling in architectural diagrams.

In the next sections, the related approaches are described based on their affiliation to the textual approaches in Section 7.2.1, visual approaches in Section 7.2.2 and structural approaches in Section 7.2.3.

7.2.1. Textual Approaches

The main goal of textual approaches is usually to provide structured and comprehensive information of a set of patterns from a certain domain, in order to be used as a reference. Textual approaches are typically based on textual description templates.

The most common way to document design patterns is to capture them in a book, which is a kind of a pattern catalogue. There is a significant amount of books on design patterns. Usually the books describe patterns from the same application domain, for example, object-oriented design patterns or security patterns.

Some of the most common pattern catalogues of this type are: "Design Patterns. Elements of Reusable Object-Oriented Software" by Gamma et al. [28], "A System of Patterns: Pattern-Oriented Software Architecture" by Buschmann et al. [29], "Pattern-Oriented Software Architecture: A Pattern Language for Distributed Computing" by Buschmann et al. [31], "Patterns of Enterprise Application Architecture" by Fowler [58] or "Security Patterns: Integrating Security and Systems Engineering" by Schumacher et al. [61]. These are just some few examples of the pattern catalogue books.

Each of the book catalogues follows its own description template. While inside of one book, such template is helpful for quicker understanding of patterns, different templates for patterns of different domains complicate understanding and working with the design patterns. To the author's best knowledge, there is neither an established standard, nor a re-usable template available for the description of design patterns in the catalogue.

The majority of the other approaches to document the design patterns are based on such book catalogues, e.g. following the description template out of books or deriving the information out of them. Also the AM3D approach follows this tendency, both, being inspired by the description template and using the content of the books. Wikis

Another subtype of textual approaches are the purified catalogues, e.g. by Tichy [186], who organizes the patterns based on the problems they solve, or online catalogues, such as catalogue by Fowler [187], who organizes patterns of enterprise application architecture in a short online catalogue based on the pattern goals. Such catalogues typically provide shorter information and/or are available online. Other examples are a catalogue at Sourcemaking [188] and a catalogue at OO Design [189].

Since the main goal of these approaches is to provide a reference on design patterns, other aspects of the AM3D approach are not covered.

7.2.2. Visual Approaches

This group of descriptive approaches is based on graphical representations, such as UML and UML profiles or Role-Connector modelling. These approaches usually focus on pattern visualisation in architectural models. Such visualisation can be seen as a way of documenting pattern design decisions, with the focus on structural representation of taken decisions, which is also a subpart of the AM3D approach.

A large part of approaches concentrate on UML pattern representation and its extensions. So, already in 2000, Sunye et al. [190] and Guennec et al [191] have proposed modification to the UML notation to better support design pattern modelling. Sunye et al. [190] proposed to extend the parametrized collaborations in UML to better support the semi-automatic application of design patterns, and Guennec et al [191] target was to improve automatic processing of pattern applications within CASE (Computer-Aided Software Engineering) tools. Mak et al. [192] propose extension of UML with stereotypes to allow a specification of patterns without over-specifying the information.

In [193] Kamal et al. provide the evaluation of ADLs on modelling design patterns for software architecture. They comment, that despite UML is a kind of standard, it provides little support to model architectural patterns. The authors evaluate UML 2.0 [194,195], ACME [196], Wright [197], UniCon [198], xADL [199] and AESOP
[200] with the help of the developed evaluation framework.

Dong et al. [64] propose extension of UML with pattern UML-profile. The goal of the approach is to support visualization of design patterns in UML diagrams. UML model elements can be annotated with different tags related to pattern application, such as role in the pattern or name of a pattern. Such visualisation annotation is an implicit documentation of pattern design decisions in design models, however, the authors actually do not concentrate on this aspect. Other relevant to the AM3D approach aspects, such as a reusable catalogue, pattern decision evaluation, or documentation of rationale, are not supported.

Kamal et al. [65] propose UML profiles to model patterns in UML models with the help of a set of architectural primitives, such as callback, indirection, aggregation cascade etc.. The primitives are defined as extensions of existing meta-classes using stereotypes, tagged values, and constraints. They provide examples for Pipes and Filters, Model View Controller and Layers. This work is extended by Kamal et al. in [201] to support variability in modelling of pattern solutions.

A method of design pattern instantiation support in code and architectural model is proposed by Kajsa et al. [202]. The authors extend UML and define transformation from models to UML models, and then to code.

Another approach to pattern visualisation is the presentation of design patterns with the help of role-connector concept. This concept was first proposed by Mary Shaw at the end of the 90s, and has been regularly used to depict design patterns in architectural diagrams since then.

For example, a UML-based pattern specification language called "Role-based Metamodeling Language" (RBML) is proposed by Kim et al. [60,

69]. The approach defines design patterns as a solution domain in terms of roles at the meta-model level. The goal of the RBML is to "support the development of precise pattern specifications that can be used for the development of pattern tools", and in particular, in UML-based tools. It is possible to generate architectural model stubs (for UML) of design patterns. The RBML deals with various design perspectives of patterns, such as static structure, interactions, and state-based behaviours. Roles are played by UML model elements, such as classes, and can be represented either graphically or textually in the OCL (Object Constraint Language, [148]).

Another example is approach by Elaasar et al. [62], which uses the role and connector notation in their meta-modelling approach, described in detail in the next section.

Finally, some modelling tools, such as Rational Software Architect by IBM [203], support modelling of some of design patterns (e.g., so-called GoF patterns, from Gamma et al. [28]) through predefined models available in their repositories.

The number of approaches in this area is high, and this section lists only several exemplary approaches. The AM3D approach relies on the state-of-the-art and uses role-connector mechanism together with the UML notations as utilized by Gamma et al. [28] to depict pattern structures.

7.2.3. Structural Approaches

This group of descriptive approaches for pattern documentation is called structural approaches. These approaches are based on ontologies or meta-models, which structure the information about patterns, and thus formalize pattern application.

An example of ontology-based approach is the approach proposed by Pavlic et al. [66], who formalize design pattern specifications in order to organize design patterns in a Web-based repository. The repository supports searching for and proposing potentially useful design patterns. Pavlic et al. propose to use questions in order to guide the selection of patterns for certain design situations. The answers to the questions are pre-defined, and depending on what answer the user selects, one of the patterns is recommended with a certain probability (see also Section 7.4.2 for related work on expert systems). Pavlic et al. do not consider potential quality influence of patterns and pattern application decision documentation.

Another ontology-based approach is by Dietrich et al. [69, 204]. The authors use OWL (Web Ontology Language, [205]) to describe patterns with the goal to "facilitate the use of patterns as knowledge artefacts shared by the software engineering community". One of their envisioned goals is to enable discover of pattern definitions in social networks, to define and to publish patterns, to rate patterns, to establish the trustworthiness of patterns found, and finally search for pattern instances in Java projects.

Besides the ontology-based approaches, another subtype of the structural pattern documentation approaches are approaches based on the meta-models. Albin-Amiot et al. [206] propose to formalise design patterns with the help of the meta-model. The goal of the formalisation is to enable code generation and design pattern detection. The meta-model does not focus on the general information about patterns, but on how the patterns are used, their relations and structural representation. Pattern selection, pattern application decision evaluation and documentation, and potential quality influence are out of the work's scope.

Schaefer et al. [67] propose another specification of software patterns based on the meta-model. The goal is to support pattern description and management. This meta-model, similar to the AM3D meta-model, is also based on the description template from the Gamma et al. book [28]. It supports pattern variants, relations between patterns, and general description information. The information includes data on the pattern's intent and consequences, as in Gamma et al.. The patterns can be structured by keywords and category. The meta-model is thought as aid for students working with patterns during the course at the Paderborn University. It does not support pattern selection or evaluation and documentation of pattern application decisions.

Henninger et al. [63] propose a hybrid approach based on an ontology-based meta-model for design patterns. The goal of the approach is to formalise pattern specifications in order to create a pattern catalogue and to support pattern languages for composite design based on patterns. Since the approach is ontology-based, it supports search for patterns (probably based on keywords). Note, that the concept of the meta-model in Henninger et al. is different from the AM3D definition of the meta-model. In terms of the AM3D approach the meta-model of Henninger et al. would be rather a pure ontology. The approach does not support pattern selection or evaluation and documentation of pattern application decisions. Influence on quality probably can be depicted through the concept of "forces", however, it is not explained in the paper and can only be assumed.

Elaasar et al. [62] propose a Pattern Modeling Framework (PMF), which is a meta-modelling approach for pattern specification and detection. The authors define an "Epattern" meta-model, that allows for pattern specification at a model level. The PMF focuses on the architectural details of patterns, in particular, on their modelling in EMOF-compatible models. The authors state that the notation for Epattern is based on the notation of the class and composite structure diagrams of UML 2.0.. Elaasar et al. use role and connector notation for pattern depiction, extended with Port, Association and Constraint.

El Boussaidi et al. [207] propose an interesting concept, where pattern applications are divided into three areas: Problem area, solution area and transformations area, which is a rule-based representation of the transformations for the application of the pattern. While, usually the problem is depicted through the requirements-issue relationships, the authors propose a modelling language for definition of problem space.

Mapelsden et al. [59, 69] define a Design Pattern Modelling Language (DPML) is a meta-model and a notation for specifying pattern solutions and instances within object models to support modelling and reuse of patterns. The DPML allows to define patterns and to instantiate them in UML. While pattern definition remains the same, instances can be changed according to the needs and then attached to the UML model elements.

A language-independent formalization of patterns is proposed by Bottoni et al. [68] to support language-independent modelling. It allows for transformation into other modelling notations, such as models by meta-model-based approaches, and others.

7.3. Formalisation and Capture of Design Decisions and Rationale

This section is structured based on the in Section 7.1 proposed classification scheme, and focuses on the approaches for design decision formalisation and documentation. Approaches dedicated to decisions on pattern application are also a part of this section. Under documentation of design decisions the collection and capture of information on decision decisions is understood in the section.

Most of the approaches do not distinguish between types of design decisions, and do not consider reusable solutions to support rationale documentation. The somewhat simplified view on design decisions is also an outcome of the analysis by Bu et al. in [208], where they provide an analysis of decision-centric architectural design approaches, based on the case study. The authors investigate support for design reasoning from three perspectives: (1) architectural knowledge modelling, (2) decision making techniques, and (3) design rationale management. The conclusion is that most approaches assume that architecturally significant requirements are given and clear, and that the design reasoning is based only one dimension.

In the next sections, the related approaches are described based on their affiliation to the textual approaches in Section 7.3.1, visual approaches in Section 7.3.2 and structural approaches in Section 7.3.3.

7.3.1. Textual Approaches

One of the most common ways to document design decisions is to capture them in a textual document, which is specific for each project. The decisions can be captured as unstructured text, however, there is usually a description template to follow.

If there are some links to requirements or rationale descriptions, than usually these are textual references to the requirement numbers or textual descriptions of the rationale.

The common problem with such approaches is that capture of design decisions, and in particular rationales and links to requirements, requires significant effort. Once requirements or decisions change, the maintenance of such documents becomes even more complicated, as all the changes have to be done manually. It is easy to oversee decisions that need to be re-evaluated, as no automated triggers are possible.

Tyree et al. [45] propose a textual architecture decision description template, which is based on REMAP (Representation and Maintenance of Process Knowledge) and DRL (Decision Representation Language) metamodels. The decision template can be used to describe any kind of decisions, although, the authors do not distinguish between decision types. All information, including the rationale, has to be written in textual form and cannot be reused or derived from solutions.

The architecture design decision support system tool (ADDSS) by Capilla et al. [46] supports capturing and documenting architectural design based on a template. The approach supports relationships between decisions, and to other project context element, such as links to requirements and architecture diagrams.

Architectural Decision Knowledge Wiki (ADkwik) is proposed by Schuster et al. [47, 209] (quoted from Shahin [57]) and is a model-based collaboration system that implements the approach proposed by Zimmermann et al. [48, 210, 211] and explained later on. ADkwik is a classical wiki, and supports reusing decisions from the architectural decision repository, import and export of decision content, search of decisions by various attributes and support collaboration features [57]. Another Wiki-based approach is proposed by Bachmann et al. [212], and describes a Wiki-based tool for documentation of software architectures, and, in particular, for documentation of design decisions.

7.3.2. Visual Approaches

Another very common way to document design decisions are diagram-based approaches, whereby design decisions are typically implicitly captured in the system architecture and design documents [45]. Some of the approaches, however, support explicit documentation of decisions with the help of annotations to the model elements.

Nevertheless, the common problem with such approaches is that the rationale for the decisions, as well as links to the triggers and other contextual information are often completely omitted and this kind of information is lost. Moreover, the architectural documents are seldom updated, and typically quickly become out of date and practically useless.

Zhu et al. [49] propose a UML profile for modelling design decisions and an associated UML profile for modelling non-functional requirements in a generic way. In both cases, the elements in question are treated as first-class entities. Modelled design decisions refer to existing architectural elements to maintain traceability.

An ontology-driven visualization of architectural design decisions is proposed by Boer et al. [213]. The ontology is based on quality criteria, and their effects. The supported usage scenarios are: Trade-off analysis, impact analysis, and if-then scenario (what would happen if another option would be selected in previous scenarios).

A specialised decision view in additions to classical views on software architecture was proposed by Kruchten [123] and Kruchten et al. in [24].

Van Heesch et al. [214] extended the work of Kruchten and a documentation framework for architecture decisions. This framework consists of four viewpoints based on the ISO/IEC/IEEE 42010 standard describing system and software architectures. The four viewpoints are: Decision Detail viewpoint, Decision Relationship viewpoint, Decision Chronology viewpoint, and Decision Stakeholder Involvement viewpoint.

7.3.3. Structural Approaches

The last group of approaches for documentation of design decisions and rationale are structural approaches, based on the ontologies, models and meta-models. A survey by Shahin et al. [57] provides on overview of some of the existing model-based approaches to formalize and to document design decisions, such as mature approaches by Kruchten [130], Zimmermann [48], Lee et al. [215], Tang et al. [133]. These approaches, as well as others, are discussed in detail in this section from the perspective of the AM3D approach.

Most of these approaches focus on the general class of design decisions and are a foundation for our AM3D approach. The few of the related approaches that treat the design patterns as a class of design decisions are presented at the end of the section.

Although the original goal of the approach by Dutoit et al. [216] is different from this Section's topic (the approach main focus is on integrating rationale with requirements engineering), the authors present an interesting concept model in detail describing decisions and elements leading to the decisions. A decision is triggered by the issues, which result from different requirement types. Decisions include solution alternatives (called Options in the model), which are assessed based on provided arguments and quality requirements. Question concept depicts "needs to be solved for the requirements process to proceed", and can "indicate a design issue, a request for clarification or a possible defect".

Kruchten [130] proposed an ontology of architectural design decisions for software-intensive systems. The goal of the ontology is to capture decisions and all their interdependencies in order to support the evolution and maintenance of the systems. Kruchten distinguishes between different higher-order types of decisions, such as existence decisions, property decisions, and executive decisions. Decisions may have textual rationale. In [50], Kruchten et al. enhance the previous work and describe a use-case model for an architectural knowledge base and updated ontology. The meta-model based on the ontology by Kruchten was a foundation for the development of the decision meta-model of the AM3D approach.

Baniassad et al. [217] propose a graph-based approach to connect pattern design with the code, and to represent such connections in a graphical form. In particular, Design Pattern Rationale Graphs (DPRG) are proposed to make the design pattern rationale accessible to developers with the help of links between elements in code with rationale from common patterns.

Boer et al. [51, 218, 219] define a "core model" of architectural knowledge, with the goal to establish a standardized terminology in the area of architectural knowledge management, and to define which elements belong to the models in the area. The approach does not consider architectural solutions directly, but offers a class for "alternatives", which are implicit design solutions. Design patterns and quality influences (or other influences) of design decisions are also excluded from the approach.

Gu et al. [220] focus on the process decisions in the SOA domain, and map these decisions against the above described "core model". The authors propose an extension of the "core model", which deals with the SOA-specific concepts and does not include the above mentioned elements.

Babar et al. [221] present a data model for development of knowledge sharing repositories. A model of architectural design decisions for making such decisions more explicit is proposed by Choi et al. [222]. A fuzzy-logic-based approach for design decision making and documentation is developed by Lytra et al. [223].

Tang et al. [133] propose AREL, an approached based on a rationale-based architectural model for design traceability and reasoning. The model captures design decisions, their rationale and constraints. The main focus is on support of traceability between elements. The model supports extensive project context, such as requirements, architectural models and environment descriptions. It also supports trade-off and risks analyses, based on the textual annotations. The alternatives are encapsulated into the rationale, and the rationale can have various types (quantitative and qualitative).

Interestingly, a large cluster of approaches (including those, listed above) does not consider connection between the concept of the architectural solution and architectural decisions. The decisions and solutions, actually, are treated as synonyms or solutions are simply omitted. Some of the few approaches, which separate both of the concepts are listed in the following.

Carignano et al. [52] propose another model to capture the design rationale. The model also includes means for description of some of the project context information, such as Requirements, Stakeholders, Quality Attributes and others. Architectural solutions are explicitly considered by the model, but are not first-class entities, but a sub-class of architectural design decisions and are included into decisions.

A solution recommendation approach is envisioned in the work of Zhang et al. [53], who also propose a meta-model for modelling design decisions. The goal of the approach is to select a set of the most suitable solutions, so that the quality goals of the system are the most satisfied.

Van der Ven et al. [224] propose an approach for explicit modelling of design decisions in the architecture. The authors discuss the rationale behind the architecture, and the way to capture it through decisions modelling. They explicitly distinguish between solutions and decisions. The proposed approach is based on the Archium, which is a tool combining an architectural description language together with the decision model. Archium is described later on. In this approach, the documentation of decisions and rationale, are however, still a manual process with no reuse facilitation.

Finally, there are few approaches considering design patterns as a type of design decisions. Jansen et al. [54, 126] view software architecture as a composition of a set of explicit decisions, and propose a model and a meta-model for architectural decisions reflecting this view. The meta-model is a base for their approach and tool-support called Archium. Archium approach by Jansen et al. [126] considers design patterns first class in the realization, and not as sub-sets of predefined decisions.

Harrison et al. [225, 226] suggest that architectural design patterns can support documentation of design decisions. The authors write that pattern selection helps to relate decisions with each other and that pattern description is comparable to the design description templates, besides the fact that the pattern descriptions focus on timeless and generic knowledge, and can be used for the decision documentation. The authors provide a comparison of patterns and decisions in terms of documentation. The paper describes the idea, but does not provide a concrete approach. To our best knowledge, there are no follow up approaches by these authors. The AM3D approach extends the idea by Harrison et al. and proposes its implementation.

Zimmermann et al. [48,72,210,211] propose a decision framework based on reusable architectural decision models. Design patterns are a type of decision described through decision alternatives. The approaches use requirements models and decision templates to instantiate decision models. The templates describe knowledge collected in other projects, e.g. utilizing the same architectural style. The purpose is to avoid decisions being done solely based on the experience of an architect, to support the collaboration and exchange of rationale between project teams. The decisions modelled in the model refer to the design elements in the architectural models. The approach by Zimmermann et al. is close to the AM3D approach. It makes use of already available information, in order to support decision making. It follows similar main steps in the decisions making process – decision identification, decision making and decision enforcement. However, it focuses on reuse of decisions and decision information itself, and not on the reuse of solutions and reuse of rationale through the solutions. The solutions are actually included into decision and are not treated as separate (first class) entities. The decision making is carried out though decision supporting techniques, such as SWOT tables [227] and "formal alternative scoring algorithms" [228] (quoted from [211]). The decision enforcement is done through the code injection through Eclipse JET Templates. In [229], Zimmermann et al. describe a way to reuse certain decisions based on the analysis of applied design patterns. The authors also provide an excerpt of a generic Meta issue catalogue, which is independent of application domain. The idea here is that some issues do reoccur, and therefore, the design decisions for these issues reoccur. The idea of the AM3D approach is to support evaluation of pattern application and to reuse properties of design patterns for decision documentation, and in particular, for the rationale generation.

Capilla et al. [56] extend the work further on, and introduces meta-model extensions to capture and to share architectural decisions in order to support evolution of decisions, decision identification, decision making and to support runtime decisions. The extension adds links to design artefacts, support for decision history and support of modification during runtime, such as changes of operation mode or routes of service invocations.

An approach "Software Engineering Using Rationale" (SEURAT) was proposed by Burge et al. [21, 230, 231] and extend for design patterns by Wang et al. [55] . The main goal of SEURAT is documentation of design decisions together with the rationale in the project context with the focus on software maintenance support. The support for the rationale is extensive, and includes capture of intent of developers and capture of all considered alternatives together with the decisions-making process (arguments for and against solutions). Besides other features, SEURAT has a pre-defined argument ontology, which contains a hierarchy of common arguments that serve as types of claims that can be used for communication of properties in the system. SEURAT also defines a concept of questions that need to be answered as part of the decision-making process. The questions in SEURAT have other purpose than in AM3D approach, they indicate "what information is required before making the decisions and by specifying the source of the information needed or used to answer the question". The rationale can be also linked to code, as developers are the main targets of the approach.

UNICASE [113] UNICASE is a "CASE-Tool integrating models from the different development activities, such as requirements, use cases, UML models, schedules, bug and feature models into a unified model". It support traceability between various artefacts, and allows the viewing and editing of various models in various representations. The tool was recently extended to support decisions on design patterns and their application. The main goal of UNICASE is to support a set of project-related activities, such as requirements engineering and UML modelling, and to integrate these various actions into one tool environment. Thus, its goals differ from the goals of the AM3D approach. UNICASE can be rather seen as a complementary approach, and a good tool-base for integration with the AM3D approach, which is a subject for future work.

The extension added by Wang et al. [55] has a pre-defined pattern library and used the non-functional requirements to guide the selection of patterns. Each pattern is seen as an alternative solution in the decision made, and decisions are captured with the rationale recorded. This extension has several levels to distinguish between patterns: Pattern categories, design problem categories, affected quality attributes and decisions required to adopt a pattern and their alternative patterns. List of potential pattern candidates can be generated based on the defined criteria. The catalogue of patterns is based on the other sources, such as Microsoft MSDN.

The major difference between the AM3D approach and other related approaches is that the goal of the AM3D approach is to only to support documentation of design decisions, and in particular of those connected to design patterns, but also to support re-evaluation of decisions and to reuse the architectural solution descriptions for the semi-automated documentation of decision rationales. The AM3D approach also allows for the architectural constraint checks in order to enforce correct pattern solution modelling. This combination of decision re-evaluation, documentation together with the rationale and of support during the modelling makes the AM3D approach, differentiates our approach from the related approaches.

7.4. Reasoning About and Selection of Patterns

Multiple approaches are introduced to reason about and to select suitable design patterns. A survey and comparison of eight existing decision-making techniques for general decision making approaches is provided by Falessi et al. in [78]. This section focuses solely on selection and reasoning about design patterns. Approaches that support search for and selection of patterns based on quality attributes and category definitions are discussed in Section 7.4.1. Approaches that support search for and selection of patterns based on guiding questions are discussed in Section 7.4.2.

7.4.1. Quality- and Category-Based Approaches

Among the approaches supporting search for and selection of design patterns are the approaches based on the quality attributes and on potential quality influence of design patterns.

For example, Pena-Mora et al. [23] proposed a methodology to combine design rationale and design patterns and developed a design recommendation and intent model already in 1997. The methodology focuses on the code level and covers patterns from Gamma et al. [28].

A solution recommendation approach is envisioned in the work of Zhang et al. [53]. The approach is based on the meta-model for modelling design decisions. The approach calculates quality value vectors for different candidate solutions, as well as quality weight vector. The quality goals are derived from requirements. The final goal is to select a set of solutions that satisfies the defined quality goals the most.

Gross et al. [70] researched the influence of non-functional properties of the patterns on the application of design patterns, and proposed a way for reasoning about the design patterns based on the non-functional requirements. The non-functional aspects of descriptions of patterns are systematically considered when applying patterns during design. Hereby, the known non-functional requirements to the system (treated as design goals) are compared with available solutions, and how these solutions can achieve the defined goals. The approach supports documentation of claims both for and against different choices.

Svahnberg et al. [228] propose a framework for comparison of different solution candidates based on quality attributes via Analytic Hierarchy Process (AHP), and allows comparing benefits and liabilities to evaluate resulting decision. The framework was tested on five patterns from Buschmann et al. [29], being examples of architectural solutions. The software quality attributes need to be prioritized in order to carry out the comparison. The final comparison is carried out by participants.

An approach to support selection of patterns based on desired quality attributes by Zdun et al. [71] is based on formalisation of the pattern relationships in a pattern language grammar. The grammar is annotated with effects on quality goals. The defined relationships between patterns allow for pattern selection. Patterns are considered to be design solutions. The influence of quality goals is defined on a five-point scale, from a very positive influence to a very negative influence. The approach uses a questions, options, and criteria notation (from MacLean et al. [232]) to visualize alternatives for design decisions and related design considerations. The questions highlight the key issues to be considered in a design situation (they describe a pattern category or domain), options are the possible answers to the questions, and criteria are the reasons that argue for or against the possible options of a question. The goal of this notation is to support a detailed analysis of each decision, and to "provide a detailed decision map" for a design decision.

Zimmermann et al. [72] propose an approach that supports domain-specific pattern selection based on the provided requirement models, and provides traceability from platform-independent patterns to platform-specific decisions.

Bode et al. [233] refine and map quality goals to properties of design patterns to improve the design. For this, the authors evaluate a set of architectural patterns and provide a calculation scheme to enable the evaluation of the patterns to support design decisions. To select suitable solutions (design patterns), the authors first propose to use architectural constraints to eliminating all unsuitable solutions. Afterwards, all left solutions are evaluated and ranked regarding the relevant quality goals. The ranking is calculated based on the predefined values for the solutions.

Ameller et al. [234] propose a tool ArchiTech for decision-making based on quality attributes. ArchiTech proposes alternative architectural decisions based on the quality requirements. First, the architect specifies the quality requirements and constraints. These are used by the tool to generate a prioritized list of decisions that satisfy the provided requirements. The architect selects from the list decisions to be applied. The tool analyses selected decisions, and, if applicable, notifies the architect about possible issues with decisions and actions to resolve them. Finally, the process to proceed with decisions may be generated.

The extension to the SEURAT approach proposed by Wang et al. [55] allows for generating a list of potentially suitable pattern candidates based on the defined criteria. The approach is described in Section 7.3.3.

More of related approaches can be found in surveys by Birukou [76] and by Thabasum et al. [77].

7.4.2. Question-Based Approaches and Expert Systems

A large class of related work can be described as expert or recommendation systems for pattern selection.

One of the approaches is KARaCAs by Garbe et al. [73]. KARaCAs is an expert system based on the Bayesian Belief Network, where questions are used to select the most appropriate pattern. Such approaches aim to support software engineer to select the right pattern for their design problem. These approaches are complementary to our approach, because our approach is not indented to be used as an expert system for pattern selection itself. Once a pattern is selected, our approach helps to evaluate the applicability of this pattern and captures the pattern decision with its rationale. One has to keep in mind that most of the expert systems bear the drawback that the "right" answer ("the right pattern") might be negatively weighted or even excluded early in the decision making process due to the wrongly answered introductory questions.

Zdun et al. [71] support a selection of patterns based on quality attributes of pattern relationships, and questions for definitions of problem spaces (categories and domains). This approach is described in the previous section.

In [74] Moudam et al. present a support system for making decision to choose design patterns. The authors define a modelling language (XML- and XMI-based) to define patterns to support their design pattern management system. The system captures data on applicability of design patterns and allows for searching for suitable patterns based on the situations in which desired design pattern could be used. First, users select a set of keywords that match the scope of the user interest, and in the next step, selection of situations relevant for the user, which are proposed based on the selected keywords. Finally, once the situations are selected, a list of suitable design patterns is generated.

Mueller et al. [75] propose a question-based approach for efficiently finding architecture candidates using annotated pattern and style catalogues. Questions guide the selection of solution candidates form the catalogue. The solution candidates in catalogue are extended with rated questions, and answering these reduces the candidate space. The authors propose the following rating for the solutions based on questions: A solution contributes positively (0, 1.0) to a problem, a solution contributes negatively (–1.0, 0) to a problem, a solution contradicts the problem. The final evaluation of candidate solution is based on the evaluation of architectural instances, whereby quality requirements and the constraints are analysed.

More of related approaches can be found in surveys by Birukou [76] and by Thabasum et al. [77].

7.5. Goal-Oriented Architecture-Driven Requirements Engineering

The related work in this section is described according to our overview in publications [3, 11].

Goal-oriented architecture-driven requirements engineering is a rather new research area. The related work in the area typically focus on "closing the gap" between requirements and architecture, rather than contributing to requirements engineering via software design.

The influence of existing architecture and reusable elements on requirements has been evaluated and confirmed in several studies, such as Boer [79] or Ferrari et al. [40, 41, 235]. The later explore the influence of existing architecture on requirements in multiple steps, finishing with a case study on a large-scale prototypical project in [41]. Neither of them, however, considers a practical approach to inform the requirement engineering from architectural design.

Engelsman et al. [236] investigate elicitation of requirements from the existing architecture and architecture-based requirement specification reuse. The focus is on obtaining specifications for the development of the new systems, based on the similar previously developed systems.

A Goal Solution Scheme [237] was proposed to map quality goals and goal refinements to architectural principles and solutions. However, it does not consider requirements elicitation. The KARaCAs approach by Garbe et al. [73] is as well focused on establishing the connection from requirements into architectural solutions. Gruenbacher et al. [238] propose an approach called CBSP to establish and to maintain a connection between requirements and architectural elements. Hesse et al. [239] propose a model for decisions supporting the intertwined documentation of related requirements and architecture knowledge.

The idea to use architecture as a basis for further requirement discovery and determination of the alternative design solutions was first proposed by Nuseibeh [42] and Woods [240]. In particular, Nuseibeh proposes to use the view on models, prototypes and commercially available software to emerge new requirements. There are few details about the method itself. Another method using a similar idea is [241]. It uses information extraction to improve the architecture evolution process by mining architecture and design patterns. However, its goal is to support the system's evolution and to extract general scenarios for it.

Petrov et al. [242] propose to integrate decision analysis into requirements engineering. The authors deal with specific information sources that can contribute to requirements specification – contextual environment concerns and architectural patterns and heuristics (architectural patterns, in this case, are a kind of "macro-architectural" best practices). These additional information sources can be used complimentary to the AM3D approach proposed in this thesis, as it does not consider "macro-architectural requirements" explicitly.

Koziolek discusses the relationship of design space exploration and quality requirements prioritization in [43] and proposes a method to systematically support quality requirements prioritization [80]. In the area of software architecture optimization, a large number of approaches have been suggested to improve a given design with respect to several quality properties at once [3]. However, as to [3], none of the approaches discusses the feedback that multi-criteria optimization can give to the requirements decisions of other than quantifiable quality requirements. As to the prioritisation of quality requirements and software architecture, methods like ATAM [165] help to qualitatively uncover quality requirements conflicts and find appropriate trade-offs [3].

A prior to this thesis, we have briefly investigated into the possibility to use the design patterns for the elicitation of non-functional requirements in [4]. Further on, we have together extended the work by Koziolek [43,80] in [3], focusing on the interplay of design space exploration with other design decisions and general requirements decisions, i.e. considers more than quality requirements.

An overview of some additional related approaches can be further on found in [40,41].

7.6. Summary

This chapter provided an overview of the related approaches, which were structured according to the proposed classification scheme. The scheme defines the following related research areas: Formalisation and documentation of design patterns, formalisation and documentation of design decisions and rationale, reasoning about and selection of design patterns, and goal-oriented architecture-driven requirements engineering. Furthermore, approaches to formalisation and documentation of design patterns and formalisation and documentation of design decisions and rationale are classified based on the formalisation method they use: Textual, Visual and structural approaches. Approaches to reasoning about and selection of design patterns are classified based on their underlying methodology: Quality- and category-based and question-based approaches.

The AM3D approach builds upon several state of the art approaches, such as approaches by Kruchten [130], Zimmermann et al. [72], Burge et al. [21], Wang et al. [55], Nuseibeh [42] and Koziolek [43,80].

One of the most related approaches to the AM3D approach is the SEURAT approach proposed by Burge et al. [21,231] and extended by Wang et al. [55]. It, however, has a different focus. While it support documentation of design decisions and selection of design patterns trough quality attributes, it does not support evaluation of such pattern design decisions beyond the quality attributes, and does not generate rationale for the decisions. A textual rationale may be provided manually. The approach supports requirements capture, management and usage in trace links, however, support of requirements elicitation and prioritisation is out of its focus.

Other closely related approach is UNICASE [113]. The main goal of UNICASE is to support a set of project-related activities, which differs from the goals of the AM3D approach. Similar to the SEURAT, UNICASE approach does not focus on evaluation of decisions or extraction of rationale, as well as on-demand requirements elicitation and prioritisation. AREL approach by Tang et al. [133] captures decisions, rationale and constraints in order to support of traceability between elements. The approach requires a manual input of design rationale, and does not focus on evaluation of design solutions. The approach by Mueller et al. [75] evaluates candidate solutions based on the evaluation of architectural instances, whereby quality requirements and the constraints are analysed. KARaCAs approach by Garbe et al. [73] is an expert system using questions to select the most appropriate pattern. Both of these approaches use questions in a way typical for the expert systems, which differs from the AM3D approach. For the detailed discussion of the difference between the AM3D approach and expert systems please refer to Section 3.5.

As to the architecture-driven requirements elicitation area, the most related are the approaches by Nuseibeh [42] and Koziolek [43, 80]. The AM3D approach continues these work, and in particular, work proposed by Koziolek in cooperation in [3] and in this thesis.

To summarise, the main novelty of the AM3D approach is the concept of the question annotations to reusable design solutions. Such question annotations allow for evaluation of solutions, semi-automated generation of rationale for decisions on design solutions and trigger on-demand requirements elicitation and prioritisation. Thus, unlike questions in the expert systems, they do not guide a user to a solution, but rather support the user in solution evaluation and documentation of decision on a solution. In addition to decision documentation and management, supported by the above mentioned approaches, the AM3D approach adds support for the semi-automated decision generation and simplified capture of the trace links between requirements, decisions and architecture. Trace links are triggered in the process of answering the questions. Finally, in addition to requirements capture and management, also supported by the above mentioned approaches, the AM3D approach also triggers on-demand elicitation and prioritisation of requirements that are relevant to the current architectural design. All of these benefits are, in fact, achieved through the concept of question annotations.

8. Conclusion

This chapter concludes the thesis, summarizing the main contributions, benefits and validation results in Section 8.1. Section 8.2 summarises the assumptions and limitations of the approach and the conducted validations. Section 8.3 discusses open research questions and directions for future work, structured according to the three categories: Short-term user-relevant open questions and future work (Section 8.3.1); long-term user-relevant open questions and future work (Section 8.3.2); and empirical user-relevant open questions and future work (Section 8.3.3).

8.1. Summary

This thesis addresses the problems with elicitation and prioritisation of requirements, application of design patterns and documentation of the decisions about the application of design patterns. In particular, the decisions to apply design patterns similar to the decisions on other reusable architectural solutions are often a result of a spontaneous process and not of a systematic approach. The outcome depends on the experience of the software engineer. Our survey showed that even experienced software engineers face problems with design pattern application, and in particular, they are not always sure which pattern is the most appropriate for a problem and are often underestimating potential drawbacks of design patterns (see Section 6.4). According to the survey, even the experienced software engineers had problems with the correct architectural implementation of patterns and faced problems with poor documentation of pattern decisions. Indeed, the decisions on pattern application, together with other design decisions, often are only implicitly documented. The rationale is typically not captured and there is no traceability between various artefacts, such as requirements, decisions and architectural model elements. All these factors may result in poor and undocumented designs, which are overly complicated due to the wrongly applied design patterns, and expose unexpected and rather negative design properties. The maintenance of such systems and such design documentation is accordingly complicated. As to requirements engineering, elicitation and prioritisation of requirements prior to design is complicated, since it is not clear how much and with what level of detail the requirements shall be elicited. The initial prioritisation of requirements seldom holds for all subsystems. Moreover, there is a high risk of discovering really relevant requirements late during the system design, which leads to expensive design corrections.

The solution, proposed in this thesis, is called the AM3D approach. The AM3D approach supports the goal-oriented architecture-driven requirements engineering, lightweight evaluation of design decisions on pattern application and semi-automated documentation of the rationale, together with trace links to requirements and architectural elements.

8.1.1. Contributions

The contributions towards the proposed approach are summarized as follows (for more details on contributions, please refer to Section 1.2):

1. Extension of the general development process with the *lightweight process for goal-oriented requirements engineering and simplified documentation of rationale for the design decisions on design pattern application.* Besides the documentation of rationale and elicitation of requirements, the developed process supports several other design and evolution scenarios, proving corresponding sub-processes to be incorporated into the main development process. It is compatible with all process models that have an explicit design phase. It can

also be embedded into agile methods, such as Scrum, as documentation of decisions and rationale happens on demand as a by-product of a single design step and is neither planned in advance, nor detached from the engineer's activities. The developed process is detailed for several defined application scenarios (see Section 3.2.2), each provided with a specialised process to follow when applying the AM3D approach. These scenarios reflect the needs of software engineers during design and evolution.

2. *A new type of design pattern catalogue with the rationale question annotations,* allowing for a more appropriate use of design patterns, supporting the documentation of rationale for the design decisions, documentation of trace links between various project artefacts, such as design model elements and requirements; and supporting goal-oriented elicitation of requirements and evaluation of decisions on the pattern application. The catalogue is described in detail in Section 4.

3. *An exemplary design pattern catalogue:* An exemplary design pattern catalogue with the rationale question annotations was developed based on the defined process and formalisation and is provided in Section 5. The catalogue contains common design patterns, documented following the approach proposed in this thesis. The exemplary catalogue provides a reference for the creation of the catalogues based on the AM3D approach. It represents an expert knowledge in the area structured in terms of the AM3D approach. The developed exemplary catalogue was also used for the validation of the approach in the conducted controlled experiment (see Section 6.5). The subjects used the catalogue during the experiment to solve tasks on design pattern application and maintenance.

8.1.2. Publications

The contributions of the approach have been partially published in various peer-reviewed conferences and workshops.

Co-authored [14] provides a state of the initial research of software evolution problems of the long-living systems. It describes some of the root causes, one of which is that longevity is not considered during the construction. The other cause is that approaches tend to focus on symptoms of evolution problems, rather than on the real causes of those problems. This line of research is continued in co-authored [5, 7, 12]. Among others, the developed sustainability guidelines for the evolution support are first proposed and then reported. In parallel, an extensive state-of-the-art survey was carried out and an overview is provided in the co-authored [17]. This line of research contributed to a better understanding of software evolution and practical needs in the area. The AM3D approach was tangled according to the gained insights.

In [13], a relationship between agile methods and architectural modelling is discussed. An initial version of the AM3D approach is proposed to drive requirements elicitation through the use of patterns and components. The publication received a CompArch Young Investigator Award. The reviewed version was then published in [10], and validation possibilities for the proposed approach are discussed and published in [9]. The discussion of architectural design and agile methods is continued in [6], where results of the survey on agile methods and architectural documentation are also presented. The research on the goal-oriented elicitation of requirements with the AM3D approach is continued in [11] and in co-authored [3]. In the latter, the effects of design decisions on requirements engineering are discussed and the AM3D approach is joined with a design space exploration approach as a new approach for design-informed requirement elicitation and prioritisation.

In [4], the AM3D approach is extended to support documentation of design decisions during architectural modelling. Finally, in [1, 15], the approach idea is presented in detail, together with the initial results of the survey, which is also one of the validations of the AM3D approach (described in Section 6.4). An integrated approach, which includes support for software evolution, starting from requirements through decisions up to the code, is presented in the co-authored [2].

Part of the research on the supporting meta-models is published in [16]. The paper outlines a generic approach for a meta-model- and domain- independent model variability, with one of the approach's application examples being variants of design patterns and their modelling. Another part is co-authored in [8], where problems arising through the requirement to connect the existing architectural meta-models with the meta-models of the AM3D approach in a non-invasive way (currently done as a decorator pattern) are described and a potential solution is proposed.

8.1.3. Benefits

The main goal of the AM3D approach is to support the evolution of software systems. The specific benefits of the proposed approach are:

- Documented rationale of design decisions on the pattern application
- Semi-automated documentation of trace links between requirements, decisions and architectural elements
- A more appropriate use of design patterns and design pattern variants
- Goal-oriented architecture-driven requirements engineering

In the following, the benefits are explained in more detail:

- **Documented rationale of design decisions on the pattern application:** Design decisions on pattern application documented together with the rationale provide positive effects on software evolution. In particular, the AM3D approach contributes to detection and supports the re-evaluation of outdated decisions on design pattern application. The re-evaluation is based on the captured rationale behind design decisions on design pattern application. The rationale is semi-automatically captured through the answers provided by software engineers to the pattern question annotations during design. The validation of the AM3D approach could not demonstrate a statistical significance in this benefit; nevertheless, an improvement with 70% probability as compared to the classical documentation can be considered an encouraging result (the benefit, of course, requires further empirical validation).

- **Semi-automated documentation of trace links between requirements, decisions and architectural elements:** Answers to the question annotations are justified with the existing requirements to the system. The users have certain system requirements in mind while replying to the questions. Therefore, they are more likely to choose to provide links (in the form of IDs) to the most important requirements, contributing to the answers to the questions, in order to justify their answers. By doing so, the AM3D approach receives information about the connection between a decision to apply or to withdraw a design pattern, and the requirements contributing to this decision. Moreover, if a decision is met to apply a design pattern candidate, the candidate is then instantiated in the architectural model. In this case, the design decision is related with the corresponding architectural elements. While instantiation of the pattern itself requires manual actions from the users (see Section 3.1 and Section 8.3 for discussion about manual and automated instantiation), trace links from decisions to the corresponding architectural elements can be generated automatically, as this can be facilitated though the meta-model design. Details on the traceability support are provided in Section 3.3. Details on architectural instantiation of design patterns are provided in Section 4.2.3.

Thus, the AM3D approach supports establishing a connection between several project artefacts via the documentation of trace links: First, the requirements in the requirement specification are related to the design documentation, and second, they are then related to the architectural model elements. The requirements are linked to the architectural elements via documented design decisions and their rationale.

- **A more appropriate use of design patterns and design pattern variants:** A more appropriate use of design patterns is validated to be achieved for the less experienced software engineers in the example of students who participated in the conducted empirical study (see Section 6.5). More appropriate use is achieved through the AM3D pattern catalogue question annotations provided for each pattern in the catalogue and describing its core properties (both desired and undesired). We argue this benefit is also viable for more experienced engineers, since the data from our survey indicates that experienced software engineers also face problems with design pattern application (see Section 6.4 for details on the survey).

  In addition, the AM3D approach automatically supports a more correct architectural pattern application, as explained in Section 4.2.3. Each design pattern in the AM3D catalogue contains information on its architectural structure, expressed through roles and connectors [62]. This information allows for an automatic check of architectural models, where patterns are instantiated with the help of defined OCL constraints. Engineers can be notified in case the architectural structure is incorrect during the design or if it is occasionally violated during system evolution. The AM3D approach supports structural checks at the architectural level and, in the current version, does not apply to the code level, which is a subject of future work.

- **Goal-oriented architecture-driven requirements engineering:** The AM3D approach supports a goal-oriented architecture-driven requirements engineering method. The requirements directly connected to the current design decisions are elicited and prioritised on demand. The elicitation and prioritisation are triggered by the question annotations to design patterns, and when the available information (such as system requirements) is not sufficient to answer certain questions. In such cases, an engineer may contact stakeholders (e.g., requirements engineers) in order to be provided with additional information in the missing area. Thus, the information is elicited and prioritised on demand and is highly relevant to the current design state, unlike in a non-triggered requirement elicitation process. This benefit of the AM3D approach was not empirically validated. However, we have successfully published several publications on the topic [3, 11].

8.1.4. Validation

The validation of the AM3D approach is described in detail in Chapter 6. The overall validation of the AM3D approach consists of three steps:

1. **A survey:** A survey based on structured interviews was conducted to validate the motivation of the AM3D approach and to evaluate the feasibility of the proposed example from the annotated pattern catalogue as a solution to some of the problems with design patterns. This is a "Type 0 validation", which evaluated the *Feasibility* of the approach (see Section 6.1 for the description of validation types). The survey subjects were 25 software engineers employed in industry and academia. The survey results confirmed that even experienced software engineers do face various problems with design patterns and their application. The AM3D approach was evaluated as potentially

feasible to solve some of the problems, such as documentation of design patterns and selection of the most appropriate design patterns. Moreover, the survey results evaluated that question annotations can be successfully understood by the persons who were not involved into the creation of the catalogue. The survey is described in detail in Section 6.4.

2. **Application on a common example:** The developed artefacts and process of the AM3D approach were applied on the CoCoME-based example to demonstrate their appropriateness for the goals of the approach. This is a "Type I validation", which evaluated the *Appropriateness* of the approach. All artefacts and the process could be applied to model the example and to perform the evolution scenario. The application on example is presented in Section 3.6.

3. **An empirical study:** An empirical study based on a controlled experiment was conducted to validate the following benefits of the approach: The design patterns annotated with questions could be better understood and applied more correctly, as compared to the design pattern catalogue based on the standard approach (common books); Decisions documented with rationale generated from answers to the questions can be re-evaluated more easily during system maintenance. This is a "Type II validation", which evaluated the *Applicability* of the approach. The experiment subjects were 20 students, who were divided semi-randomly into two groups – the treatment group and the control group. The experiment results showed that design patterns annotated with questions can be better understood and applied more correctly, as compared to the standard approach, with a statistically significant difference. The re-evaluation of design decisions, as well, was shown to be more correct, even though the result did not pass the statistically significant difference border. In this case, the probability was about 70%. Altogether, the treatment group per-

formed significantly better than the control group. The experiment is described in detail in Section 6.5.

8.1.5. Overall Summary

To summarise, this thesis provides several insights into the area of architecture-driven requirements elicitation and prioritisation (more efficient on-demand elicitation and prioritisation, see Section 3.4), design decision evaluation on design pattern application and documentation of their rationale (semi-automated generation and documentation of rationale for design decisions on pattern application, see Section 4), and establishment of trace links between requirements, decisions and architectural elements (see Section 3.3). The thesis is focused on design patterns, as a subclass of reusable architectural solutions.

First of all, despite a significant amount of research in the area of design pattern application and documentation, the transfer to the application in industry is not yet complete, as also shown in the survey. There are still open research questions left in the area.

The design patterns, as a subclass of reusable solutions, can be used to trigger and support documentation of design decisions connected to their application. Moreover, they can be used to support evaluation of correctness of design decisions. For this, they have to be captured in a new kind of design pattern catalogue – the AM3D catalogue, which is a new format to describe design patterns. It enables the derivation of documentation of project-specific design decisions from the pattern-specific and project-independent questions to design patterns. These questions are called AM3D pattern question annotations, and they can be seen as rationale fragments attached to design patterns in the catalogue. Such question annotations allow for goal-oriented questioning not only about the reasons behind a potential decision, but also about the requirements of the system. Missing requirements can be thus elicited on demand, altogether contributing to a more lightweight software design. While answering the questions, the trace links between elements of various artefacts are established in a semi-automated way. These elements include requirements, decisions and architectural elements.

To profit from the proposed approach, an investment into the initial development of the design pattern catalogue according to the AM3D approach is required. In return on this investment, the catalogue then supports more correct software design with fewer design mistakes connected to design pattern application (both for inappropriately applied design patterns and for inappropriately applied structure of patterns). Moreover, there is also an improvement in the maintenance of the systems developed according to the AM3D approach through fewer design mistakes and a more lightweight design documentation.

8.2. Assumptions and Limitations

This section discusses assumptions and limitations of this thesis. Some of them were discussed in detail in the previous chapters of the thesis; in such cases, the references to the chapters and sections are provided. The assumptions and limitations of the AM3D approach are the following:

- **Presence of explicit design phase and design documentation:** The main assumption of the AM3D approach is the presence of an explicit design phase, which includes explicit architectural modelling, since the AM3D approach is operating at the architectural level. The AM3D process presented in this thesis is assumed to be integrated into the development process that has or is compatible with a design phase. This is a feasible assumption, since (1) the main goal of the AM3D approach is to support evolution of software systems, and (2) an explicit design and its documentation is of particular importance for a bearable evolution of larger and long-living software systems [18, 19, 24, 26].

The AM3D pattern catalogue can be used for evaluation of design decisions on pattern application also without an explicit design or modelling. In this case, however, the benefit of semi-automated documentation of decisions and rationale is lost due to the absence of design artefacts.

- **Necessity of design documentation maintenance:** Once design documentation is created, it has to be maintained. This is another important assumption of the AM3D approach. The maintenance of the design documentation of often not the case in practice, however, as there is tendency in interest towards having updated documentation. The approach provides support in maintenance of documentation of design decisions on pattern application, however it is not completely automated. Once documentation becomes out of date, the benefit of documented decisions is lost. In this case the AM3D approach can still be used to support new decisions on design pattern application and their documentation together with the rationale.

- **Necessity for engineers to answer question annotations:** The AM3D approach supports the evaluation and documentation of design decisions. This is, however, based on the assumption that the engineers use the AM3D catalogue with question annotations to design patterns and do reply on these questions. Thus, it is assumed that the engineers are ready to reply to the questions in the catalogue if they want to use the AM3D approach.

- **Dependency of trace links on software engineers:** Similar to the previous assumption, the engineers have to be eager to provide rationale, such as links to the triggering requirements and links to the implementing elements in the architecture. The AM3D approach supports these actions, but does not completely automate them.

- **Necessity for an initial AM3D catalogue:** Another assumption of the AM3D approach is the presence of the initial AM3D catalogue in order to profit from the AM3D approach. Such a catalogue has to be provided for the start of the design phase, and then shall be regularly extended to include design patterns or other reusable solutions that are regularly used throughout the projects or for other projects. Clearly, the catalogue is a rather significant initial investment. A cost-benefit evaluation shall be conducted to validate the benefits of the AM3D approach (such as a more correct design) over the initial costs of creating the catalogue. However, a catalogue with common reusable solutions can be reused between projects and even between organisations, and an effort for its creation can be distributed in an open source project, which is a part of future work. Moreover, an initial AM3D catalogue is provided in this thesis as a starting point for the development.

- **Limitations of natural language:** The common limitation in the area of architectural knowledge management is the natural language that is used in the majority of artefacts (e.g., requirement specifications, design documentation, rationale descriptions). Such descriptions are not precise, may be misinterpreted, and the possibilities of their automated processing are limited.

  The description of design patterns in the AM3D catalogue and the question annotations are captured in a natural language. The language of the questions and the text quality strongly influences the usability of such questions for the pattern selection, evaluation and documentation. Answered questions serve as a rationale for the pattern usage, and naturally misleading questions may form a wrong rationale. However, this problem is common and affects other language-dependent approaches, such as expert systems or ontologies.

Although formal pattern specifications have been proposed, for example expressed in a LISA formal specification language [243], there is no empirical evaluation on the effort required for understanding such formal definitions and the application of them. The overtaking of such strict formal methods to the wide industrial design practice seems rather questionable. However, an investigation of possibilities of usage of strict formal definitions n the AM3D approach can be a part of future work.

In order to reduce potential ambiguities in descriptions of design patterns in the AM3D catalogue, a description template was defined and used throughout the sample catalogue, provided in this thesis. Some parts of the information from the template are linked to the glossary, which limits a natural language subset to a so-called controlled natural language (see Section 2.5.3 for more information on controlled natural languages). The same approach is also used for the definitions of question annotations. They are formulated in semi-formal language, which is explained in Section 4.3.3.

Since such natural language descriptions influence the understandability of question annotations, this was defined to be one of the research questions during the survey validation of the AM3D approach. In particular, the understandability of questions was evaluated for persons who were not involved into the AM3D approach and catalogue designs. The survey results have shown high understandability of the provided questions. The positive results can be explained through the review process, which the catalogue entries have undergone. A two-step review process of question annotations to design patterns shall reduce this threat.

- **Indeterminacy in the process of adding question annotations:** Creation of question annotations is a creative process. Its outcome depends on the experience of the software engineer following it.

Therefore, the review process of question annotations (discussed in Section 4.3.5) is important to assure the quality and understandability of the annotations. The results of our validations show that the questions are understandable to the uninvolved persons, and are sufficient to support correct decisions on pattern application.

- **Ambiguity in question annotations types:** The question annotation types described in Section 4.3.3 are a limitation of the AM3D approach, as they provide a non-excluding categorisation of the pattern properties described by the questions. This means that some questions can be referred to in more than one question type category. In particular, this might be the case for questions about the goals and intent of design patterns. The focus of the categorisation was placed in an extensive description of all the properties of a pattern (the question types are sufficient to describe any property), while possible overlaps in some question types are considered to be acceptable.
- **Dependency of the design documentation quality on the quality of the catalogue entries:** Since the design decisions documentation is partially based on the catalogue entries (the decisions rationale is semi-automatically generated from the answers to question annotations), the quality of the catalogue entries influences the quality of the documentation. Therefore, a review process for the catalogue entries is recommended before the catalogue is used. The initial AM3D catalogue provided in this thesis has undergone a review process and was also used for the validation of the approach.
- **Dependency of documentation quality on software engineers:** Similar to the previous limitation, the quality of the design documentation is influenced by the answers provided by the engineer using the approach and the catalogue. The ambiguities in answers to the question annotations and correctness of trace links to other artefacts can be checked only to a limited extent. This is a general issue with

all documentation approaches, as documentation highly depends on the willingness and cooperation of software engineers.

- **Potential deficiency of quality classification:** One of the limitations of the AM3D approach is that used quality classification can be insufficient to for some specific domains. However, the quality aspects in the meta-model formalisation can be easily extended or replaced with the required quality classification. This is also true for the used requirement classification, and in particular, the classification of quality requirements.

- **Potential deficiency of selected architectural representation:** Another limitation of the AM3D approach is that the selected architectural modelling method is based on the Palladio Component Model (PCM, [152]), and its system modelling part. The roles and connectors modelling formalism of design pattern representation is compatible with the PCM. It is also compatible with other UML-like modelling notations, where a system can be represented through components and connectors, or similar modelling units, e.g. through classes. The selected modelling mechanism allows for automated checks of the pattern structure, as information on the pattern structure is saved in the catalogue together with the pattern description and question annotations.

  Behavioural modelling representations and others would require extension of the AM3D modelling formalism. They are not supported by the current state of the AM3D approach.

- **Threats to validity and limitations of the validation:** Threats to validity and limitations of the carried out validations are carefully discussed in the chapter dedicated to the AM3D approach's validation. For the discussion of threats to validity and limitations of the validation for the survey, please refer to Section 6.4.6. For the discussion of threats to validity and limitations of the validation for the experiment, please refer to Section 6.5.6.

8.3. Open Questions and Future Work

This section discusses open research questions and ideas for future work. It is structured according to the three categories: Short-term user-relevant open questions and future work (Section 8.3.2), long-term user-relevant open questions and future work (Section 8.3.1), and empirical user-relevant open questions and future work (Section 8.3.3).

8.3.1. Short-Term User-Relevant Open Questions and Future Work

The following actions can be undertaken to extend and to improve the AM3D approach in the short-term:

- **Extension to an expert system:** First of all, the approach can be extended to support pattern selection triggered through the question annotations, thus implementing an expert system. For a detailed explanation of the difference between the current state of the AM3D approach and the expert systems please refer to Section 3.5. The current purpose of the question annotations in the AM3D catalogue is to support the evaluation of applicability of a pattern and to document decisions on pattern application. However, the questions to the patterns are already available and are structured according to the four types of design pattern properties (see Section 4.3.3). Therefore, it is possible to extend the AM3D approach to implement an expert system, which would support selection of design patterns starting from the design problem. In this case, the selection will be based on the proposed pattern catalogue, similar to [73]. The entry top-level questions will be general pattern questions from the catalogue, and the further refinement can be done by intent and consequences questions. Finally, the choice between pattern variants could be performed by the pattern variant questions.

Another way to extend the functions of the AM3D approach to an expert system is to add the filtering of the pattern proposals based on quality goals, similar to the [55] and [233]. By doing this, the choice of the patterns would be guided through the defined and prioritized list of quality requirements (quality goals) to the system. Ideally, both of these extensions shall be implemented to enable a better proposal of patterns, which is would be tailored to the current system requirements and engineer's needs.

A more far line of research connected to this area would be a semi-automated proposal of design pattern solutions based on the architectural models, for example as in [244, 245], or in code, as proposed by [2]. However, here a full automation is questionable, as a final decision on pattern application still has to be met by the engineers.

- **Extension of proposing of alternative pattern candidates:** Together with the extension to expert systems, the AM3D approach can extended to support better proposing of alternative pattern candidates, once a patten candidate under consideration has proven to be suboptimal. The current version of the AM3D approach may propose better pattern candidates, if the question is shared by two or more design patterns, and is answered negatively in one of the cases. The additional featured to be add may include automated check for ambiguities in the answers to design patterns, when answers to the questions in fact contradict each other or are suboptimal for the pattern solutions in question. Such an extension would require conceptual work for the extension of question annotations formalisation, and, potentially, modification of the question annotation formalisation in the meta-model.

- **Generalisation to other reusable solutions:** Despite the fact that this thesis focuses on the architectural design patterns, it does not exclude support of other pattern types or support of other architectural design solutions, and in particular, support of reusable architectural solutions, such as third-party components and Web services. The current support for components includes components as means of instantiation of design patterns (design pattern instances are assigned to the implementing components). Although reusable third-party components can be annotated with questions already in the current version of the approach, the support was not detailed. For example, different types of third-party components and their potential influence of question styles were not investigated. The AM3D approach can be also extended to support design solutions that are invisible at or cross-cutting to the system architecture.

  Once a solution is reusable (can be unmodified used more than once, similar to design patterns), its properties are known in advance. In such case it can be described with the help of question annotations, and then be used to evaluate the solution and to document related decisions with the rationale generated out of answers to the questions.

  Such an extension will require modification in the formalisation of the approach (however, the formalisation was already designed with the possible extensions in mind). It will also require replication of validation for the new supported solution types. Once new architectural solutions types are supported by the approach, the formalisation has to be extended to support new design decision types connected to these solutions.

- **Tool support improvement:** The current tool support of the AM3D approach is a research prototype. Even though the catalogue can be used without any tool support, a mature tool support would bring the benefits of the AM3D approach that are connected to the automation. In particular, a mature tool support with a user-friendly GUI would ease semi-automated documentation of design decisions with generated rationale, and would assure architectural checks on correct pattern application.

The current research prototype is based on Eclipse. It is thinkable to create extensions for other languages that would use the same core (the AM3D pattern catalogue, saved in an XML format).

- **UNICASE integration:** As part of the tool support improvement, the AM3D approach and its supporting artefacts can be integrated into one of the existing open-source tools. UNICASE [113] is an open-source CASE-tool that operates with different artefacts of a project. It already supports "requirements, use cases, UML models, schedules, bug and feature models", which are integrated into one unified model. It has a mature implemented client that allows for viewing and editing of these artefacts in various visualization forms. Besides its functionality and maturity, UNICASE is Eclipse-based and utilises EMF. These features do it to a good candidate for the integration with AM3D approach. The initial investigation conducted on this topic has shown a high potential of such an integration.

- **Extension of the exemplary AM3D pattern catalogue:** The exemplary AM3D patter catalogue presented in this thesis shall be extended to contain more of the common design pattern descriptions, in order to be applicable in the industrial practice. Ideally, the catalogue shall be extended to describe all of the common design patterns presented in Gamma et al. [28] and in Buschmann et al. [29].

8.3.2. Long-Term User-Relevant Open Questions and Future Work

The following actions can be undertaken to extend and to improve the AM3D approach in the long term:

- **Automated instantiation in architectural models and code:** The current implementation of the AM3D approach requires the user of the approach to decide manually which design pattern shall be implemented by which components in the architectural models. The AM3D approach guides the user and supports structural checks through the OCL constrains, however, it does not instantiate patterns on its own, as discussed in Section 3.1. A complete automated instantiation of design patterns in architectural models could be the next step. However, such automated instantiation of design patterns (both in architecture and code) was left out of focus of the AM3D approach on purpose. The main reason was that analysis techniques in order to assure a correct integration of design patterns into the existing model are a rather large research question, which is sufficient for a separate PhD thesis.

  The main problem is to obtain the context from the design model and to automatically derive a proper design pattern application place and order. In the simplest case, which can be also supported by the AM3D approach, a new architectural model element is generated for every element form the architectural pattern description (for roles and connectors). It is then placed in the model and the user connects it to the rest of the elements. However, often, a design pattern part shall become a part of the other already existing architectural element or even elements. In this case, an automated analysis and the correct automated pattern application is a non-trivial task, since behavioural aspects shall be extracted from the existing design sand correctly considered for the pattern application.

- **Traceability of design patterns and design decisions to code and reversed:** Similar to the previous point, another possibility to extend the AM3D approach would be its extension to support reverse engineering of design decisions on pattern application (and not only) from the code level for the systems that were not developed using the AM3D approach. Also here, an additional contribution would be reverse of trace links from design decisions in code back to the decisions making on requirement and decision changes. Research work in this direction is currently held by Konersmann et al. in [2].

- **Extension to support behavioural models:** The AM3D approach, at the moment, only supports UML-like component diagrams, and similar to those. It can be extended to support the behavioural information on design patterns in order to enable checks of during the pattern application, and to enable automated pattern instantiation, as described above.

- **Integration of the AM3D pattern catalogue into a Wiki:** An automated import and export functionality for the AM3D pattern catalogue to and from a Wiki form for design pattern description may be beneficial. Such form would allow a larger community to contribute to the extension of the AM3D catalogue and to review the catalogue entries in a structured review process.

- **Reverse engineering and reverse traceability of design patterns and design decisions from architectural models:** The current version of the AM3D approach supports only forward design. However, it could be plausible to extend the approach to support reverse engineering of the architectural models in order to extract design decisions on pattern application (and not only) for the systems that were not developed using the AM3D approach. Another potential contribution here would be enabling of reverse trace links from design decisions back to the decisions making on requirement and decision changes. This is a kind of design decision change impact detection and notification, similar research work in this direction is currently held by Küster et al. in [246].

8.3.3. Empirical Open Questions and Future Work

The following actions can be undertaken to extend and to improve the AM3D approach:

- **Cost-benefit validation of the approach:** The usage of an AM3D pattern catalogue and the documentation of design rationales involve additional overhead and costs. Such overhead might not pay off for smaller or short-living systems. However, the AM3D approach enables semi-automated documentation of decisions on design pattern application, and the rationale behind those decisions. Such automation saves the effort required for manual documentation of the taken pattern decisions and their rationale. The AM3D approach is therefore assumed to be most beneficial for the development of large, complex or long-living systems. However, the appropriateness of this assumption shall undergo a cost-benefit empirical validation. As explained in Section 6.1, the cost-benefit validation in the area of architectural knowledge management is connected to extremely high effort and costs. However, it would also provide insight in the usability of the AM3D approach in the long term compared to the investment costs.

  There are several potential difficulties in the validation design that can already be anticipated. First, the starting point of the validation can vary from an existing AM3D catalogue, to a new project-specific catalogue. It is unclear, who shall be responsible for the initial creation of the catalogue, since it is also likely to be an open source solution in the future. It is unclear how many design patterns the initial catalogue shall contains. Moreover, it is unclear if the catalogue entries shall be limited to the design patterns, or, which is more realistic, shall also include other reusable solutions, such as third party components. This would cause differences in the initial costs. Second, it is unclear, of the validation shall run only for one system, which shall be then monitored and evolved over time, or if it shall include several systems, since the catalogue can be reused between projects. Then, it is unclear if there are differences in the extent of the design pattern use depending on the problem domain. In this case, the validation results can be seriously disturbed into a positive or a negative side. These factors are just some of the variables of the cost-benefit validation, which provide a strong influence on the validation outcome.

- **Effort validation of the approach:** Besides the cost-benefit validation, an additional validation on the effort connected to the use of the AM3D approach as compared to the classical approach shall be conducted. Initial results obtained during the controlled experiment (described in Section 6.5) indicate that the AM3D approach application is actually connected to less effort, than the application of the classical approach. However, this aspect shall be re-validated more carefully, based on the time measurements, in addition to the qualitative statistics obtained during the conducted experiment.

- **Extension of the question annotations formalisation:** The general formalisation of question annotations can be further extended. In the current state of the AM3D approach a simplified notation based on the controlled natural languages was used. It can be extended to implement one of the common used controlled languages (see Section 2.5.3 for an overview of natural controlled languages) to better support automated processing and filtering. In the body of this work, also the approach to and the rules to formulate pattern questions can be further refined.

This chapter provided a summary of the AM3D approach. Although the presented AM3D approach has limitations and there are open research questions, which are listed above, it provides a foundation for the further improvement of the poor documentation of design decisions rationale on design pattern application and trace links between requirements, decisions and architectural elements. It also provides an improvement on the inappropriate use of design patterns and their variants, which was demonstrated to be statistically significant by the approach's validation, and contributes to a more-focused requirements elicitation and prioritisation.

A. Appendix. Survey Documentation

This Appendix is the questionnaire that was used for the survey. In consists of the introduction, general questions, general questions, pattern-specific questions for three sample patterns, general questions about pattern application and questions to retrieve additional information. Survey parts are:

- **Introduction:** The introduction gives an overview of the survey. It explains the goals, gives an introduction to the AM3D approach, explains how to fill in the questions and gives information on the data privacy.
- **I. General questions:** This section contains general questions on pattern application experience of the participants.
- **II. Pattern-specific questions:** This section contains questions to elicit the opinion on the proposed pattern catalogue on the example of three sample patterns – Model-View-Controller (MVC), Thick Client and Single Table Inheritance. For each pattern there is an excerpt of several catalogue questions listed in order to evaluate questions to the patterns.
- **III. General questions about pattern application:** This section contains questions to elicit a generalized opinion on the proposed approach.
- **IV. Additional information:** This section contains questions to elicit participant's background information.

The text of the survey questionnaire is included in the following.

24/08/12

PATTERN APPLICATION QUESTIONNAIRE

Introduction

In this survey, we would like to collect the opinions on the potential applicability of an approach utilizing pattern catalogue (containing patterns annotated with pattern-specific questions) in general, and, more specifically, the appropriateness of the questions for the application by software engineers in practice.

Software patterns are approved solutions for reoccurring problems, e.g. Model-View-Controller, Factory, Observer, Iterator, etc.

We propose an approach to support software engineers in evaluating if selected patterns are really suitable for application, and if so, which variant of the pattern is the most appropriate. The approach is based on a pattern catalogue, where each pattern is annotated with pattern-specific questions. These catalogue questions provide hints on the basic properties of the pattern, its intent and consequences.

* Here and later: "Catalogue questions" are pattern-specific questions that are stored together with the pattern in the proposed pattern catalogue, and "Questions" are the questions of this questionnaire.

The general idea of the proposed approach is the following:

- First, the software engineer selects a pattern that is potentially suitable to solve a problem of software engineering. The selection is based either on own experience or is proposed by a pattern expert system (if any in use).
- Second, the software engineer answers the catalogue questions connected to the selected patterns. The catalogue questions shall be answered by a software engineer before the decision to apply a pattern. If the software engineer cannot answer some catalogue question (for example, because the system functionality is not fully defined), he or she should translate the catalogue question to the responsible requirements engineer, who can elicit new requirements to answer the question.
- Finally, if the answers to questions have confirmed the appropriateness of the selected pattern, the pattern can be implemented in architecture and code.

Although the proposed approach is based on catalogue questions to the patterns, its intent is not pattern selection itself (not an expert system), but support of evaluation of applicability of a selected pattern for the given problem.

Given the proper automation, answers to the catalogue questions can be automatically saved as rationale for the selected or discarded pattern. This information can be later used to support system evolution.

Data Privacy Information

Please note that this survey collects some data on your education and experience. Your participation in this survey is anonymous, unless you choose to provide your E-Mail address. Your E-Mail address will be solely used to provide you the survey results, it and the other data will be kept confidential and will not be disclosed by us.

Information collected in this questionnaire, except your E-Mail address, may be disclosed (in anonymous form) in research reports and will be used for research purposes only. For any further information about the usage of your data feel free to contact one of the investigators listed below.

List of investigators:

- M. Sc. Zoya Durdik, PhD at Karlsruhe Institute of Technology (KIT), Karlsruhe, Germany. Email: zoya.durdik@kit.edu.
- Prof. Dr. Ralf Reussner, Professor at Karlsruhe Institute of Technology (KIT), Karlsruhe, Germany. Email: ralf.reussner@kit.edu.

Organizational

Please answer all questions, unless they are marked as optional. The questionnaire takes 20 minutes to complete in total and is organized in four sections.
Thank you very much for your collaboration.

1

24/08/12

I. General questions:
This section deals with general questions about pattern application.

1. How would you estimate your experience with applying patterns:

- Very low (I have not applied any)
- Low (I have applied patterns during one or two test or study projects)
- Medium (From time to time I am applying patterns during my work)
- High (I am regularly applying design patterns)
- Very high (My work is connected to design patterns, I am proficient in application of design patterns, I regularly apply design pattern from different domains)

2. How many patterns have you applied (approximately)?

I have applied ca. ___________ patterns

3. Please estimate usefulness of patterns for better quality of software (e.g., maintainability, non-functional properties, extendability) from your point of view:

- Very low
- Low
- Medium
- High
- Very high

4. Please specify if you have ever experienced some problems while applying or working with patterns:

- ☐ Yes, it happened to me to overlook some properties of a pattern or some consequences of a pattern application and then to discover that the choice was non optimal
- ☐ Yes, I was unsure which pattern (of several appropriate patterns I knew) was the most suitable for the problem
- ☐ Yes, I didn't know which pattern could be used to solve my problem
- ☐ Yes, the structure of the pattern was unclear
- ☐ Yes, the implementation of the pattern was unclear
- ☐ Yes, while modifying the system or code I have not noticed that there was a pattern applied, and modified its structure
- ☐ No, never
- ☐ Other, please specify: ___________________________________

5. If you have not answered no in the previous question, then were the encountered problems due to ...:

- ☐ ... few experience with patterns
- ☐ ... insufficient understanding of requirements to the system
- ☐ ... low experience in programming in general
- ☐ Other, please specify: ___________________________________

6. Inappropriate use of patterns I have encountered in _____ percent of projects I have worked in.

7. Inappropriate documentation of patterns I have encountered in _____ percent of projects I have worked in.

8. Have you experienced problems with patterns in systems that you have not developed yourself but you had to maintain?

- ☐ No
- ☐ Yes
- ☐ Other, please specify: ___________________________________

If you answered yes, please specify with which patterns: ____________________

____

9. (Optional) Please provide your opinion if it is difficult to apply patterns and why (e.g. insufficient documentation, large amount of known patterns, lack of appropriate training, ..)?

____

____

2

24/08/12

II. Pattern-specific questions:
This section contains repeating questions to 3 different patterns: (A) Model-View-Controller, (B) Fat (Thick) Client and (C) Single Table Inheritance.
For each pattern we have listed an excerpt of 5 catalogue questions (factors) per pattern (typically there are 7-8 catalogue questions). We would like you to evaluate the provided catalogue questions (factors).

A. Model-View-Controller (MVC)

1. Are you familiar with this pattern?

- No
- Somewhat (I have read about it)
- Yes (I have applied it several times)

2. The following factors (listed in the table) describe properties of the pattern. Would you consider these influence factors as important for the appropriate application of this design pattern?
You have the following answer options for each factor:

You have the following answer options for each factor:

- Relevant (I believe this factor is the defining property of the pattern)
- Somewhat relevant (I believe this factor is an indicator for appropriate pattern application)
- Irrelevant (I believe this factor has nothing to do with the pattern application)
- I don't know
- I haven't understood the factor

Please read these factors carefully even if you are not familiar with the pattern, but please only provide answers to the Question # 2 if you are somewhat familiar or familiar with this pattern.

Example how to fill in the answers (for the Observer pattern):

Factor	Relevant	Somewhat relevant	Irrelevant	I don't know	I haven't understood the factor
If one object changes its state, would you like other objects to be notified about this change?	YES	☐	☐	☐	☐
If your application has a strict layered architecture, will a potential violation of this style be a problem?	☐	YES	☐	☐	☐

Factors for the Model-View-Controller:

#	Factor	Relevant	Somewhat relevant	Irrelevant	I don't know	I haven't understood the factor
	Would you like to present the same information in different ways e.g., through multiple views?	☐	☐	☐	☐	☐
	The data in the model is not changed through the views, and this will not be an issue in the future?	☐	☐	☐	☐	☐
	Would you like to add new views at run-time or delete existing views?	☐	☐	☐	☐	☐
	Do you plan to exchange underlying data model or views representing this data? (Design Time)	☐	☐	☐	☐	☐
	Are potential delays of view updates (because of larger amounts of data) acceptable?	☐	☐	☐	☐	☐

3. (Optional question) were any important factors forgotten in the question #2?

____

____

3

24/08/12

B. Fat (Thick) Client (Mobile applications)

1. Are you familiar with this pattern?

- No
- Somewhat (I have read about it)
- Yes (I have applied it several times)

2. The following factors (listed in the table) describe properties of the pattern. Would you consider these influence factors as important for the appropriate application of this design pattern?
You have the following answer options for each factor:

You have the following answer options for each factor:

- Relevant (I believe this factor is the defining property of the pattern)
- Somewhat relevant (I believe this factor is an indicator for appropriate pattern application)
- Irrelevant (I believe this factor has nothing to do with the pattern application)
- I don't know
- I haven't understood the factor

Please read these factors carefully even if you are not familiar with the pattern, but please only provide answers to the Question # 2 if you are somewhat familiar or familiar with this pattern.

Factors for the Fat (Thick) Client:

#	Factor	Relevant	Somewhat relevant	Irrelevant	I don't know	I haven't understood the factor
	Would you like a client to be able to perform the functionality in circumstances of potential disconnection to the main server /service?	☐	☐	☐	☐	☐
	Would you like to reduce the load on your main server or network through the higher processing and capacity demands to the client devices?	☐	☐	☐	☐	☐
	Is working offline essential for your application?	☐	☐	☐	☐	☐
	Are you building upon an existing architecture with already available devices?	☐	☐	☐	☐	☐
	Will the application be running on powerful devices and porting to low-performance devices can be excluded in the future?	☐	☐	☐	☐	☐

3. (Optional question) were any important factors forgotten in the question #2

____

____

4

24/08/12

C. Class Table Inheritance (Root-leaf mapping in relational databases)

1. Are you familiar with this pattern?

- No
- Somewhat (I have read about it)
- Yes (I have applied it several times)

2. The following factors (listed in the table) describe properties of the pattern. Would you consider these influence factors as important for the appropriate application of this design pattern?
You have the following answer options for each factor:

You have the following answer options for each factor:

- Relevant (I believe this factor is the defining property of the pattern)
- Somewhat relevant (I believe this factor is an indicator for appropriate pattern application)
- Irrelevant (I believe this factor has nothing to do with the pattern application)
- I don't know
- I haven't understood the factor

Please read these factors carefully even if you are not familiar with the pattern, but please only provide answers to the Question # 2 if you are somewhat familiar or familiar with this pattern.

Factors for the Single Table Inheritance

#	Factor	Relevant	Somewhat relevant	Irrelevant	I don't know	I haven't understood the factor
	Would you like to present an inheritance hierachy of classes in relational database?	☐	☐	☐	☐	☐
	Is complex data mapping between table required to be computed in your application?	☐	☐	☐	☐	☐
	Is the final amount of tables in the database structure limited (small) and is this unlikely to change in the future?	☐	☐	☐	☐	☐
	Will the tables repectively the fields hierarchy not be subject to frequent change in the future?	☐	☐	☐	☐	☐
	Are potential performabce bottlenecks with joints or multi-querying caused by retrieving larger amounts of data acceptable?	☐	☐	☐	☐	☐

3. (Optional question) were any important factors forgotten in the question #2

5

24/08/12

III. General questions about pattern application:
This section asks questions on your opinion about the proposed approach.

1. Please provide estimation how such a catalogue of patterns (containing sets of questions for each pattern, similar to the section II of this questionnaire) could be helpful during pattern application:

- ☐ It might solve documentation problem, if answers to the questions are automatically documented
- ☐ It might help clarifying properties and consequences of a pattern
- ☐ It might help to select the most suitable pattern between several candidate patterns
- ☐ It might help to find a pattern that the person doesn't know
- ☐ It might help to better apply a pattern, through explicit hits to the pattern's structure or implementation
- ☐ It will not solve any problems connected to the pattern application
- ☐ Other: ______________________________

2. Consider the following evolution scenario: The requirements have changed and a new functionality needs to be added. The questions for the patterns and provided answers to the questions are documented in an accessible form together with the applied pattern.

Please provide your estimation as to what degree such a catalogue of patterns with questions could improve / ease software evolution in case of the following tasks:

Task A. Find a location where functionality needs to be changed

- Low (No improvement)
- Medium (Some improvement)
- High (Noticeable Improvement)

If you like, provide a comment: ______________________________

Task B. Decide whether an applied pattern is outdated or not due to the requirement change.

- Low (No improvement)
- Medium (Some improvement)
- High (Noticeable Improvement)

If you like, provide a comment: ______________________________

6

24/08/12

IV. Additional information:
This section asks questions on your background.

1. Please indicate your industrial experience:

- Practice during my studies
- I participated in industrial projects
- I have worked in industry for about a year
- I have worked in industry for about 1 – 5 years
- I have worked in industry for more than 5 years
- No experience
- Other: ______________________________

2. Please select your current academic degree:

- Undergraduate
- Graduate (Bachelor)
- Graduate (Master /Diplom)
- PhD
- No academic degree
- Other: ______________________________

3. Please specify your occupation (or previous occupation if unemployed):

- Industry
- Research division of a company
- Student
- Doctoral researcher
- Post-Doctoral researcher
- Professor
- Both academia and industry mixed

4. (Optional) Other comments and suggestions:

____

____

5. (Optional) If you would like to receive the survey results, please provide your E-Mail-address (Your E-Mail address will be used only to send you the survey results):

____

Thank you!

7

B. Appendix. Experiment Documentation

In order to enable replication of the validation experiment, the complete set of experiment documentation is included in this Appendix B. The three groups of artefacts were used for the experiment preparation and execution: Introduction materials, questionnaires with tasks and artefacts handled to each student, which are required in addition to questionnaires with tasks. In the following they are explained in detail.

I. Introduction materials:

- **Introduction Texts for Groups A and B:** Introduction texts to the experiment tasks and the pattern catalogue. The texts were read out during the slide demonstration with three goals: To forward better comparability between two groups, to avoid mistakes during explanations and to improve traceability in case of extraordinary experiment results. The texts for two groups A and B had common build ing blocks, but were adopted according to the artefacts each of the groups was supposed to use during the experiment. Each of the texts was read by the experiment group moderator before the main task part.
- **Introduction Slides Group A:** The slides that were used for the introduction in Group A, accompanied by the above explained introduction text for Group A.
- **Introduction Slides Group B:** The slides that were used for the introduction in Group A, accompanied by the above explained introduction text for Group B.

II. Questionnaires with tasks:

- **Pre-Experiment (Warm-Up) Tasks:** The questionnaire with warm-up tasks, which were asked before the experiment tasks. The goal of these easy tasks is to help students get familiar with the available artefacts and navigation through them.
- **Experiment Tasks for Group A:** Two tasks for the validation experiment for the Group A using the proposed method (pattern catalogue with annotations). The questionnaire contains integrated list of design decisions documented according to the proposed method and a screen-shot of the system diagram of to be changed PSE system as a reminder.
- **Experiment Tasks for Group B:** Two tasks for the validation experiment for the Group B using the standard method (pattern catalogue without annotations, such as books or Wikipedia). The questionnaire contains integrated list of design decisions documented according to the standard method and a screen-shot of the system diagram of to be changed PSE system as a reminder.
- **Post-Experiment (Cool-Down) Tasks:** Questionnaire with cool-down tasks. These tasks are the so-called control tasks to collect the background information about the experiment subjects, about their experience in software engineering fields, to evaluate the understandability of the main experiment artefacts and tasks, and to collect the feedback to the experiment from the experiment subjects.

III. Artefacts handled to each student, which are required in addition to questionnaires with tasks:

- **List of System Requirements for Groups A and B:** A paper version of requirements to the PSE system. Experiment subjects have worked with these requirements during the system implementation, thus they were familiar with the requirements and the list was a mere reminder.

- **List of System Decisions for Group A:** A full list of architectural decisions to the PSE system for the group A. Experiment subjects have worked with these requirements during the system implementation and were familiar with the decisions. The decisions in this list are documented according to the proposed method (pattern catalogue with annotations).
- **List of System Decisions for Group B:** A full list of architectural decisions to the PSE system for the group B. Experiment subjects have worked with these requirements during the system implementation and were familiar with the decisions. The decisions in this list are documented according to the standard method (pattern catalogue without annotations, such as books or Wikipedia).
- **Pattern Catalogue for Group A:** A pattern catalogue documented according to the proposed method (pattern catalogue with annotations) containing descriptions of 12 patterns. Not all of these patterns were relevant to solve the task, which was done on purpose to achieve a more real-life problem environment.
- **Pattern Catalogue for Group B:** A pattern catalogue documented according to the standard method (pattern catalogue without annotations, such as books or Wikipedia) containing descriptions of 12 patterns. Not all of these patterns were relevant to solve the task, which was done on purpose to achieve a more real-life problem environment. These pattern description were taken from the standard pattern catalogues, such as by Gamma et al. [28], Fowler [58] and Buschmann et al. [29] and Wikipedia description articles. Therefore, in the appendix are listed only several sample pages: sample first pages of the standard catalogue entrees for Multi-Tier Style, Model View Controller pattern and Facade pattern (pages number 6, 10 and 51 of the standard catalogue), "Table of Content" (page 1) and disclaimer about material sources (page 107).

- **Experiment Time Table:** Time table of the experiment, including precise schedule with introduction and tasks sessions, assigned rooms and responsible moderators.

Please note that the following artefacts were developed together with the colleges (Erik Buerger, Matthias Huber, Martin Kuester, Max Kramer and Johannes Stammel): Pre-experiment (warm-Up) tasks, post-experiment (cool-down) tasks, list of system requirements for groups A and B, lists of system decisions, introduction slides for groups A and B and experiment time table.

Gruppe A:

Einführung, Zoya (Zum Vorlesen)

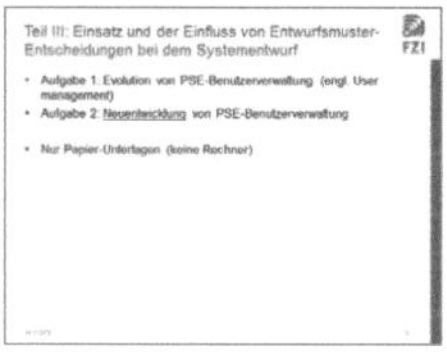

Im drittem Teil werden Sie den Einsatz und den Einfluss von Entwurfsmusterentscheidungen (engl. Pattern design decisions) im Systementwurf und Evolution evaluieren.
Sie bekommen 2 Aufgaben.
Die erste Aufgabe behandelt die **System-Evolution** der Benutzerverwaltung. Dabei evaluieren Sie die Gültigkeit der getroffenen Entwurfsmuster-Entscheidungen nach den Änderungsanfragen an das User Management.
Die Aufgabe 2 behandelt die **Neuentwicklung** und sucht nach passendem Entwurfsmuster um die angegebenen Probleme zu lösen. Wir nehmen dabei an, dass die Benutzerverwaltung neu entwickelt wird.

Für diesen Teil des Experimentes werden Sie nur Papierunterlagen benötigen.

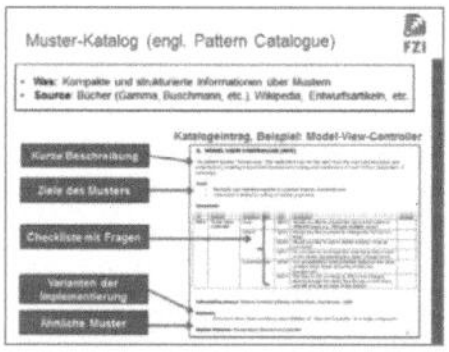

Für den dritten Teil bekommen Sie einen Muster Katalog, in dem die für die Aufgaben benötigten Muster beschrieben sind.

Was ist ein Pattern Katalog?
Ein Pattern Katalog enthält Kompakte und strukturierte Informationen über Patterns die aus den Bücher, wie z.B. Gamma, oder Artikeln kommen.
Für jedes Muster wird jeweils eine kurze Beschreibung und das Ziel des Musters eingegeben, eine Checkliste mit Fragen, mögliche Varianten der Musterimplementierung, wenn es welche gibt, und ähnliche Muster, die das ähnliche Problem auf eine andere Art und Weise lösen.

Diese **Fragen** beschreiben das Ziel (engl. goal), die beabsichtigte Eigenschaften (engl. intent), die mögliche Konsequenzen (engl. consequences) einer Muster-Anwendung. Diese Fragen sollen einem Entwickler eine schnelle Auskunft über das Muster und dessen Eigenschaften geben.
Die Fragen sind als **„Ja/Nein"** Fragen gestellt. **Antwort „Ja"** bedeutet dass diese Eigenschaft bei der Musterauswahl Ihnen wichtig ist. **Antwort „nein"** bei den Intent-Fragen bedeutet, dass diese Eigenschaft nicht im Vordergrund steht. Die Antwort **„Nein"** bei den Konsequenz-Fragen bedeutet, dass das Muster einen oder anderen Bedienungen (z.B. Anforderungen) nicht passt und evtl. ein anderes Muster eingesetzt werden sollte. Je mehr **„Nein"** Antworten Sie bei einem Muster machen, je wahrscheinlicher passt dieses Muster für Ihr Problem nicht.
Keine Antwort bedeutet, dass diese Eigenschaft Ihnen nicht wichtig ist, bzw. dass es keine Anforderungen dazu gibt.

Wie nutzt man den Katalog?
Wir haben folgendes Problem: *„Die Daten sollen in der App in unterschiedlichen GUIs (je Betriebssystem) angezeigt werden. Dabei soll es möglich sein die GUIs auszutauschen. Keine Business-App, daher keine besonderen Anforderungen an die Performanz."*
Evtl. könnte das MVC Muster für dieses Problem passen. Wir öffnen den „MVC" Katalogeintrag und lesen das Ziel des Musters durch.
Das klingt passend, daher gehen wir die Checkliste mit den Fragen durch und versuchen diese Fragen für uns zu beantworten. Die besonders relevante Fragen mit „**Ja**", die die nicht stimmen mit **„Nein"**.
Z.B. hier: **„Ja"**, wir wollen die gleichen Informationen unterschiedlich präsentieren.
Keinen Antwort, da es keine Anforderungen zum „Run-Time" gibt.
„Ja", weil die GUI-Austauschbarkeit im Problem gefordert wird. **Ja**, weil keine Performanz Anforderungen gestellt sind. Und **Keine Antwort**, weil es keine Anforderungen dazu gibt.

Wenn es z.B. eine Performanzanforderung geben würde, hätten wir hier **„Nein"** ausgewählt. „Nein" bei den Konsequenzen bedeutet, dass das MVC Muster evtl. für das Problem nicht ganz passend ist. Man kann das Muster trotzdem verwenden oder ein anderes verwandtes Muster anschauen („Similar patterns"), oder eine andere Lösung ohne einem Muster verwenden.
Gehen Sie so bei der Lösung der **Aufgabe 2** aus dem dritten Teil vor.
Wenn Sie sich für das Muster entscheiden, sind Ihre Antworten auf Fragen eine Begründung (Rationale) für die Anwendung dieses Musters und werden mit der Muster-Entscheidung mitgespeichert. Während der System-Evolution braucht man so eine Begründung bei den Wartungsaufgaben.

26 August 2013 1

Wie verwendet man die Muster-Begründung (engl. rationale)?
Bei der **Aufgabe 1** aus dem dritten Teil bekommen Sie eine Liste mit den getroffenen Muster-Entscheidungen.
In dieser Liste sind für jede Entscheidung eine allgemeine Begründung, beteiligte Architektur-Elemente und Anforderungen festgehalten.
Außerdem gibt es für jede Muster-Entscheidung noch eine zusätzliche Muster-Begründung in Form der beantworteten Fragen aus dem Katalog wie vorher erklärt.
Diese Muster-Begründung wurde von einem Architekt beim Entwurf angegeben. Mit deren Hilfe kann man überprüfen, falls es Änderungsanfragen an das System gibt, ob die Muster-Entscheidung danach noch gültig ist.

Im Beispiel hier sehen Sie einen Auszug aus dem Papier-Entscheidungsdokument PSE-Entscheidungen. In einer Muster-Entscheidung wurde „Class Table Inheritance" als Variante des OR-Mappings ausgewählt, mit dem das Mapping zwischen Klassen und Datenbank in Hibernate konfiguriert wird.

Nehmen wir, an jetzt kommt eine Änderungsanfrage:
„Es soll ein neuen Benutzer-Typ „App-Admin" unterstützt werden, der in das Domain Model eingepflegt werden muss. In Zukunft wird es häufige Änderungen des Domain-Modells geben".
Lesen wir die Begründung von dem Muster in der Entscheidung durch. Laut Q074 ging man bei der Entscheidung davon aus, dass es keine häufigen Domain-Modell-Änderungen geben wird. **Daher wird diese Entscheidung durch die Änderungsanfrage potenziell getroffen und sollte evtl. überdacht werden.** Allerdings, wenn wir mit dem Muster nicht sehr gut vertraut sind, können wir uns auch an den Katalog wenden, um die Muster-Beschreibung schnell zu überfliegen.

In dem Fragebogen, den Sie bekommen, sollen Sie solche Entscheidung dann als „soll überdacht werden" markieren. Es bedeutet nicht, dass die Entscheidung verworfen wird und aus dem System entfernt wird, sondern dass über diese Entscheidung nachgedacht werden muss. Vergessen Sie nicht bei der Aufgabenlösung eine kurze Begründung, z.B. mit dem Muster und dem Fragen IDs einzutragen.

26 August 2013 2

Einführung ins Experiment, Zoya (Zum Vorlesen)

Gruppe B:

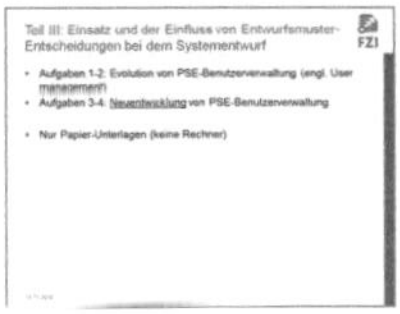

Im drittem Teil werden Sie den Einsatz und den Einfluss von Entwurfsmusterentscheidungen (engl. Pattern design decisions) im Systementwurf und Evolution evaluieren.
Sie werden 2 Aufgaben bekommen.
Die erste Aufgabe behandelt die **System-Evolution** der Benutzerverwaltung. Dabei evaluieren Sie die Gültigkeit der getroffenen Entwurfsmuster-Entscheidungen nach den Änderungsanfragen an User Management.
Die Aufgabe 2 behandelt die **Neuentwicklung** und sucht nach passenden Entwurfsmustern um die angegebenen Probleme zu lösen. Wir nehmen dabei an, dass die Benutzerverwaltung neu entwickelt wird.

Für diesen Teil des Experimentes werden Sie nur Papierunterlagen benötigen.

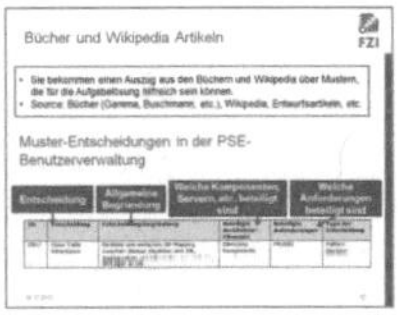

Bei der **Aufgabe 1** aus dem dritten Teil bekommen Sie einen Auszug aus Büchern und Wikipedia, in dem die für die Aufgabe benötigten Muster beschrieben sind, und eine Liste mit getroffenen Muster-Entscheidungen.

In dieser Liste sind für jede Entscheidung eine Begründung, beteiligte Architektur-Elemente und Anforderungen festgehalten.
Diese Begründung wurde von einem Architekt beim Benutzerverwaltung-Entwurf getroffen. Mit deren Hilfe kann man überprüfen, falls es Änderungsanfragen an System gibt, ob die Muster-Entscheidung danach noch gültig ist

Wie verwendet man die Entscheidungs-Begründung (engl. rationale)?
Im Beispiel hier sehen Sie einen Auszug aus dem Papier-Entscheidungsdokument PSE-Entscheidungen. In einer Muster-Entscheidung wurde „Class Table Inheritance" als Variante des OR-Mappings ausgewählt, mit dem das Mapping zwischen Klassen und Datenbank in Hibernate konfiguriert wird.

Nehmen wir, an jetzt kommt eine Änderungsanfrage:
„Es soll ein neuen Benutzer-Typ „App-Admin" unterstützt werden, der in das Domain Model eingepflegt werden muss. In Zukunft wird es häufige Änderungen des Domain-Modells geben".
Lesen wir die Begründung von dem Muster in der Entscheidung durch.
Wenn wir mit dem Muster nicht sehr gut vertraut sind, wenden wir uns ans Buch und überfliegen **schnell** die Beschreibung.
Wir sehen dort (Seite 262) „Any refactoring of fields up or down the hierarchy causes database changes".
Laut der Änderungsanfrage werden aber häufigen Domain-Modell-Änderungen geben. **Daher wird diese Entscheidung durch die Änderungsanfrage potenziell getroffen und sollte evtl. überdacht werden.**

Das bedeutet, dass die Änderungsanfrage potenzielle Auswirkungen auf diese Entscheidung haben kann, weil neue Objekte eingefügt werden sollen. In dem Fragebogen, den Sie bekommen, sollen Sie solche Entscheidung dann als „soll überdacht werden" markieren. Es bedeutet nicht, dass die Entscheidung verworfen wird und aus dem System entfernt wird, sondern dass über diese Entscheidung nachgedacht werden muss. Vergessen Sie nicht bei der Aufgabenlösung eine kurze Begründung, in denen Sie z.B. Seiten Aus dem Buch referenzieren.

26 August 2013 3

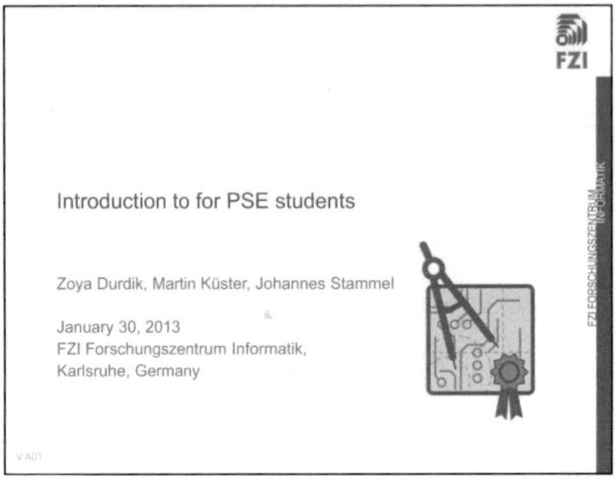
FZI
Introduction to for PSE students
Zoya Durdik, Martin Küster, Johannes Stammel
January 30, 2013
FZI Forschungszentrum Informatik,
Karlsruhe, Germany
FZI FORSCHUNGSZENTRUM INFORMATIK

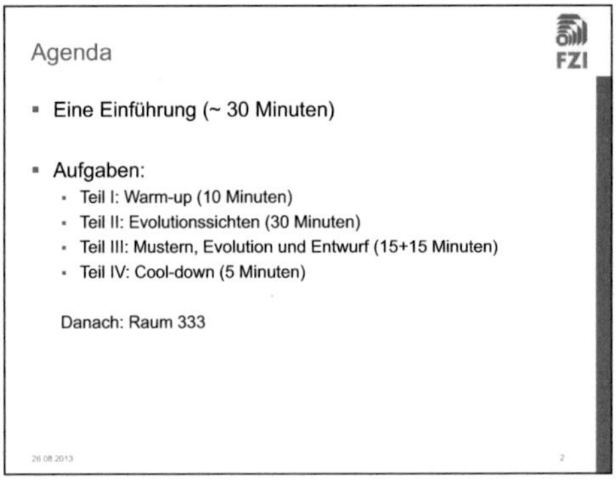
Agenda
FZI
Eine Einführung (~ 30 Minuten)
Aufgaben:
Teil I: Warm-up (10 Minuten)
Teil II: Evolutionssichten (30 Minuten)
Teil III: Mustern, Evolution und Entwurf (15+15 Minuten)
Teil IV: Cool-down (5 Minuten)
Danach: Raum 333
2

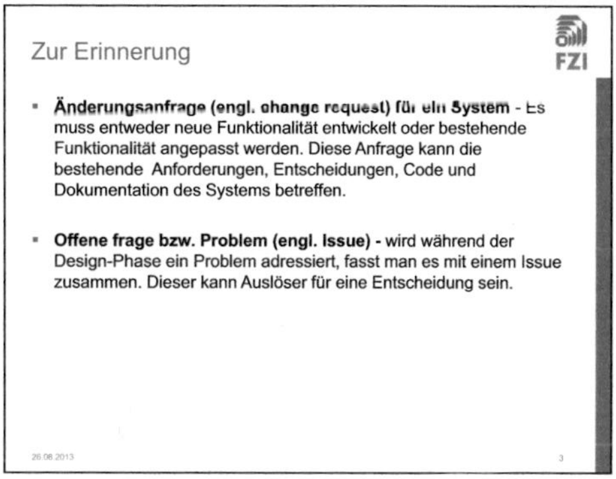
Zur Erinnerung
FZI
▪ **Änderungsanfrage (engl. change request) für ein System** - Es muss entweder neue Funktionalität entwickelt oder bestehende Funktionalität angepasst werden. Diese Anfrage kann die bestehende Anforderungen, Entscheidungen, Code und Dokumentation des Systems betreffen.
▪ **Offene frage bzw. Problem (engl. Issue) -** wird während der Design-Phase ein Problem adressiert, fasst man es mit einem Issue zusammen. Dieser kann Auslöser für eine Entscheidung sein.
26.08.2013
3

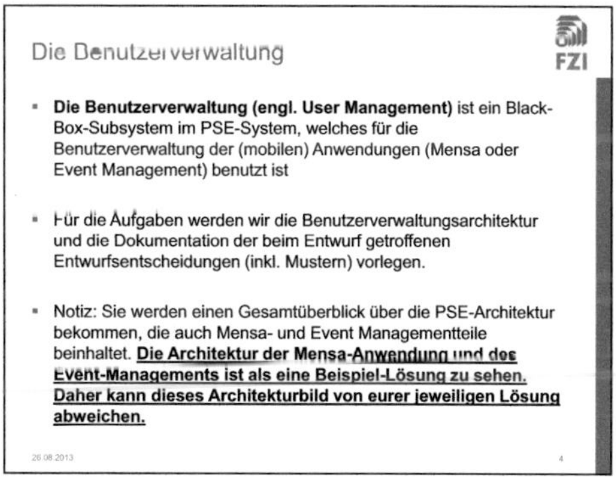
Die Benutzerverwaltung
FZI
▪ **Die Benutzerverwaltung (engl. User Management)** ist ein Black-Box-Subsystem im PSE-System, welches für die Benutzerverwaltung der (mobilen) Anwendungen (Mensa oder Event Management) benutzt ist
▪ Für die Aufgaben werden wir die Benutzerverwaltungsarchitektur und die Dokumentation der beim Entwurf getroffenen Entwurfsentscheidungen (inkl. Mustern) vorlegen.
▪ Notiz: Sie werden einen Gesamtüberblick über die PSE-Architektur bekommen, die auch Mensa- und Event Managementteile beinhaltet. **Die Architektur der Mensa-Anwendung und des Event-Managements ist als eine Beispiel-Lösung zu sehen. Daher kann dieses Architekturbild von eurer jeweiligen Lösung abweichen.**
26.08.2013
4

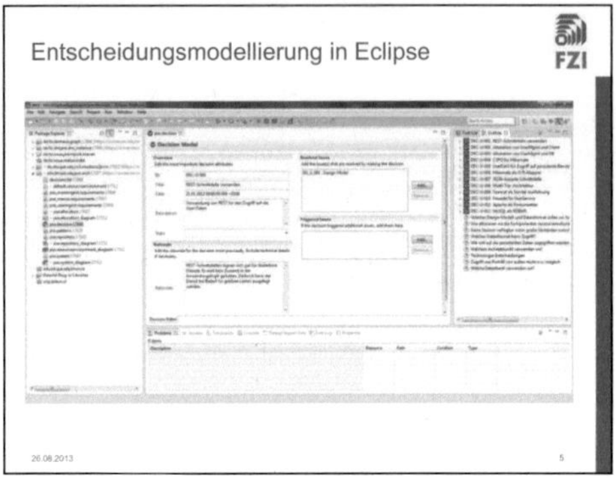
Entscheidungsmodellierung in Eclipse
FZI
26.08.2013
5

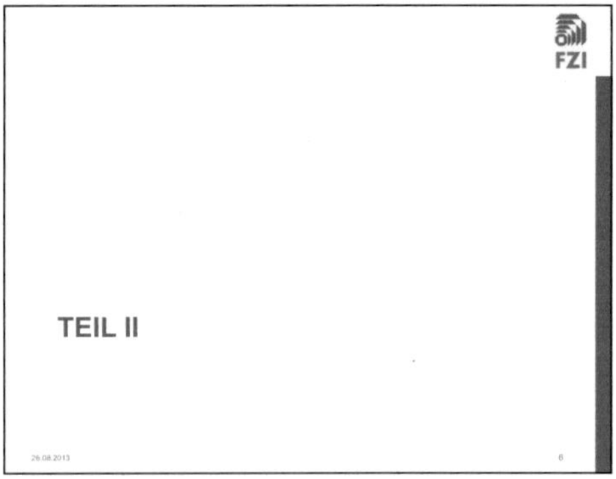
FZI
TEIL II
26.08.2013
6

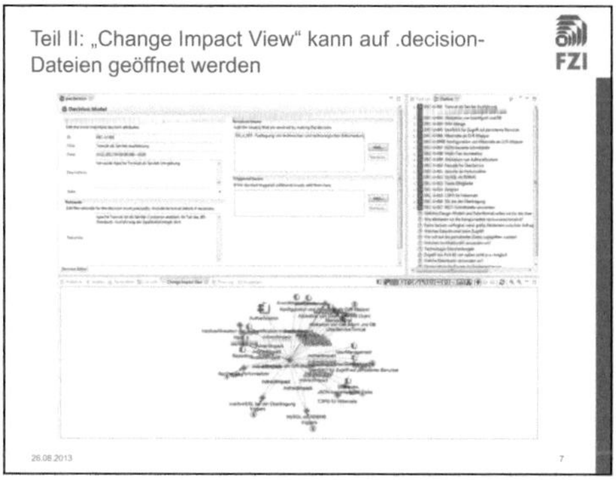
Teil II: „Change Impact View“ kann auf .decision-Dateien geöffnet werden
FZI
26.08.2013
7

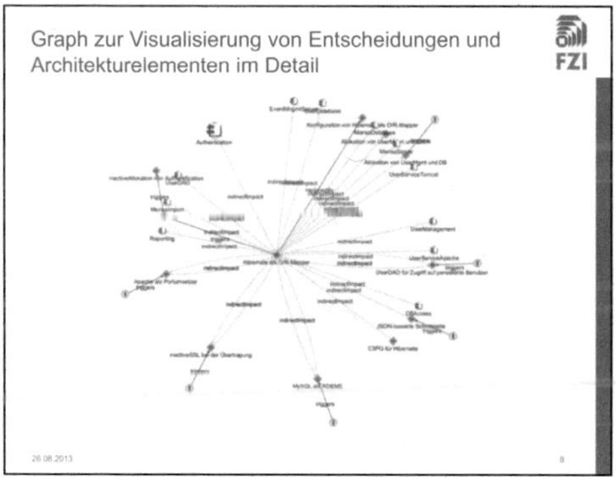
Graph zur Visualisierung von Entscheidungen und Architekturelementen im Detail
FZI
26.08.2013
8

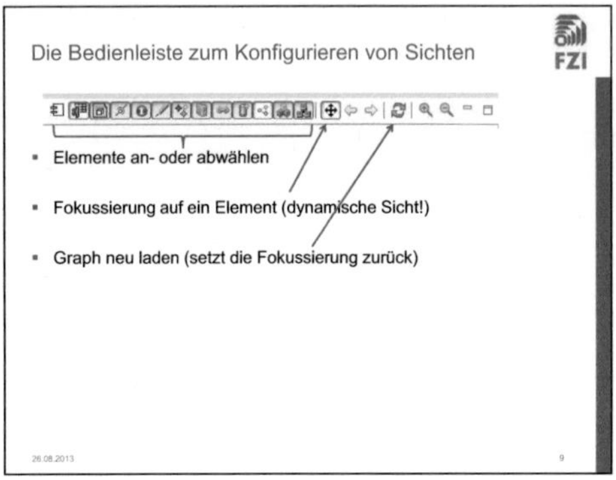
Die Bedienleiste zum Konfigurieren von Sichten
FZI
Elemente an- oder abwählen
Fokussierung auf ein Element (dynamische Sicht!)
Graph neu laden (setzt die Fokussierung zurück)
26.08.2013
9

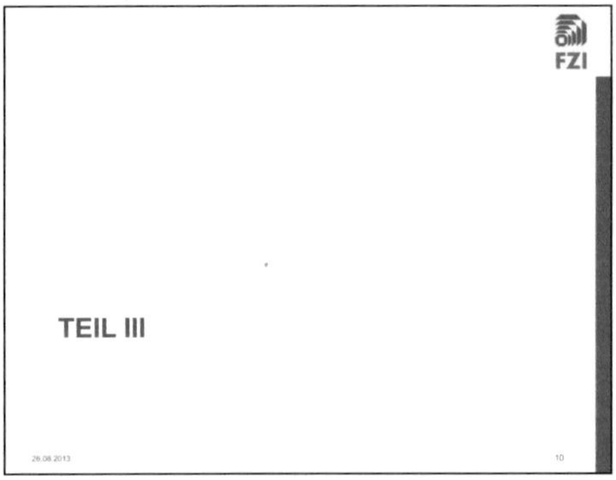
FZI
TEIL III
26.08.2013
10

Teil III: Einsatz und der Einfluss von Entwurfsmuster-Entscheidungen bei dem Systementwurf

FZI

- Aufgabe 1: Evolution von PSE-Benutzerverwaltung (engl. User management)
- Aufgabe 2: Neuentwicklung von PSE-Benutzerverwaltung

- Nur Papier-Unterlagen (keine Rechner)

26.08.2013 11

Muster-Katalog (engl. Pattern Catalogue)

FZI

- **Was:** Kompakte und strukturierte Informationen über Mustern
- **Source:** Bücher (Gamma, Buschmann, etc.), Wikipedia, Entwurfsartikeln, etc.

Katalogeintrag, Beispiel: Model-View-Controller

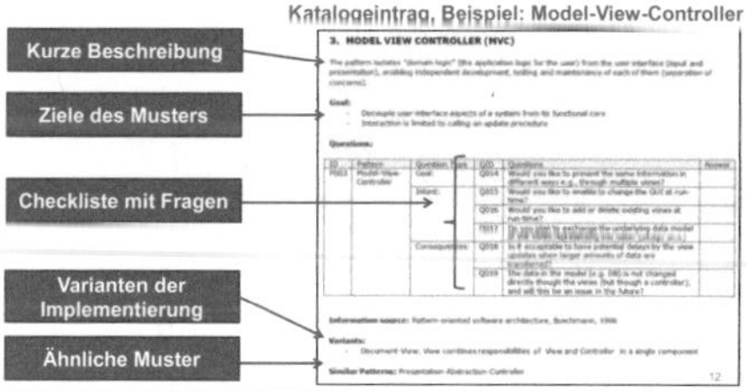

12

Fragen im Katalog

Checkliste für die Musteranwendung

FZI

Ziel | **Absicht** | **„Ja" / „Nein" Fragen**

Question Type	QID	Questions	Answer
Goal:	Q014	Would you like to present the same information in different ways e.g., through multiple views?	
Intent:	Q015	Would you like to enable to change the GUI (views) at run-time?	„Ja"
	Q017	Do you plan to exchange the underlying data model or the views representing this data? (design time)	
Consequences:	Q018	Is it acceptable to have potential delays by the view updates when larger amounts of data are transferred?	„Nein"
	Q019	The data in the model (e.g. DB) is not changed directly though the views (but though a controller), and will this be an issue in the future?	„---"

Konsequenzen

- **„Ja"** = Besonders wichtig
- **„Nein"** = Nicht der Absicht (bei den Absicht-Fragen)
  = Evtl. ein falsches Muster
  (bei den Konsequenzen-Fragen)
- **„Kein Antwort"** = die Eigenschaft spielt bei der Musterauswahl keine besondere Rolle (oder es gibt keine Anforderung dazu)

26.08.2013 13

Wie nutzt man den Katalog bei der Neuentwicklung

FZI

Problem? Die Daten sollen in der App in unterschiedlichen GUIs (je Betriebssystem) angezeigt werden. Dabei soll es möglich sein die GUIs auszutauschen. Keine Business-App, daher keine besonderen Anforderungen an die Performanz."

Model-View-Controller

✓

Question Type	QID	Questions	Answer
Goal:	Q014	Would you like to present the same information in different ways e.g., through multiple views?	„Ja"
Intent:	Q015	Would you like to enable to change the GUI (views) at run-time?	„---"
	Q017	Do you plan to exchange the underlying data model or the views representing this data? (design time)	„Ja"
Consequences:	Q018	Is it acceptable to have potential delays by the view updates when larger amounts of data are transferred?	„Ja"
	Q019	The data in the model (e.g. DB) is not changed directly though the views (but though a controller), and will this be an issue in the future?	„---"

26.08.2013 14

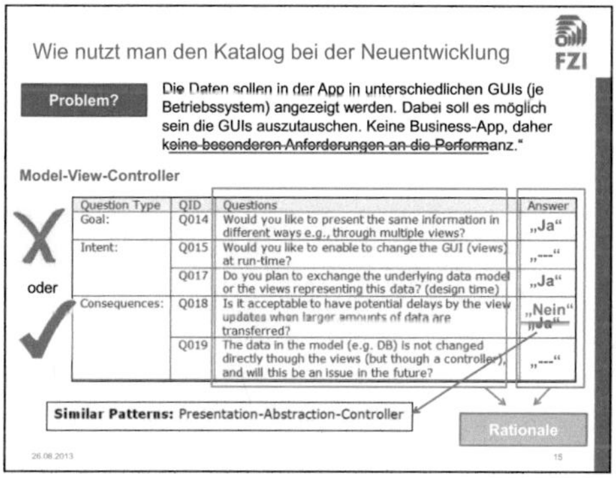
Wie nutzt man den Katalog bei der Neuentwicklung
FZI
Problem?
Die Daten sollen in der App in unterschiedlichen GUIs (je Betriebssystem) angezeigt werden. Dabei soll es möglich sein die GUIs auszutauschen. Keine Business-App, daher keine besonderen Anforderungen an die Performanz."
Model-View-Controller
oder
Question Type
QID
Questions
Answer
Goal:
Q014
Would you like to present the same information in different ways e.g., through multiple views?
„Ja"
Intent:
Q015
Would you like to enable to change the GUI (views) at run-time?
„---"
Q017
Do you plan to exchange the underlying data model or the views representing this data? (design time)
„Ja"
Consequences:
Q018
Is it acceptable to have potential delays by the view updates when larger amounts of data are transferred?
„Nein"
„Ja"
Q019
The data in the model (e.g. DB) is not changed directly though the views (but though a controller), and will this be an issue in the future?
„---"
Similar Patterns: Presentation-Abstraction-Controller
Rationale
26.08.2013
15

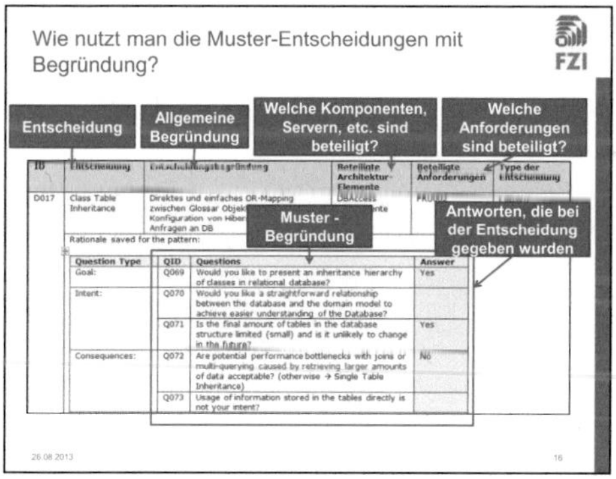
Wie nutzt man die Muster-Entscheidungen mit Begründung?
FZI
Entscheidung
Allgemeine Begründung
Welche Komponenten, Servern, etc. sind beteiligt?
Welche Anforderungen sind beteiligt?
ID
Beteiligte Architektur-Elemente
Beteiligte Anforderungen
Type der Entscheidung
D017
Class Table Inheritance
Direktes und einfaches OR-Mapping
Anfragen an DB
Muster - Begründung
Antworten, die bei der Entscheidung gegeben wurden
Rationale saved for the pattern:
Question Type
QID
Questions
Answer
Goal:
Q069
Would you like to present an inheritance hierarchy of classes in relational database?
Yes
Intent:
Q070
Would you like a straightforward relationship between the database and the domain model to achieve easier understanding of the Database?
Q071
Is the final amount of tables in the database structure limited (small) and is it unlikely to change in the future?
Yes
Consequences:
Q072
Are potential performance bottlenecks with joins or multi-querying caused by retrieving larger amounts of data acceptable? (otherwise → Single Table Inheritance)
No
Q073
Usage of information stored in the tables directly is not your intent?
26.08.2013
16

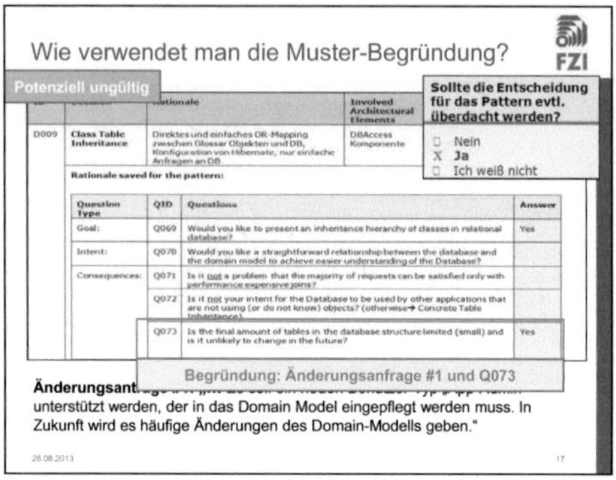
Wie verwendet man die Muster-Begründung?
FZI
Potenziell ungültig
Sollte die Entscheidung für das Pattern evtl. überdacht werden?
Nein
X Ja
Ich weiß nicht
Involved Architectural Elements
D009
Class Table Inheritance
Direktes und einfaches OR-Mapping zwischen Glossar Objekten und DB, Konfiguration von Hibernate, nur einfache Anfragen an DB
DBAccess Komponente
Rationale saved for the pattern:
Question Type | QID | Questions | Answer
Goal: | Q069 | Would you like to present an inheritance hierarchy of classes in relational database? | Yes
Intent: | Q070 | Would you like a straightforward relationship between the database and the domain model to achieve easier understanding of the Database?
Consequences: | Q071 | Is it not a problem that the majority of requests can be satisfied only with performance expensive joins?
Q072 | Is it not your intent for the Database to be used by other applications that are not using (or do not know) objects? (otherwise→ Concrete Table Inheritance)
Q073 | Is the final amount of tables in the database structure limited (small) and is it unlikely to change in the future? | Yes
Begründung: Änderungsanfrage #1 und Q073
Änderungsant
unterstützt werden, der in das Domain Model eingepflegt werden muss. In Zukunft wird es häufige Änderungen des Domain-Modells geben."
26.08.2013
17

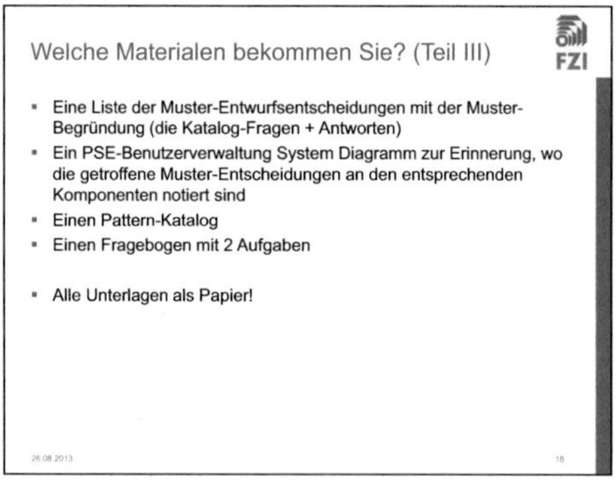
Welche Materialen bekommen Sie? (Teil III)
FZI
Eine Liste der Muster-Entwurfsentscheidungen mit der Muster-Begründung (die Katalog-Fragen + Antworten)
Ein PSE-Benutzerverwaltung System Diagramm zur Erinnerung, wo die getroffene Muster-Entscheidungen an den entsprechenden Komponenten notiert sind
Einen Pattern-Katalog
Einen Fragebogen mit 2 Aufgaben
Alle Unterlagen als Papier!
26.08.2013
18

Und los geht's!

FZI

FZI FORSCHUNGSZENTRUM INFORMATIK

Introduction for PSE students

Zoya Durdik, Martin Küster, Johannes Stammel

January 30, 2013
FZI Forschungszentrum Informatik,
Karlsruhe, Germany

V 801

Agenda

FZI

- Eine Einführung (~ 30 Minuten)
- Aufgaben:
  - Teil I: Warm-up (10 Minuten)
  - Teil II: Evolutionssichten (30 Minuten)
  - Teil III: Mustern, Evolution und Entwurf (30 Minuten)
  - Teil IV: Cool-down (5 Minuten)

26.08.2013 2

Zur Erinnerung

FZI

- **Änderungsanfrage (engl. change request) für ein System** - Es muss entweder neue Funktionalität entwickelt oder bestehende Funktionalität angepasst werden. Diese Anfrage kann die bestehende Anforderungen, Entscheidungen, Code und Dokumentation des Systems betreffen.

- **Offene frage bzw. Problem (engl. Issue) -** wird während der Design-Phase ein Problem adressiert, fasst man es mit einem Issue zusammen. Dieser kann Auslöser für eine Entscheidung sein.

26.08.2013 3

Die Benutzerverwaltung

FZI

- **Die Benutzerverwaltung (engl. User Management)** ist ein Black-Box-Subsystem im PSE-System, welches für die Benutzerverwaltung der (mobilen) Anwendungen (Mensa oder Event Management) benutzt ist

- Für die Aufgaben werden wir die Benutzerverwaltungsarchitektur und die Dokumentation der beim Entwurf getroffenen Entwurfsentscheidungen (inkl. Mustern) vorlegen.

- Notiz: Sie werden einen Gesamtüberblick über die PSE-Architektur bekommen, die auch Mensa- und Event Managementteile beinhaltet. **Die Architektur der Mensa-Anwendung und des Event-Managements ist als eine Beispiel-Lösung zu sehen. Daher kann dieses Architekturbild von eurer jeweiligen Lösung abweichen.**

26.08.2013 4

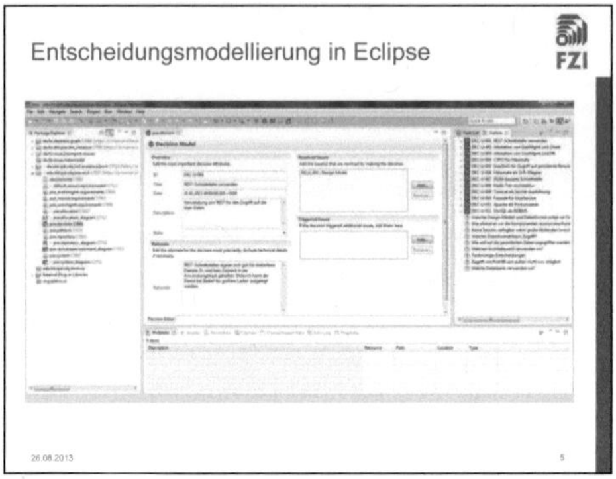
Entscheidungsmodellierung in Eclipse
FZI
26.08.2013
5

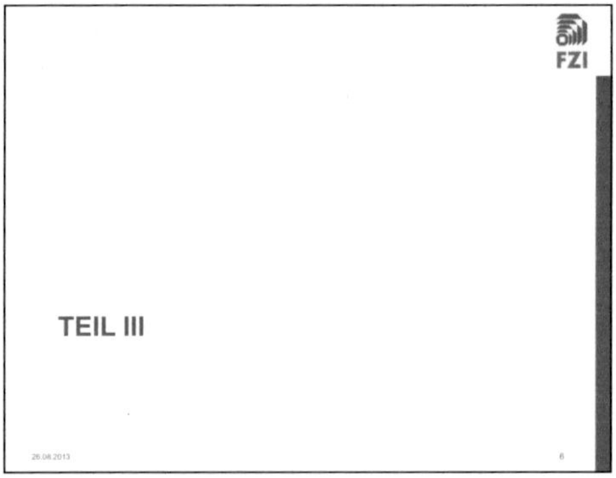
FZI
TEIL III
26.08.2013
6

Teil III: Einsatz und der Einfluss von Entwurfsmuster-Entscheidungen bei dem Systementwurf

FZI

- Aufgabe 1: Evolution von PSE Benutzerverwaltung (engl. User management)
- Aufgabe 2: <u>Neuentwicklung</u> von PSE-Benutzerverwaltung
- Nur Papier-Unterlagen (keine Rechner)

26.08.2013 7

Bücher und Wikipedia Artikeln

FZI

- Sie bekommen einen Auszug aus den Büchern und Wikipedia über Mustern, die für die Aufgabenlösung hilfreich sein können.
- Source: Bücher (Gamma, Buschmann, etc.), Wikipedia, Entwurfsartikeln, etc.

Muster-Entscheidungen in der PSE-Benutzerverwaltung

Entscheidung

Allgemeine Begründung

Welche Komponenten, Servern, etc. sind beteiligt?

Welche Anforderungen sind beteiligt?

ID	Entscheidung	Entscheidungsbegründung	Beteiligte Architektur-Elemente	Beteiligte Anforderungen	Type der Entscheidung
D017	Class Table Inheritance	Direktes und einfaches OR-Mapping zwischen Glossar Objekten und DB, Konfiguration von Hibernate, nur einfache Anfragen an DB	DBAccess Komponente	FRU002	Pattern Decision

26.08.2013 8

Wie verwendet man die Begründung?

FZI

PSE-Entscheidung:

ID	Entscheidung	Entscheidungsbegründung	Beteiligte Architektur-Elemente	Beteiligte Anforderungen	Type der Entscheidung
D017	Class Table Inheritance	Direktes und einfaches OR-Mapping zwischen Glossar Objekten und DB, Konfiguration von Hibernate, nur einfache Anfragen an DB	DBAccess Komponente	FRU002	Pattern Decision

Potenziell ungültig

Änderungsanfrage #1: „... Es soll ein neuen Benutzer-Typ „App-Admin" unterstützt werden, der in das Domain Model eingepflegt werden muss. In Zukunft wird es häufige Änderungen des Domain-Modells geben."

Buch-Auszug:

Class Table Inheritance

Seite 262: „Weaknesses:... Any refactoring of fields up or down the hierarchy causes database changes".

Im Fragebogen:

Sollte die Entscheidung für das Pattern evtl. überdacht werden?

- ☐ Nein
- X Ja
- ☐ Ich weiß nicht

Begründung: Änderungsanfrage #1 und Buchauszug Seite 262, Text unterstr.

26.08.2013

Welche Materialen bekommen Sie?

FZI

- Eine Liste der Muster-Entwurfsentscheidungen mit Begründung (engl. rationale)
- Ein PSE-Benutzerverwaltung System Diagramm zur Erinnerung, wo die getroffene Muster-Entscheidungen an entsprechenden Komponenten notiert sind
- Einen Buch-Auszug
- Ein Fragebogen mit vier Aufgaben
- Alle Unterlagen als Papier!
- Für die Aufgaben 3 und 4 brauchen Sie die PSE-Entscheidungen und das System nicht, die werden Ihnen wieder entnommen.

26.08.2013 10

FZI
Und los geht's!
26.08.2013
11

Aufgaben für die Übung im Rahmen der Veranstaltung
"Praxis der Software-Entwicklung"

Karlsruhe Institute of Technology

TEIL I

[10 Minuten]

Version 1.0

Veröffentlichung: 30.01.2013

Autor

Zoya Durdik

Martin Küster

Aufgaben für die Übung im Rahmen der Veranstaltung "Praxis der Software-Entwicklung"

Autor: Zoya Durdik, Martin Küster Stand: 28.01.2013 Version: 1.0

Karlsruhe Institute of Technology

Wichtig: Alle Aufgaben beziehen sich auf die vorliegenden Artefakte (Architekturmodelle, Anforderungen, etc.), die von Ihrem PSE-Entwurf etwas abweichen können. Schauen Sie sich bitte beiliegenden Artefakte an, um die Aufgaben zu beantworten.

Die Fragen sollen Ihnen die Möglichkeit geben, sich mit den Artefakten und dem System vertraut zu machen.

Geben Sie bitte Ihre ID ein: ___________________

Fragen:

1. Welche Schnittstelle (engl. Interface) wird von den beiden PSE-Applikationen (Mensa und EventManagement) gemäß dem vorgelegten Architekturmodell benutzt?

(Tipp: In ausgegebenen Workspace in Eclipse öffnen Sie z.B. das Diagramm „pse.repository_diagramm" im Projekt „edu.kit.ipd.sdq.pse.arch". Allerdings, Sie können den PropertiesView durch „ShowProperties" im Kontext-Menu aufrufen, falls Sie die Properties von den Elementen anschauen wollen)

Die beiden Apps benutzen ___________________ (Name) Interface

2. Wie viele Felder hat der Datentype „User" gemäß dem vorgelegten Architekturmodell des User-Management Systems? (Tipp: Öffnen Sie z.B. das Modell „pse.repository" im Projekt „edu.kit.ipd.sdq.pse.arch" und suchen Sie nach dem CompositeDataType „User" in Baumeditor.)

Der Datentype „User" hat _____ (Anzahl) Felder.

3. Wie viele assemblierte Komponenten hat das UserManagement-System? (Tipp: Öffnen Sie das Diagramm „pse.system_diagramm" im Projekt „edu.kit.ipd.sdq.pse.arch")

Das UserManagement System hat _____ (Anzahl) Komponenten.

4. Auf wie vielen Servern ist das PSE-System laut vorgelegten Architekturmodellen im Einsatz (engl. Deployment)? (Tipp: Öffnen Sie z.B. das Diagramm „pse.allocation_diagramm" im Projekt „edu.kit.ipd.sdq.pse.arch")

Das PSE System ist auf _____ (Anzahl) Servern zum Einsatz gebracht.

5. Finden Sie das Muster „Model-View-Control" (MVC) in den ausgegebenen Materialen. Wie viele Varianten des MVC-Musters gibt es gemäß diesen Materialeien? (Tipp: Schauen sie die Angaben unter „Variants" in Kapitel/Sektion MVC an)

Es gibt _____ (Anzahl) Implementierungsvarianten des MVC Muster.

Falls Sie Fragen haben, wenden Sie sich bitte an uns. Geben Sie uns bitte Bescheid, wenn Sie mit den Aufgaben fertig sind. Sie bekommen dann den weiteren Aufgabenblock. Danke!

Status: Final – öffentlich – Seite 1/2

Aufgaben für die Übung im Rahmen der Veranstaltung "Praxis der Software-Entwicklung"

Karlsruhe Institute of Technology

TEIL III, Aufgabe 1

Muster-Entscheidungen und Evolution

[15 Minuten]

Version 1.0

Veröffentlichung: 30.01.2013

Autor

Zoya Durdik

Teil III. Code: A02

Karlsruhe Institute of Technology

Sie haben [15 Minuten] **Geben Sie bitte Ihre ID ein: ________________**

AUFGABE 1. Prüfen Sie, ob die im Vorfeld bereits getroffenen Entwurfsmusterentscheidungen (engl. pattern design decisions) nach den aufgelisteten Änderungsanfragen (engl. change requests) überdacht werden sollten.

Vorgehensweise:

Für jede Entwurfsentscheidung aus Tabelle I „Aufgabe"

1. Die Begründung für die Entscheidung in Tabelle II „PSE-Muster-Entscheidungen" lesen.
2. Das Muster in einem Musterkatalog (engl. pattern catalogue) kurz überfliegen
3. Die Liste der Änderungsanfragen in der Tabelle III „Änderungsanfragen" durchgehen und entscheiden „Sollte die Entscheidung für das Pattern evtl. überdacht werden"
   - „**Ja**" oder „**Nein**" in der Tabelle I ausfüllen.
   - Bitte markieren Sie mit „**Ja**" wenn die Eigenschaften des Musters verletzt werden oder wenn Voraussetzungen für den Einsatz des Musters nicht mehr erfüllt werden, oder wenn das Muster der Einsatz des Musters nochmal detailliert überdacht werden muss.
   - Bitte markieren Sie mit „**Nein**" wenn einfache Code-Anpassungen vorgenommen werden müssen, die die Semantik des Musters oder die Art der Implementierung des Musters nicht verändern, bzw. wenn das Muster nicht betroffen ist.
   - Eine kurze Begründung zu der Antwort in Tabelle I schreiben (ggf. IDs der Änderungsanfragen, der Mustern, der Muster-Fragen, etc. mitnotieren).

Tipp: Eine Änderungsanfrage führt nicht unbedingt zur Ungültigkeit von den Entwurfsmusterentscheidungen. Es müssen nicht alle von den gelisteten Entwurfsmuster-Entscheidungen durch die Änderungsanfragen betroffen sein.

Tabelle I. Aufgabe

ID*	Entwurfs-entscheidung*	Sollte die Entscheidung für das Pattern evtl. überdacht werden?	Begründung
D009	Class Table Inheritance **Beispiel**	☐ Nein X **Ja** ☐ Ich weiß nicht	*Laut **Beispiel CR000 (siehe Folien)** soll die DB ein neues Objekt unterstützen, wofür das Muster Class Table Inheritance laut dem Pattern Catalogue Eintrag 10 QID073 nicht gut geeignet ist*
D005	**Façade**	☐ Nein ☐ Ja ☐ Ich weiß nicht	
D006	**Singleton**	☐ Nein ☐ Ja ☐ Ich weiß nicht	
D007	**Thin client**	☐ Nein ☐ Ja ☐ Ich weiß nicht	
D002	**Multi-Tier Architektur**	☐ Nein ☐ Ja ☐ Ich weiß nicht	

* Siehe Tabelle II für Entscheindunsgbegründung und relevante Komponenten.

Tabelle III. Änderungsanfragen (engl. change requests):

ID	Änderungsanfrage
CR001	Das Login dauert teilweise zu lang, daher muss eine Session-Verwaltung in die UserServiceTomcat Komponente eingebaut werden, um die Wartezeiten bei der Re-Authentifizierung zu reduzieren.
CR002	Der Client (Mensa oder Event Management) der auf mobilen Geräten läuft, soll auch im Falle temporärer Funknetzausfalle funktionsfähig bleiben.
CR003	Das User Management soll einen neuen Report-Typ „Benutzerstatistiken" unterstützen, der Informationen über Benutzer und deren durchschnittliches Alter abfragt und einen allgemeinen Report daraus erstellt.

Seite 1/11

Teil III. Code: A02

Nachfragen zu der Aufgabe 1.

1. Es fiel mir leicht die Gültigkeit von Entwurfsmuster-Entscheidungen zu prüfen

- ☐ Richtig (Ich habe die Aufgabestellung gut verstanden und bin bei den meisten meiner Antworten sicher)
- ☐ Teilweise richtig (Ich konnte nicht alle Entwurfsmuster-Entscheidungen sicher bewerten, habe aber am Ende die passenden Antworten gefunden und ich bin bei den meisten meiner Antworten sicher)
- ☐ Teilweise falsch (Ich konnte nicht alle Entwurfsmuster-Entscheidungen sicher bewerten, und bin nicht bei den allen meinen Antworten sicher)
- ☐ Falsch (Ich bin bei den meisten Antworten nicht sicher)

Kommentar ____

2. Hat Ihnen der beigelegte Muster-Katalog bei der Aufgabenlösung geholfen?

- ☐ Die beantworteten Fragen aus dem Katalog, die mit den Entscheidungen gespeichert waren, waren ausreichend und haben mich bei der Aufgabenlösung unterstützt.
- ☐ Ich fühlte mich durch den Katalog gut unterstützt.
- ☐ Ich fühlte mich durch den Katalog unterstützt, hätte aber ein Buch oder das Internet gebrauchen können, bzw. ich hatte zusätzlichen Materialen gebraucht.
- ☐ Ich konnte den Katalog für die Aufgabenlösung zwar teilweise verwenden, die Informationen waren aber überwiegend nicht ausreichend.
- ☐ Der Katalog konnte mir bei der Aufgabenlösung nicht helfen.
- ☐ Die Aufgabe war so einfach, ich habe den Katalog nicht gebraucht.
- ☐ Sonstiges ______________________________________

3. Sonstige Kommentare?

____

____

____

Geben Sie uns bitte Bescheid, wenn Sie mit diesen Aufgaben fertig sind, um weitere Aufgaben zu bekommen.

Seite 2/11

Teil III. Code: A02

Tabelle II. Liste der PSE—Muster-Entscheidungen

ID	Decision	Rationale	Involved Architectural Elements	Involved Requirements	Decision Type
D001	**Client-Server Architektur**	Austauschbarkeit. Grundlegende Entscheidung über Architektur.	alle	FRA001	Pattern Decision
	Rationale saved for the pattern: No additional rationale saved				

ID	Decision	Rationale	Involved Architectural Elements	Involved Requirements	Decision Type
D002	**Multi-Tier-Architektur**	Multi Tier-Architektur eignet sich aus folgenden Gründen: 1) Abstraktion von Persistenz durch Layering. 2) Erfahrung im JEE-Bereich (JBoss etc.) 3) Clients leicht austauschbar.	alle	FRA001	Pattern Decision
	Rationale saved for the pattern:				

QID	Questions	Answer
Q007	Would you like to be able to add or modify specific parts instead of reworking the whole application?	Yes
Q008	Would you like to structure the system according to the underlying physical infrastructure?	
Q009	Would you like to prevent the client to access data directly?	Yes
Q010	Would you like to have a linear communication model in your system, where each tier can communicate only with 2 neighboring tiers in a strong linear hierarchy?	
Q012	Are you aware that all communication will run through a middle tier, which can become a bottleneck?	Yes
Q013	Potential involvement of multiple communication protocols with different evolution cycles is not an issue in the future?	
	See questions for Client-Server architecture	

ID	Decision	Rationale	Involved Architectural Elements	Involved Requirements	Decision Type
D003	**Component-based Architektur**	Austauschbarkeit. Grundlegende Entscheidung über Architektur	alle	-	Pattern Decision
	Rationale saved for the pattern: No additional rationale saved				

Seite 3/11

Teil III. Code: A02

ID	Decision	Rationale	Involved Architectural Elements	Involved Requirements	Decision Type
D004	**Proxy**	Apache vor dem Tomcat wegen Portumsetzung. Apache implementiert Reverse-Proxy als Port-Mapper. Anbindung des Apache über mod_jk an den Tomcat via AJP-Protokoll.	UserServiceApache Komponente	FRA003, NFRU005	Pattern Decision

Rationale saved for the pattern:

No additional rationale saved

ID	Decision	Rationale	Involved Architectural Elements	Involved Requirements	Decision Type
D005	**Façade**	UserServiceTomcat Komponente als Façade für Reporting, Authentifizierung und User-Management. Einfacher Zugriff auf die verschiedenen Funktionen der Benutzerverwaltung, inkl. Authentisierung, Reporting und Anfragen an das User-Management-Systems.	UserServiceTomcat Komponente	FRU008, NFRU001	Pattern Decision

Rationale saved for the pattern:

Question Type	QID	Questions	Answer
Goal:	Q042	Would you like to provide a unified interface to a set of interfaces in a subsystem?	Yes
Intent:	Q043	Would you like to minimize the communication and dependencies between subsystems?	
	Q046	An additional functionality wrapped into the unified interface is not your intent? (otherwise → Proxy)	Yes
	Q047	Is a stateless unified interface your intent? (otherwise → Proxy)	Yes
	Q048	Is it desired that subsystem classes know nothing about the facade object(s)? (otherwise → Mediator)	
	Q049	A new interface for an object is not your intent? (otherwise → Adaptor)	
Consequences:	Q050	Is a potential performance bottleneck not an issue?	Yes

Seite 4/11

Teil III. Code: A02

ID	Decision	Rationale	Involved Architectural Elements	Involved Requirements	Decision Type
D006	**Singleton**	Kontrollierter Zugriffskontrol	Authentifizierung Komponente	FRU009	Pattern Decision

Rationale saved for the pattern:

Question Type	QID	Questions	Answer
Goal:	Q064	Would you like to ensure that a class has only one instance?	Yes
Intent:	Q065	Would you like to make class instance easily accessible (globally)?	
Consequences:	Q066	If you are developing a distributed application, it is not an issue that the data stored in the instance cannot change too often?	Yes
	Q067	Having a global access to the class instance is not a potential threat to the application?	
	Q068	You are not developing a multi-thread application, respectively you have extended singleton for this case?	Yes

ID	Decision	Rationale	Involved Architectural Elements	Involved Requirements	Decision Type
D007	**Thin Client**	Zugriff auf die Funktionalität des Servers	EventManagement App, Mensa App	FRA002, FRA003, NFRM004, NFRM006, NFRE011	Pattern Decision

Rationale saved for the pattern:

Question Type	QID	Questions	Answer
Goal:	Q027	Would you like a client to put responsibility for data computation, persistence, etc. on the server side?	Yes
Intent:	Q028	Would you like to keep SW updates centralized?	Yes
	Q030	Is your infrastructure heterogeneous?	
	Q031	Would you like to support low-performance devices?	Yes
Consequences:	Q032	Working offline is not essential for your application? (otherwise → Fat Client)	Yes
	Q033	Are main changes (SW updates) expected to be on the server side? (otherwise → Fat Client)	

Seite 5/11

Teil III.   Code: A02

ID	Decision	Rationale	Involved Architectural Elements	Involved Requirements	Decision Type
D008	**DAO**	UserDAO für Zugriff auf persistente Benutzer. DAO ist ein etabliertes Muster aus dem JEE-Umfeld.	UserDAO Komponente		Pattern Decision
	Rationale saved for the pattern: No additional rationale saved				

ID	Decision	Rationale	Involved Architectural Elements	Involved Requirements	Decision Type
D009	**Class Table Inheritance**	Direktes und einfaches OR-Mapping zwischen Glossar Objekten und DB, Konfiguration von Hibernate, nur einfache Anfragen an DB	DBAccess Komponente	FRU002	Pattern Decision

Rationale saved for the pattern:

Question Type	QID	Questions	Answer
Goal:	Q069	Would you like to present an inheritance hierarchy of classes in relational database?	Yes
Intent:	Q070	Would you like a straightforward relationship between the database and the domain model to achieve easier understanding of the Database?	
Consequences:	Q071	Is it <u>not</u> a problem that the majority of requests can be satisfied only with performance expensive joins?	
	Q072	Is it <u>not</u> your intent for the Database to be used by other applications that are not using (or do not know) objects? (otherwise→ Concrete Table Inheritance)	
	Q073	Is the final amount of tables in the database structure limited (small) and is it unlikely to change in the future?	Yes

Seite 6/11

Teil III.   Code: A02

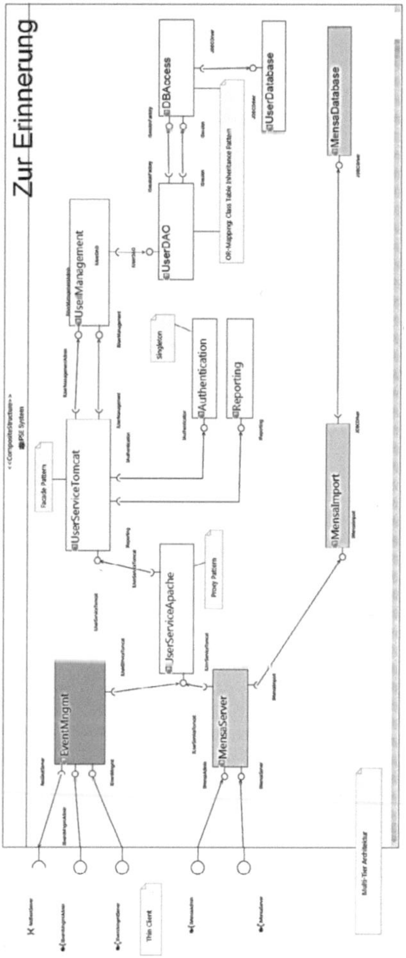

Seite 7/11

Teil III. Code: A02

Aufgaben für die Übung im Rahmen der Veranstaltung "Praxis der Software-Entwicklung"

Karlsruhe Institute of Technology

TEIL III, Aufgabe 2

Muster-Entscheidungen und Neue Entwicklung

[15 Minuten]

Version 1.0

Veröffentlichung: 30.01.2013

Autor

Zoya Durdik

Seite 8/11

Teil III. Code: A02

KIT Karlsruhe Institute of Technology

Sie haben [15 Minuten] **Geben Sie bitte Ihre ID ein:** ____________

AUFGABE 2. Wählen Sie welche Entwurfsmustern (engl. design patterns) zu den angegebenen Problemen (engl. issues) passen.

Wir betrachten dasselbe PSE-System, gehen aber davon aus, dass diese neu Entwickelt wird. **Stellen Sie sich also vor, dass Sie ein neues PSE-System mit neuen Anforderungen entwickeln.**

Vorgehensweise:

Für jedes Problem (engl. issue) aus Tabelle I „Zu lösende Probleme":

1. Das Problem aufmerksam lesen, alle Details berücksichtigen.
2. Für jede angegebene mögliche Lösung: Das Muster in dem Musterkatalog (engl. pattern catalogue) kurz nachschlagen
3. Entscheiden welche Lösung (Muster) angesichts der Problem-Details und der im Katalog gelisteten Muster-Eigenschaften am passendsten ist.
4. Eine Begründung ggfls. mit Vorteilen und Nachteilen zu Ihrer Lösung in Tabelle I eintragen. Die Begründung sollte ggf. Muster und Muster-Fragen IDs (aus dem Katalog) enthalten.
5. Zu dem nächsten Problem in der Tabelle I übergehen.

Tipp: Die Mustern lösen zwar jeweils ähnliche Probleme, unterscheiden sich aber in Details. **Für die Details schauen Sie im Katalog nach,** und tragen Sie die Details in der Begründung ein. Vergessen Sie nicht, dass Sie sich in der PSE-Neuentwicklung befinden!

Tabelle I. Zu lösende Probleme (engl. issues):

ID	Problem	Kreuzen Sie die richtige Lösung an	Begründung
P000	Die Data im App soll in unterschiedlichen GUIs (je Betriebssystem) angezeigt werden. Dabei soll es möglich sein die GUIs oder die Data Model voneinander unabhängig auszutauschen. **Beispiel**	□ PAC □ MVA X **MVC** □ Keins davon	*Eintrag im Pattern Catalogue #3: QID Q014, QID Q017*
P001	Das User Management soll eine zentrale Schnittstelle anbieten, welche die Sub-Komponente austauschbar hält. Die Schnittstelle soll die Session-Verwaltung übernehmen.	□ Adaptor □ Facade □ Proxy □ Keins davon	
P002	Der Client (Mensa oder Event Management) soll auf mobilen Geräten laufen können. Auch ältere Geräte (ältere Generation) sollen möglichst von den Apps unterstützt werden. Aufgrund der häufigen gesetzlichen Änderungen müssen evtl. häufige Änderungen an der Software vorgenommen werden.	□ Fat Client □ Thin Client □ Keins davon	
P003	Die Applikation soll auf dem Port 1022 laufen, jedoch können die ATIS-Server auf Port 0..1023 nichts empfangen, daher sollen die Applikationen andere Ports benutzen.	□ Adaptor □ Facade □ Proxy □ Keins davon	
P004	Es sollen normale Benutzer, Premium-Benutzer und Admin-Benutzer geben. Auf den Daten den normalen Benutzer sollte man schnell zugreifen können. Es wird eine andere Anwendung geben die ohne Objekte zu kennen auf den Daten zugreifen können muss.	□ Class Table Inheritance □ Single Table Inheritance □ Concrete Table Inheritance □ Keins davon	

Teil III. Code: A02

Nachfragen zu der Aufgabe 2.

1. Es fiel mir leicht die richtigen Entwurfsmuster auszuwählen

- ☐ Richtig (Ich habe die Aufgabenstellung gut verstanden und bin bei den meisten meiner Antworten sicher)
- ☐ Teilweise richtig (Ich konnte nicht alle Entwurfsmuster sicher auswählen, habe aber am Ende die passenden Antworten gefunden und ich bin bei den meisten meiner Antworten sicher)
- ☐ Teilweise falsch (Ich konnte nicht alle Entwurfsmustern sicher auswählen, und bin nicht bei allen meinen Antworten sicher)
- ☐ Falsch (Ich bin mir bei den meisten Antworten nicht sicher)

Kommentar ______________________________

2. Hat Ihnen der beigelegte Muster-Katalog bei der Aufgabenlösung geholfen?

- ☐ Ich fühlte mich durch den Katalog gut unterstützt.
- ☐ Ich fühlte mich durch den Katalog unterstützt, hätte aber ein Buch oder das Internet gebrauchen können, bzw. ich hatte zusätzlichen Materialen gebraucht.
- ☐ Ich konnte den Katalog für die Aufgabenlösung zwar teilweise verwenden, die Informationen waren aber überwiegend nicht ausreichend.
- ☐ Der Katalog konnte mir bei der Aufgabenlösung nicht helfen.
- ☐ Die Aufgabe war so einfach, ich habe den Katalog nicht gebraucht.
- ☐ Sonstiges ______________________________

3. Sonstige Kommentare?

____

____

____

ENDE DER TEIL III

Seite 10/11

Aufgaben für die Übung im Rahmen der Veranstaltung "Praxis der Software-Entwicklung"

Karlsruhe Institute of Technology

TEIL III, Aufgabe 1

Muster-Entscheidungen und Evolution

[15 Minuten]

Version 1.0

Veröffentlichung: 30.01.2013

Autor

Zoya Durdik

Teil III. Code: B01

Sie haben [15 Minuten] Geben Sie bitte Ihre ID ein: ________________

AUFGABE 1. Prüfen Sie, ob die im Vorfeld bereits getroffenen PSE-Entwurfsmuster-Entscheidungen (engl. pattern design decisions) nach den aufgelisteten Änderungsanfragen (engl. change requests) überdacht werden sollten.

Vorgehensweise:

Für jede Entwurfsentscheidung aus Tabelle I „Aufgabe"

1. Die Begründung für die Entscheidung in Tabelle II „PSE-Muster-Entscheidungen" lesen.
2. Das Muster in einem Buch kurz überfliegen
3. Die Liste der Änderungsanfragen in der Tabelle III „Änderungsanfragen" durchgehen und entscheiden „Sollte die Entscheidung für das Pattern evtl. überdacht werden"
   - „**Ja**" oder „**Nein**" in der Tabelle I ausfüllen.
   - Bitte markieren Sie mit „**Ja**" wenn die Eigenschaften des Musters verletzt werden oder wenn Voraussetzungen für den Einsatz des Musters nicht mehr erfüllt werden, oder wenn das Muster der Einsatz des Musters nochmal detailliert überdacht werden muss.
   - Bitte markieren Sie mit „**Nein**" wenn einfache Code-Anpassungen vorgenommen werden müssen, die die Semantik des Musters oder die Art der Implementierung des Musters nicht verändern, bzw. wenn das Muster nicht betroffen ist.
   - Eine kurze Begründung zu der Antwort in Tabelle I schreiben (ggf. IDs der Änderungsanfragen, und Buchseitennummer, etc. mitnotieren).

Tipp: Eine Änderungsanfrage führt nicht unbedingt zur Ungültigkeit von den Entwurfsmusterentscheidungen. Es müssen nicht alle von den gelisteten Entwurfsmuster-Entscheidungen durch die Änderungsanfragen betroffen sein.

Tabelle I. Aufgabe

ID*	Entwurfs-entscheidung*	Sollte die Entscheidung für das Pattern evtl. überdacht werden?	Begründung
D009	Class Table Inheritance **Beispiel**	□ Nein X **Ja** □ Ich weiß nicht	*Laut **Beispiel CR000 (siehe Folien)** soll die DB ein neues Objekt unterstützen, wofür das Muster Class Table Inheritance laut dem Buch Seite 85 nicht gut geeignet ist.*
D005	**Façade**	□ Nein □ Ja □ Ich weiß nicht	
D006	**Singleton**	□ Nein □ Ja □ Ich weiß nicht	
D007	**Thin client**	□ Nein □ Ja □ Ich weiß nicht	
D002	**Multi-Tier Architektur**	□ Nein □ Ja □ Ich weiß nicht	

* Siehe Tabelle II für Entscheindunsgbegründung und relevante Komponenten.

Tabelle III. Änderungsanfragen (engl. change requests):

ID	Änderungsanfrage
CR001	Das Login dauert teilweise zu lang, daher muss eine Session-Verwaltung in die UserServiceTomcat Komponente eingebaut werden, um die Wartezeiten bei der Re-Authentifizierung zu reduzieren.
CR002	Der Client (Mensa oder Event Management) der auf mobilen Geräten läuft, soll auch im Falle temporärer Funknetzausfalle funktionsfähig bleiben.
CR003	Das User Management soll einen neuen Report-Typ „Benutzerstatistiken" unterstützen, der Informationen über Benutzer und deren durchschnittliches Alter abfragt und einen allgemeinen Report daraus erstellt.

Seite 1/8

Teil III. Code: B01

Tabelle II. Liste der PSE—Muster-Entwurfsentscheidungen

ID	Decision	Rationale	Involved Architectural Elements	Involved Requirements	Decision Type
D001	**Client-Server Architektur**	Austauschbarkeit. Grundlegende Entscheidung über Architektur.	alle	FRA001	Pattern Decision
D002	**Multi-Tier-Architektur**	Multi-Tier-Architektur eignet sich aus folgenden Gründen: 1) Abstraktion von Persistenz durch Layering. 2) Erfahrung im JEE-Bereich (JBoss etc.) 3) Clients leicht austauschbar.	alle	FRA001	Pattern Decision
D003	**Component-based Architektur**	Austauschbarkeit. Grundlegende Entscheidung über Architektur	alle	FRA001	Pattern Decision
D004	**Proxy**	Apache vor dem Tomcat wegen Portumsetzung. Apache implementiert Reverse-Proxy als Port-Mapper. Anbindung des Apache über mod_jk an den Tomcat via AJP-Protokoll.	UserServiceApache Komponente	FRA003, NFRU005	Pattern Decision
D005	**Façade**	UserServiceTomcat Komponente als Façade für Reporting, Authentifizierung und User-Management. Einfacher Zugriff auf die verschiedenen Funktionen der Benutzerverwaltung, inkl. Authentisierung, Reporting und Anfragen an das User-Management-Systems.	UserServiceTomcat Komponente	FRU008, NFRU001	Pattern Decision
D006	**Singleton**	Kontrollierte Zugriffskontrolle	Authentifizierung Komponente	FRU009	Pattern Decision
D007	**Thin Client**	Zugriff auf die Funktionalität des Servers	EventManagement App, Mensa App	FRA002, FRA003, NFRM004, NFRM006, NFRE011	Pattern Decision
D008	**DAO**	UserDAO für Zugriff auf persistente Benutzer. DAO ist ein etabliertes Muster aus dem JEE-Umfeld.	UserDAO Komponente		Pattern Decision
D009	**OR-Mapping: Class Table Inheritance**	Hibernate, um das Binding zwischen persistierten Objekten in der Datenbank und den objektorientierten Ralisierungen zu ermöglichen. Direktes und einfaches OR-Mapping zwischen Glossar Objekten und DB, Konfiguration von Hibernate, nur einfache Anfragen an DB.	DBAccess Komponente	FRU002	Pattern Decision

Seite 2/8

Teil III. Code: B01

Karlsruhe Institute of Technology

Nachfragen zu der Aufgabe 1.

1. Es fiel mir leicht die Gültigkeit von Entwurfsmuster-Entscheidungen zu prüfen

- ☐ Richtig (Ich habe die Aufgabestellung gut verstanden und bin bei den meisten meiner Antworten sicher)
- ☐ Teilweise richtig (Ich konnte nicht alle Entwurfsmuster-Entscheidungen sicher bewerten, habe aber am Ende die passenden Antworten gefunden und ich bin bei den meisten meiner Antworten sicher)
- ☐ Teilweise falsch (Ich konnte nicht alle Entwurfsmuster-Entscheidungen sicher bewerten, und bin nicht bei den allen meinen Antworten sicher)
- ☐ Falsch (Ich bin bei den meisten Antworten nicht sicher)

Kommentar ____

2. Hat Ihnen der beigelegte Pattern Buch-Auszug bei der Aufgabenlösung geholfen?
- ☐ Ich fühlte mich durch das Buch gut unterstützt.
- ☐ Ich fühlte mich durch das Buch unterstützt, hätte aber ein anderes Buch oder das Internet gebrauchen können, bzw. ich hatte zusätzlichen Materialen gebraucht.
- ☐ Ich konnte das Buch für die Aufgabenlösung zwar teilweise verwenden, die Informationen waren aber überwiegend nicht ausreichend.
- ☐ Das Buch konnte mir bei der Aufgabenlösung nicht helfen.
- ☐ Die Aufgabe war so einfach, ich habe das Buch nicht gebraucht.
- ☐ Sonstiges ______________________________________

3. Sonstige Kommentare?

____

____

____

Geben Sie uns bitte Bescheid, wenn Sie mit diesen Aufgaben fertig sind, um weitere Aufgaben zu bekommen.

Seite 3/8

Teil III. Code: B01

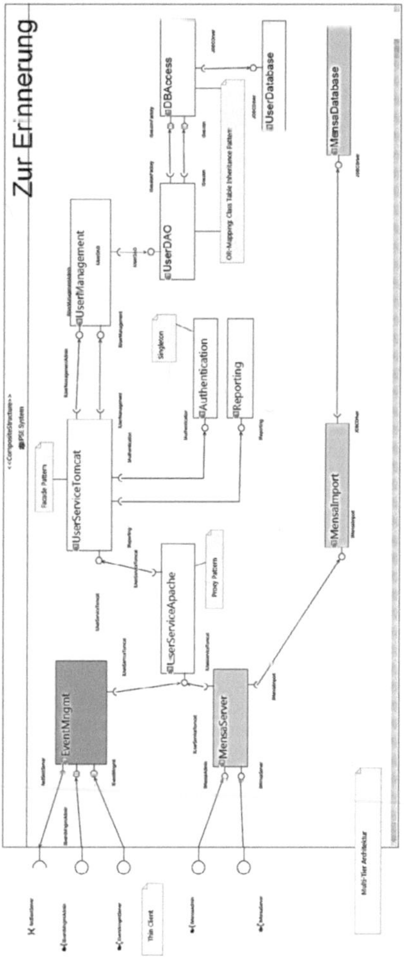

Seite 4/8

Teil III. Code: B01

Karlsruhe Institute of Technology

Aufgaben für die Übung im Rahmen der Veranstaltung "Praxis der Software-Entwicklung"

Karlsruhe Institute of Technology

TEIL III, Aufgabe 2

Muster-Entscheidungen und Neue Entwicklung

[15 Minuten]

Version 1.0

Veröffentlichung: 30.01.2013

Autor

Zoya Durdik

Seite 5/8

Teil III. Code: B01

Karlsruhe Institute of Technology

Sie haben [15 Minuten] **Geben Sie bitte Ihre ID ein: ________________**

AUFGABE 2. Wählen Sie welche Entwurfsmustern (engl. design patterns) zu den angegebenen Problemen (engl. issues) passen.

Wir betrachten dasselbe PSE-System, gehen aber davon aus, dass diese neu Entwickelt wird. **Stellen Sie sich also vor, dass Sie ein neues PSE-System mit neuen Anforderungen entwickeln.**

Vorgehensweise:
Für jedes Problem (engl. issue) aus Tabelle I „Zu lösende Probleme":

1. Das Problem aufmerksam lesen, alle Details berücksichtigen.
2. Für jede angegebene mögliche Lösung: Das Muster in dem Buch kurz nachschlagen
3. Entscheiden welche Lösung (Muster) angesichts der Problem-Details und der im Buch gelisteten Muster-Eigenschaften am passendsten ist.
4. Eine Begründung ggfls. mit Vorteilen und Nachteilen zu Ihrer Lösung in Tabelle I eintragen. Die Begründung sollte ggf. Buchseiten enthalten.
5. Zu dem nächsten Problem in der Tabelle I übergehen.

Tipp: Die Mustern lösen zwar jeweils ähnliche Probleme, unterscheiden sich aber in Details. **Für die Details schauen Sie im Buch nach**, und tragen Sie die Details in der Begründung ein. Vergessen Sie nicht, dass Sie sich in der PSE-Neuentwicklung befinden!

Tabelle I. Zu lösende Probleme (engl. issues):

ID	Problem	Kreuzen Sie die richtige Lösung an	Begründung
P000	Die Data im App soll in unterschiedlichen GUIs (je Betriebssystem) angezeigt werden. Dabei soll es möglich sein die GUIs oder die Data Model voneinander unabhängig auszutauschen. **Beispiel**	□ PAC □ MVA X **MVC** □ Keins davon	*Im Buch, Seite 10: Ziel des Musters ist ..., Seite 26:Konsequenzen ..*
P001	Das User Management soll eine zentrale Schnittstelle anbieten, welche die Sub-Komponente austauschbar hält. Die Schnittstelle soll die Session-Verwaltung übernehmen.	□ Adaptor □ Facade □ Proxy □ Keins davon	
P002	Der Client (Mensa oder Event Management) soll auf mobilen Geräten laufen können. Auch ältere Geräte (ältere Generation) sollen möglichst von den Apps unterstützt werden. Aufgrund der häufigen gesetzlichen Änderungen müssen evtl. häufige Änderungen an der Software vorgenommen werden	□ Fat Client □ Thin Client □ Keins davon	
P003	Die Applikation soll auf dem Port 1022 laufen, jedoch können die ATIS-Server auf Port 0..1023 nichts empfangen, daher sollen die Applikationen andere Ports benutzen.	□ Adaptor □ Facade □ Proxy □ Keins davon	
P004	Es sollen normale Benutzer, Premium-Benutzer und Admin-Benutzer geben. Auf den Daten den normalen Benutzer sollte man schnell zugreifen können. Es wird eine andere Anwendung geben die ohne Objekte zu kennen auf den Daten zugreifen können muss.	□ Class Table Inheritance □ Single Table Inheritance □ Concrete Table Inheritance □ Keins davon	

Seite 6/8

Teil III. Code: B01

Karlsruhe Institute of Technology

Nachfragen zu der Aufgabe 2.

1. Es fiel mir leicht die richtigen Entwurfsmuster auszuwählen

- ☐ Richtig (Ich habe die Aufgabenstellung gut verstanden und bin bei den meisten meiner Antworten sicher)
- ☐ Teilweise richtig (Ich konnte nicht alle Entwurfsmuster sicher auswählen, habe aber am Ende die passenden Antworten gefunden und ich bin bei den meisten meiner Antworten sicher)
- ☐ Teilweise falsch (Ich konnte nicht alle Entwurfsmustern sicher auswählen, und bin nicht bei allen meinen Antworten sicher)
- ☐ Falsch (Ich bin mir bei den meisten Antworten nicht sicher)

Kommentar ______________________________

2. Hat Ihnen der beigelegte Pattern Buch-Auszug bei der Aufgabenlösung geholfen?

- ☐ Ich fühlte mich durch das Buch gut unterstützt.
- ☐ Ich fühlte mich durch das Buch unterstützt, hätte aber ein anderes Buch oder das Internet gebrauchen können, bzw. ich hatte zusätzlichen Materialen gebraucht.
- ☐ Ich konnte das Buch für die Aufgabenlösung zwar teilweise verwenden, die Informationen waren aber überwiegend nicht ausreichend.
- ☐ Das Buch konnte mir bei der Aufgabenlösung nicht helfen.
- ☐ Die Aufgabe war so einfach, ich habe das Buch nicht gebraucht.
- ☐ Sonstiges ______________________________

3. Sonstige Kommentare?

____

____

____

ENDE DER TEIL III

Seite 7/8

Aufgaben für das Experiment im Rahmen der Veranstaltung
"Praxis der Software-Entwicklung"

Karlsruhe Institute of Technology

TEIL IV

[5 Minuten]

Version 1.0

Veröffentlichung: 30.01.2010

Autor

Zoya Durdik

Martin Küster

Aufgaben für die Übung im Rahmen der Veranstaltung "Praxis der Software-Entwicklung"

Autor: Zoya Durdik, Martin Küster Stand: 28.01.2013 Version: 1.0

Geben Sie bitte Ihre ID ein: ____________________

Fragen:

1. Sie sind derzeit:
- ☐ Bachelor (Informatik) Student
- ☐ Master (Informatik) Student
- ☐ Diplom (Informatik) Student
- ☐ Sonstiges und zwar ____________________

2. In welchem Fachsemester sind Sie jetzt?
Ich bin im _____ Fachsemester

3. Haben Sie je gegen Entgelt Software entwickelt?
- ☐ Ja
- ☐ Nein

4. Haben Sie bereits praktische Programmiererfahrungen sammeln können? (Mehrfachnennung möglich)
- ☐ Nein, PSE ist mein erstes Software-Entwicklungsprojekt
- ☐ Ja und zwar ich habe bereits in _____ (Anzahl) Entwicklungs-Projekten während des Studiums mitgearbeitet
- ☐ Ja und zwar ich habe bereits in _____ (Anzahl) Entwicklungs-Projekten außerhalb des Studiums mitgearbeitet

Davon waren _____ (Anzahl) Projekte aus der Domäne der mobilen Anwendungen

5. Welche Architekturmodellierungssprachen kennen Sie? Haben Sie die praktisch in Projekten verwendet?

Ich kenne (aus Vorlesung oder Büchern):
- ☐ UML Komponentendiagramme
- ☐ Palladio Component Model
- ☐ Sonstiges und zwar ____________________

Ich habe praktisch verwendet (Modelle erstellt oder geändert):
- ☐ UML Komponentendiagramme
- ☐ Palladio Component Model
- ☐ Sonstiges und zwar ____________________

6. Haben Sie bereits praktische SW-Architekturentwurfs- und Architekturmodellierungserfahrungen sammeln können? (Mehrfachnennung möglich)
- ☐ Nein, PSE ist mein erstes Software-Entwicklungsprojekt
- ☐ Ja und zwar ich habe bereits in _____ (Anzahl) Entwurf-Projekten während des Studiums mitgearbeitet
- ☐ Ja und zwar ich habe bereits in _____ (Anzahl) Entwurf-Projekten außerhalb des Studiums mitgearbeitet

Aufgaben für die Übung im Rahmen der Veranstaltung "Praxis der Software-Entwicklung"

Autor: Zoya Durdik, Martin Küster Stand: 28.01.2013 Version: 1.0

Karlsruhe Institute of Technology

7. Kennen Sie sich mit Entwurfsmustern aus? Welche der folgenden Aussagen treffen auf Sie zu? (Mehrfachnennung möglich)

- ☐ Nein, ich weiß nichts über Entwurfsmuster.
- ☐ Ja, ich habe über Entwurfsmuster in einer oder mehreren Vorlesung(en) gehört und kenne ca. _____ (Anzahl) Entwurfsmustern.
- ☐ Ja, ich habe mich persönlich mit der theoretischen Seite beschäftigt (z.B. Bücher gelesen, im Internet gesucht) und kenne ca. _____ (Anzahl) Entwurfsmuster
- ☐ Ja, ich habe Entwurfsmuster praktisch selbst eingesetzt (z.B. während des Praktikums oder als studentische Hilfskraft) und zwar folgende ______________________

  ______________________ (Namen) Entwurfsmuster
- ☐ Kommentar: ______________________

8. Gab es Artefakte, bei den Sie Verständnisprobleme hatten?

- ☐ Nein, keine
- ☐ Ja, mit folgenden Artefakten ______________________

Konnten diese geklärt werden?

- ☐ Ja, die wurden geklärt
- ☐ Nein, folgende sind noch offen geblieben ______________________

9. Hatten Sie Verständnisprobleme mit den Aufgaben oder mit der englischen Sprache während der Übung?

- ☐ Nein, keine
- ☐ Ja, mit folgende Aufgabe ______________________

Konnten diese geklärt werden?

- ☐ Ja, die wurden geklärt
- ☐ Nein, folgende sind noch offen geblieben ______________________

10. Würden Sie gerne uns irgendetwas mitteilen wollen? (Kommentare, Wünsche, Fragen, Probleme, etc.)

____
____
____
____
____

Wir bedanken uns ganz herzlich!

ZUR ERRINERUNG: LISTE DER PSE-ANFORDERUNGEN (ENGL. REQUIREMENTS)

Allgemeine Funktionale Anforderungen
* FRA001. Client-Server-Anwendung. Zugriff durch verschiedene Clients möglich.
* FRA002. Zugriff soll über Internet möglich sein. HTTP.
* FRA003. Daten sollen von außen zugreifbar sein. Zugriff von außerhalb ATIS-Netz
* FRA004. Brücke zwischen Value-Objekten und persistierten Objekten, Einführung von Transaktionen / Sessions
* FRA005. Glossarterms: „User", „Event", „Food", „Vote"
* FRA006. Benutzerdaten sollen gespeichert sein
* FRA007. OR-Mapping nach gängigen Standards.

BugFix Anfragen
* BX0001. Sessions laufen über / sind nicht mehr gültig

Benutzerverwaltung, Funktionale Anforderungen
* FRU001. Benutzerdaten sollen dauerhaft gespeichert werden.
* FRU002. Ein Benutzer besteht aus (Vorname, Nachname, Nickname, E-Mail-Adresse, Geburtsdatum, Passwort)
* FRU003. Ein Benutzer wird eindeutig durch E-Mail-Adresse ODER Nickname identifiziert, d.h. beide Einträge erfüllen die Schlüsseleigenschaft.
* FRU004. Zugriff auf die Details eines Benutzers sollen nur möglich sein, wenn das Passwort mit übertragen wird.
* FRU005. Die Möglichkeit einer externen Authentifikation soll möglich sein (Facebook, Google, ...). In diesem Fall soll dem System der Benutzer bekannt gemacht werden.
* FRU006. Der Zugriff auf die Daten soll über das Web (von außerhalb des Uni-Netzes) möglich sein.
* FRU007. Einem mobilen Klienten soll es möglich sein, auf die Daten zuzugreifen.
* FRU008. Nach außen soll nur eine Schnittstelle sichtbar sein, die Subkomponente sollen austauschbar sin.
* FRU009. Authentifizirung für Benutzer sollte nur an einer Stelle passieren (merfache Instanziirung vermeiden)

Benutzerverwaltung, Nicht-funktionale Anforderungen
* NFRU001. Der Zugriff auf die Daten soll durch eine schlanke Schnittstelle erfolgen.
* NFRU002. Die bestehende Infrastruktur der ATIS soll verwendet werden (Virtuelle Maschine im Uni-Netz)
* NFRU003. Das System soll in Java implementiert werden.
* NFRU004. Performance: Eine Anfrage an das System nach einem einzelnen Benutzer soll nicht länger als 1 Sek dauern.
* NFRU005. ATIS-Server können nicht auf Port 0..1023 hören, daher die Applikationen sollen andere Ports benutzen

Mensa, Funktionale Anforderungen
* FRM001. Der Client soll das aktuelle Angebot der Mensa sowie Bewertungen anzeigen.
* FRM002. Benutzer sollen die Möglichkeit haben, zu Angeboten der Mensa Bewertungen abzugeben.
* FRM003. Ein Essen kann unter mehreren Namen angeboten werden; dies soll von der Anwendung berücksichtigt werden.
* FRM004. Benutzer sollen die Möglichkeit haben Essen zusammen zu legen.
* FRM005. Benutzer sollen die Möglichkeit haben, zu Essen der Mensa Bilder hochzuladen.

Mensa, Nicht-funktionale Anforderungen
* NFRM001. Die Serveranwendung soll in Java geschrieben werden und in einem Apache Tomcat Servlet-Container ausgeführt werden.
* NFRM002. Die Serveranwendung soll eine bereits vorhandene Benutzerverwaltung verwenden.
* NFRM003. Die Serveranwendung soll über Hibernate mit einer Datenbank kommunizieren.
* NFRM004. Die Clientanwendung soll eine nativ auf dem Apple iPhone lauffähige Anwendung sein.
* NFRM005. Die Clientanwendung soll einfach bedienbar und durch eine ansprechende graphische Benutzerführung leicht zugänglich sein.
* NFRM006. Die Datenhaltung soll vom Server übernommen werden. Auf den Clients sollen lediglich Zugangsdaten gespeichert werden.
* NFRM007. Sicherheit: z.B. Passwörter nicht im Klartext speichern.
* NFRM008. Evtl. verschlüsselte Kommunikation zwischen Client und Server.

1

26 August 2013

Event Management, Funktionale Anforderungen

* FRE001. Die Zuteilung soll der Teilnehmer unter Berücksichtigung der Nutzerpräferenzen sowie der zeitlichen Beschränkungen erfolgen.
* FRE002. Die Anwendung soll so gestaltet werden, dass sie für ein einzelnes Anwendungszenario, das aus zwei Anwendungsfällen besteht eingesetzt werden kann.
* FRE003. Das Szenario könnte in dieser einfachen Form z.B im Rahmen von Konferenzen, Workshops, Tagungen, Tutorien etc. auftreten.
* FRE009 Die Eigenheiten dieser Veranstaltungen sollen jedoch nicht berücksichtigt werden und keine entsprechenden Verfeinerungen oder Zusatzfunktionen umgesetzt werden.
* FRE010. Mehrere Veranstaltungen sollen die Dienste der Anwendung ungestört voneinander in Anspruch nehmen können.
* FRE011. Beim ersten starten der App muss sich der Benutzer neu registrieren oder mit einem bestehenden Account anmelden.
* FRE012. Die Anmeldedaten werden auf dem Gerät gespeichert sodass sich der Nutzer auf diesem Gerät nicht erneut anmelden muss.
* FRE013. Die App soll eine Möglichkeit bieten Veranstaltungen zu erstellen. Bei der Erstellung der Veranstaltung müssen folgende Angaben gemacht werden: Name jeder Veranstaltung, Minimale und maximale Teilnehmer je Veranstaltung, Anzahl paralleler Veranstaltungen, Anzahl hintereinander folgender Sitzungen, E-Mailadressen der Teilnehmer
* FRE014. Bei der Erstellung der Veranstaltung können optional folgende Funktionalitäten realisiert werden: Teilnehmer aus dem Adressbuch des Android Gerätes einladen, Manuelle Anpassung der automatischen Zuteilung vor der Übermittlung an die Teilnehmer, Festlegung welche Teilnehmer bei der Zuteilung besonders zu berücksichtigen sind Festlegung fixer Termine für einzelne Veranstaltungen
* FRE015. Bei der Anmeldung zu einer Veranstaltung müssen folgende Angaben gemacht werden: Nutzerpräferenzen zu jeder Veranstaltung
* FRE016. Bei der Anmeldung zu einer Veranstaltung können optional folgende Funktionalitäten realisiert werden: Anzeige der anderen Teilnehmer und deren Präferenzen (wenn durch Veranstalter erlaubt), Feste Zuteilung zu einer Veranstaltung statt Präferenzangabe (z.B. für Vortragende) (u.U. im Verwaltungsanwendungsfall statt im Nutzeranwendungsfall anzusiedeln)
* FRE017. Die Anwendung soll aus einer mobilen App für Android-Geräte und einem Java Servlet bestehen.
* FRE018. Die Oberfläche der Android-App soll für die bereitgestellten Tablets optimiert werden.
* FRE019. Die App kann optional für ein Android Smartphone optimiert werden.
* FRE020. Die Kommunikation zwischen Android-App und Server soll mittels HTTP-Anfragen unter Verwendung des Datenformates JSON stattfinden.
* FRE021. Zum Betrieb der Serveranwendung soll eine bestehende Plattform mit einer MySQL-Datenbank und einem Apache Tomcat Servlet-Container benutzt werden.
* FRE022. Die Serveranwendung soll als Java Servlet realisiert werden und POJOs mittels Hibernate persistieren.
* FRE023. Benutzerdaten dürfen nicht im Servlet verarbeitet werden sondern sind zwingend in einer dafür bereitgestellten Komponente zu verwalten.

Event Management, Nicht-funktionale Anforderungen

* NFRE009. Die Clientanwendung soll einfach bedienbar, und durch eine ansprechende graphische Benutzerführung leicht zugänglich sein.
* NFRE010. Die Datenhaltung und Geschäftslogik soll vom Server übernommen werden.
* NFRE011. Auf den Clients sollen lediglich Zugangsdaten gespeichert werden.
* NFRE012. Die Zuteilungsberechnung soll sowohl auf einfachste Weise auf dem Server durchgeführt werden können als auch durch Absenden einer Anfrage an einen externen Server realisiert werden.
* NFRE013. Sicherheit: z.B. Passwörter nicht im Klartext speichern.
* NFRE014. Evtl. verschlüsselte Kommunikation zwischen Client und Server.

26 August 2013 2

Geben Sie bitte Ihre ID ein: ____________________

TABELLE II. LISTE DER PSE—MUSTER-ENTWURFSENTSCHEIDUNGEN

(ENGL. DESIGN DECISIONS)

ID	Decision	Rationale	Involved Architectural Elements	Involved Requirements	Decision Type
D001	Client-Server Architektur	Austauschbarkeit. Grundlegende Entscheidung über Architektur.	alle	FRA001	Pattern Decision

Rationale saved for the pattern:

No additional rationale saved

ID	Decision	Rationale	Involved Architectural Elements	Involved Requirements	Decision Type
D002	Multi-Tier-Architektur	Multi-Tier-Architektur eignet sich aus folgenden Gründen: 1) Abstraktion von Persistenz durch Layering. 2) Erfahrung im JEE-Bereich (JBoss etc.) 3) Clients leicht austauschbar.	alle	FRA001	Pattern Decision

Rationale saved for the pattern:

Question Type	QID	Questions	Answer
Goal:	Q007	Would you like to be able to add or modify specific parts instead of reworking the whole application?	Yes
Intent:	Q008	Would you like to structure the system according to the underlying physical infrastructure?	
	Q009	Would like to prevent the client to access data directly?	Yes
	Q010	Would you like to have a linear communication model in your system, where each tier can communicate only with 2 neighboring tiers in a strong linear hierarchy?	
	Q011	Are you developing a web application?	Yes
Consequences:	Q012	Are you aware that all communication will run through a middle tier, which can become a bottleneck?	Yes
	Q013	Potential involvement of multiple communication protocols with different evolution cycles is not an issue in the future?	

ID	Decision	Rationale	Involved Architectural Elements	Involved Requirements	Decision Type
D003	Component-based Architektur	Austauschbarkeit. Grundlegende Entscheidung über Architektur	alle	-	Pattern Decision

Rationale saved for the pattern:

No additional rationale saved

26 August 2013 1

ID	Decision	Rationale	Involved Architectural Elements	Involved Requirements	Decision Type
D004	**Proxy**	Apache vor dem Tomcat wegen Portumsetzung. Apache implementiert Reverse-Proxy als Port-Mapper. Anbindung des Apache über mod_jk an den Tomcat via AJP Protokoll	UserServiceApache Komponente	FRA003, NFRU005	Pattern Decision

Rationale saved for the pattern:

No additional rationale saved

ID	Decision	Rationale	Involved Architectural Elements	Involved Requirements	Decision Type
D005	**Façade**	UserServiceTomcat Komponente als Façade für Reporting, Authentifizierung und User-Management. Einfacher Zugriff auf die verschiedenen Funktionen der Benutzerverwaltung, inkl. Authentisierung, Reporting und Anfragen an das User-Management-Systems.	UserServiceTomcat Komponente	FRU008, NFRU001	Pattern Decision

Rationale saved for the pattern:

Question Type	QID	Questions	Answer
Goal:	Q042	Would you like to provide a unified interface to a set of interfaces in a subsystem?	Yes
Intent:	Q043	Would you like to minimize the communication and dependencies between subsystems?	Yes
	Q046	Are the encapsulated subsystems stateless? (otherwise → Proxy)	Yes
	Q047	An additional functionality wrapped into the common interface is not desired? (otherwise → Proxy)	Yes
	Q048	Is it desired that subsystem classes know nothing about the facade object(s)? (otherwise → Mediator)	
	Q049	A wrapper for multiple objects or a new interface design for an object is not your intent? (otherwise → Adaptor)	
Consequences:	Q050	Is a potential performance bottleneck not a problem?	
	Q051	A potential God Class smell of the interface is not a problem? (Goad Class smell = A single overlarge class implementing a lot of functionality)	Yes

ID	Decision	Rationale	Involved Architectural Elements	Involved Requirements	Decision Type
D006	Singleton	Kontrollierter Zugriffskontrol	Authentifizierung Komponente	FRU009	Pattern Decision

Rationale saved for the pattern:

Question Type	QID	Questions	Answer
Goal:	Q064	Would you like to ensure that a class has only one instance?	Yes
Intent:	Q065	Would you like to make class instance easily accessible (globally)?	
Consequences:	Q066	If you are developing a distributed application, it is not an issue that the data stored in the instance cannot change too often?	Yes

26 August 2013 2

		Q067	Having a global access to the class instance is not a potential threat to the application?	
		Q068	You are not developing a multi-thread application, respectively you have extended singleton for this case?	Yes

ID	Decision	Rationale	Involved Architectural Elements	Involved Requirements	Decision Type
D007	Thin Client	Zugriff auf die Funktionalität des Servers	EventManagement App, Mensa App	FRA002, FRA003, NFRM004, NFRM006, NFRE011	Pattern Decision

Rationale saved for the pattern:

Question Type	QID	Questions	Answer
Goal:	Q027	Would you like a client to put responsibility for data computation, persistence, etc. on the server side?	Yes
Intent:	Q028	Would you like to keep SW updates centralized?	Yes
	Q030	Is your infrastructure heterogeneous?	
	Q031	Would you like to support low-performance devices?	Yes
Consequences:	Q032	Working offline is not essential for your application? (otherwise → Fat Client)	Yes
	Q033	Are main changes (SW updates) expected to be on the server side? (otherwise → Fat Client)	

ID	Decision	Rationale	Involved Architectural Elements	Involved Requirements	Decision Type
D008	**DAO**	UserDAO für Zugriff auf persistente Benutzer. DAO ist ein etabliertes Muster aus dem JEE-Umfeld.	UserDAO Komponente		Pattern Decision

Rationale saved for the pattern:

No additional rationale saved

ID	Decision	Rationale	Involved Architectural Elements	Involved Requirements	Decision Type
D009	Class Table Inheritance	Direktes und einfaches OR-Mapping zwischen Glossar Objekten und DB, Konfiguration von Hibernate, nur einfache Anfragen an DB	DBAccess Komponente	FRU002	Pattern Decision

Rationale saved for the pattern:

Question Type	QID	Questions	Answer
Goal:	Q069	Would you like to present an inheritance hierarchy of classes in relational database?	Yes
Intent:	Q070	Would you like a straightforward relationship between the database and the domain model to achieve easier understanding of the Database?	
	Q071	Is the final amount of tables in the database structure limited (small) and is it unlikely to change in the future?	Yes
	Q072	Usage of information stored in the tables directly is your intent?	Yes

26 August 2013 3

Consequences:	Q073	Are potential performance bottlenecks with joins or multi-querying caused by retrieving larger amounts of data acceptable? (otherwise → Single Table Inheritance)	Yes

26 August 2013

4

Geben Sie bitte Ihre ID ein: ____________________

TABELLE II. LISTE DER PSE–MUSTER-ENTWURFSENTSCHEIDUNGEN

(ENGL. DESIGN DECISIONS)

ID	Decision	Rationale	Involved Architectural Elements	Involved Requirements	Decision Type
D001	**Client-Server Architektur**	Austauschbarkeit. Grundlegende Entscheidung über Architektur.	alle	FRA001	Pattern Decision
D002	**Multi-Tier-Architektur**	Multi-Tier-Architektur eignet sich aus folgenden Gründen: 1) Abstraktion von Persistenz durch Layering. 2) Erfahrung im JEE-Bereich (JBoss etc.) 3) Clients leicht austauschbar.	alle	FRA001	Pattern Decision
D003	**Component-based Architektur**	Austauschbarkeit. Grundlegende Entscheidung über Architektur	alle	FRA001	Pattern Decision
D004	**Proxy**	Apache vor dem Tomcat wegen Portumsetzung. Apache implementiert Reverse-Proxy als Port-Mapper. Anbindung des Apache über mod_jk an den Tomcat via AJP-Protokoll.	UserServiceApache Komponente	FRA003, NFRU005	Pattern Decision
D005	**Façade**	UserServiceTomcat Komponente als Façade für Reporting, Authentifizierung und User-Management. Einfacher Zugriff auf die verschiedenen Funktionen der Benutzerverwaltung, inkl. Authentisierung, Reporting und Anfragen an das User-Management-Systems.	UserServiceTomcat Komponente	FRU008, NFRU001	Pattern Decision
D006	**Singleton**	Kontrollierter Zugriffskontrol	Authentifizierung Komponente	FRU009	Pattern Decision
D007	**Thin Client**	Zugriff auf die Funktionalität des Servers	EventManagement App, Mensa App	FRA002, FRA003, NFRM004, NFRM006, NFRE011	Pattern Decision
D008	**DAO**	UserDAO für Zugriff auf persistente Benutzer. DAO ist ein etabliertes Muster aus dem JEE-Umfeld.	UserDAO Komponente		Pattern Decision
D009	**OR-Mapping: Class Table Inheritance**	Hibernate, um das Binding zwischen persistierten Objekten in der Datenbank und den objektorientierten Ralisierungen zu ermöglichen. Direktes und einfaches OR-Mapping zwischen Glossar Objekten und DB, Konfiguration von Hibernate, nur einfache Anfragen an DB.	DBAccess Komponente	FRU002	Pattern Decision

26 August 2013 1

Karlsruhe Institute of Technology

Geben Sie bitte Ihre ID ein: ____________

MUSTER KATALOG (PATTERN CATALOGUE)

Sie können gerne Ihre Fragen-Antworten im Katalog eintragen oder Text unterstreichen, z.B. :

Model-View-Controller

Question Type	QID	Questions	Answer
Goal:	Q014	Would you like to present the same information in different ways e.g., through multiple views?	„Ja"
Intent:	Q015	Would you like to enable to change the GUI (views) at run-time?	„---"
	Q017	Do you plan to exchange the underlying data model or the views representing this data? (design time)	„Ja"
Consequences:	Q018	Is it acceptable to have potential delays by the view updates when larger amounts of data are transferred?	„Ja"
	Q019	The data in the model (e.g. DB) is not changed directly though the views (but though a controller), and will this be an issue in the future?	„---"

oder

Model-View-Controller

Question Type	QID	Questions	Answer
Goal:	Q014	Would you like to present the same information in different ways e.g., through multiple views?	„Ja"
Intent:	Q015	Would you like to enable to change the GUI (views) at run-time?	„---"
	Q017	Do you plan to exchange the underlying data model or the views representing this data? (design time)	„Ja"
Consequences:	Q018	Is it acceptable to have potential delays by the view updates when larger amounts of data are transferred?	„Nein"
	Q019	The data in the model (e.g. DB) is not changed directly though the views (but though a controller), and will this be an issue in the future?	„---"

PATTERN CATALOGUE

The catalogue contains a brief description of patterns, together with the checklists that summarize the goal, intent and consequences of pattern use. Checklists can be used to check if the pattern is appropriate to solve your problem, and capture the rationale for pattern use. If you use the catalogue to solve the task, please provide the pattern ID and the questions ID(s) involved in the solution.

Question types: Pattern goal, Pattern intent, Possible negative consequences of a pattern

TABLE OF CONTENT:

26 August 2013

1. CLIENT-SERVER STYLE

Structure the system into servers (centralized systems) and clients referring to that system and using its resources though a connecting network.

Goal:
- Structure the system as distributed system with independent clients and servers and a connecting network between them
- Provide a centralized source to store the data and centralized access to it

Questions:

ID	Pattern	Question Type	QID	Questions	Answer
P001	Client-Server Style	Goal:	Q001	Would you like to design a distributed system with independent servers (capture resources), clients (demand resources) and a network connection between them?	
		Intent:	Q002	Would you like to have central data storage and a centralized access to the system data?	
			Q003	Is a better control over security essential for your system?	
			Q005	Would you like multiple clients to have access to the data?	
			Q006	Would you like to support different client types or different devices?	

Information source: Wikipedia, design articles

Variants:
- Not listed

Similar patterns: Not listed

2. MULTI-TIER STYLE

A Client-Server architecture, in which presentation, application processing and data management functions are logically separated.

Goal:
- Logically separate functions so that specific layers can be added or modified, instead of reworking the entire application
- Separate system according to physical structure of an infrastructure

Questions:

ID	Pattern	Question Type	QID	Questions	Answer
P002	Multi-Tier Style	Goal:	Q007	Would you like to be able to add or modify specific parts instead of reworking the whole application?	
		Intent:	Q008	Would you like to structure the system according to the underlying physical infrastructure?	
			Q009	Would you like to prevent the client to access data directly?	
			Q010	Would you like to have a linear communication model in your system, where each tier can communicate only with 2 neighboring tiers in a strong linear hierarchy?	
		Consequences:	Q012	Are you aware that all communication will run through a middle tier, which can become a bottleneck?	
			Q013	Potential involvement of multiple communication protocols with different evolution cycles is not an issue in the future?	
			+	See questions for Client-Server architecture	

Information source: Wikipedia, design articles

Variants:
- Not listed

Similar patterns: Layered architectural style

26 August 2013

2

3. MODEL VIEW CONTROLLER (MVC)

The pattern Isolates "domain logic" (the application logic for the user) from the user interface (input and presentation), enabling independent development, testing and maintenance of each of them (separation of concerns).

Goal:
- Decouple user-interface aspects of a system from its functional core
- Interaction is limited to calling an update procedure

Questions:

ID	Pattern	Question Type	QID	Questions	Answer
P003	Model-View-Controller	Goal:	Q014	Would you like to present the same information in different ways e.g., through multiple views?	
		Intent:	Q015	Would you like to enable to change the GUI (views) at run-time?	
			Q017	Do you plan to exchange the underlying data model or the views representing this data? (design time)	
		Consequences:	Q018	Is it acceptable to have potential delays by the view updates when larger amounts of data are transferred?	
			Q019	The data in the model (e.g. DB) is not changed directly though the views (but though a controller), and will this be an issue in the future?	

Information source: Pattern-oriented software architecture, Buschmann, 1996

Variants:
- Document-View: View combines responsibilities of View and Controller in a single component

Similar Patterns: Presentation-Abstraction-Controller

4. FAT CLIENT

The pattern describes a computer (client) in a client–server architecture that provides rich functionality independently of the central server.

Goal:
- Provide (partial) independence of the client from the server
- Assure ability to work offline (at least partially)
- Improve performance of complex computations on the client side

Questions:

ID	Pattern	Question Type	QID	Questions	Answer
P004	Fat (Thick) Client	Goal:	Q020	Would you like a client to be able to perform the functionality in circumstances of potential disconnection to the main server?	
		Intent:	Q021	Would you like to reduce the load on your main server or network offloading the higher processing and capacity demands to the client devices?	
			Q022	Is working offline essential for your application?	
		Consequences:	Q023	Will the application be running on powerful devices and porting to low-performance devices can be excluded in the future? (otherwise → Thin Client)	
			Q024	Is your infrastructure limitedly heterogeneous and this is unlikely to change in the future? (otherwise → Thin Client)	
			Q025	Is potential slower start-up of the application acceptable?	

Information source: Wikipedia, design articles

Variants:
- Fat Client with Cache for connectivity problems
- Mixed thin and fat (thick) client implementation

Similar Patterns: Thin client

5. THIN CLIENT

The pattern describes a computer (client) in client–server architecture that heavily depends on the functionality provided by a central server.

Goal:
- Put role responsibilities on the server (e.g. computation, persistence, or even GUI rendering)
- Keep updates centralized and simplify the maintenance of computational services

Questions:

ID	Pattern	Question Type	QID	Questions	Answer
P005	Thin Client	Goal:	Q027	Would you like a client to put responsibility for data computation, persistence, etc. on the server side?	
		Intent:	Q028	Would you like to keep SW updates centralized?	
			Q030	Is your infrastructure heterogeneous?	
			Q031	Would you like to support low-performance devices?	
		Consequences:	Q032	Working offline is <u>not</u> essential for your application? (otherwise → Fat Client)	
			Q033	Are main changes (SW updates) expected to be on the server side? (otherwise → Fat Client)	

Information source: Wikipedia, design articles

Variants:
- Not listed

Similar Patterns: Fat (Thick) client

26 August 2013

4

6. PROXY

Provide a representative (a placeholder) for another object to control access to it.

Goal:
- Provide an interface to some other object, resource, network connection, etc.

Questions:

ID	Pattern	Question Type	QID	Questions	Answer
P006	Proxy	Goal:	Q034	Would you like to provide an interface to some other object, resource, network connection, etc.?	
		Intent:	Q035	Would you like to provide or to restrict the access to functionalities provided by another object or server?	
			Q036	Would you like to provide an interface with some additional functionality, e.g. management of objects state, etc.?	
			Q037	Would you like to provide a representative for an object in different address-space?	
		Consequences:	Q039	You are not wishing to be able to extend the object's properties dynamically? (otherwise → Decorator)	
			Q040	Is a potential performance bottleneck not a problem?	
			Q041	Is a higher level of indirection not a problem?	

Information source: Gamma, Wikipedia

Variants:
- Remote proxy provides a local representative for an object in a different address space.
- Virtual proxy creates expensive objects on demand
- Protection proxy controls access to the original object

Similar Patterns: Façade, Mediator, Adaptor

7. FACADE

Provide a unified interface to a set of interfaces in a subsystem.

Goal:
- Minimize the communication and dependencies between subsystems
- Simplify a number of complicated interfaces with a subsystem into a single interface

Questions:

ID	Pattern	Question Type	QID	Questions	Answer
P007	Façade	Goal:	Q042	Would you like to provide a unified interface to a set of interfaces in a subsystem?	
		Intent:	Q043	Would you like to minimize the communication and dependencies between subsystems?	
			Q046	An additional functionality wrapped into the unified interface is not your intent? (otherwise → Proxy)	
			Q047	Is a stateless unified interface your intent? (otherwise → Proxy)	
			Q048	Is it desired that subsystem classes know nothing about the facade object(s)? (otherwise → Mediator)	
			Q049	A new interface for an object is not your intent? (otherwise → Adaptor)	
		Consequences:	Q050	Is a potential performance bottleneck not an issue?	

Information source: Gamma, Posa 1

Variants:
- Singleton Façade (implemented through singleton pattern)
- Multiple Façade objects provide the same interfaces to the same set of subsystems
- Multiple Façades provide different interfaces to the same set of subsystems

Similar Patterns: Proxy, Mediator, Adaptor

8. ADAPTOR

Convert an interface of a class into another interface clients expect.

Goal:

- Convert the interface of a class into another interface clients expect
- Adapter lets classes work together, that could not otherwise because of incompatible interfaces

Questions:

ID	Pattern	Question Type	QID	Questions	Answer
P008	Adaptor	Goal:	Q052	Would you like to convert an interface of a class (or an object) into another interface clients expect?	
		Intent:	Q053	Would you like to make interfaces of incompatible classes compatible?	
			Q054	Would you like to change an interface of an existing object (a new interface design for an object)? (otherwise → Proxy or Decorator)	
		Consequences:	Q055	Are you aware of the size of the code you have to write and maintain to adapt the class?	

Information source: Gamma, Wikipedia

Variants:

- Object Adaptor, contains an instance of class it wraps and makes calls into the instance of wrapped object
- Class Adapter, includes multiple polymorphic interfaces by implementing or inheriting both the interface that is expected and the interface that is pre-existing

Similar Patterns: Proxy, Façade, Mediator

9. SINGLETON

Restrict the instantiation of a class to one object.

Goal:

- Ensure a class only has one instance
- Provide a global point of access to it.

Questions:

ID	Pattern	Question Type	QID	Questions	Answer
P009	Singleton	Goal:	Q064	Would you like to ensure that a class has only one instance?	
		Intent:	Q065	Would you like to make class instance easily accessible (globally)?	
		Consequences:	Q066	If you are developing a distributed application, it is <u>not</u> an issue that the data stored in the instance cannot change too often?	
			Q067	Having a global access to the class instance is not a potential threat to the application?	
			Q068	You are not developing a multi-thread application, respectively you have extended singleton for this case?	

Information source: Gamma, Wikipedia

Variants:

- Singleton permits a number of its instances, the number can be configured in the Class

Similar Patterns: Not specified

26 August 2013

6

10.CLASS TABLE INHERITANCE

Represents an inheritance hierarchy of classes with one table for each class. Database structure maps clearly to objects and allow links anywhere in the inheritance structure.

Goal:
- Map fields in inheritance hierarchy to a relational database
- Straightforward relationship between Database and domain model
  Tables are easy to understand and don't waste space

Questions:

ID	Pattern	Question Type	QID	Questions	Answer
P010	Class Table Inheritance	Goal:	Q069	Would you like to present an inheritance hierarchy of classes in relational database?	
		Intent:	Q070	Would you like a straightforward relationship between the database and the domain model to achieve easier understanding of the Database?	
		Consequences:	Q071	Is it not a problem that the majority of requests can be satisfied only with performance expensive joins?	
			Q072	Is it not your intent for the Database to be used by other applications that are not using (or do not know) objects? (otherwise→ Concrete Table Inheritance)	
			Q073	Is the final amount of tables in the database structure limited (small) and is it unlikely to change in the future?	

Information source: Fowler, EAA p.285, 2005

Variants:
- Not listed

Similar Patterns: Single Table Inheritance, Concrete Table Inheritance

11.SINGLE TABLE INHERITANCE

Represents an inheritance hierarchy of classes in a relational database as a single table that has columns for all the fields of the various classes. Maps all fields of all classes of an inheritance structure into a single table. Each class stores relevant data to it in one single row.

Goal:
- Map fields in inheritance hierarchy to a relational database
- Minimize joins

Questions:

ID	Pattern	Question Type	QID	Questions	Answer
P011	Single Table Inheritance	Goal:	Q074	Would you like to present an inheritance hierarchy of classes in relational database?	
		Intent:	Q075	Would you like to keep all data in a single table? (otherwise → Class Table Inheritance or Concrete Table Inheritance)	
			Q076	It is important to avoid joins in retrieving data?	
		Consequences:	Q077	Frequent locks on one table are not an issue?	
			Q078	A non-straightforward relationship between database and domain model is not a problem?	
			Q079	Is it not your intent for the Database to be used by other applications that are not using (or do not know) objects? (otherwise→ Concrete Table Inheritance)	

Information source: Fowler, EAA p.278, 2005

Variants:
- Additional tables - add separate index tables that either list keys of rows that have a certain property.

Similar Patterns: Class Table Inheritance, Concrete Table Inheritance

26 August 2013

7

12.CONCRETE TABLE INHERITANCE

Represents an inheritance hierarchy of classes in a relational database with one table for each concrete class. Database structure maps clearly to objects and allow links anywhere in the inheritance structure.

Goal:

- Map fields in inheritance hierarchy to a relational database
- Assure each table is self-contained and has no irrelevant fields
- Spread the load between tables
- Assure that Database can be used by other applications that aren't using the objects

Questions:

ID	Pattern	Question Type	QID	Questions	Answer
P012	Concrete Table Inheritance	Goal:	Q080	Would you like to present an inheritance hierarchy of classes in relational database?	
		Intent:	Q081	Shall one database table be used for each concrete class in the hierarchy and no tables for abstract classes?	
			Q082	Would you like to spread the request load between the tables?	
			Q083	Would you like the Database to be used by other applications that are not using (or do not know) objects?	
		Consequences:	Q084	Are there few changes to the objects (classes) expected?	
			Q085	Is data collection (retrieval) from all of the tables seldom demanded in your application? (otherwise → Single Table Inheritance)	

Information source: Fowler, EAA p.293, 2005

Variants:

- Not listed

Similar Patterns: Single Table Inheritance, Class Table Inheritance

26 August 2013

8

Geben Sie bitte Ihre ID ein: ____________________

MUSTER BUCH- UND WIKIPEDIA- AUSZUG

Sie können gerne den Text unterstreichen.

Seitennummer sieht folgend aus und ist in der unteren rechten Ecke der Seite zu finden: **PAGE NUMBER: 1**

TABLE OF CONTENT:

27 August 2013

Multitier architecture - Wikipedia, the free encyclopedia

PAGE NUMBER: 6

Three-tier architecture

Three-tier[3] is a client–server architecture in which the user interface, functional process logic ("business rules"), computer data storage and data access are developed and maintained as independent modules, most often on separate platforms. It was developed by John J. Donovan in Open Environment Corporation (OEC), a tools company he founded in Cambridge, Massachusetts.

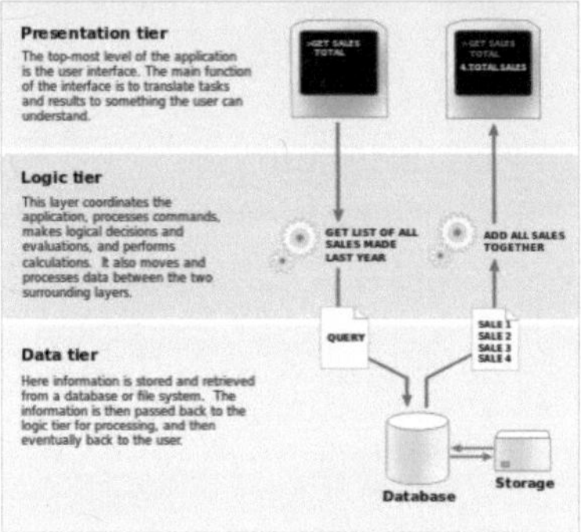

Visual overview of a Three-tiered application

The three-tier model is a software architecture pattern.

Apart from the usual advantages of modular software with well-defined interfaces, the three-tier architecture is intended to allow any of the three tiers to be upgraded or replaced independently in response to changes in requirements or technology. For example, a change of operating system in the *presentation tier* would only affect the user interface code.

Typically, the user interface runs on a desktop PC or workstation and uses a standard graphical user interface, functional process logic that may consist of one or more separate modules running on a workstation or application server, and an RDBMS on a database server or mainframe that contains the computer data storage logic. The middle tier may be multi-tiered itself (in which case the overall architecture is called an "n-tier architecture").

Three-tier architecture has the following three tiers:

Presentation tier
: This is the topmost level of the application. The presentation tier displays information related to such services as browsing merchandise, purchasing and shopping cart contents. It communicates with other tiers by outputting results to the browser/client tier and all other tiers in the network.

Application tier (business logic, logic tier, data access tier, or middle tier)
: The logical tier is pulled out from the presentation tier and, as its own layer, it controls an application’s functionality by performing detailed processing.

Data tier

PAGE NUMBER: 6

PAGE NUMBER: 10

Model-View-Controller

The *Model-View-Controller* architectural pattern (MVC) divides an interactive application into three components. The model contains the core functionality and data. Views display information to the user. Controllers handle user input. Views and controllers together comprise the user interface. A change-propagation mechanism ensures consistency between the user interface and the model.

Example Consider a simple information system for political elections with proportional representation. This offers a spreadsheet for entering data and several kinds of tables and charts for presenting the current results. Users can interact with the system via a graphical interface. All information displays must reflect changes to the voting data immediately.

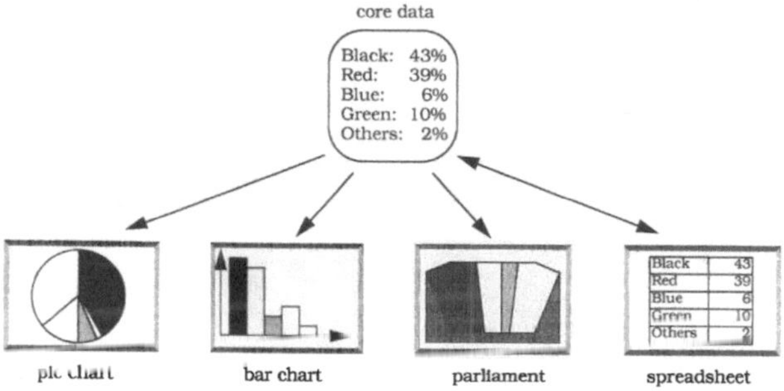

It should be possible to integrate new ways of data presentation, such as the assignment of parliamentary seats to political parties, without major impact to the system. The system should also be portable to platforms with different 'look and feel' standards, such as workstations running Motif or PCs running Microsoft Windows 95.

PAGE NUMBER: 10

Facade

SEARCH

Help | Intro | Case Study | Pattern Catalog | Conclusion

Facade

Object Structural

| Contents | Guide to Readers | Glossary | Notation | Foundation | Bibliography | Index | Pattern Map |

Intent
Motivation
Applicability
Structure
Participants
Collaborations
Consequences
Implementation
Sample Code
Known Uses
Related Patterns

▾ Intent

Provide a unified interface to a set of interfaces in a subsystem. Facade defines a higher-level interface that makes the subsystem easier to use.

▾ Motivation

Structuring a system into subsystems helps reduce complexity. A common design goal is to minimize the communication and dependencies between subsystems. One way to achieve this goal is to introduce a **facade** object that provides a single, simplified interface to the more general facilities of a subsystem.

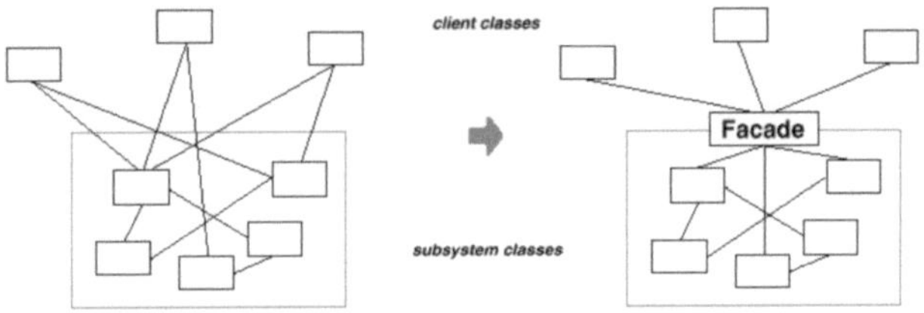

Consider for example a programming environment that gives applications access to its compiler subsystem. This subsystem contains classes such as Scanner, Parser, ProgramNode, BytecodeStream, and ProgramNodeBuilder that implement the compiler. Some specialized applications might need to access these classes directly. But most clients of a compiler generally don't care about details like parsing and code generation; they merely want to compile some code. For them, the powerful but low-level interfaces in the compiler subsystem only complicate their task.

To provide a higher-level interface that can shield clients from these classes, the compiler subsystem also includes a Compiler class. This class defines a unified interface to the compiler's functionality. The Compiler class acts as a facade: It offers clients a single, simple interface to the compiler subsystem. It glues together the classes that implement compiler functionality without hiding them completely. The compiler facade makes life easier for most programmers without hiding the lower-level functionality from the few that need it.

PAGE NUMBER: 51

PAGE NUMBER: 107

These materials were taken from:

Books:

- "Design Patterns: Elements of Reusable Object-Oriented Software" by Erich Gamma, Richard Helm, Ralph Johnson and John Vlissides (1994), Addison-Wesley Professional
- "Patterns of Enterprise Application Architecture" by Martin Fowler (2002), Addison-Wesley Professional
- "Pattern-Oriented Software Architecture Volume 1: A System of Patterns" by Frank Buschmann, Regine Meunier, Hans Rohnert and Peter Sommerlad (1996), Wiley; Volume 1 edition (1996)

Wikipedia articles on: Thin client, thick client, client-server architecture, multitier architecture

PAGE NUMBER: 107

Zeitplan, 30.01

Zeit	Gruppe A, Raum -142 (Martin, Zoya)		Zeit	Gruppe B, Raum -143 (Johannes)
16:00 - 16:05 (5)	(Puffer)		16:00 - 16:05 (5)	(Puffer)
16:05 - 16:15 (10)	Allgemeine Schulung		16:05 - 16:15 (10)	Allgemeine Schulung
16:15 - 16:35 (20)	Patterns und Views Schulung		16:15 - 16:40 (25)	KAMP Schulung
16:35 - 16:45 (10)	**Fragebogen I**			
16:45 - 17:15 (30)	**Fragebogen II (Martin)**		16:40 - 16:50 (10)	**Fragebogen I**
17:15 - 17:20 (5)	(Puffer)		16:50 - 17:20 (30)	**Fragebogen II (Martin)**
17:20 - 17:50 (30)	**Fragebogen III (Zoya)**		17:20 - 17:50 (30)	**Fragebogen III (Zoya)**
17:50 - 18:00 (10)	**Fragebogen IV**		17:50 - 18:00 (10)	**Fragebogen IV**

26 August 2013 1

List of Figures

List of Tables

Bibliography

[1] Z. Durdik and R. Reussner, "On the Appropriate Rationale for Using Design Patterns and Pattern Documentation," in *Proceedings of the 9th ACM SIGSOFT International Conference on the Quality of Software Architectures (QoSA 2013)*, June 2013.

[2] M. Konersmann, Z. Durdik, M. Goedicke, and R. Reussner, "Towards Architecture-Centric Evolution of Long-Living Systems (The ADVERT Approach)," in *Proceedings of the 9th ACM SIGSOFT International Conference on the Quality of Software Architectures (QoSA 2013)*, June 2013.

[3] Z. Durdik, A. Koziolek, and R. Reussner., "How the understanding of the effects of design decisions informs requirements engineering," in *Second International Workshop on the Twin Peaks of Requirements and Architecture (TwinPeaks 2013) @ ICSE2013*, 2013.

[4] Z. Durdik and R. Reussner, "Position Paper: Approach for Architectural Design and Modelling with Documented Design Decisions (ADMD3)," in *Proceedings of the 8th international ACM SIGSOFT conference on Quality of Software Architectures (QoSA 2012)*, 2012.

[5] Z. Durdik, B. Klatt, H. Koziolek, K. Krogmann, J. Stammel, and R. Weiss, "Sustainability guidelines for long-living software systems," in *Proceedings of the 28th IEEE International Conference on Software Maintenance (ICSM 2012)*, 2012.

[6] C. Prause and Z. Durdik, "Architectural Design and Documentation: Waste in Agile Development?" in *Proceedings of the Interna-*

tional Conference on Software and Systems Process (ICSSP 2012) (co-located with ICSE 2012), June 2012, to appear.

[7] B. Klatt, Z. Durdik, K. Krogmann, H. Koziolek, J. Stammel, and R. Weiss, "Identify Impacts of Evolving Third Party Components on Long-Living Software Systems," in *Proceedings of the 16th Conference on Software Maintenance and Reengineering (CSMR'12)*, Szeged, Hungary, March 2012, pp. 461–464.

[8] M. E. Kramer, Z. Durdik, M. Hauck, J. Henss, M. Küster, P. Merkle, and A. Rentschler, "Extending the Palladio Component Model using Profiles and Stereotypes," in *Palladio Days 2012 Proceedings (appeared as technical report)*, ser. Karlsruhe Reports in Informatics ; 2012,21, S. Becker, J. Happe, A. Koziolek, and R. Reussner, Eds. Karlsruhe: KIT, Faculty of Informatics, 2012, pp. 7–15. [Online]. Available: http://digbib.ubka.uni-karlsruhe.de/volltexte/documents/2350659

[9] Z. Durdik, "A Proposal on Validation of an Agile Architecture-Modelling Process," in *Proceedings of Software Engineering 2011 (SE2011), Doktoranden-Symposium*, 2011.

[10] Z. Durdik, "Towards a process for architectural modelling in agile methods," in *Proceedings of 7th Int. Conf. on the Quality of Software Architectures (QoSA 2011)*, 2011.

[11] Z. Durdik, "An architecture-centric approach for goal-driven requirements elicitation," in *Proceedings of the European Software Engineering Conference and the ACM SIGSOFT Symposium on the Foundations of Software Engineering 2011 (ESEC/FSE 2011), Doctoral Symposium*, Szeged, Hungary, September 2011.

[12] H. Koziolek, R. Weiss, Z. Durdik, J. Stammel, and K. Krogmann, "Towards Software Sustainability Guidelines for Long-living Indus-

trial Systems," in *Proceedings of Software Engineering (Workshops), 3rd Workshop of GI Working Group Long-living Software Systems (L2S2), Design for Future*, ser. LNI, vol. 184. GI, 2011, pp. 47–58.

[13] Z. Durdik, "Architectural modeling in agile methods," in *Proceedings of the Fifteenth International Workshop on Component-Oriented Programming (WCOP 2010)*, ser. Interne Berichte, B. Bühnová, R. H. Reussner, C. Szyperski, and W. Weck, Eds., vol. 2010-14. Karlsruhe, Germany: Karlsruhe Institue of Technology, Faculty of Informatics, June 2010, pp. 23–30, CompArch Young Investigator Award 2010. [Online]. Available: http://digbib.ubka.uni-karlsruhe.de/volltexte/1000018464

[14] R. Weiss, H. Koziolek, J. Stammel, and Z. Durdik, "Evolution problems in the context of sustainable industrial software systems," in *Proceedings of 2nd Workshop of GI Working Group "Long-living Software Systems" (L2S2)*, 2010.

[15] Z. Durdik and R. Reussner, "On the Appropriate Rationale for Using Design Patterns and Pattern Documentation," in *Proceedings of Software Engineering 2014 (SE2014)*, 2014.

[16] Z. Durdik, K. Krogmann, and F. Schad, "Towards a generic approach for meta-model- and domain- independent model variability," KIT, Karlsruhe, Germany, Karlsruhe Reports in Informatics 2012,5, ISSN: 2190-4782, 2012. [Online]. Available: http://digbib.ubka.uni-karlsruhe.de/volltexte/1000026207

[17] J. Stammel, Z. Durdik, K. Krogmann, R. Weiss, and H. Koziolek, "Software Evolution for Industrial Automation Systems: Literature Overview," Karlsruhe, Germany, Karlsruhe Reports in Informatics 2011,2, 2011. [Online]. Available: http://digbib.ubka.uni-karlsruhe.de/volltexte/1000022262

[18] A. Tang, M. A. Babar, I. Gorton, and J. Han, "A survey of architecture design rationale," *Journal of Systems and Software*, vol. 79, 2006.

[19] M. Babar, A. Tang, I. Gorton, and J. Han, "Industrial perspective on the usefulness of design rationale for software maintenance: A survey," *Proceedings of Sixth International Conference on Quality Software (QSIC 2006)*, pp. 201 – 208, 2006.

[20] A. Nkwocha, J. G. Hall, and L. Rapanotti, "Design rationale capture for process improvement in the globalised enterprise: An industrial study," *Software and Systems Modeling*, vol. 12, no. 4, pp. 825–845, Oct. 2013. [Online]. Available: http://dx.doi.org/10.1007/s10270-011-0223-y

[21] J. E. Burge and D. C. Brown, "SEURAT: Integrated Rationale Management," in *Proceedings of the 30th International Conference on Software Engineering (ICSE 2008)*. New York, NY, USA: ACM, 2008, pp. 835–838. [Online]. Available: http://doi.acm.org/10.1145/1368088.1368215

[22] J. Burge and J. Kiper, "Capturing decisions and rationale from collaborative design," in *Design Computing and Cognition 2008*, J. Gero and A. Goel, Eds. Springer Netherlands, 2008, pp. 221–239. [Online]. Available: http://dx.doi.org/10.1007/978-1-4020-8728-8_12

[23] F. Pena-Mora and S. Vadhavkar, "Augmenting design patterns with design rationale," *Artificial Intelligence for Engineering Design, Analysis and Manufacturing*, vol. 11, pp. 93–108, 1997.

[24] P. Kruchten, R. Capilla, and J. Dueas, "The decision view's role in software architecture practice," *Software, IEEE*, vol. 26, no. 2, pp. 36–42, 2009.

[25] J. E. Burge, J. M. Carroll, R. McCall, and I. Mistrik, *Rationale-Based Software Engineering*. Springer Berlin Heidelberg, 2008.

[26] M. Mirakhorli and J. Cleland-Huang, "Tracing architectural concerns in high assurance systems (nier track)," in *Proceedings of the 33rd International Conference on Software Engineering*, ser. ICSE '11. New York, NY, USA: ACM, 2011, pp. 908–911. [Online]. Available: http://doi.acm.org/10.1145/1985793.1985942

[27] M. Mirakhorli and J. Cleland-Huang, "A pattern system for tracing architectural concerns," *Proceedings of the Pattern Languages of Programming (PLoP 2011)*, 2011.

[28] E. Gamma, R. Helm, R. Johnson, and J. Vlissides, *Design Patterns. Elements of Reusable Object-Oriented Software*. Addison-Wesley Longman, Amsterdam, 1995.

[29] F. Buschmann, R. Meunier, H. Rohnert, and P. Sommerlad, *A System of Patterns: Pattern-Oriented Software Architecture*. John Wiley & Sons, 1996, vol. 1.

[30] M. Fowler, *Patterns of Enterprise Application Architecture*. Addison-Wesley Professional, 2005.

[31] F. Buschmann, K. Henney, and D. C. Schmidt, *Pattern-Oriented Software Architecture: A Pattern Language for Distributed Computing*. John Wiley & Sons, 2007.

[32] M. Vokac, W. Tichy, D. I. K. Sjoberg, E. Arisholm, and M. Aldrin, "A controlled experiment comparing the maintainability of programs designed with and without design patterns - a replication in a real programming environment," *Emp. S. Eng.*, vol. 9, no. 3, 2004.

[33] E. Freeman, E. Freeman, B. Bates, and K. Sierra, *Head First Design Patterns*. O' Reilly & Associates, Inc., 2004.

[34] Z. Li, J. Hall, and L. Rapanotti, "On the systematic transformation of requirements to specifications," *Requirements Engineering*, pp. 1–23, 2013. [Online]. Available: http://dx.doi.org/10.1007/s00766-013-0173-8

[35] K. Pohl, *Requirements engineering: fundamentals, principles, and techniques.* Springer Publishing Company, Incorporated, 2010.

[36] L. M. Cysneiros and J. C. S. do Prado Leite, "Non-functional requirements: From elicitation to modelling languages," in *Proceedings of the 24th International Conference on Software Engineering*, ser. ICSE '02. New York, NY, USA: ACM, 2002, pp. 699–700. [Online]. Available: http://doi.acm.org/10.1145/581339.581452

[37] S. Ullah, M. Iqbal, and A. Khan, "A survey on issues in non-functional requirements elicitation," in *International Conference on Computer Networks and Information Technology (ICCNIT 2011)*, July 2011, pp. 333–340.

[38] A. Matoussi and R. Laleau, "A survey of non-functional requirements in software development process," *Laboratory of Algorithmic, Complexity, and Logic. Technical Report. TR–LACL–2008–7*, 2008.

[39] L. Xu, H. Ziv, D. Richardson, and Z. Liu, "Towards modeling non-functional requirements in software architecture," in *In Proceedings of Aspect-Oriented Software Design, Workshop on AspectOriented Requirements Engineering and Architecture Design*, 2005.

[40] J. A. Miller, R. Ferrari, and N. H. Madhavji, "Characteristics of new requirements in the presence or absence of an existing system architecture," *17th IEEE International Requirements Engineering Conference (RE 2009)*, pp. 5 – 14, 2009.

[41] R. Ferrari, O. Sudmann, C. Henke, J. Geisler, W. Schafer, and N. H. Madhavji, “Requirements and systems architecture interaction in a prototypical project: Emerging results,” *Proceedings of 16th International Working Conference on Requirements Engineering: Foundation for Software Quality (REFSQ 2010)*, vol. Volume 6182/2010, pp. 23 – 29, 2010.

[42] B. Nuseibeh, “Weaving together requirements and architectures,” *Computer*, vol. 34 , Issue:3, pp. 115 – 119, 2001.

[43] A. Koziolek, “Research preview: Prioritizing quality requirements based on software architecture evaluation feedback,” in *Req. Eng.: Foundation for SW Quality*, ser. Lecture Notes in Comp. Science, vol. 7195, 2012.

[44] A. van Lamsweerde, “Goal-oriented requirements engineering: a guided tour,” in *Fifth IEEE International Symposium on Requirements Engineering, 2001*, 2001, pp. 249–262.

[45] J. Tyree and A. Akerman, “Architecture decisions: demystifying architecture,” *Software, IEEE*, vol. 22, no. 2, pp. 19–27, 2005.

[46] R. Capilla, F. Nava, J. Montes, and C. Carrillo, “Addss: Architecture design decision support system tool,” in *Proceedings of 23rd IEEE/ACM International Conference on Automated Software Engineering (ASE 2008)*, 2008, pp. 487–488.

[47] N. Schuster and O. Zimmermann. (2008) Architectural decision knowledge wiki. http://www.alphaworks.ibm.com/tech/adkwik (February 2014). [Online]. Available: http://www.alphaworks.ibm.com/tech/adkwik

[48] O. Zimmermann, “Architectural decisions as reusable design assets,” *Software, IEEE*, vol. 28 Issue 1, pp. 64 – 69, 2010.

[49] L. Zhu and I. Gorton, "Uml profiles for design decisions and non-functional requirements," in *Proceedings of the Second Workshop on SHAring and Reusing architectural Knowledge Architecture, Rationale, and Design Intent*. IEEE Computer Society, 2007, p. 8.

[50] P. Kruchten, P. Lago, and H. Vliet, "Building up and reasoning about architectural knowledge," in *Quality of Software Architectures*, ser. Lecture Notes in Computer Science, C. Hofmeister, I. Crnkovic, and R. Reussner, Eds. Springer Berlin Heidelberg, 2006, vol. 4214, pp. 43–58. [Online]. Available: http://dx.doi.org/10.1007/11921998_8

[51] R. C. Boer, R. Farenhorst, P. Lago, H. Vliet, V. Clerc, and A. Jansen, "Architectural knowledge: Getting to the core," in *Software Architectures, Components, and Applications*, ser. Lecture Notes in Computer Science, S. Overhage, C. Szyperski, R. Reussner, and J. Stafford, Eds. Springer Berlin Heidelberg, 2007, vol. 4880, pp. 197–214. [Online]. Available: http://dx.doi.org/10.1007/978-3-540-77619-2_12

[52] M. Carignano, S. Gonnet, and H. Leone, "A model to represent architectural design rationale," in *Proceedings of Joint Working IEEE/IFIP Conference on Software Architecture, 2009 European Conference on Software Architecture (WICSA/ECSA 2009)*, 2009, pp. 301–304.

[53] L. Zhang, Y. Sun, Y. Peng, X. Cui, and H. Mei, "Towards quality based solution recommendation in decision-centric architecture design." in *SEKE*, 2011, pp. 776–781.

[54] A. Jansen, J. van der Ven, P. Avgeriou, and D. Hammer, "Tool support for architectural decisions," in *Software Architecture, 2007. WICSA '07. The Working IEEE/IFIP Conference on*, 2007, pp. 4–4.

[55] W. Wang and J. E. Burge, “Using rationale to support pattern-based architectural design,” in *ICSE Workshop on Sharing and Reusing Architectural Knowledge*, 2010.

[56] R. Capilla, O. Zimmermann, U. Zdun, P. Avgeriou, and J. M. Küster, “An enhanced architectural knowledge metamodel linking architectural design decisions to other artifacts in the software engineering lifecycle,” in *ECSA*, ser. Lecture Notes in Computer Science, I. Crnkovic, V. Gruhn, and M. Book, Eds., vol. 6903. Springer, 2011, pp. 303–318.

[57] M. Shahin, P. Liang, and M. Khayyambashi, “Architectural design decision: Existing models and tools,” in *European Conf. on Softw. Architecture. WICSA/ECSA 2009.*, 2009, pp. 293 –296.

[58] M. Fowler, D. Rice, M. Foemmel, E. Hieatt, R. Mee, and R. Stafford, *Patterns of Enterprise Application Architecture*. Addison-Wesley Professional, 2002.

[59] D. Mapelsden, J. Hosking, and J. Grundy, “Design pattern modelling and instantiation using dpml,” in *Proceedings of the Fortieth International Conference on Tools Pacific: Objects for Internet, Mobile and Embedded Applications*, ser. CRPIT ’02. Darlinghurst, Australia, Australia: Australian Computer Society, Inc., 2002, pp. 3–11. [Online]. Available: http://dl.acm.org/citation.cfm?id=564092.564094

[60] D.-K. Kim, R. B. France, S. Ghosh, and E. Song, “A role-based metamodeling approach to specifying design patterns,” in *COMPSAC*. IEEE Computer Society, 2003.

[61] M. Schumacher, E. Fernandez-Buglioni, D. Hybertson, F. Buschmann, and P. Sommerlad, *Security Patterns: Integrating Security and Systems Engineering*. WILEY, 2005.

[62] M. Elaasar, L. C. Briand, and Y. Labiche, "A metamodeling approach to pattern specification," in *Proceedings of the 9th international conference on Model Driven Engineering Languages and Systems (MoDELS 2006)*, ser. MoDELS'06, 2006, pp. 484–498.

[63] S. Henninger and P. Ashokkumar, "An ontology-based metamodel for software patterns," in *18th Int. Conf. on SW Eng. and Knowl. Eng. (Seke2006)*, 2006.

[64] J. Dong, S. Yang, and K. Zhang, "Visualizing design patterns in their applications and compositions," *IEEE Transactions on Software Engineering*, vol. 33, pp. 433–453, 2007.

[65] A. W. Kamal, P. Avgeriou, and U. Zdun, "Modeling architectural pattern variants," in *EuroPLoP*, ser. CEUR Workshop Proceedings, T. Schümmer, Ed., vol. 610. CEUR-WS.org, 2008.

[66] L. Pavlic, M. Hericko, and V. Podgorelec, "Improving design pattern adoption with ontology-based design pattern repository," in *30th International Conference on Information Technology Interfaces (ITI 2008)*, 2008.

[67] W. Schaefer. (2010) Specification of Software Patterns for Pattern-Oriented Software Development: Meta-model. PG POSE student project.

[68] P. Bottoni, E. Guerra, and J. de Lara, "A language-independent and formal approach to pattern-based modelling with support for composition and analysis," *Information and Software Technology*, vol. 52, no. 8, pp. 821–844, Aug. 2010. [Online]. Available: http://dx.doi.org/10.1016/j.infsof.2010.03.005

[69] T. Taibi, *Design Pattern Formalization Techniques*. IGI Publishing, 2007.

[70] D. Gross and E. Yu, "From non-functional requirements to design through patterns," *Requirements Engineering*, vol. 6, pp. 18–36, 2000.

[71] U. Zdun, "Systematic pattern selection using pattern language grammars and design space analysis," *Software: Practice and Experience*, vol. 37, no. 9, pp. 983–1016, 2007.

[72] O. Zimmermann, U. Zdun, T. Gschwind, and F. Leymann, "Combining pattern languages and reusable architectural decision models into a comprehensive and comprehensible design method," in *Proceedings of Seventh Working IEEE/IFIP Conference on Software Architecture (WICSA 2008)*, 2008, pp. 157–166.

[73] H. Garbe, C. Janssen, C. Moebus, H. Seebold, and H. de Vries, "KARaCAs: Knowledge Acquisition with Repertory Grids and Formal Concept Analysis for Dialog System Construction," in *Managing Knowledge in a World of Networks*. Springer, 2006.

[74] Z. Moudam and N. Chenfour, "Design pattern support system: Help making decision in the choice of appropriate pattern," *Procedia Technology*, vol. 4, no. 0, pp. 355 – 359, 2012, proceedings of 2nd International Conference on Computer, Communication, Control and Information Technology(C3IT-2012). [Online]. Available: http://www.sciencedirect.com/science/article/pii/S2212017312003337

[75] M. Müller, B. Kersten, and M. Goedicke, "A question-based method for deriving software architectures," in *Software Architecture*, ser. Lecture Notes in Computer Science, I. Crnkovic, V. Gruhn, and M. Book, Eds. Springer Berlin Heidelberg, 2011, vol. 6903, pp. 35–42. [Online]. Available: http://dx.doi.org/10.1007/978-3-642-23798-0_4

[76] A. Birukou, "A survey of existing approaches for pattern search and selection," in *Proceedings of the 15th European Conference on Pattern Languages of Programs (EuroPLoP 2010)*, 2010.

[77] S. Thabasum and M. Sundar, "A survey on software design pattern tools for pattern selection and implementation," in *Int. Journal of Comp. Science and Communication Networks (IJCSCN)*, vol. Volume 2, Issue 4, 2012.

[78] D. Falessi, G. Cantone, R. Kazman, and P. Kruchten, "Decision-making techniques for software architecture design: A comparative survey," *ACM Computer Survey*, vol. 43, no. 4, pp. 33:1–33:28, Oct. 2011. [Online]. Available: http://doi.acm.org/10.1145/1978802.1978812

[79] R. C. de Boer and H. van Vliet, "On the similarity between requirements and architecture," *Journal of Systems and Software*, vol. 82, 2009.

[80] A. Koziolek, "Architecture-driven quality requirements prioritization," in *First International Workshop on the Twin Peaks of Requirements and Architecture (TwinPeaks 2012)*. IEEE Computer Society, 2012.

[81] W. Dröschel and M. Wiemers, *Das V-Modell 97*. Oldenbourg, 1999.

[82] R. Pressman, *Software engineering: a practitioner's approach*, ser. McGraw-Hill higher education. McGraw-Hill Higher Education, 2010.

[83] P. Kruchten, *The Rational Unified Process: An Introduction*. Addison-Wesley Professional, 2003.

[84] K. Schwaber and M. Beedle, *Agile Software Development with Scrum*. Pearson Studium, 2008.

[85] R. Böhme and R. Reussner, "Validation of Predictions with Measurements," in *Dependability Metrics*, ser. Lecture Notes in Computer Science. Springer-Verlag Berlin Heidelberg, 2008, vol. 4909, ch. 3, pp. 14–18. [Online]. Available: http://www.springerlink.com/content/662rn13014r46269/fulltext.pdf

[86] H. Koziolek, "Parameter dependencies for reusable performance specifications of software components," Ph.D. dissertation, University of Oldenburg, Germany, March 2008.

[87] I. Sommerville, *Software Engineering*, 8th ed., ser. International computer science series. Addison Wesley, 2007. [Online]. Available: http://books.google.de/books?id=B7idKfL0H64C

[88] R. Pichler, *Agile Product Management with Scrum: Creating Products that Customers Love.* Addison-Wesley Signature Series (Cohn), 2010.

[89] K. Beck and C. Andres, *Extreme Programming Explained: Embrace Change*, 2nd ed. Addison-Wesley, 2004.

[90] A. Cockburn, *Crystal Clear: A Human-Powered Methodology for Small Teams.* Addison-Wesley Longman, Amsterdam, 2004.

[91] S. R. Palmer, M. Felsing, and S. Palmer, *A Practical Guide to Feature-Driven Development.* Prentice Hall International, 2002.

[92] J. A. Highsmith and K. Orr, *Adaptive Software Development: A Collaborative Approach to Managing Complex Systems.* Dorset House Publishing Co Inc.,U.S., 1999.

[93] O. Salo and P. Abrahamsson, "Agile methods in european embedded software development organisations: a survey on the actual use and usefulness of extreme programming and scrum," *Software, IET*, vol. 2 , Issue:1, pp. 58 – 64, 2008.

[94] B. Sheth, "Scrum 911! using scrum to overhaul a support organization," *Agile Conference, 2009. AGILE '09.*, pp. 74 – 78, 2009.

[95] C. Mann and F. Maurer, "A case study on the impact of scrum on overtime and customer satisfaction," *In the Proceedings of the Agile Conf., 2005.*, pp. 70 – 79, 2005.

[96] T. Dingsoyr, G. K. Hanssen, T. Dyba, G. Anker, and J. O. Nygaard, "Developing software with scrum in a small cross-organizational project," *Lecture Notes in Computer Science*, vol. Volume 4257/2006, pp. 5–15, 2006.

[97] K. Long and D. Starr, "Agile supports improved culture and quality for healthwise," *Conference Agile, 2008. AGILE '08.*, pp. 160 – 165, 2008.

[98] A. Cockburn and J. Highsmith, "Agile software development, the people factor," *Computer*, vol. Volume: 34 , Issue: 11, pp. 131 – 133, 2001.

[99] H. Hulkko and P. Abrahamsson, "A multiple case study on the impact of pair programming on product quality," *Proceedings of the Software Engineering, 2005. ICSE 2005. 27th International Conference*, pp. 495–504, 2005.

[100] S. Maranzano, J.F.and Rozsypal, G. Zimmerman, G. Warnken, P. Wirth, and D. Weiss, "Architecture reviews: practice and experience," *Software, IEEE*, vol. 22 , Issue: 2, pp. 34 – 43, 2005.

[101] K. Beck, M. Beedle, A. van Bennekum, A. Cockburn, W. Cunningham, M. Fowler, J. Grenning, J. Highsmith, A. Hunt, R. Jeffries, J. Kern, B. Marick, R. C. Martin, S. Mellor, K. Schwaber, J. Sutherland, and D. Thomas, "Agile manifesto," 2001, http://agilemanifesto.org/.

[102] IEEE, *IEEE Systems and software engineering – Life cycle processes – Requirements engineering – 29148-2011*, IEEE Std., 2011.

[103] I. Sommerville and P. Sawyer, *Requirements Engineering: A Good Practice Guide*. New York, NY, USA: John Wiley & Sons, Inc., 2003.

[104] M. Glinz, “On non-functional requirements,” in *15th IEEE International Requirements Engineering Conference (RE ’07)*, 2007.

[105] J. Robertson and S. Robertson, “Volere requirements specification template,” The Atlantic Systems Guild, Tech. Rep., 2010.

[106] S. Robertson and J. Robertson, *Mastering the Requirements Process*. Addison-Wesley Professional; 3 edition, 2012.

[107] M. Cohn, *Agile Estimating and Planning (Robert C. Martin)*. Prentice Hall International, 2005.

[108] M. Cohn, *User Stories Applied: For Agile Software Development*. Addison-Wesley Professional; 1 edition, 2004.

[109] IBM. Ibm rational doors, a requirements management tool. http://www-03.ibm.com/software/products/en/ratidoor/ (December 2013). [Online]. Available: http://www-03.ibm.com/software/products/en/ratidoor/

[110] IBM. Ibm rational requisitepro, a requirements management tool. http://www-03.ibm.com/software/products/en/reqpro/ (December 2013). [Online]. Available: http://www-03.ibm.com/software/products/en/reqpro/

[111] Polarion. Polarion requirements, a web requirements management tool. http://www.polarion.com/products/requirements/index.php (December 2012). [Online]. Available: http://www.polarion.com/products/requirements/index.php

[112] A. Smith, P. Spencer, and ideaStub. Open source requirements management tool. http://sourceforge.net/projects/osrmt/ (December 2013). [Online]. Available: http://sourceforge.net/projects/osrmt/

[113] I. f. C. S. Software Engineering Heidelberg. Unicase, an open source case-tool for modeling artifacts in a software engineering project. University of Heidelberg, TU Muenchen. http://se.ifi.uni-heidelberg.de/research/projects/unicase.html (February 2014). [Online]. Available: http://se.ifi.uni-heidelberg.de/research/projects/unicase.html

[114] P. Avgeriou, J. Grundy, J. G. Hall, P. Lago, and I. Mistrík, Eds., *Relating Software Requirements and Architectures.* Springer, 2011.

[115] R. N. Taylor, N. Medvidovic, and E. M. Dashofy, *Software Architecture: Foundations, Theory, and Practice.* Wiley, 2009.

[116] P. Clements, F. Bachmann, L. Bass, and D. Garlan, *Documenting Software Architectures: Views and Beyond (SEI Series in Software Engineering).* Addison-Wesley Longman, 2002.

[117] N. Rozanski and E. Woods, *Software Systems Architecture: Working With Stakeholders Using Viewpoints and Perspectives.* Addison-Wesley Professional, 2009.

[118] D. J. Paulish and L. Bass, *Architecture-Centric Software Project Management: A Practical Guide.* Boston, MA, USA: Addison-Wesley Longman Publishing Co., Inc., 2001.

[119] D. Soni, R. L. Nord, and C. Hofmeister, "Software architecture in industrial applications," in *Proceedings of the 17th International Conference on Software Engineering*, ser. ICSE '95. New York, NY, USA: ACM, 1995, pp. 196–207. [Online]. Available: http://doi.acm.org/10.1145/225014.225033

[120] G. Booch, J. Rumbaugh, and I. Jacobson, *The Unified Modeling Language User Guide*. Addison-Wesley Longman, 2005.

[121] P. Dissaux, M. F. Amine, and P. Michel, *Architecture Description Languages: IFIP TC-2 Workshop on Architecture Description Languages (WADL), World Computer Congress*. Springer Verlag, 2004.

[122] ISO, *Systems and software engineering – Architecture description, ISO/IEC/IEEE 42010:2011*, ISO/IEC/IEEE Std.

[123] P. Kruchten, "The 4+1 view model of architecture," *IEEE Software*, vol. Volume 12 , Issue 6, pp. 42 – 50, 1995.

[124] D. Garlan, "Software architecture: a roadmap," *Proceedings of the Conference on The Future of Software Engineering*, pp. 91 – 101, 2000.

[125] J. Tyree, "Architectural design decisions session report," in *Proceedings of the 5th Working IEEE/IFIP Conference on Software Architecture*, ser. WICSA '05. Washington, DC, USA: IEEE Computer Society, 2005, pp. 285–286. [Online]. Available: http://dx.doi.org/10.1109/WICSA.2005.14

[126] A. Jansen and J. Bosch, "Software architecture as a set of architectural design decisions," in *Proceedings of the 5th Working IEEE/IFIP Conference on Software Architecture*, ser. WICSA '05. Washington, DC, USA: IEEE Computer Society, 2005, pp. 109–120. [Online]. Available: http://dx.doi.org/10.1109/WICSA.2005.61

[127] O. Zimmermann, S. Milinski, M. Craes, and F. Oellermann, "Second generation web services-oriented architecture in production in the finance industry," in *Companion to the 19th Annual ACM SIGPLAN Conference on Object-oriented Programming Systems, Languages, and Applications*, ser. OOPSLA '04. New York,

NY, USA: ACM, 2004, pp. 283–289. [Online]. Available: http://doi.acm.org/10.1145/1028664.1028772

[128] M. A. Babar, T. Dingsyr, P. Lago, and H. van Vliet, *Software Architecture Knowledge Management: Theory and Practice*, 1st ed. Springer Publishing Company, Incorporated, 2009.

[129] J. Bosch, "Software architecture: The next step," in *Software Architecture*, ser. Lecture Notes in Computer Science, F. Oquendo, B. Warboys, and R. Morrison, Eds. Springer Berlin Heidelberg, 2004, vol. 3047, pp. 194–199. [Online]. Available: http://dx.doi.org/10.1007/978-3-540-24769-2_14

[130] P. Kruchten, "An Ontology of Architectural Design Decisions in Software Intensive Systems," in *2nd Groningen W. Software Variability*, 2004, pp. 54–61.

[131] D. E. Perry and A. L. Wolf, "Foundations for the study of software architecture," *ACM SIGSOFT Software Engineering Notes*, vol. 17, no. 4, pp. 40–52, Oct. 1992. [Online]. Available: http://doi.acm.org/10.1145/141874.141884

[132] J. Lee, "Design rationale systems: Understanding the issues," *IEEE Expert: Intelligent Systems and Their Applications*, vol. 12, no. 3, pp. 78–85, May 1997. [Online]. Available: http://dx.doi.org/10.1109/64.592267

[133] A. Tang, Y. Jin, and J. Han, "A rationale-based architecture model for design traceability and reasoning," *Journal of Systems and Software*, vol. 80, no. 6, pp. 918 – 934, 2007.

[134] R. H. Reussner, S. Becker, J. Happe, J. Henss, A. Koziolek, H. Koziolek, M. Kramer, and K. Krogmann, *Modeling and Simulating Software Architectures with Palladio*. To appear, 2015, Chapter 4: Ar-

chitectural Reuse. Chapter 4 Authors: Ralf Reussner, Zoya Durdik, Oliver Hummel, Benjamin Klatt and Florian Meyerer.

[135] D. Schmidt, M. Stal, H. Rohnert, and F. Buschmann, *Pattern-Oriented Software Architecture – Volume 2 – Patterns for Concurrent and Networked Objects.* WILEY, 2000.

[136] M. Kircher and P. Jain, *Pattern-Oriented Software Architecture: Patterns for Distributed Services and Components.* John Wiley and Sons Ltd, 2004.

[137] B. P. Douglass, *Real-Time Design Patterns*, ser. Object Technology Series. Addison-Wesley Professional, 2002.

[138] T. Erl, *SOA Design Patterns.* Prentice Hall PTR, 2009.

[139] C. Szyperski, *Component Software: Beyond Object-Oriented Programming*, 2nd ed. Boston, MA, USA: Addison-Wesley Longman Publishing Co., Inc., 2002.

[140] T. Stahl, M. Voelter, and K. Czarnecki, *Model-Driven Software Development: Technology, Engineering, Management.* John Wiley & Sons, 2006.

[141] T. Goldschmidt, "View-based textual modelling," Ph.D. dissertation, Karlsruhe Institute of Technology (KIT), Karlsruhe, 2011. [Online]. Available: http://digbib.ubka.uni-karlsruhe.de/volltexte/1000022234

[142] A. Khakulov, "Pattern instantiation and visualisation in palladio," Master's thesis, Department of Informatics Institute for Program Structures and Data Organization (IPD), Karlsruhe Institute of Technology (KIT), 2012, reviewer: Prof. Dr. R. H. Reussner, Prof. Dr. W. F. Tichy, Advisor: Z. Durdik, A. Rentschler.

[143] ModelWare. (2007) Information society technologies (ist) sixth framework programme: Glossary. http://www.modelware-ist.org/index.php?option=com_rd_glossary&Itemid=55 (February 2014). [Online]. Available: http://www.modelware-ist.org/index.php?option=com_rd_glossary&Itemid=55

[144] H. Stachowiak, *Allgemeine Modelltheorie*. Springer-Verlag, 1973.

[145] J. Ernst. (1999) What is metamodeling, and what is it good for? http://infogrid.org/wiki/Reference/WhatIsMetaModeling/ (August 2008 by T. Goldschmidt). [Online]. Available: http://infogrid.org/wiki/Reference/WhatIsMetaModeling/

[146] O. M. G. (OMG). (2012) The metaobject facility specification (mof). http://www.omg.org/mof/ (February 2014). [Online]. Available: http://www.omg.org/mof/

[147] E. Foundation. Eclipse Modeling Framework Project (EMF). http://www.eclipse.org/modeling/emf/ (February 2014). [Online]. Available: http://www.eclipse.org/modeling/emf/

[148] O. M. G. (OMG). (2012) Object constraint language (ocl). http://www.omg.org/spec/OCL/2.3.1 (December 2013). [Online]. Available: http://www.omg.org/spec/OCL/2.3.1

[149] E. Foundation. Graphical Editing Framework (GEF). http://www.eclipse.org/gef/ (February 2014). [Online]. Available: http://www.eclipse.org/gef/

[150] E. Foundation. Graphical Modelling Framework(GMF). http://www.eclipse.org/modeling/gmp/ (February 2014). [Online]. Available: http://www.eclipse.org/modeling/gmp/

[151] O. O. M. Group). (2008) Semantics of business vocabulary and business rules (sbvr), v1.0. http://www.omg.org/spec/SBVR/1.0/

PDF (February 2014). [Online]. Available: http://www.omg.org/spec/SBVR/1.0/PDF

[152] S. Becker, H. Koziolek, and R. Reussner, "The Palladio component model for model-driven performance prediction," *Journal of Systems and Software*, vol. 82, pp. 3–22, 2009. [Online]. Available: http://dx.doi.org/10.1016/j.jss.2008.03.066

[153] F. Brosch, H. Koziolek, B. Buhnova, and R. Reussner, "Architecture-based reliability prediction with the palladio component model," *Transactions on Software Engineering*, vol. 38, no. 6, 2011.

[154] SDQ. Palladio software architektur simulator. http://www.palladio-simulator.com (February 2014). [Online]. Available: http://www.palladio-simulator.com

[155] S. Herold, H. Klus, Y. Welsch, C. Deiters, A. Rausch, R. Reussner, K. Krogmann, H. Koziolek, R. Mirandola, B. Hummel, M. Meisinger, and C. Pfaller, *The Common Component Modeling Example*, ser. LNCS. Springer, 2008, vol. 5153, ch. CoCoME.

[156] V. Grassi, R. Mirandola, E. Randazzo, and A. Sabetta, "The common component modeling example," in *CoCoME - The Common Component Modeling Example*, A. Rausch, R. Reussner, R. Mirandola, and F. Plášil, Eds. Berlin, Heidelberg: Springer-Verlag, 2008, ch. KLAPER: An Intermediate Language for Model-Driven Predictive Analysis of Performance and Reliability, pp. 327–356. [Online]. Available: http://dx.doi.org/10.1007/978-3-540-85289-6_13

[157] M. Malohlava, P. Hnetynka, and T. Bures, "Sofa 2 component framework and its ecosystem," *Electronic Notes in Theoretical Computer Science (ENTCS)*, vol. 295, pp. 101–106, May 2013. [Online]. Available: http://dx.doi.org/10.1016/j.entcs.2013.04.009

[158] SDQ. (2014) The Common Component Modeling Example (cocome) palladio component models (pcm). http://svnserver.informatik.kit.edu/i43/svn/code/CoCoME-SPP/ (February 2014). [Online]. Available: http://svnserver.informatik.kit.edu/i43/svn/code/CoCoME-SPP/

[159] T. Kuhn, "A survey and classification of controlled natural languages," *Computational Linguistics*, 2013.

[160] R. Schwitter, "Controlled natural languages for knowledge representation," in *Proceedings of the 23rd International Conference on Computational Linguistics: Posters*. Association for Computational Linguistics, 2010, pp. 1113–1121.

[161] J. F. Sowa, "Common logic controlled english," jfsowa.com, Tech. Rep., 2004, draft. [Online]. Available: http://www.jfsowa.com/clce/specs.htm

[162] N. E. Fuchs, "First-order reasoning for attempto controlled english," in *CNL*, ser. Lecture Notes in Computer Science, M. Rosner and N. E. Fuchs, Eds., vol. 7175. Springer, 2010, pp. 73–94.

[163] ANSI/NISO Z39.19-2005 (R2010) Guidelines for the Construction, Format, and Management of Monolingual Controlled Vocabularies. (2005) ANSI/NISO 2005. http://www.niso.org/ (February 2014). [Online]. Available: http://www.niso.org/

[164] M. Heller, "A patterns-based modeling process with traced design rationale," Master's thesis, Karlsruhe Institute of Technology (KIT), 2012, reviewer: Prof. Dr. R. H. Reussner, Prof. Dr. W. F. Tichy, Advisor: Z. Durdik, M. Küster.

[165] R. Kazman, M. Klein, and P. Clements, "ATAM: Method for architecture evaluation," Software Engineering Institute, Tech. Rep.,

Sep. 05 2000. [Online]. Available: http://www.sei.cmu.edu/pub/documents/00.reports/pdf/00tr004.pdf

[166] J. Viega and G. McGraw, *Building Secure Software: How to Avoid Security Problems the Right Way.* Addison-Wesley Professional, 2001.

[167] N. Leveson, *Safeware: System Safety and Computers.* Addison-Wesley Professional, 1995.

[168] M. Fowler, *UML Distilled: A Brief Guide to the Standard Object Modeling Language, Third Edition.* AW, 2003.

[169] S. Ambler, *The Elements of UML(TM) 2.0 Style.* Cambridge University Press, 2005, vol. 15.

[170] S. Werfel, "Eine Methode zur architekturzentrierten Unterstützung von Software Evolution durch Dokumentation von Entwurfsentscheidungen und ihrer Begründungen," Master's thesis, Karlsruhe Institute of Technology (KIT), 2013, reviewer: Prof. Dr. R. H. Reussner, Jun.-Prof. Dr. A. Koziolek, Advisor: Z. Durdik, P. Merkle.

[171] M. MSDN. oftware architecture and design, chapter 3: Architectural patterns and styles. https://msdn.microsoft.com/en-us/library/ee658117.aspx (February 2015). [Online]. Available: https://msdn.microsoft.com/en-us/library/ee658117.aspx

[172] V. R. Basili, "Software modeling and measurement:The Goal/Question/Metric paradigm," University of Maryland, College Park, MD, USA, Computer Science Technical Report Series CS-TR-2956 (UMIACS-TR-92-96), 1992.

[173] A. Preece, "Evaluating verification and validation methods in knowledge engineering," *Industrial Knowledge Management*, pp. 123–145, 2001.

[174] W. F. Tichy, "Hints for reviewing empirical work in software engineering," *Empirical Softw. Engg.*, vol. 5, no. 4, pp. 309–312, 2000.

[175] A. Fink, *The Survey Handbook, 2nd edition.* SAGE, Thousand Oaks/London, 2003.

[176] C. Wohlin, P. Runeson, M. Höst, M. C. Ohlsson, B. Regnell, and A. Wesslén, *Experimentation in software engineering: an introduction.* Norwell, MA, USA: Kluwer Academic Publishers, 2012.

[177] K. Punch, *Introduction to Social Research: Quantitative and Qualitative Approaches.* Sage Publications Ltd, 2005.

[178] R. Yin, *Case Study Research: Design and Methods.* Sage Publications, Beverly Hills, 2009.

[179] Wikipedia. Student's t-test. http://en.wikipedia.org/wiki/Student's_t-test (February 2014). [Online]. Available: http://en.wikipedia.org/wiki/Student's_t-test

[180] Wikipedia. Wilcoxon signed-rank test. http://en.wikipedia.org/wiki/Wilcoxon_signed-rank_test (February 2014). [Online]. Available: http://en.wikipedia.org/wiki/Wilcoxon_signed-rank_test

[181] J. Chambers and colleagues. The R Project for Statistical Computing. Bell Laboratories. http://www.r-project.org/ (February 2014). [Online]. Available: http://www.r-project.org/

[182] M. A. Babar, "An exploratory study of architectural practices and challenges in using agile software development approaches," *Proceedings of Joint Working IEEE/IFIP Conference on Software Architecture, 2009 & European Conference on Software Architecture (WICSA/ECSA 2009)*, pp. 81 – 90, 2009.

[183] A. Tang, P. Avgeriou, A. Jansen, R. Capilla, and M. A. Babar, "A comparative study of architecture knowledge management tools,"

Journal of Systems and Software, vol. 83, no. 3, pp. 352 – 370, 2010. [Online]. Available: http://www.sciencedirect.com/science/article/pii/S0164121209002295

[184] R. Capilla, F. Nava, S. Pérez, and J. C. Dueñas, "A web-based tool for managing architectural design decisions," *ACM SIGSOFT Software Engineering Notes*, vol. 31, 2006.

[185] A. Jansen, T. Vries, P. Avgeriou, and M. Veelen, "Sharing the architectural knowledge of quantitative analysis," in *Quality of Software Architectures. Models and Architectures*, ser. Lecture Notes in Computer Science, S. Becker, F. Plasil, and R. Reussner, Eds. Springer Berlin Heidelberg, 2008, vol. 5281, pp. 220–234. [Online]. Available: http://dx.doi.org/10.1007/978-3-540-87879-7_14

[186] W. F. Tichy, "A catalogue of general-purpose software design patterns," in *Proceedings of the Tools-23: Technology of Object-Oriented Languages and Systems (TOOLS 1997)*, 1997.

[187] Z. Durdik and R. Reussner. Pattern survey, Google Docs. https://docs.google.com/spreadsheet/viewform?formkey=dGVlMFdoel9PUnNuVFp4SnlLSUkwSUE6MA (February 2014).

[188] Sourcemaking. Design patterns at sourcemaking. http://sourcemaking.com/design_patterns (January, 2014). [Online]. Available: http://sourcemaking.com/design_patterns

[189] OODesign.com. (Object Oriented Design Patterns) http://www.oodesign.com (January, 2014). [Online]. Available: http://www.oodesign.com

[190] G. Sunye, A. L. Guennec, and J.-M. Jezequel, "Design patterns application in uml," in *Proceedings of the 14th European Conference on Object-Oriented Programming*, ser. Springer-Verlag London. Lecture, 2000, pp. 44–62.

[191] A. L. Guennec, G. Sunye, and J. marc Jezequel, "Precise modeling of design patterns," in *Proceedings of UML 2000*. Springer Verlag, 2000, pp. 482–496.

[192] J. K. H. Mak, C. S. T. Choy, and D. P. K. Lun, "Precise modeling of design patterns in uml," in *Proceedings of the 26th International Conference on Software Engineering*, ser. ICSE '04. Washington, DC, USA: IEEE Computer Society, 2004, pp. 252–261. [Online]. Available: http://dl.acm.org/citation.cfm?id=998675.999430

[193] A. W. Kamal and P. Avgeriou, "An evaluation of adls on modeling patterns for software architecture," in *Proceedings of the 4th International Workshop on Rapid Integration of Software Engineering techniques (RISE)*. Springer LNCS, 2007. [Online]. Available: http://www.cs.rug.nl/~paris/papers/RISE07.pdf

[194] M. Bjerkander and C. Kobryn, "Architecting systems with uml 2.0," *Software, IEEE*, vol. 20, no. 4, pp. 57–61, 2003.

[195] N. Medvidovic, D. S. Rosenblum, D. F. Redmiles, and J. E. Robbins, "Modeling software architectures in the unified modeling language," *ACM Transactions on Software Engineering and Methodology (TOSEM)*, vol. 11, no. 1, pp. 2–57, Jan. 2002. [Online]. Available: http://doi.acm.org/10.1145/504087.504088

[196] D. Garlan, R. Monroe, and D. Wile, "ACME: An Architecture Description Interchange Language," in *Proceedings of CASCON 1997*, 1997, pp. 169–183.

[197] R. Allen and D. Garlan, "A formal basis for architectural connection," *ACM Transactions on Software Engineering and Methodology (TOSEM)*, pp. 213–249, 1997.

[198] M. Shaw, R. DeLine, D. V. Klein, T. L. Ross, D. M. Young, and G. Zelesnik, "Abstractions for software architecture and tools to sup-

port them," *IEEE Transactions on Software Engineering*, vol. 21, pp. 314–335, 1995.

[199] E. Dashofy, A. van der Hoek, and R. Taylor, "A highly-extensible, xml-based architecture description language," in *Proceedings of Working IEEE/IFIP Conference on Software Architecture*, 2001, pp. 103–112.

[200] D. Garlan, R. Allen, and J. Ockerbloom, "Exploiting style in architectural design environments," in *Proceedings of the 2Nd ACM SIGSOFT Symposium on Foundations of Software Engineering*, ser. SIGSOFT 1994. New York, NY, USA: ACM, 1994, pp. 175–188. [Online]. Available: http://doi.acm.org/10.1145/193173.195404

[201] A. W. Kamal and P. Avgeriou, "Modeling the variability of architectural patterns," in *SAC*, S. Y. Shin, S. Ossowski, M. Schumacher, M. J. Palakal, and C.-C. Hung, Eds. ACM, 2010, pp. 2344–2351.

[202] P. Kajsa, L. Majtás, and P. Návrat, "Design pattern instantiation directed by concretization and specialization," *Comput. Sci. Inf. Syst.*, vol. 8, no. 1, pp. 41–72, 2011.

[203] IBM. IBM Rational System Architect. http://www.ibm.com/software/products/en/ratisystarch/ (December 2013). [Online]. Available: http://www.ibm.com/software/products/en/ratisystarch/

[204] J. Dietrich, N. Jones, and J. M. Wright, "Using social networking and semantic web technology in software engineering - use cases, patterns, and a case study," *Journal of Systems and Software*, vol. 81, no. 12, pp. 2183–2193, 2008.

[205] W3C. (2004) Owl web ontology language overview. http://www.w3.org/TR/owl-features (February 2014). [Online]. Available: http://www.w3.org/TR/owl-features

[206] H. Albin-Amiot, Y.-G. Gueheneuc, and R. A. Kastler, "Meta-modeling design patterns: Application to pattern detection and code synthesis," in *Proceedings of ECOOP Workshop on Automating Object-Oriented Software Development Methods 2001*, 2001, pp. 01–35.

[207] G. El Boussaidi and H. Mili, "A model-driven framework for representing and applying design patterns," in *Proceedings of the 31st Annual International Computer Software and Applications Conference*, ser. COMPSAC '07, vol. Volume 01. Washington, DC, USA: IEEE Computer Society, 2007, pp. 97–100. [Online]. Available: http://dx.doi.org/10.1109/COMPSAC.2007.31

[208] W. Bu, A. Tang, and J. Han, "An analysis of decisioncentric architectural design approaches," Swinburne University of Technology, Tech. Rep., 2009.

[209] N. Schuster, "ADkwik - a Collaborative System for Architectural Decision Modeling and Decision Process Support based on Web 2.0 Technologies," Master's thesis, Hochschule der Medien, Stuttgart, 2007.

[210] O. Zimmermann, J. Koehler, and F. Leymann, "The role of architectural decisions in model-driven soa construction," in *4th International Workshop on SOA and Web Services (OOPSLA 2006)*, 2006.

[211] O. Zimmermann, T. Gschwind, J. Küster, F. Leymann, and N. Schuster, "Reusable architectural decision models for enterprise application development," in *Software Architectures, Components, and Applications*, ser. Lecture Notes in Computer Science, S. Overhage, C. Szyperski, R. Reussner, and J. Stafford, Eds. Springer Berlin Heidelberg, 2007, vol. 4880, pp. 15–32. [Online]. Available: http://dx.doi.org/10.1007/978-3-540-77619-2_2

[212] F. Bachmann and P. Merson, "Experience using the web-based tool wiki for architecture documentation," Software Engineering Institute, Carnegie Mellon University, Tech. Rep., 2005.

[213] R. de Boer, P. Lago, A. Telea, and H. Van Vliet, "Ontology-driven visualization of architectural design decisions," in *Proceedings of Joint Working IEEE/IFIP Conference on Software Architecture, 2009 European Conference on Software Architecture (WICSA/ECSA 2009)*, 2009, pp. 51–60.

[214] U. van Heesch, P. Avgeriou, and R. Hilliard, "A documentation framework for architecture decisions," *J. Syst. Softw.*, vol. 85, no. 4, pp. 795–820, Apr. 2012. [Online]. Available: http://dx.doi.org/10.1016/j.jss.2011.10.017

[215] L. Lee and P. Kruchten, "Customizing the capture of software architectural design decisions," in *Canadian Conf. on Electrical and Computer Engineering*, 2008.

[216] A. H. Dutoit and B. Paech, "Rationale-based use case specification," *Proceedings of Requirements Engineering (RE 2002)*, vol. 7, no. 1, pp. 3–19, 2002. [Online]. Available: http://dx.doi.org/10.1007/s007660200001

[217] E. Baniassad, G. Murphy, and C. Schwanninger, "Design pattern rationale graphs: Linking design to source," in *Proceedings of 25th International Conference on Software Engineering, 2003*, 2003, pp. 352–362.

[218] R. C. D. Boer, R. Farenhorst, V. Clerc, J. S. V. D. Ven, R. Deckers, P. Lago, and H. V. Vliet, "Structuring software architecture project memories, submitted," in *Proceedings of the 8th International Workshop on Learning Software Organizations (LSO 2006)*, 2006.

[219] R. Farenhorst and R. C. de Boer, "Core concepts of an ontology of architectural design decisions," Vrije University Amsterdam, Tech. Rep. IR-IMSE-002, 2006.

[220] Q. Gu and P. Lago, "Soa process decisions: New challenges in architectural knowledge modeling," in *Proceedings of the 3rd International Workshop on Sharing and Reusing Architectural Knowledge*, ser. SHARK '08. New York, NY, USA: ACM, 2008, pp. 3–10. [Online]. Available: http://doi.acm.org/10.1145/1370062.1370065

[221] M. Babar, I. Gorton, and B. Kitchenham, "A framework for supporting architecture knowledge and rationale management," in *Rationale Management in Software Engineering*, A. Dutoit, R. McCall, I. Mistrík, and B. Paech, Eds. Springer Berlin Heidelberg, 2006, pp. 237–254. [Online]. Available: http://dx.doi.org/10.1007/978-3-540-30998-7_11

[222] H. Choi, Y. Choi, and K. Yeom, "An integrated approach to quality achievement with architectural design decisions." *Journal of Software*, vol. 1, no. 3, pp. 40–49, 2006.

[223] I. Lytra and U. Zdun, "Supporting architectural decision making for systems-of-systems design under uncertainty," in *Proceedings of the First International Workshop on Software Engineering for Systems-of-Systems*, ser. SESoS '13. New York, NY, USA: ACM, 2013, pp. 43–46. [Online]. Available: http://doi.acm.org/10.1145/2489850.2489859

[224] J. Ven, A. Jansen, J. Nijhuis, and J. Bosch, "Design decisions: The bridge between rationale and architecture," in *Rationale Management in Software Engineering*, A. Dutoit, R. McCall, I. Mistrík, and B. Paech, Eds. Springer Berlin Heidelberg,

2006, pp. 329–348. [Online]. Available: http://dx.doi.org/10.1007/978-3-540-30998-7_16

[225] N. Harrison, P. Avgeriou, and U. Zdun, "Using patterns to capture architectural decisions," *Software, IEEE*, vol. 24, no. 4, pp. 38–45, 2007.

[226] N. Harrison and P. Avgeriou, "Pattern-driven architectural partitioning: Balancing functional and non-functional requirements," in *Digital Telecommunications, 2007. ICDT '07. Second International Conference on*, 2007, pp. 21–21.

[227] Wikipedia. Swot analysis. http://en.wikipedia.org/wiki/SWOT_analysis (February 2014). [Online]. Available: http://en.wikipedia.org/wiki/SWOT_analysis

[228] M. Svahnberg, C. Wohlin, L. Lundberg, and M. Mattsson, "A quality-driven decision-support method for identifying software architecture candidates," *International Journal of Software Engineering and Knowledge Engineering*, vol. 13, no. 05, pp. 547–573, 2003.

[229] O. Zimmermann, "Architectural decision identification in architectural patterns," in *Proceedings of the Working IEEE / IFIP Conference on Software Architecture/European Conference on Software Architecture 2012, Companion Volume*, ser. WICSA/ECSA '12. New York, NY, USA: ACM, 2012, pp. 96–103. [Online]. Available: http://doi.acm.org/10.1145/2361999.2362021

[230] J. Burge, "Software engineering using rationale," Ph.D. dissertation, Worcester Polytechnic Institute, 2005.

[231] J. Burge and D. Brown, "Software Engineering Using RATionale," *Journal of Systems and Software*, vol. 81, no. 3, pp. 395 – 413, 2008, selected Papers from the 2006 Brazilian Symposia on

Databases and on Software Engineering. [Online]. Available: http://www.sciencedirect.com/science/article/pii/S0164121207001203

[232] A. MacLean, R. M. Young, V. M. E. Bellotti, and T. P. Moran, “Questions, options, and criteria: Elements of design space analysis,” *Hum.-Comput. Interact.*, vol. 6, no. 3, pp. 201–250, Sep. 1991. [Online]. Available: http://dx.doi.org/10.1207/s15327051hci0603&4_2

[233] S. Bode and M. Riebisch, “Impact evaluation for quality-oriented architectural decisions regarding evolvability,” in *Software Architecture*, ser. Lecture Notes in Computer Science, M. Babar and I. Gorton, Eds. Springer Berlin Heidelberg, 2010, vol. 6285, pp. 182–197. [Online]. Available: http://dx.doi.org/10.1007/978-3-642-15114-9_15

[234] D. Ameller, O. Collell, and X. Franch, “Architech: Tool support for nfr-guided architectural decision-making,” in *Proceedings of 20th IEEE International Requirements Engineering Conference (RE 2012)*, 2012, pp. 315–316.

[235] J. Miller, R. Ferrari, and N. Madhavji, “Architectural effects on requirements decisions: An exploratory study,” *Seventh Working IEEE/IFIP Conf. on Software Architecture, 2008*, pp. 231 – 240, 2008.

[236] W. Engelsman, H. Jonkers, H. M. Franken, and M.-E. Iacob, “Architecture-driven requirements engineering,” in *Advances in Enterprise Engineering II*, ser. Lecture Notes in Business Information Processing, 2009, vol. 28.

[237] M. Riebisch, “Problem-Solution Mapping for Evolution Support of Software Architectural Design,” in *Proceedings of Software Engineering 2011*, 2011.

[238] P. Gruenbacher, A. Egyed, E. Egyed, and N. Medvidovic, "Reconciling software requirements and architectures with intermediate models," in *Software and Systems Modeling*. Springer, 2003, pp. 202–211.

[239] T.-M. Hesse and B. Paech, "Supporting the collaborative development of requirements and architecture documentation," in *Twin Peaks of Requirements and Architecture (TwinPeaks), 2013 3rd In ternational Workshop on the*, July 2013, pp. 22–26.

[240] E. Woods and N. Rozanski, "How software architecture can frame, constrain and inspire system requirements," in *Relating Software Requirements and Architectures*. Springer Berlin Heidelberg, 2011.

[241] L. Zhu, M. A. Babar, and R. Jeffery, "Mining patterns to support software architecture evaluation," *4th Working IEEE/IFIP Conference on Software Architecture (WICSA 2004)*, pp. 25 – 34, 2004.

[242] P. Petrov, U. Buy, and R. Nord, "Enhancing the software architecture analysis and design process with inferred macro-architectural requirements," in *Twin Peaks of Requirements and Architecture (Twin Peaks), 2012 IEEE First International Workshop on the*, sept. 2012, pp. 20 –26.

[243] G. Buchgeher and R. Weinreich, "Automatic tracing of decisions to architecture and implementation," in *Software Architecture (WICSA), 2011 9th Working IEEE/IFIP Conference on*, 2011, pp. 46–55.

[244] L. Briand, Y. Labiche, and A. Sauve, "Guiding the application of design patterns based on uml models," in *Software Maintenance, 2006. ICSM '06. 22nd IEEE International Conference on*, Sept 2006, pp. 234–243.

[245] H. Albin-Amiot, P. Cointe, Y.-G. Gueheneuc, and N. Jussien, "Instantiating and detecting design patterns: putting bits and pieces together," in *Automated Software Engineering, 2001. (ASE 2001). Proceedings. 16th Annual International Conference on*, Nov 2001, pp. 166–173.

[246] M. Kuester, "Architecture-centric modeling of design decisions for validation and traceability," in *Proceedings of the 7th European Conference on Software Architecture (ECSA '13)*, ser. Lecture Notes in Computer Science, K. Drira, Ed., vol. 7957. Springer Berlin Heidelberg, 2013, pp. 184–191. [Online]. Available: http://dx.doi.org/10.1007/978-3-642-39031-9_16

The Karlsruhe Series on Software Design and Quality

Edited by Prof. Dr. Ralf Reussner // ISSN 1867-0067

Band 1 **Steffen Becker**
Coupled Model Transformations for QoS Enabled Component-Based Software Design. 2008
ISBN 978-3-86644-271-9

Band 2 **Heiko Koziolek**
Parameter Dependencies for Reusable Performance Specifications of Software Components. 2008
ISBN 978-3-86644-272-6

Band 3 **Jens Happe**
Predicting Software Performance in Symmetric Multi-core and Multiprocessor Environments. 2009
ISBN 978-3-86644-381-5

Band 4 **Klaus Krogmann**
Reconstruction of Software Component Architectures and Behaviour Models using Static and Dynamic Analysis. 2012
ISBN 978-3-86644-804-9

Band 5 **Michael Kuperberg**
Quantifying and Predicting the Influence of Execution Platform on Software Component Performance. 2010
ISBN 978-3-86644-741-7

Band 6 **Thomas Goldschmidt**
View-Based Textual Modelling. 2011
ISBN 978-3-86644-642-7

Die Bände sind unter www.ksp.kit.edu als PDF frei verfügbar oder als Druckausgabe bestellbar.

The Karlsruhe Series on Software Design and Quality

Edited by Prof. Dr. Ralf Reussner // ISSN 1867-0067

The Karlsruhe Series on Software Design and Quality

Edited by Prof. Dr. Ralf Reussner // ISSN 1867-0067

Band 13 **Michael Hauck**
Automated Experiments for Deriving Performance-relevant Properties of Software Execution Environments. 2014
ISBN 978-3-7315-0138-1

Band 14 **Zoya Durdik**
Architectural Design Decision Documentation through Reuse of Design Patterns. 2016
ISBN 978-3-7315-0292-0